Walter Money

The First And Second Battles of Newbury

And the Siege of Donnington Castle During the Civil War

Walter Money

The First And Second Battles of Newbury
And the Siege of Donnington Castle During the Civil War

ISBN/EAN: 9783744724135

Printed in Europe, USA, Canada, Australia, Japan

Cover: Foto ©ninafisch / pixelio.de

More available books at **www.hansebooks.com**

THE

FIRST AND SECOND

BATTLES OF NEWBURY

AND THE

SIEGE OF DONNINGTON CASTLE

DURING THE CIVIL WAR,

A.D. 1643-6.

BY

WALTER MONEY, F.S.A.

Illustrated with Portraits, Plans, and Views.

LONDON:
SIMPKIN, MARSHALL, AND CO., STATIONERS' HALL COURT.
NEWBURY: W. J. BLACKET, NORTHBROOK STREET.

MDCCCLXXXI.

Dedication.

TO

THE RIGHT HONOURABLE HENRY HOWARD MOLYNEUX,

EARL OF CARNARVON,

D. C. L., F. R. S.,

PRESIDENT OF THE SOCIETY OF ANTIQUARIES,

&c., &c., &c.

WHOSE Ancestors took a prominent part in the Great Civil War, with which this Volume deals, and under Whose auspices the FALKLAND MEMORIAL,- raised to record the names of those who fell fighting in their Country's Cause, was successfully completed and inaugurated, this Book is, with his Lordship's Permission, respectfully and gratefully dedicated by

THE AUTHOR.

PREFACE.

PERHAPS no part of the Military transactions and operations of the Great Civil War in the time of Charles I. has been so cursorily dealt with and so confusedly treated as that relating to the Two Battles fought in the neighbourhood of the ancient town of Newbury, in the years 1643 and 1644.

Although the chief incidents of that stormy period are related by Clarendon and other writers of the time, the local circumstances and traditions of those two important engagements have not by any means been fully chronicled.

The value of placing on record, in a connected form, all that could be gathered together relating to the period in question requires no comment. Year by year as books have multiplied, and civilization has increased, commercial activity has penetrated from the great centres of industry into the rural districts, and has resulted in the gradual obliteration of many an old landmark, in the removal or alteration of many an historical building, and in the dying-out of many an old tradition.

To supply this want in our chronicles, to record as faithfully as possible all that can be obtained, both locally and generally, about the history of these Battles, which will always be memorable in our annals, and should be attractive to all classes of Englishmen, I have undertaken this work.

Born almost under the shadow of the grey walls of Donnington Castle, near which my ancestors dwelt during the occurrence of these stirring events, I have naturally felt a special interest in anything that concerns the varied fortunes and associations of the old fortress, which figures so prominently in these local, but at the same time national, transactions.

To those numerous friends, who have helped me by their advice and information, I wish to express my cordial thanks; especially to PROFESSOR T. RUPERT JONES, F.R.S., Staff College, Sandhurst; CAPTAIN C. COOPER KING, R.M.A., F.G.S., Professor of Tactics, Administration, &c., Royal Military College, Sandhurst; COLONEL J. L. CHESTER, LL.D.; CHARLES TRICE MARTIN, Esq., F.S.A., and WALFORD D. SELBY, Esq., of the Public Record Office; all of whom have materially contributed to lighten my labours and add pleasure to this self-imposed task.

Finally I have to tender my sincere acknowledgements to those who assisted in the establishment of the Memorial to Lord Falkland and the patriots who fell with him, the proposal to erect which I was led to originate by the study of that section of English History which this volume endeavours to illustrate and explain.

WALTER MONEY.

Newbury, March 15th, 1881.

ADDENDA ET CORRIGENDA.

Page 25, foot-note,   *for* Orry's *read* Orrery's.
— 31, line 10 from bottom, *for* auxilliaries *read* auxiliaries.
— 48, line 7 from top, With regard to BERNARD BROCAS, and the flag taken by him at the First Battle of Newbury, Reginald Brocas, Esq., has obligingly favoured me with the following particulars:—"An ancestor of mine, Sir Thomas Brocas, of Beaurepaire, had eight sons, seven of whom fell in the Civil War, fighting for the King. The one (Bernard) who captured the flag at the Battle of Newbury was the fifth son of the said Sir Thomas; and the affair happened thus. He, Bernard Brocas, being in love with a daughter of Lord Sandes, of the Vyne (a property which adjoins the Beaurepaire property, and once formed part of it), took every opportunity of passing his time with his fair mistress, much to the dislike of all his relatives, who were staunch Royalists, and many of whom had fought at Edgehill,—in fact, four of his brothers were there. Refusing to give up his Intended, and being told that his loyalty was distrusted, and that his mistress would wean him away to her father's side, he took an oath that he would give substantial proof, in the next engagement, of his loyalty, and would either bring back a standard, or stay on the field. He did both! He took the flag, killed the bearer (who is said to have been one of the Hazleriggs), and was found on the field after the battle, dead, with the flag beside him.

"After all was over the flag was taken and given to the Sandes family; and it was at the Vyne when Chaloner Chute, the Speaker to the House of Commons, took it from Lord Sandes. He gave it to my ancestor; and we have had it ever since. I myself have had it for over thirty years in my possession.

"The mistake in the date 'August,' instead of 'September,' was owing to my brother, who amused himself in putting the writing under the flag, having substituted the date of the promise to take the flag for the date of the battle."

— 70, line 8 from bottom, *for* Blagne *read* Blague.
— 72. Since the text was printed, some fresh information has been obtained with regard to Lord Belasyse and his Monument mentioned in the Appendix to the First Battle. The Inscription mentioned in the text as having been copied from his Monument, on the authority of Maitland's "History and Survey of London," has since been found to be inaccurate. The Monument is still to be seen on the outside of the east wall of the Church of St. Giles in the Fields, with the following inscription :

"This monument was erected in the year of our Lord 1736, by the pious direction of the honourable Dame

Barbara Webb, wife of Sir John Webb, of Cranford Magna in the county of Dorset, baronet, and the honourable Catharine Talbot, wife of the honourable John Talbot, of Longford in the county of Salop, esquire, surviving daughters and co-heirs of the right honourable John, Lord Belasyse, second son of Thomas, Lord Viscount Fauconberg, in memory of their most dear father, his wives, and children.

"Who, for his loyalty, prudence, and courage, was promoted to several commands of great trust by their majesties King Charles I. and II., viz., having raised six regiments of horse and foot in the civil wars, he commanded a tertia in his Majestie's armies at the battles of Edge-hill, Newbury, and Knavesby; at the sieges of Reading and Bristol: and afterwards, being made governor of York, and commander-in-chief of all his Majestie's forces in Yorkshire, he fought the battle of Selby, with the lord Fairfax. And being lieutenant-general of the counties of Lincoln, Nottingham, Derby, and Rutland, and governor of Newark, he valiantly defended that garrison against the English and Scotch armies, till his Majesty came in person to the Scotch quarters, and commanded the surrender of it. At which time he also had the honour of being general of the King's horse-guards; in all which services during the war, and other achievements, he deported himself with eminent courage and conduct, and received many wounds, sustained three imprisonments in the Tower of London; and after the happy restoration of Charles II., he was made lord-lieutenant of the east-riding of the County of York, governor of Hull, general of his Majesties forces in Africa, governor of Tangier, captain of his majestie's guard of gentlemen pensioners, and first lord commissioner of the treasury to King James II. He died the 10th of September, A.D. 1689, whose remains are deposited in this vault." The remainder of the inscription refers to his marriages and issue.

Page 72, line 8 from top, *for* Fanconberg *read* Fauconberg.
— 73, line 17 from bottom. With reference to the death of Richard Brydges, which is stated in the text, on the authority of Jacob's "Peerage," to have been in 1548, it is evident that, as Queen Mary was not crowned until 1553, the person referred to as being made K.B. at her coronation was Sir Richard Brydges, M.P. for Berkshire in 1554.
— 75, third paragraph. *Read thus*—BERNARD BROCAS. Of Beaurepaire, near Sherborne St. John, Hants, He was the fifth son of Sir Thomas Brocas (son of Sir Pexall Brocas) by Elizabeth, daughter of Robert Wingfield, of Upton, Co. Northampton.
— 78, line 4 from top. Colonel Daniel O'Neill. This officer was Lieutenant-Colonel of Prince Rupert's regiment of horse; afterwards groom of the bedchamber to the King.
— 85, first line, *insert* § 2. *before* PARLIAMENTARIAN.

TABLE OF CONTENTS.

	PAGE.
Dedication	iii
Preface	v
Addenda et Corrigenda	vii
Table of Contents	ix
List of Plans and Illustrations	xii
THE FIRST BATTLE AT NEWBURY, SEPTEMBER 20TH, 1643	1

APPENDIX.

	PAGE.
I. A list of those Regiments of Trained-Bands and Auxiliaries of the City of London, which were engaged at the First Battle of Newbury	55
II. The Attack on Essex's Rear the day after the First Battle of Newbury	58
III. The presence of Queen Henrietta Maria at the Battle (disproved).	61
IV. A case of Witch-murder at Newbury	63
IV.* The Discovery of the Coffin and Remains of the Vault of Robert Devereux, third Earl of Essex, in the Chapel of St. John the Baptist in Westminster Abbey, June 1879	65
V. Biographical Notices of Officers and others mentioned in connection with the First Battle of Newbury	67
§ 1. Royalist Officers	67

	PAGE.		PAGE.
Patrick Ruthven, Earl of Forth	67	Sir Thomas Aston	76
Prince Rupert	67	Sir Anthony Mansel	76
Sir John Byron	67	Sir Edward Stradling	76
Lord Wilmot	68	Sir Michael Wodehouse	76
Earl of Caernarvon	68	Sir Jacob Astley	76
Earl of Lindsey	69	Sir John Frechville	76
Earl of Northampton	69	Sir John Hurry	77
Earl of Nottingham	70	Major-Gen. George Porter	77
Earl of Cleveland	70	Col. St.-John	77
Earl of Holland	70	Col. Edward Villiers	77
Earl of Bedford	71	Col. Will. Legge	77
Earl of Clare	71	Col. Daniel O'Neill	viii and 78
John, Lord Belasyse (see also List of *Corrigenda*)	vii, 72	Col. Morgan	78
Lord Chandos	73	Col. Thomas Eure	78
Lord Molyneux	„ 73	Col. Richard Platt	78
Hon. Henry Bertie	73	Col. Charles Gerard	78
Sir Charles Lucas	74	Col. Thomas Bagehot	79
Sir George Lisle	74	Capt. Basil Woodd	79
Sir Edward Waldegrave	75	Capt. Clifton	79
Bernard Brocas	„ vii & 75	Capt. Newman	79
Sir Lewis Kirke	75	Capt. Gwynne	80
Sir Henry Slingsby	75	Henry Spencer, Earl of Sunderland	80
Sir William Vavasour	76	Lord Falkland	81

TABLE OF CONTENTS.

§ 2. Parliamentarian Officers and others 85

	PAGE.		PAGE.
Earl of Essex	85	Colonel Sheffield	88
Lord Robartes or Roberts	85	Col. John Meldrum	88
Lord Grey of Groby	85	Col. Norton	88
Sir John Meyrick	85	Col. Dalbier	88
Sir Philip Stapleton	85	Captain Hunt	88
Sir William Constable	86	Capt. Francis St.-Barbe	88
Sir William Balfour	87	Capt. Hammond	88
Sir Samuel Luke	87	Capt. Charles Fleetwood	89
Sir Arthur Godwin	87	Capt. Charles Pym	89
Major-General Skippon	87	William Twisse, D.D.	89
Major-General Deane	87	Robert Codrington	89
Lieut.-General Middleton	88		

VI. Extracts from the Certificates or Returns of those Persons who, pursuant to the Order of the House of Commons, made the Protestation in the County of Berks, 30th July, 1641 90

	PAGE.		PAGE.
Brimpton Parish	91	Kintbury	92
Chaddleworth—	91	Leckhampstead	92
Chieveley—	91	Midgham	92
Compton—	91	Newbury	92
Enborne—	91	Peasemore	92
Frilsham—	91	Shaw-cum-Donnington	92
Greenham (a Tything of Thatcham)	91	Little Shefford	93
		Great Shefford	93
Hamsted-Marshall	91	Speen	93
Hampsted-Norris	91	Wasing	93
West Ilsley	92	Welford	93
East Ilsley	92	Winterborne-Danvers	93
Inkpen	92		

VII. List of the Sequestrators of the Estates of "Delinquents, Papists, Spyes, and Intelligencers," for the County of Berks, appointed under Ordinance of the Lords and Commons, April 1, 1643 93

	PAGE.		PAGE.
Sir Francis Pile	93	Roger Knight	94
Sir Francis Knollys, junior	93	Henry Powle	94
Peregrine Hoby	94	Thomas Fettiplace	95
Harry Marten	94	Tanfield Vachell	95

VII.* The Commissioners for raising Money and Forces within the County of Berks, and for Maintenance of Garrisons within the said County for use of Parliament, appointed June 27, 1644 95

	PAGE.		PAGE.
William Lenthall	95	Richard Browne	98
Sir Robert Pye	96	John Packer	99
Sir Benjamin Rudyerd	96	Robert Packer	99
Edmund Dunch	97	Cornelius Holland	99
Daniel Blagrave	98		

TABLE OF CONTENTS. xi

	PAGE.
VIII. Ship Money	99
IX. State of Public Feeling in the County in 1643	102
X. Agreement between Charles I. and the County of Berks respecting a Contribution to be levied for the support of the King's Army	104

THE SECOND BATTLE AT NEWBURY, OCTOBER 27TH, 1644 .. 107

APPENDIX. 162
    I. The King's March to Newbury 162
    II. The King's Stay at Newbury 163
    III. Red Heath and Red Hill 165
    IV. Account of the Second Battle of Newbury, from a MS. belonging to the Earl de la Warr 167
    V. Newbury Church as a Prison and Hospital .. 167
    VI. Boxford 168
    VII. Bucklebury 169
    VIII. License of War 169
    IX. Capture of Lady Forth, Countess of Brentford 173
    X. Captain Knight's Relation of the Siege of Donnington Castle 177
    XI. Depositions of Witnesses at the Trial of King Charles I., as to the presence of the King at the Two Battles of Newbury 185
    XII. Biographical Notices of some of the Officers and others mentioned in connection with the Second Battle of Newbury 187
        A. Royalist Officers 187

	PAGE.		PAGE.
Prince Maurice	187	Sir John Owen	192
Duke of Richmond	187	Sir Thomas Hooper	192
Lord Bernard Stuart	187	Sir Richard Page	192
Earl of Newport	188	Sir Thomas Basset	192
Earl of Berkshire	188	Sir Humphrey Benett	192
Earl Rivers	188	Sir John Granville	192
Lord Capel	188	Sir Joseph Wagstaffe	192
Lord Hopton	189	Sir Charles Lloyd	192
Lord Colepeper	189	Sir Edward Walker	192
Lord Goring	190	Colonel Leke	192
Sir John Boys	190	Col. Anthony Thelwall	193
Sir Bernard Astley	191	Col. Giles Strangeways	193
Sir William Brouncker	191	Col. Houghton	193
Sir William Ashburnham	191	Captain Catelyn	193
Sir William St.-Leger	191	Robert Stradling	193

        B. Parliamentarian Officers 194

	PAGE.		PAGE.
Earl of Manchester	194	Lieut.-Gen. Ludlow	195
Sir William Waller	194	Colonel Norton	196
Sir Arthur Hesilrige	195	Col. Sir Richard Ingoldsby	196
Major-General Crawford	195	Col. John Birch	196
Lieut.-Gen. Middleton	195		

    XIII. Historical Notices of the Manor and Castle of Donnington 197

INDEX 212

LIST OF THE PLANS AND ILLUSTRATIONS.

1 Portrait of LORD FALKLAND. (Frontispiece.) Opposite title-page.
2 ,, PRINCE RUPERT .. .. Opposite page 8
3 View of DONNINGTON CASTLE .. .. .. ,, 18
4 Portrait of the EARL OF ESSEX .. .. ,, 22
5 ,, ,, BRENTFORD or BRAINFORD .. ,, 28
6 ,, ,, SUNDERLAND .. .. ,, 38
7 Copy of the COFFIN-PLATE of the EARL OF ESSEX .. ,, 66
8 Portrait of the EARL OF CAERNARVON .. ,, 68
9 Plan of the FIRST BATTLE OF NEWBURY .. .. ,, 106
10 Plan of the DEFENCES OF DONNINGTON CASTLE ,, 108
11 Portrait of the EARL OF MANCHESTER .. .. ,, 118
12 View of SHAW HOUSE . .. .. ,, 122
13 Portrait of SIR WILLIAM WALLER .. .. ,, 132
14 ,, SIR JOHN BOYS .. .. .. ,, 160
15 Plan of the SECOND BATTLE OF NEWBURY .. .. ,, 212

THE FIRST BATTLE AT NEWBURY,

September 20th, 1643.

In order to understand the political situation of the precise period of English History under review, a brief description of the previous operations of the hostile armies, which resulted in the Two Battles of Newbury, is necessary, because the narrative will then be rendered more complete. At the same time the means will be provided of rightly estimating the value and effect of these engagements on the fortunes of the two combatants.

After the assault of Bristol and its surrender to the Royalists under Prince Rupert, in July, 1643, the King again joined the camp; and, having sent Prince Maurice with a detachment into Devonshire, he deliberated how to employ his remaining forces in an enterprize of moment. Some of his followers proposed that he should march direct to London, where everything was in confusion, though this undertaking, by reason of the great strength of the London Militia or Trained Bands, was thought to be attended with great difficulties; but Gloucester, lying within 20 miles of Bristol, presented a possibly easier conquest. This was the only remaining garrison possessed by the Parliament in the west of the kingdom; and, by interrupting the communications of the royal armies between the south-west and north-east, prevented these from acting in concert. Hence the King at last assented to the plan of besieging this important town. The questionable policy of this measure is thus noticed by one of Charles's most faithful adherents, Sir Philip Warwick;—" One (or the like) councill in both quarters, north and west, soon blasted the prosperity in each place; for the King pitcht upon that fatall resolution, recommended to him, it is said, by the Lord Culpeper (who wanted no loyalty), of beseiging Glocester, who thought it a good policy not to leave a strong towne behind him. But the counsell proved fatall; for had the King at that time resolv'd in himself to have struck at the proud head of London and had had authority enough at that time to have required the Earl of Newcastle to have joyned with him, ...humanely speaking, he had rais'd such confusion among the two Houses and the Londoners, that they had either sent

B

him his owne terms, or if they had fought him, most probably he had bin victorious......But the King fixes on Gloucester, and the Earle of Newcastle as fatally about the same time setts down before Hull."* This was by the advice of Lt.-Gen. King, whose loyalty was suspected.

After all, it is by no means certain that Charles' march to London would have been so effectual and so little opposed as it is here taken for granted it would have been.

On the 10th August,† the King's army, under his immediate command, occupied the heights above the City of Gloucester. The town was defended by a garrison of only fifteen hundred men, besides the inhabitants; and the Governor (Massey) was peremptorily summoned to surrender, two hours being allowed for an answer. Before the expiration of that time, two deputies from the city, Sergeant-Major ‡ Pudsey and a citizen, presented themselves at the camp. They were pale, thin men, dressed in black, and closely shaven: "We bring to the Majesty," said they, "an answer from the godly city of Gloucester;" and, on being introduced to the King, they read a letter, which ran thus: "We, the inhabitants, magistrates, officers, and soldiers within the garrison of Gloucester unto his Majesty's gracious message return this humble answer, "That we do keep this city, according to our oath and allegiance, to and for the use of his Majesty signified by both houses of Parliament: and are resolved by God's help, to keep this city accordingly."

On hearing this brief reply, delivered in a firm, clear tone, and perceiving the strange appearance of the messengers, who stood motionless before the King awaiting his answer, a movement at once of surprise, derision, and anger was about to manifest itself on the part of the courtiers; but Charles, as grave as his enemies, repressed it with a gesture, and dismissed the deputies with these words: "If you expect help you are deceived; Waller is extinct, and Essex cannot come." The deputation had no sooner entered the city, than the inhabitants set fire to the suburbs, and left themselves nothing to defend but what was within the walls. For twenty-six days, from Aug. 10th to Sept. 5th, the citizens, by their indefatigable exertions, frustrated all the efforts of the besiegers. Except a hundred and fifty men kept in reserve, the whole garrison were constantly on foot. In all their labours, in all their dangers, the people took part with the soldiers, the women with their husbands, the children with their mothers. Massey even made frequent sallies, and only three men took

---

* Sir Ph. Warwick's 'Memoires,' pp. 260—2.

† The "Old Style" of reckoning was employed in England at this period and long afterwards, though the "New Style" according to the Gregorian Calendar was in general use on the Continent.

‡ "Sergeant-Major" formerly signified the officer now styled Major, and the "Sergeant-Major General" was what is now called Major-General.

advantage of them to desert. Tired of so long a delay, attended by neither glory nor rest, the royal army in a spirit of revenge licentiously devastated the country round, the officers frequently employing their men to carry off from his house some rich farmer or peaceable freeholder of the other side, who only regained his liberty on payment of ransom.*

The news of the siege of Gloucester caused the greatest consternation in London; and the Parliament, seeing the absolute necessity of relieving the town as the only means of supporting their cause, now exerted to the utmost their power and authority. Trading was for a time suspended, in order that none should decline military service upon whom the lot should fall. The relief of Gloucester was urged in every pulpit. A force of 8000 horse and 4000 foot was expeditiously put into a condition of marching against the King; and a committee, comprising some of the warmest partisans of war, went to the Earl of Essex on the 4th August to inform him of the measures that had been taken to recruit and make full provision for his army, and to enquire what else he needed. In a word they entrusted the destiny of the country to his hands, with assurance of the complete confidence reposed in him by Parliament. The Earl, in a letter to the Speaker, assured the House he would never desert the cause "as long as I have any blood in my veins, until this kingdom may be made happy by a blessed peace (which is all honest men's prayers) or to have an end by the sword." †

On the 24th August the Earl of Essex mustered his forces on Hounslow Heath; and, after a solemn review in the presence of nearly all the Members of both Houses, marched by way of Colnbrook, Beaconsfield, and Aylesbury to the assistance of Gloucester. On the 1st of September he arrived at Brackley Heath, the general rendezvous, where he was joined by a reinforcement of horse and a train of artillery, which brought his force up to about 14,000 men. He then proceeded by way of Bicester, Chipping Norton, and Stow-on-the-Wold; here he was attacked by a detached corps of cavalry under Prince Rupert, who vainly endeavoured to stop him; but the Earl advanced, without suffering himself to be turned from his road, driving the enemy before him. He was already within a few miles of the Royalist Camp, already the King's horse had fallen back on the advanced posts of his infantry, when, in the hope of delaying the Earl, if only for a day, Charles sent him a messenger with proposals of peace. "The Parliament," answered Essex, "gave me no commission to treat, but to relieve Gloucester; I will do it, or leave my body beneath its walls!" "No propositions: no propositions!" shouted the soldiers, when they heard of

---

* Clarendon's 'Hist. of the Rebellion,' vol. ii, p. 341.
† Carte's MS. Letters; Bibl. Bodl.

the arrival of a trumpeter from the King. So Essex continued his march, and on the 5th Sept. he appeared on Prestbury Hills within view of the city. Here the thunder of his cannon announced to the beleaguered citizens that their deliverance had come; and soon the sight of the King's quarters in flames informed them that the siege was raised.

The important services performed by Massey and the garrison at Gloucester called forth the thanks of Parliament, who granted £1,000 to the governor, and proportionate largess to the officers and soldiers; and, in order to preserve the memory of the transaction, the 5th of September was ordered by the Mayor and Corporation to be observed as an annual holiday, and was so kept until the Restoration. The south gate of the city, which had been battered down during the siege, was rebuilt the same year, with these mottoes inscribed round the arch: on one side "A CITY ASSAULTED BY MAN, BUT SAVED BY GOD;" and on the other side, next the city, "EVER REMEMBER THE VTH SEPT. 1643—GIVE GOD THE GLORY." At the Restoration these inscriptions were effaced, and the royal arms substituted. The walls and fortifications of the city were destroyed by order of King Charles II.; and that monarch likewise deprived the citizens of their charter, but subsequently granted a new one. Massey eventually left the Parliament's service and joined Prince Charles in Holland, under whose standard he fought at Worcester; but, being taken prisoner, he was committed to the Tower. He managed however to escape, and, after the death of Cromwell, he undertook to seize Gloucester, but was taken in the attempt. A second time he slipped from his captors; and, on the restoration of the secluded Members in 1660, he appeared in Parliament, and represented Gloucester the two following years, in the last of which he was knighted.

The easy success gained by Essex in this march may be attributed to supineness on the part of his adversary; but it is probable that, as Clarendon says, the Royalists could not believe he was coming, and "laid their account" in the nearly thirty miles of champaign country that he would have to traverse, after the King's soldiers had eaten it bare; and where, if he attempted the expedition, the royal horse would perpetually infest his march and probably destroy his army.*

The day the Parliamentary General entered Gloucester had been set apart for a public fast, but on his arrival it was turned into a day of ardent rejoicing. Provisions of all kinds were conveyed to the city, the Governor Massey and his soldiers were loaded with praise, the citizens congratulated on their courage, and the Earl was received everywhere with demonstrations of gratitude.

The march of Essex to Gloucester was considered one of the

---

* Clarendon's 'Hist. of the Rebellion,' vol. ii, p. 343.

most able exploits of the whole war; for his troops were untrained and ill-disciplined, and for the greater part of the way he was in the enemy's country. From Brackley to Prestbury, Wilmot and four other royalist commanders were hanging on his rear; and in the encounter at Stow, Prince Rupert with 4,000 horse made a desperate attempt to cut off his advanced guard, but in vain. It would appear from the following remarks by Lord Orrery that there was more of a fight here than the historians have mentioned: he says "When Essex marched to relieve Gloucester, Prince Rupert advanced with his cavalry to meet the relieving army on the Downs: which doubtless he had defended, had not some brigades of Essex's infantry done wonders on that day."*

At Gloucester Essex left his heavy ordnance with 40 barrels of powder and the greater part of his baggage, the better to expedite his march over an unusually hilly country. Having strengthened and victualled the garrison, which had been driven to great extremities, his mission was accomplished; but, fearing an engagement with the enemy on account of their superiority in cavalry, the Lord General determined to manœuvre his way back to London without risking a battle. The London trained-bands and auxiliaries too, supposing their work already done, earnestly desired to direct their footsteps homewards.

On the third day after his arrival in Gloucester, Essex, with the object of dividing the King's forces, made a demonstration, as though he intended to proceed northward to Worcester; but, changing his route on a sudden, he marched to Tewkesbury, where, having thrown a bridge over the Severn and dispatched a body of troops to Upton as a feint, he quartered till Friday, 15th September. Succeeding by this skilful manœuvre in drawing the King's attention towards Worcester, Essex with the remainder of his army took advantage of a dark night, and moved away for Cirencester. His vanguard, arriving in the town about 1 a.m. on Saturday morning, surprised two newly raised regiments of Royal horse, intended for service in Kent and commanded by Sir Nicholas Crispe and Col. Spencer, both of whom were then absent. In the fight which ensued the Parliamentarians took 300 prisoners, 400 horses, with six stands of colours; and, what was of more consequence, obtained possession of a large store of provisions; thus enabling the Earl to refresh his exhausted forces, and perhaps mainly contributing to his success at Newbury. This skirmish is referred to in Corbet's "Relation of the Siege of Gloucester" in the following terms: "The forlorn hope entered Cirencester, whilst the rest surrounded it, killed the centinell sleeping, march'd up to the market-house without opposition (the enemy supposing them Prince Maurice his forces, that night expected) till they entered the houses and surprised them in bed,

---

* Orrery's 'Art of War,' p. 180.

took 400 men and 30 cart-loads of bread and cheese and other provisions, a great relief in a wasted country, and the only support of the soldiers against the battle of Newbury."

The royalist troopers taken prisoners at Cirencester were secured in the fine old parish church, which, fortunately, escaped injury during the siege in the previous year, the inhabitants having carefully protected it by suspending woodpacks around the exterior. After a few hours' rest, Essex was again on the march, his means being augmented on the way by the addition of some 1,000 sheep and 60 head of cattle, which had been taken from "malignants and papists" *en route*. These were afterwards lost during the action on Aldbourne Chase, "every man's care then being to secure himself." On Saturday night the halt was at Cricklade, and on Sunday at Swindon, where a religious service was held. Next morning the march was resumed towards Hungerford, where the Earl intended quartering for the night. In a contemporary letter from Lord George Digby, Essex is said to have had 2,000 horse and 5,000 foot when he marched from Tewkesbury; but he had left some of his troops at Gloucester and others at Upton, and had lost a number of his men in several skirmishes; and this will account to some extent for the diminution of the force with which he had left London. There were also numerous stragglers on the march; and many of the Parliamentary soldiers, who remained behind drinking and who neglected to march with the colours; were slain by the Royalists on entering the towns and villages, or were taken prisoners. Essex's numerical strength, however, afterwards at Newbury was evidently beyond Lord Digby's computation; for when the Earl marched from Brackley he had an army of about 14,000 men, and no regular engagement had taken place to account for a diminution to the extent of *one-half* of his available force.

To the royal cause the raising of the siege of Gloucester was a fatal blow. Since retiring from before the city, the defeated King had halted in the neighbourhood of Winchcombe and at Sudeley Castle, about eight miles from Gloucester, awaiting the motions of the enemy. It is mentioned in Warburton's 'Memoirs and Correspondence of Prince Rupert,' that the latter had sent notice of the movements of Essex to his Majesty; but he, believing himself better informed, allowed the enemy twenty-four hours advantage before he followed him. But there appears to be some discrepancy between the statements here made and those of Lord Byron[*] in a letter to Lord Clarendon [†] wherein he says:—"that had Prince Rupert been pleased to credit my intelligence, the advantage which Essex gained might have been prevented; which neglect obliged the army to go so

---

[*] For memoirs of persons of note, see APPENDIX.

[†] Lord Byron's account of the Battles of Newbury, in a letter to Lord Clarendon, in MS. Clar. State Papers, in Bodleian Lib., no. 1738.

hasty and painful a march, that before he reached Newbury there was about 2000 horse and as many foot lost by the way." This is corroborated by Capt. John Gwynne, who says,* "And when we drew off from Gloucester it proved to be most tempestuous rainy weather so that few or none could take little or no rest on the hills where they were, the winds next morning soon dryed up our through-wet clothes we lay pickled in all night (as a convenient washing for us at our coming from the trenches), and we made such haste in pursuit of Essex's army that there was an account of 1,500 foot quite tired and spent, not possible to come up to their colours before we engaged the enemy * * * We were like to drop down every step we made with want of sleepe, yet notwithstanding we marcht on till we overtook the enemy's army at Newbury town end."

As soon, however, as the King felt assured as to Essex's march and route, he dispatched Prince Rupert with a strong body of horse† to overtake him before he should get so far in advance as to form a junction with Waller's army, which was daily expected to leave London. The Prince accordingly, mustering his cavalry on Broadway Down, gave immediate pursuit, and marching all that night and the next day reached Faringdon, but was unable to overtake the enemy.

Whilst refreshing his weary troopers here, Rupert sent on Sir John Hurry to reconnoïtre, and soon learnt that Essex was passing over Aldbourne Chase, expecting to enter Newbury that night, Saturday 16th September, 1643.

The force at the disposal of the King at this time may be estimated at 10,000 men. According to Rapin,‡ he commanded when before Gloucester about "8,000 horse and foot;" but this may probably be read as 8,000 of each arm, since, from the facts that such a considerable deduction has to be made for stragglers, and that a garrison of 3,000 infantry and 500 cavalry was left in Reading after the Newbury battle, and in addition a force was placed in Donnington Castle, it certainly seems that the army of the Royalists was far more numerous than the historian would lead us to believe. Rudge, in his 'History of Gloucester,' indeed, computes the King's forces as 30,000 strong, which is doubtless an exaggeration; and Lord Byron states that the army before Gloucester was the greatest the King had during the war; so that the estimate of 10,000 men for the Royalist force that fought afterwards at Newbury is probably fairly accurate. Clarendon also bears this out in his statement that the King's army contained "above 8,000 horse" when his Majesty left Gloucester. ||

---

* Gwynne's 'Milit. Memoirs,' pp. 36—37.
† E. Warburton's 'Prince Rupert,' vol. ii. 291.
‡ Rapin's 'Hist. Eng.', vol. ii p. 478.
|| Clarendon, 'Life,' vol. i. p. 164.

Prince Rupert's detachment, therefore, may well have numbered 3,000 sabres, exclusive of the regiments sent, as will be seen hereafter, under Hurry to harass the rear of the Parliamentary forces; and their order of march was such as to offer every advantage to such a dashing cavalier as the nephew of King Charles. Essex's column of infantry was moving with wide intervals "between their divisions;" and his cavalry, though in actual presence of the enemy, did little to ascertain where that enemy was. The opportunity was a good one for a bold and intelligent adversary; for a force of all arms indifferently accustomed to combined action would, as all history tells us, be subject to grave disadvantage if attacked under these circumstances. Lord Byron, after describing the position of the Parliamentary Army on Aldbourne Chase as of "great advantage for our horse," says "we were so placed that we had it in our power both to charge their horse in flank and at the same time to have sent another party to engage their artillery, yet that fair occasion was omitted, and the enemy allowed to join all their forces together, and then we very courageously charged them." It is a most noticeable fact that the Parliamentary army was singularly unaccustomed, at this time, to the movement of mixed bodies. To keep so great a distance between the different fractions was, from every point of view, likely to lead to disaster, inasmuch as each might be taken individually, and thus the value of the united force be entirely destroyed.

This skirmish, which took place on the open down about two miles to the north-west of the village of Aldbourne, is graphically referred to in two contemporary tracts, which give both the Royalist and Parliamentarian version of the affair. In Robert Codrington's "Life and death of the Earl of Essex," the author, after an account of the siege of Gloucester, relates that "From hence [Cirencester] his Excellence marched into Wiltshire, and, being advanced towards Auburn Hills, he had a sight of his Majesty's horse, which appeared in several great bodies, and were so marshalled to charge our army of foot, being then on their march in several divisions; which caused our foot to unite themselves into one gross, our horse perpetually skirmishing with them, to keep them off the foot. In the meantime, the dragoons on both sides gave fire in full bodies on one another, on the side of the Hill, that the woods above, and the vallies below, did echo with the thunder of the charge. There were about fourscore slain upon the place, and more than as many more were sorely wounded.

"Our horse also made great impression upon the Queen's regiment of horse, and charged them again and again, and cut in pieces many of her life-guard. In this service, the Marquis of Vivile was taken prisoner: it seems he would not be known who he was; but endeavouring to rescue himself from a Lieutenant

PRINCE RUPERT.

From the portrait by VANDYKE.

that took him Prisoner, and thereupon, having his head almost cloven asunder with a pole ax, he acknowledged himself, in the last words he spoke, which were, *Vous voyez un grand Marquis mourant;* that is, *You see a great Marquis dying.* His dead body was carried to Hungerford by the Lord General's command. It had not been long there, but the King did send a Trumpet to his Excellency, conceiving that the Marquis had been wounded only, and taken Prisoner, and desired that his Chirurgeons and Doctors might have free Access unto him for his Recovery. His Excellency certified the Trumpet that he was dead, and returned his Body to the King, to receive those funeral rites as his Majesty would give it. Some say, that his body was ransomed for three hundred Pieces of Gold." This latter statement is borne out by Whitelock in his Memoirs, who further narrates that the money was divided by Essex among his soldiers: and that this statement, as to the disposal of the body of the Marquis, is probable may be inferred from the fact that the registers of the Parish Church of Hungerford, though containing records of the burial of soldiers, make no reference to any who are of higher rank or greater note.*

Monsieur de Larrey observes in reference to the Marquis:— "The French, who never fail of illustrating the actions of their countrymen, extol the prowess of Chartre, Persans, and Beaveau, [and Vieuville†] four of their heroes who were in this engagement near Hungerford. These came over with the Count de Harcourt, whom the young King Lewis the 14th, or rather the Queen Regent, sent into England, in quality of Ambassador Extraordinary, to negociate a reconciliation between the King and the Parliament; these four lords suffering themselves to be carried away with the fire natural to their nation, and forgetting the occasion of their journey, came and offer'd their services to the King, and were actually in the battle. It cost the Marquis of Vieuville his life, for he was killed by Col. Kilson, whom he had wounded and was pursuing with too much obstinacy; and the bravery of these four adventurers was the occasion of the Ambassador's negociation proving abortive. For the Parliament, resenting his partiality, would not hearken to his proposals. This was what they signified to him by the Earls of Stamford and Salisbury, who were deputed by the two Houses. The ambassador excus'd it as an imprudent action, which he said could not be imputed to him; and for which the other had been

---

* The Aldbourne Registers are blank during the period of the Civil War, and they do not recommence until 1646; but in the Hungerford Registers, are the following entries: 1643, Sept. 18, buried four soldiers: Sept 25, buried another soldier: Oct. 4, Henry Chorbley a soldier. It would seem from the dates that these were some of the victims of the skirmish above described. Had de Vieuville been interred there, doubtless it would have been mentioned.

† This name is omitted in the text, but referred to in a marginal note. See Clarendon's Hist. v. ii, p. 346.

sufficiently punish'd by the death of one of their companions: but these excuses were rejected. Even he himself was accus'd as coming rather as a spy than an ambassador, and with a design rather to foment the troubles than to appease them." *

The Royalist's account is somewhat more lengthy, as may be expected, and they evidently view the affair of Aldbourne Chase as a minor victory, though the success was so partial as scarcely to make it worth claiming. Still their preliminary movements were not unskilfully taken, for while Col. Hurry with 1,000 troopers was dispatched to harass the rear, the remainder of the cavalry under Rupert himself moved off to intercept and assail the head of the hostile column. Here let the Royalist writer, "a noble person from the South," tell the story in his own words. "It was our good lucke to cross his army just as our party had overtaken it upon the open Downe, two miles on the *north-west* side of *Auburne*. The Rebells descrying us drew up in Battalia, leaving onely a body of some 200 Horse upon a Hill, somewhat distant from the Grosse of their Army, which we found means so to steale upon with Hurryes party, as to charge and rout them, and taking two Cornetts, and killing forty or fifty Men, without any losse on our part, we beat them into their Foot, and Cannon; upon which occasion we discovered such evident symptomes of feare and distraction in their whole Army, as that the Prince was well nigh tempted from his temper, and was once resolved to have charged with three thousand Horse alone; their whole Army consisting of two thousand Horse, and five thousand Foot at least, and store of Cannon. But newes arriving at the instant, That our Foot was beyond expectation, advanced within six or seven Miles of us, it imposed upon his Highnesse prudence this caution, not to adventure upon halfe our strength, that rest, which the next day he might be sure to fight for with double power: Upon which consideration he made a stand, resolving that night, onely to attend them and hinder their March. We had not stood long, when we discovered that the enemy prepared for a retreat, and by degrees drew away their Baggage first, then their Foot, leaving their Horse at a good distance from them. The Prince his designe hereupon, was, to have charged them, when halfe their forces should have been drawne off the field into those Lanes whereunto their Baggage was already advanced, But their Motions being so very slow, and the Night drawing on; upon second thoughts, his Highnesse judged it the best course, to try if by a small party he could ingage their Horse, which was then grown to be a good distance from their Foot. This party he committed to the care of Hurrey, with two Regiments onely neer at hand to second

---

* History of the Reign of King Charles I, Lond. 1716, vol ii., pp 165—6. An excellent portrait of the Marquis de Vieuville was formerly in the collection of the Duke of Buckingham at Stowe.

him, keeping the Body of his Horse at such a distance, as might incourage the enemy to venture on that sever'd part, which they did with a little too much incouragement, for to say the truth, the Regiment that should have seconded Hurrey, not doing their part so well as they ought, forced his party almost to make somewhat a disorderly retreat, and the Prince to send hasty succours to them; which the Queenes Regiment (commanded by my Lord Jermine) was ordered to doe, which his Lordship performed with much galantry, being received very steadily by a strong Body of the enemies' Horse, and with a composednesse in the Officer that commanded them, very remarkable, for his Lordship advancing before his Regiment, with the Marquesse of *Viville* on one hand, and the Lord *Digby* on the other, the enemies volley of Carbines (given them smartly at lesse than ten yards) being past, the Commander (somewhat forwarder than the rest) was plainly seen to prye into their Countenances, and removing his levell from one to another to discharge his Pistoll, as it were by election at the Lord Digbyes head, but without any more hurt (saving onely the burning of his face) then he himselfe received by my Lord *Jerman's* sword, who (upon the Lord *Digbyes* Pistoll missing fire) ran him with it into the back: but he was as much beholding there to his Arms, as the Lord Digby to his head-piece. Immediately upon this shock, the Queene's Regiment was so charged in the reare by a fresh body of theirs, that the greatest part of it shifting for themselves, the Lord *Jermine* accompanied with the French Marquesse, and the Officers onely of his regiment thought it as safe a way, as well as the most honourable to venture forward through their whole Army, rather than to charge back through those that invironed him, and so with admirable successe (the unhappy losse of that gallant *Marquesse* excepted) he brought himselfe, foure Coullers, and all his Officers off safe, having made their way round through the grosse of the Enemies foot. The Lord *Digby* (being stunn'd and for the present blinded with his shot,) was fortunately received out of the middle of a Regiment of the Enemies by a brave Charge, which Prince *Rupert* in Person made upon them with His own Troope, where in His Highnesse Horse was shot in the Head under Him; but yet by God's blessing brought him off. And so the Enemies' Horse being beaten quite up to their Foot and Cannon, the night comming upon us, gave a Period to that action."*

After this the Royalists proceeded towards Newbury, and the Parliamentarians to Hungerford, where crossing the Kennet they also prepared for a further advance towards the former town, though by the opposite bank of the stream. It is evident that Essex had originally designed to proceed to Reading by the London Road on the left bank of the river, but the sudden irruption of

---

* A Copy of a Letter written to his Excellence the Marquesse of Newcastle by a noble person from the South, &c., &c., 1643, p. 5, *et seq.*

Rupert's Cavalry led him of necessity to change his plan. If the skirmish was not completely successful, it at any rate forced the Parliamentarians off their direct road and compelled them to place an obstacle between themselves and their pursuers. Throughout it must be borne in mind that Essex's chief desire was to reach London. To fight his way there was apparently not his intention, if it could be avoided. But the cavalry action delayed him by driving him off the London Road, and enabled the King's Infantry to reach Newbury, and thus the Royal Army appeared in menacing force on the flank of the line of march of the Parliamentarians, obliging the Earl to form front to his flank and attempt to defeat the King before he continued his advance towards the Capital. Probably he hoped to pass the Kennet at Newbury; but having failed there, he chose the next available passage, that of Padworth, after the battle on the 20th September had been decided in his favour. The skirmish, however, though well conceived and, as we have seen, partially successful, was but feebly executed. The opportunity afforded by the lengthy division of the Earl's column of march on open ground, for a demoralizing blow at the Army of the Parliament was almost lost through the want of order and method of the attack.

"The Armies" writes Byron again, "were then drawne so near together that it was impossible the enemy could avoid fighting with us if we pleased, and hereupon a fourth error may be observed, for notwithstanding the necessity there was of fighting (at least if they persisted in their marching to London and we in ours of preventing them) yet no orders were given out for the manner of our fighting and how the army should be embattled as usually is done on the like occasions." Skill must be combined with courage to reap the full fruits of victory; and these only partially rested with the troopers of the King, for the army of the Parliament made good its march to Hungerford though it left behind it according to the 'Mercurius Aulicus' "17 carts heavily laden with ammunition and victual, three whereof were bullet, the rest wheat and other provisions, leaving there also the 1,000 sheep (previously mentioned) tyed by the legs, 200 whereof were at once restored to their owners, the rest left till those who had a just right to them should come and claim them."* Both sides suffered considerable loss in this encounter. Of the officers of the Parliament, Capt. Middleton and Capt. Hacket are recorded as being slain. Whitelock estimates the killed on both sides at about 80; and the 'True Informer' of September 23rd, 1643, says "Of persons of note slain on the King's side in the skirmish was the Marquis of Vieuville, his son, and Sir John Throgmorton," but this appears to be one of the frequent exaggerations of party pamphleteers. Sir Robert Throckmorton held the title at this

---

* 'Mercurius Aulicus,' Friday, October 6th, 1643.

THE FIRST BATTLE OF NEWBURY. 13

time and died in 1650. Two of the Throckmortons, Colonels Ambrose and Thomas, were in the service of King Charles, but it is not recorded in any other account of the skirmish that either fell here, or that the Marquis de Vieuville had a son killed in the action. Some traces of the fight were found in May, 1815, when the workmen, in widening the turnpike road from Swindon to Hungerford, exhumed sixty skeletons on removing a bank at Preston at the spot where the parishes of Aldbourne and Ramsbury join, a few yards from the turning leading to the latter place. The skeletons were those of young men and lay scattered about two feet below the surface. The bones were placed in carts and conveyed to the churchyards of Aldbourne and Ramsbury where they were re-interred. If, as in all probability, these remains were those of the soldiers slain in the skirmish on the Chase, it is a singular coincidence that the boundary-line of two parishes should have been chosen, as at Newbury, for the place of burial for the slain. It is probable that as this "running fight" extended over both parishes, the parochial authorities undertook jointly to gather up and inter the dead, the union point of their respective parishes being selected as significant of the mutual character of their obligation, and also as an enduring landmark. A considerable portion of this bank, which has the appearance of having been artificially raised, still remains at the side of the road, and can be identified by a row of fir trees growing at the top. In Love's Coppice, about 1,500 yards west from where the bodies were found, a large number of silver coins of Elizabeth, James I., and Charles I. were discovered some few years ago, the greater portion of which came into the possession of the late Major Seymour, of Crowood, on whose property the wood is situate, who had them melted up and made into a tankard. A tradition exists, that during "The Troubles" many of the inhabitants of Ramsbury, fearful of being plundered and of losing their lives, took shelter in this wood; these coins may have been buried at this time by one of the refugees, and by some accident never again recovered.

To return to the King. With the foot and artillery his Majesty continued to advance steadily, and on Sunday morning, Sept. 17th, wrote to Prince Rupert, by John Ashburnham, as follows:—

"May it please your Highness, His Majesty hath commanded me to let your Highness know that he has altered his resolution of quartering this night at Burford, and now intends to quarter at Alnesscott at the Lady Ashcome's house where he will be better furnished with provisions for his army, and being the straighter way, will save three or four miles march. It is within 5 miles of Farrington, whither his Majesty desires you would advertise him this night of your proceedings. * * * Sir, your most humble Servant, JOHN ASHBURNHAM. Northleach, 12 o'clock, Sept. 17th, 1643." *

---

* E. Warburton's 'Prince Rupert,' vol. ii, 289.

The same evening another letter, written by Lord George Digby, was sent by the King:—

"May it please your Highness, The King hath received your Highness's letter written from Stamford, at five of the clock this evening, and commands me thereupon to let your Highness know, that since it appears by your intelligence that my Lord of Essex is not so far out of reach as was feared, he is desirous to make all haste towards him; his Majesty's army being all, except stragglers, well up hither to Alnesscott; his Majesty's desire therefore is that if your intelligence of the Rebells not being further advanced than Cricklade continue true, your Highness will be pleased to send speedily your opinion which way and to what place it will be fit for the King to march with his army tomorrow. As we looke uppon the map here, supposing that Essex points for Reading, we conceive Wantage will be the aptest place, but in this His Majesty conceives he is to be governed wholly by directions from your Highness according to your discoveries of their motions, or the impressions you shall make upon them, and therefore, he desires your Highness to send him speedy advertisements, of what you shall conceive best. Your Highness's most humble servant, GEORGE DIGBY. Alnesscott, at 8 at night, this Sunday. I am commanded to add, that you should consider to allow the foot here, as much rest as can well be without losing the opportunity. Sept. 17, 1643. Digby." *

The next morning Charles dispatched another missive to Rupert, in reply to a letter from the Prince, this time written by the Duke of Richmond:—

"Your Highness. I have let the King see what you writt, who approves of all in it, and will accordingly perform his part, only desires to have certain knowledge when Essex moved, or shall move from Cricklade, that if His Majesty's armie can arrive time enough (which he will the presently he receives the answer), he will take up his quarters at or about Wantage, so as to reach Newbury as you propose, but if that cannot be, he is loth to wearie the foot after so great a march as they have had, which you know infers that many are behind. Last night my Lord Digby writt to your Highness by the King's order upon the receipt of yours from Stamford, to which I can add what is only known since, that besides Vavasour and some other forces, Woodhouse will, I feel confident, come to-day with the Prince of Wales's regiment, say 700. * * * The motion of our armie depends much on the advertisement from you will give information. RICHMOND and LENOX, September 18, at 1, morning."†

After a brief halt at Faringdon, where the King dined, the troops were soon again on the move; and that evening they reached Wantage, his Majesty sleeping at the house of Sir Geo. Wilmot at Charlton. Thither Rupert sent an express messenger to the King urging him to advance with all speed in the direction of

---

* E. Warburton's 'Prince Rupert,' vol. ii, p. 290.

† The above extract has been made through the courtesy of G. A. Day, Esq., with the kind permission of V. F. Benett-Stanford, Esq., M.P., a descendant of Colonel Benett, Prince Rupert's Secretary, from one of the many original letters recently discovered at Pyt House, Wilts.

Newbury, as Essex was now fairly on his way to that place, the possession of the town being the object chiefly aimed at by the enemy. The Prince meanwhile marched with his horse from Aldbourne to Lamborne, where he refreshed his wearied troopers, and then eagerly pressed onwards to anticipate the Earl of Essex and check his progress. He was just in time, not a minute too soon; for arriving at Newbury early on Tuesday morning, the 19th September, he found the Lord General's advanced guard already in the town, engaged in preparing quarters for the on-coming troops of the Parliament.* With scarcely a moment's halt, the leading squadron of the King's troops, headed by the untiring Rupert, confronted the startled Parliament men who were ignorant of the nearness of the royal cavalry, but who, perceiving that resistance with so small a force was useless, made a precipitate flight, leaving several of their quarter-masters in the hands of the enemy. Troop after troop now poured into the town, which the Prince secured, and left Essex to the scanty resources of its immediate vicinity.

The march of the Royal Army from Gloucester had been thus conducted:—

		NIGHTS.	MILES.
"Sept. 14.	To Evisham	2	4
,, 16.	To Snowshill	1	6
,, 17.	To Norlich [Northleach] dinner, Alscot, supper	1	12
,, 18.	To Faringdon dinner, to Wantage Sir George Wilmot's, [Charlton] supper and bed	1	10
,, 19.	Dinner in the field Newbury, to supper and bed Mr. Cox's, and on Wednesday, the 20th, the great battle was struck there	4	10
,, 23.	To Oxford during pleasure ..	0	20"

Iter Carolinum.

NOTE. The actual distance from Wantage to Newbury and from the latter town to Oxford somewhat exceeds that above stated.

A few hours later, the brilliant troop of Life Guards, composed of the noblest and wealthiest cavaliers, who had no separate command, with casque and plume and glittering cuirass came moving on in stately and martial style. They heralded the approach of the ill-starred but gallant King, who, conspicuous in his steel armour, and on whose breast glittered the Star and George, rode at the head of his infantry. The young Prince of Wales (who held the rank of Captain of horse) was by his side; and for the first time during the war entered the good old town of Newbury, so soon to be associated with events of the deepest significance in connection with the great national revolution.

---

* 'Mercurius Aulicus,' September 19, 1643.

Lord Clarendon computes the amount of income possessed by this single troop as at least equal to that of all the Lords and Commons [in London] who made and maintained that war. Sir Philip Warwick, who tells us he himself "rode therein," computes this income at £100,000 per annum, equal, perhaps, to three times that sum according to our present standard.*

Newbury was the pivot, so to speak, around which much of the fighting, during the Civil War, in the southern part of England for a long period centred.

Its history goes far back into mediæval time. The Manor and Lordship, which had previously passed through a variety of hands,† were by letters patent, 1 Edward IV., 1460-1, granted by that monarch to his mother Cecilia, Duchess of York, for life, in recompense for her jointure, and from its description in this Instrument as "the manor and lordship of Newbury, with the *borough of Newbury*,"‡ the town had been probably incorporated, or was a borough by prescription, at a much earlier period than is generally supposed. Whilst held by the Crown the Manor was frequently assigned as a jointure to the Queens of England. Henry VIII. granted it to his Queen, Lady Jane Seymour; and James I. assigned it as a dower to Queen Anne, of Denmark; mother of Charles I. The latter made over the Manor to the Corporation of Newbury,§ in consideration of £50 and an annual payment of £20 4s. 2¼d., in answer to the following petition for its purchase, presented to Parliament:∥

"Rt. Honble. That the Mair, Aldermen, and Burgesses might take the Manor and liberties thereof in fee farme. Your honble. House hath bin informed that the said suite is only the desire of some few within the town, and not general, and yet that your honble. House hath bin obliged to admit the said Corporation to compound for the same, make bold to testifie your honble. House that we specially desire the said Corporation to be possessed thereof before any other. Wee having good experience of their great love and regard for the welfare of the Town and of helping to safe [save] the poor inhabitants thereof in all taxes and payments within the town that they possibly can, and in keeping the town in good order, for which your honble favour shewed to

---

* E. Warburton's 'Prince Rupert,' vol. i, p. 422.

† See " Hist. Newbury," and Godwin's " Worthies of Newbury."

‡ Rot. Pat. Edw. IV., pt. 4, m. 1. Pub. Rec. Off.

§ The lands which comprise a portion of the Manor of Newberry, Co. Cork, Ireland, are said to have been granted by the Crown to Capt. Newman, an ancestor of its present possessor, for his eminent services in the battle of the 20th September, the name of 'Newberry' being bestowed on the property in commemoration of the circumstance.

∥ Copied from a contemporary duplicate of the original in the Corporation archives.

them in their behalf, wee and all our posteritie with many more shall be each bound to pray to God for your honbles. long life and prosperous estate.

	William Howes, Mair.	
Gabriell Coxe, the elder.	Thomas Chokke.	Richard Money.
William Twisse (Rector).	William Grove.	Timothie Avery.
Thomas Dolman,	Robert Daunce.	William Wilmot.
&c.	&c.	&c.

Like many other places engaged in the staple manufacture of England—woollen cloth, the town of Newbury was well affected to the Parliament. The reasons are not far to seek. Besides being influenced by religion and a sense of independence, the inhabitants of manufacturing towns had especially suffered from the monopolies and extortions which had raised the price of necessaries and shackled the enterprise of trade. Again, the Protestant Nonconformists were a numerous and influential body, and in the same ranks, says Macaulay,[*] were to be found most of those members of the Established Church, who still adhered to the Calvinistic opinions, which, forty years before, had been generally held by the prelates and clergy. Such a man was Dr. Twisse, the Puritan Rector of Newbury, whose teaching must have exercised a decided influence in forming the opinions of the town and neighbourhood. Newbury had also, from its position on the great western road, its proximity to Oxford, the King's head-quarters, and the royal garrisons at Donnington, Basing, Faringdon, and Wallingford, suffered perhaps to a greater extent than any other town in the kingdom from the disastrous effects of this unhappy war. Its inhabitants were therefore induced by the strongest motives to espouse the cause of Parliament.

The following letters, written by members of each party, will enable the reader to form an impartial view of the proclivities of the people of Newbury at this juncture:—

Lord Grandison to Prince Rupert.
Marlboro' 8 Dec. [1642].

May itt please your High**es.** I know not how well to give credite to it, but there is two gentlemen nowe come from Newberie frighted from thence the lastt nightt by intelligence they had of some of the enemies forces were to come into Newberie *invited thether by the townsmen,* who have only reported the plague to bee there to keepe the King's troopes oute, how slight soever this may be, sure I AM THAT DISAFFECTED TOWNE CAN NOTT BEE TO MUCH PUNISHED BY YOUR HIGH**s.** for att my coming from Basingstoke they stopped all our baggage and had detained itt butt thatt they hered wee were strong enough to reveng itt. The Sherife of this Countie intends to be heer this day to order some things for his Maj**ties.** service, these same are the reasons thatt keept mee a day in this burnt and plundered quarter.   *   *   *

From your High**es** most humble faithful servant, GRANDISON.

---

[*] Hist. of Eng. vol. i, p. 106.

This letter, from the Pyt House Collection, appears to have been written immediately after the capture and plunder of Marlborough by the Royalists ("the most notoriously disaffected town of all the country," says Clarendon). This was the first garrison taken on either side; when a great part of the town was burnt. Lord Grandison died from the effects of wounds received at the siege of Bristol the following year.

Two days previously the Earl of Essex wrote to the Parliamentary Colonels Goodwin and Hurry:—

S'rs,—Since I receiv'd your letter I have had information that Marlborough has been 2 days assaulted by the King's forces [Essex here gives instructions to the two Colonels to march with all speed to its relief]. * * * *You have Newberry, a very honest towne*, to march to in ye way, where you may encourage forces to follow you, *and it is a very good place to assist you upon all occasions*. Your assured friend,

Windsor, Dec. 6, 1642, 8 o'clock at night.　　　　　　ESSEX.

Endorsed for Col. Goodwin, Col. Hurry, or either of them.*

Col. Goodwin, on his return to Newbury from Marlborough, gave the following account of his proceedings in a letter without superscription, but probably addressed to Philip, Lord Wharton, his son-in-law, with whom he was in frequent correspondence at this time:—

My Lord,—We have had many painful journies since I saw you, but none like that of Thursday, when we missed meeting the King's forces, and only because we could not get out our dragoons till noon. We went then on to Wantage, where were 3 regiments, 1 of horse, 1 of foot, 1 of dragoons, and my Lord Digby with certain ladies, they had intelligence before we came up, which was in dark night, and hasted away, we caught about 50 prisoners, my Lord Jermyn's lady and 3 or 4 other women, Sir Robt. Lee and his broth'· and there were some thirty slaine, some ammunition was left, which because we could not bring away was spoyled. I can write no more to night, the rather because I must be up by 5 in the morning to visit Andover, where my Lord Grandison is, they say, with 3,000 horse and dragoons, but I hope not so many. I think I shall run away and be with you shortly for we are all most abominable plunderers, as bad as Prince Robert [Rupert], and shall be as much hated, as when complaints come, I am ashamed to look an honest man in the face, truly, it is as bad to me as a bullet. It is now nearing morning, excuse me to all my friends: the Lord be with you all. Yours ever to command. A. G., Newbury. Sunday morninge, Dec. [12th]. P.S.—Our letters to my Lord Genl. surely are intercepted.†

In a letter written by Col. Dalbier‡ from Newbury and presented to the House of Lords by the Committee of Oxon, Bucks, and Berks, requesting the payment of the forces under his

---

* Tanner MSS., Bibl. Bodl. v. 62/2.
† Carte's MSS., Letters, Bibl. Bodl. v. 103. For particulars of this service at Marlborough and Wantage, see Waylen's Hist. Marlb., pp. 166—9.
‡ ... ... D Albier, Dalbiere, or Dulbier.

command then lying in the town, it was ordered by their Lordships, "That some course be speedily and effectually taken for the maintenance of these forces, lest they disband and be lost, and that town [Newbury] *which hath on all occasions manifested so much affection for the Parliament* come again within the power of the enemy."*

From all this it will be seen that, though the town was frequently in the Royalists' hands, and the neighbouring Castle of Donnington maintained a royal garrison during the whole of the years 1643 to 1646, the general sympathy of the people was rather with Roundhead than with Cavalier.

To the Royalist cause it was a place of great military value. Situated as it is on one of the most ancient and important passages of the Kennet, it is a place of considerable strategical importance. If occupied by an enemy, it menaced the main roads leading from the west by Reading to London; and for the Royalist Army, based as it was on Oxford, its possession enabled them to intercept any movement that might be attempted in the Kennet Valley, while their own line of retreat was completely covered. In addition to this, Donnington Castle, an ancient fortress the strength of which had been enormously increased by the construction of fieldworks of good trace and profile, further protected a retrograde movement if it became necessary, and acted, so to speak, as an advanced fort on this side of the Thames. The castle was at the time held by a staunch Royalist, Sir John Boys, and was situated about one mile north of Newbury near the Oxford road, which it completely commanded. South of the town, the ground rises gradually to a narrow plateau occupying the area between the Kennet and the En or Wash Rivulet, the western extremity of which towards Hungerford was known as Enborne Heath, and the eastern, in the immediate neighbourhood of Newbury, as Wash Common, over which the road from Oxford to Southampton passed. It was on this latter portion of the high land that the First Battle of Newbury was fought. So that while the Army of Essex, which had crossed the Kennet at Hungerford, was moving on the outer arc, as it were, to gain the passages of the stream lower down and so reach Reading, that of the King, after the cavalry skirmish just described on Aldbourne Chase, was marching by the shorter chord and had occupied the town as well as the fields to the South of it before their adversaries had reached the Wash. The option of giving or refusing battle therefore rested with the King, and as he encamped his troops on the night of 19th September in the fields below the heights his choice had evidently been made.

Meanwhile the Parliamentary General, after the engagement on Aldbourne Chase, marched to the Eastward under dis-

---

* Journal of Ho. of Lords, 8 Jan., 1645.

couraging circumstances. "We were much distressed," says one of his men, for want of sleep as also for other sustenance. It was a night of much rain and we were wet to the skin." In passing through the principal street of Aldbourne on his way to Hungerford, two of his ammunition wagons unfortunately broke down, but to prevent their falling into the hands of the enemy, matches were put to them and they were left to explode. This proved some hindrance to the pursuers, and the Earl managed to reach Chilton without further interference. Here some of his army lodged that night in the fields. Others were at Hungerford. Essex himself quartered at Chilton House.[*] The army of the Parliament suffered greatly from want of food and from exposure of the weather, and for three days could get no supplies for man or horse beyond the scanty stock they carried with them. The enemy's force followed them so closely, and the royalist horse were so far above them in number that they could not with any safety send out parties to forage, as their opponents did.

By six o'clock on Tuesday morning, 19th September, Essex and his troops again met at Hungerford [†] where what little sustenance could be obtained was portioned out to the men. The order to march was soon given, and the columns of the Parliament, with the brave Earl leading the van, advanced on their eventful enterprise.

The route taken by Essex, who appears even at this time to have been ignorant of the King's intentions, and not to have anticipated his rapid movements, was through Kintbury and Hamstead to Enborne by the road parallel with, and south of the Kennet; but on approaching Newbury, where he had designed to quarter, he found to his surprise that his advanced guard had been dislodged and driven out, and that the King occupied the town and its approaches. Thereupon he drew his army into a favourable position in the fields screened by the woods at Enborne,

---

[*] Chilton House, at this time, appears to have been the property of Mr. John Packer, proprietor of Donnington Castle. His second son, John, a Fellow of the Royal College of Physicians of London, described himse'f in his Will dated 22 June, 1703, as of Chilton-Foliatt, Wilts. It was at Dr. Packer's house at Chilton that the Marquis of Halifax, the Earl of Nottingham, and Lord Godolphin, the Commissioners appointed by James II. to treat with the Prince of Orange, slept on the night of Friday, 7th, December 1688. Chi'ton Lodge another seat in this village was the property of the eminent Cromwellian statesman Sir Bulstrode Whitelock, and here the "Memorials" and other works were chiefly written. He died at Chilton, in 1675, and was buried at Fawley, near Henley-on-Thames, but there is no memorial of him in the church. His widow, Lady Whitelock, died at Chilton in 1684.

[†] Hungerford Park, with all manorial rights within its limits, had been granted by the Crown in 1595 to the Trustees of Essex's unfortunate father, who was beheaded in 1601. There was no house in Hungerford Park when granted to the Earl of Essex, and it is not improbable he was the builder of the ancient mansion pulled down by a later owner, Mr. Dalbiac, at the east end of which were the arms of Queen Elizabeth: a large and lofty room over the servant's hall was called Queen Elizabeth's room. Lysons' *Magna Britannia*, vol. i. p. 296.

and here encamped; his men, notwithstanding all the perils and trials of a long and toilsome march, being "full of courage and in no way disheartened at their hard service." Essex himself it is said, sought shelter in a poor thatched cottage, which still stands as the Lord General's traditional resting place.*

He found himself in a position of considerable difficulty and danger. It was essential, for his plans, that he should convey his army as far as possible intact to London, and his object would have been gained by avoiding a general action altogether. But speed was also essential, and with ill disciplined troops, the inferior equipment, cumbrous artillery, baggage, and supply-trains of those times, the shortest road was more than ever the quickest. Divergence from the most direct route was not only difficult and slow of execution, both from the want of accurate maps or information, and the want of experience in directing the movements of large bodies of men, but also from the inferior nature of all the roads save those that formed the great arteries of communication. But there was yet another reason. The land was not so well drained in those days as in ours. Low lands were more liable to periodical inundations, and were therefore more generally impassable to men and horses, let alone wheeled vehicles; and naturally dry heath or high land, such as characterises the ridge of hills between the Kennet and the En Brook, afforded as a rule more ready and more certain facilities for marching. Hence it was that, even at the risk of a battle, the line of advance was directed in front of Newbury by Crockham, Greenham, and Crookham Heaths on London.

The presence of the Royalist Army at Newbury, the possession therefore of all the points of passage of the river in this neighbourhood, and the occupation of the London Road, all compelled him to execute that most difficult of all manœuvres, a flank march in the presence of the enemy.

Military criticism on the Earl's difficulties seems almost unnecessary. It is evident that to pass by the hostile force without offering battle exposed him to three dangers; an attack on his left flank as he passed, an assault on his rear after he *had* passed, and the possible capture of his baggage which would move by the best road and in rear of his columns. The first danger would lead to his defeat in detail, for the left wing would have had to stand the attack of the whole of the King's Army perhaps before the right wing could come to its assistance, thus breaking through the common principle of never offering your divided

---

* Bigg's Cottage, where local tradition records Essex slept the night before the battle, is a time-worn old tenement, apparently of an age anterior to these events, situate at the foot of Bigg's Hill (hereafter referred to) on the borders of what was formerly Enborne Heath or Down. and in about the centre of Essex's position. The occupier of the cottage states that, in clearing out a well near the spot some years since, some coins of the Caroline period and a diamond ring were found.

fractions to the blows of a vastly superior force. The second might have been still more disastrous, as the forces not arrayed in battle order and marching along several roads might have been both crushed and routed. The last danger was all important, for without supplies of ammunition, let alone food, large bodies of troops must either spread for forage and food and become disorganized and scattered, or remain concentrated and starve. There was, and is, but one way of effecting this strategic manœuvre, namely to place a sufficient obstacle between the advancing force and the enemy, such as a river, which either cannot be crossed or the passages of which are in the hands of strong detachments of the force. But these conditions did not obtain, for Newbury was then the Royal Head Quarters, so that the Parliamentary Army could not hope to pass rapidly by, while flanking detachments resisted the enemy's attempt to debouch on the exposed flank. He was prevented from marching by the roads south of the En, probably, both because of the wide detour, which would have given the Royalists time to concentrate larger forces, and, moving more rapidly than he by the better roads in the Kennet Valley, again present themselves before him under perhaps even more disadvantageous circumstances, and also by the inferior character of the roads. So it was that the Earl of Essex drew up his forces between the Kennet and Bigg's Hill, resolved to cut his way through the army of the King, should it attempt to bar his path to London.

Lord Essex's camping ground appears to have extended from the irregularly enclosed fields on the left, which protected him against a surprise by the Newbury and Kintbury Road, to Crockham Heath on the left. A natural ravine of some depth sheltered him in front, whilst his left flank had the protection of the woods at Hamstead, and of the Kennet river, and his right rested on the little river En. Here, with the rain falling in torrents, no fire! no food! the weary but resolute soldiers of the Parliament remained under arms all night "impatient of the sloth of darkness, and wishing for the morning's light to exercise their valour." Essex's dispositions were well made. An attack by the Royalists along the Kintbury-Enborne-Newbury road might have captured his baggage, and, if pushed successfully, have "turned" his left flank, cutting him off from the best road of retreat (that by Kintbury and Hungerford), and possibly driving his army back in disorder on the En Brook.To cross this by bad roads and few bridges would have led to the abandonment of his artillery and baggage,—to his being driven South and thus far off his road to London, and have increased the demoralization and disorder of his troops. Hence it is that his reserve guarded this important road and took post at Enborne, while close to it lay the strong left wing of the main army. By occupying so extended a front as that from Enborne to the En he obtained other advan-

ROBERT DEVEREUX, EARL OF ESSEX.
From a scarce print in the British Museum.

tages. His flanks, resting closely on the stream and on the wooded headland of Hamstead Park, were not liable to be turned, —that is, the enemy could not get round them and attack his flank or rear without his knowledge. Lastly with the large force at his command, it was well to utilize as many roads as possible, as at all times movement is easier by beaten tracks than across country; and, so long as his forces were not too widely disseminated, he displayed a sound appreciation of the military situation in covering the three lines of advance by the roads, Bigg's Hill—Trundle Hill, Crockham—Wash Common, by Skinner's Green, Enborne—Newbury, which led him out on to the open land where he meant to give battle to the King. It seems exceedingly probable that, though the artillery (marching by the best road as all wheeled vehicles naturally would) may have halted at the "Slings" near Enborne, it was eventually brought up to Crockham Heath, both because its advance thence could be directed by any of the roads to the front (then partly in the occupation of the cavalier outposts) which might eventually seem best, and also because, being centrally situated, it would be safer: artillery, always cumbrous, was terribly so then; guns were easily captured, and difficult to move away. There, however, they were not only in safety but, as in all times good artillery positions are on high land because the extended view thence enables the gunner to obtain the greatest possible advantage from the range the weapon has, the slow-moving guns of the Parliamentary Army were at any rate somewhat nearer their work, nearer their probable point of application, than down in the low-lying road that led from Enborne to Newbury.

Essex, having completed all his arrangements, determined to direct his attack against that position of the Royalist line on the Wash which barred the upper way to London, rather than attempt a passage through the town. In the stillness of the early dawn the Parliamentary General, favoured by the cover which sheltered his camping ground, got his men under arms; and, riding from from regiment to regiment, he told his soldiers that the enemy had all the advantages, "the Hill, the Town, Hedges, Lane, and River;" but with calm determination they unanimously cried out, "Let us fall upon them! We will, by God's assistance, beat them from them all!"* and every man prepared himself promptly for the desperate struggle.

"And you that know the gain at Newberry!
Seeing the General, how undauntedly
He then encouraged you for England's right!
When Royal forces fled, he stood the fight!"†

The disposition of the army was effected with great military

---
* Vicar's Parl. Chron.
† "A Funerall Monument to the most renowned Earl of Essex," printed in London, 1646.

skill. The right, under Major General Skippon was on the rising ground by "Biggs Hill"* and Hill Farm, extending along the Enborne Valley towards the Wash, the centre on the plateau, and the left in a more northerly direction towards Hamstead (Crockham Heath). The baggage or train was placed in or near what is now the front of Hamstead Park, opposite the Rectory, Enborne, described in the Parish Map as "The Slings,"† under the shelter of the Hamstead Woods; and here also was their reserve both of horse and foot.

It has been said "there is no sound that ever rent the air so terrible as the deep silence of suspense before the battle-word is given; it is the moment when the soul sinks under the awe of something that thrills deeper than any fear;" and during that dread pause at Newbury many a fervent prayer was doubtless offered up to the God of Battles by the true hearts that abounded in both armies. They were prayerful men in those days, though superstitious and believers in witchcraft, as will be seen by the story of the death of the witch at Newbury, given in the Appendix. Prayers were regularly put up at the head of most regiments in both armies, even when arrayed for battle, and each regiment had its own chaplain. The religious *petitions* of the Parliamentarians were frequently drawn out to a great length, while those of the Cavaliers were brief and to the purpose, such as old Sir Jacob Astley's at the battle of Edgehill, who dismounting from his horse, and taking a pike in his hand, offered up the following prayer at the head of his troops; *O Lord, Thou knowest how busy I must be this day; if I forget Thee, do not Thou forget me.—March on, boys!*

No sooner had the mists of an autumn morning disclosed the Royalists in battle array on the Wash, than Essex, anticipating their tactics, began to move forward to meet the enemy. The left division of his army under his own personal command, marched from Crockham Heath to Skinner's Green, and took possession of a neglected position of considerable military importance, a rounded hill or spur in front of the lane leading from the Wash to the Enborne road, from whence a battery could "command all the plain before Newbury."*

---

‡ *Biggs Hill.* The Hill referred to by Lord Clarendon and other writers on the Civil Wars as the spot above Essex drew up his army in order of battle. This Hill of considerable length and elevation, is near Hill Farm in the occupation of Mr. George Heath, on the line of march of Essex from Kintbury *viâ* Hamstead village and Enborne Street. Biggs Hill is not marked in the old Ordnance Map, but it comprises the portions of land marked in the Tithe Map, "The Common" and "Hill Ground." Enborne Heath, Down, or Common was enclosed about 65 years ago.

† Ludlow, in his Memoirs, refers to "Slings" as a species of Artillery used by the Parliamentarians.

* Lord Digby, in a letter written from Newbury the day after the battle, describes this elevation as "a round hill from whence a battery could command all the plain before Newbury;" this is literally the case. It is marked in the Parish Map, "Hilly Ground."

Early next morning, September 20th, the royal standard was moved forward, and floated proudly on the Wash. The King stationed his left wing and centre upon the brow of the hill sloping towards Newbury, his right wing resting on the low ground in front of the town, where it was protected by hedges lined by Dragoons.* The heavy guns were planted on a roughly raised battery, remains of which still exist,† extending from near the "Gun" public-house obliquely across the plateau, whence they could play upon any attacking column advancing up the hill, and open an enfilading fire on any flank movement of Essex, should he show himself on the brow of the opposite eminence. Whitelock corroborates this view. He states that the King had on his right hand the advantage of the river, and on the left a hill about half-a-mile from the town, *where he had planted his ordnance.* Oldmixon adds, "by reason of this disposition the Parliamentarians had no passage to them, but what was exposed to the fire of the enemy's cannon." And that this position is the true one is proved further both by the remains still existing and by the "Mercurius Aulicus," which, in relating the King's preparations the night before the battle, informs us, that "The London pamphlets gape wide upon Aulicus for saying the King at Newbury was forced to fight for a place to fight on, still alledging that His Majesty on the Tuesday night *had his cannon planted on the hill.* To which I answer once for all, that their dead bodies left behind on the place the next day manifest the contrary." As in all controversies, there are two sides to the question whether the King occupied the Common with his guns the night before the battle or not; and in the statements of either side there is a basis of truth. For though the Parliamentary writers may assert, and truthfully enough, that the King had to fight from the early morning of the 20th, in order to complete the deployment of his troops for battle, it is not the less likely that the level ground of the plateau was, at least partially, occupied the evening before. The fact that the bulk of the King's army had encamped, late on the afternoon of the 19th, after a wearisome march, on the fields south of Newbury shows that, at any rate, the front of battle taken up the next day from the En to the Kennet was not assumed until the very morning of the great fight. Yet it is probable that the entrenchment for the guns was chosen and

---

* " So called from 'Dragon,' as they fought in air or on the ground, mounted or on foot. Except in cases of surprise, however, they seldom fired on horseback, and never charged; they were, in fact, infantry with horses, to enable them to make more rapid movements: they were thrown forward to feel the way, skirmishing from behind ditches as they advanced, or covering a retreat in the same fashion: one man held 10 horses in the rear, while his comrades, their riders, fought. Their long carbines were called 'dragons' from the cock being made in that shape." *Orry's Art of War.*

† See Plan of the Battle.

prepared the evening before the battle, though possibly it was only partially armed.

The scene on Wash Common this September morning has thus been described in the picturesque language of Lord Carnarvon:— "There on the ground, the features of which to this day reflect the local incidents of the battle, the two armies were drawn up in hostile array. Could we recall that scene, how different, probably, the features in either host! On the Parliamentarian side you would have seen the Roundheads mustering in great masses on the brow of that heathy hill, with their steeple-crowned hats and basket-hilted swords, whilst from their dull-featured, but resolute ranks there ascended the hum of some psalm, invoking God, as of old, to strike for His chosen people, and to smite the enemy; or there passed from mouth to mouth the watchword, as at Marston Moor 'God with us;' or in the skilful disposition of their array you might have distinguished the different colours and insignia of each leader and his followers. Here Lord Saye-and-Sele's men in blue; there Lord Brooke's in purple; here some of Hampden's men in green; and there, perhaps, Colonel Meyrick's regiment in grey; here, Sir Arthur Haslerigg's cuirassiers, who went by the name of 'The Lobsters;' and there, the London bands—who turned the fortune of that day, and who, as an old writer says, showed that they could use a sword in the field as well as a met-wand in the shop, in their well-known red uniform; whilst in the centre of the host, under the guidance of the saturnine Essex, you might have seen his followers with their orange colours, and have heard the homely cry, with which they went to battle—'Hey for old Robin!' But if you had cast your eye to the other side of the valley, you would have witnessed a different scene. There you would have seen the cavaliers and gentlemen, with their troops of tenants, retainers, and servants, gathering fast around their standards, in all the pride of strength and birth, and high spirit, their red scarfs flaunting in the cool breeze of an autumn morning; their spurs jingling, their plumes waving, their long hair (so much abominated by the Puritan divines) floating on their shoulders; in one word, with all that exquisite grace of dress and manner which even yet breathes from the canvass of the great painter of the day. They too had their watchword, as at Marston Moor, 'God and the King:' they too stood ranged in their different battalia and under different leaders. Here Newcastle's 'Lambs' as they were called, glistened in their white dresses; there Lord Northampton's men, in green; here perhaps, rode Lunsford, as he is described in the ballad, in his blue rocket, surrounded by his fire-eating horse; while on the edge of the hill, under a black banner, edged with yellow, and bearing the arms of the Palatine, might have been seen Prince Rupert's impetuous cavalry, clothed in their black uniform—black, a fitting colour for that thunderstorm of war which broke with resistless fury on the ranks of the enemy." *

The relative situations of the two armies were greatly different. The King possessed immense advantages if they had been properly turned to account. His army was strongly posted between the enemy and London, well supplied with a great store of provisions and other necessaries both for horse and man, which the town and people of Newbury, on intelligence that Essex was advancing towards them, had provided for his troops.† The King's line of retreat was safe, and he had the town of Newbury to protect him, had he found it necessary to fall back; while the enemy was in want and shelterless, and must either fight or starve. Though sensible of the strength of the position, even the impetuous Rupert advised passive resistance instead of an advance to meet the enemy; and the King himself, even while conscious of his superiority, resolved to engage only on such terms as should ensure success.

Essex's hopes, on the other hand, when he found himself outstripped in the race, were chiefly based on the supposition that the King's troops were tired and unable to come to an actual engagement, and strengthened by a confidence that Waller (his old rival), who had been desired by the Parliament to advance to the relief of his army, would be with him that night. But at this time, Waller was quietly lying at Windsor, with 2,000 horse and as many foot, quite unconcerned as to what might befall the Earl at Newbury, as the Earl had been on his behalf at Roundway Down; otherwise, had he advanced upon the King at Newbury when the Earl was on the south side of the Kennet, the Royalists might have been in great danger of an utter defeat.

The anxiety of the Royalists to gain the passages of the Kennet on the road to London is equally evident. Referring again to Lord Byron:—he says, "the day following, both armies march't as if it had been for a wager, which should come to Newbury first, and it was our fortune to prevent them of that quarter, and likewise of Donnington Castle."

On arriving at Newbury,‡ the King, finding Essex encamped so close at hand, had no alternative but to prevent his further advance, and without loss of time took up a position extending from the town to Wash Common, where a portion of the horse

---

* 'Hampshire: Its early and later History'; being two Lectures delivered at the Basingstoke Mechanics' Institution, by the Earl of Carnarvon, 1857.

† 'The True Informer,' Sept. 23, 1643.

‡ The King during his stay in Newbury quartered at the house of the Mayor, Mr. Gabriel Coxe. Afterwards when Charles II. who had been present with his father in both engagements, visited the town in 1663, and went over the battle-fields, Mr. Coxe presented a petition to his Majesty for payment of the expenses incurred in entertaining and providing for the Royal Suite; but it seems he obtained no redress.

was already posted; his front was strengthened by several hasty entrenchments, portions of which still remain, and every disposition was made for a vigorous contest.

Wash Common, before its enclosure and the construction of modern roads, comprised a large area of land now under cultivation on both sides of the Andover Road from Newbury, thus giving at the time of the battle a much more extended field of operations than is now presented by the existing *terrain*.

The hasty advance of the Parliamentary troops seems to have led the Royalists to disregard the very common precaution of a study of the ground. They in all probability pushed beyond the town towards Wash Common by the main road leading south out of Newbury; but the value of the rounded spurs near Skinner's Lane, which commanded the whole of the low-lying ground between the Town and the Wash, had escaped their notice either through negligence or fatigue after their hasty march. Byron's account fully bears out this view, he says, "Here another error was committed, and that a most gross and absurd one, in not viewing the ground, though we had day enough to have done it, and not possessing ourselves of those hills above the town by which the enemy was necessarily to march the next day to Reading."

Owing to the close proximity of the two combatants the night before the battle, several skirmishes ensued between advanced parties of each army. In one sharp encounter between a party of Royalist horse under Hurry and a detached body of the enemy, Lord Percy was cut in the hand and Lord Jermyn had a narrow escape, his head-piece being battered about his ears and his eye injured. These attacks on the out-posts continued till dark. Scouts were employed on either side to bring in intelligence.

The Royal Army was commanded by King Charles in person; Lord Forth,* subsequently created Earl of Brentford, being the General immediately under the King. The Cavalry was led by Prince Rupert and Sir John Byron, Lord Wilmot acting as Lieutenant-General. The Foot was "ordered" by Sir Nicholas Byron (uncle to Sir John, afterwards Lord Byron). Amongst the more distinguished cavalier officers holding commands at Newbury were the following—*Earls:* Carnarvon, Lindsey, Northampton, Nottingham, Cleveland, Holland, Clare, and Bedford;—*Lords:* Bellasyse, Digby, Jermyn, Percy, Somerset (second son of Henry, first Marquis of Worcester), Andover, Chandos, and Molyneux; also the Hon. Henry Bertie, Sir Charles Lucas, Sir George Lisle, Sir Edward Waldegrave,

---

* This and many of the following names are referred to in the Biographical Appendix.

Patrick Ruthen, Earl of Brainford

Sir Bernard Brocas, Sir Lewis Kirke, Sir Henry Slingsby, Sir William Vavasour, Sir Thomas Aston, Sir Anthony Mansel, Sir Michael Wodehouse, Sir Jacob Astley, Sir John Frechville, Sir John Hurry, Major-General George Porter, and Major-General Daniel (commanding Prince of Wales' regiment); *Colonels:* Spencer, St. John, Edward Villiers, Will. Legge, Daniel O'Neill, Morgan, Eure, D'Arcy, Poole, Platt, Wheatly, Murray, Charles Gerard, Edward Gerard, and Constable;— *Captains:* Bagehot (who took the command of the Earl of Carnarvon's troop when its gallant leader fell), Basil Woodd, Panton, Sheldon, Scott (of Sir Arthur Aston's regiment), Singleton, Clifton, and Newman.

The following are mentioned as serving in the royal ranks as Volunteers:—Henry Spencer (first Earl of Sunderland), James Hay (second Earl of Carlisle), Henry Mordaunt (Earl of Peterborough), Lucius Cary (Viscount Falkland, whose duties as the King's Secretary gave him no position in the field), Sir Edward Sackville (son of Edward, fourth Earl of Dorset), severely wounded in the battle,* Sir John Russell (son of Francis, fourth Earl of Bedford), Hon. Henry Howard (son of the Earl of Berkshire and brother to Lord Andover), Colonel Richard Fielding,† and Colonel Stroud.

On the side of the Parliament, the Earl of Essex was Lord General of the army; and amongst the more conspicuous leaders were Lord Robarts or Roberts, Lord Grey of Groby, Sir John Meyrick, who "ordered" the artillery, Sir Philip Stapleton, Sir James Ramsay, Sir William Constable, Sir William Balfour, Sir William Boteler, Sir Samuel Luke, Sir William Brooks, Sir Richard Bulstrode, Sir William Springer, Sir John Meldrum, Sir Arthur Goodwin, Major-General Skippon, Major-Gen. Deane, and Lt.-General Middleton; and Colonels—Sheffield, Mainwaring, Bartley or Barclay, Norton, Dalbier, Holmsted, Tyrill, Thompson, Greaves, Langham, Draper, Brackley, Harvey, Holbourne, Tucker, White, and Fortescue.

Following up the history of the battle, we learn that the Royalists, at daybreak, were surprised to find the Parliamentarians in possession of the little hill above Cope Hall,‡ and on their side commenced hostilities by dispatching Sir John Byron with a portion of the right wing of horse and foot to assault and engage this threatening point, the circumstances of which he thus

---

* In 1645, being with a party of the King's forces, at Chawley, near Abingdon, he was taken prisoner by those of the Parliament, and stabbed to death in cold blood by a Parliamentary soldier.

† Previously governor of Reading, which he was thought to have surrendered too easily; he was tried by court martial and sentenced to be shot; but afterwards pardoned, he fought valiantly for the King.

‡ In an old terrier of the lands held by the town of Newbury, in the time of Queen Elizabeth, "Coppod Hall" is mentioned as having been given for a yearly obit by Robert Long.

narrates;—"The next day my brigade of horse was to have the van, and about 5 in the morning I had orders to march towards a little hill full of enclosures, which the enemy (through the negligence before mentioned) had possessed himself of and had brought up two small field pieces and was bringing up more, whereby, they would both have secured their march on Reading (the highway was lying hard by) and withal so annoyed our army which was drawn up in the bottom, where the King himself was, that it would have been impossible for us to have kept the ground. The hill, as I mentioned, was full of enclosures and extremely difficult for horse service, so that my orders were, only with my own and Sir Thos. Aston's regiment to draw behind the commanded foot led by Lord Wentworth and Col. George Lisle, and to be ready to second them, in case the enemy's horse should advance towards them: the rest of my brigade was by Prince Rupert commanded to the Heath, where most of the other horse and foot were drawn."

This advance of the King's right wing, which was nearest the enemy and under his fire, was a movement absolutely necessary to cover the deployment of the remainder of the army to the left over the Wash and towards the En. The advance of Rupert's cavalry to the Wash fully coincided with and supported this movement, for they could get there and block the road before the left wing and centre (of foot) could gain the heights. Meanwhile the cavalry of the right wing, unable to operate directly over the enclosed intricate land below the position occupied by the Parliamentarians, was compelled to support the advance by moving away to the left flank till the open ground of Wash Common was reached and a charge could be delivered. They could find no charging ground before this, owing to the hedgerows and escarpments which lay opposite the right flank; and even when the advance of the right was so assisted by this advance of "horse" on their left, the first attempt to force the hedgerows proved absolutely fruitless.

Simultaneous with the advance of Lord Essex's left, a corresponding movement was made by the veteran Skippon, who on Enborne Heath pushed forward the right, to co-operate with Essex; the efforts of both divisions being principally directed against the King's position on the Wash, where the storm of battle was especially maintained throughout the day; and from straggling shots the battle widened until nearly 20,000 men were engaged in deadly conflict.

The King, as previously mentioned, had determined to stand on the defensive and await the advance of Essex, but the uncontrollable ardour and impetuosity which urged on some of the young cavalier commanders frustrated his intentions and confused his whole order of battle. Scarcely had part of the Parliamentary right wing shown on Enborne Heath, when a party of the royal cavalry bore down upon them.

"Then 'spur and sword' was the battle-word, and we made
  their helmets ring,
Shouting like madmen all the while 'For God and for
  the King!'
And, though they snuffled psalms, to give the rebel dogs
  their due,
Where the roaring shot poured thick and hot they were
  stalwart men and true."
                        Song—" The Old Cavalier."

The battle soon became general, and obliged the Royalists to move to the support of these advanced troops, leaving their artillery behind them unavailable on the Common: "many of the officers flinging off their doublets in bravado and leading on their men in their shirts, as if armour was a useless encumbrance in dealing with the base-born London apprentices whom they came rather to triumph over than to fight."

The left wing of the Parliamentary army, led by Essex, and with Lord Roberts' brigade of horse in front, now advances towards the Royalist force on the Wash. Stimulated by the example of their chief, and charging gallantly up the slopes below the heath, in face of a biting fire of musquetry and grape, they sweep onward up the heights. They are gaining ground!

But at this critical moment Sir John Byron, at whose side a few minutes before had ridden the noble-hearted Falkland, now "stretched coldly in the sleep of death" under a whitethorn hedge, advanced at the head of the right wing of the royal cavalry, and, under the fire of two guns at musket distance and a deadly shower of bullets, charges them in front and flank with a determination that even the soldiers of the Parliament with all their enthusiasm and bravery are unable to withstand. Staggered by the fierce onslaught, for a moment they recoil, but it is only to rally instantly and renew the fight with undiminished resolution.

The "city red and blue regiments," largely composed of the London apprentices, are now moved away from the right, and approach to share the fight; the main body of the trained-bands and auxilliaries meanwhile fighting valiantly on Enborne Heath, with their brave old leader Skippon, under the protection of his formidable cavalry commanded by Middleton. Essex courageously leads his young citizen-soldiers fresh and ready for the struggle "up the hill." The royalists too have received a reinforcement, and Prince Rupert with his daring followers ride to the very points of the pikes. The valour and intrinsic worth of the London brigade was now to be tested, and not in vain; for the foaming squadrons of steel-clad cuirassiers came rushing forward, but these dashing troops failed again and again to penetrate those serried lines, which "stood undaunted and conquerors against all, and like a grove of pines in a day of wind and tempest, they only moved their legs, heads, or arms but kept their footing sure." The action here was long and bloody, and told fearfully on the Parliamentary ranks. Charge succeeds charge! Cheer for cheer is given! Fearless amidst the storm of battle boldly urging on his men, is seen the gallant King,* and the Royal colours for a time are borne triumphant. But the tide of battle turns, Essex's reserve of foot is near, the cavalry rally on their supports, the defiant banner of the Earl is borne aloft,† and waving his hat, with cries of "Forward! brave hearts,!" he quickly re-forms his disordered troops and again confronts the foe. A desperate *melée* ensues. The plumed helmet and the steel cap get mixed together, the combatants close and fight hand-to-hand, but at length the Parliamentary cavalry are hurled back, their scattered infantry are no longer able to support themselves, but fighting heroically to the last are driven "to the lane's end where they first came in." The royalists follow, but in their victorious excitement pursue too far, and before those who enter the lane can disengage themselves, they are nigh well cut to pieces by the Puritan troopers, who have made a stand. A tradition is preserved in the village of Enborne to this day, that the narrow lane leading to Skinner's Green became so choked with the slain that a passage had to be cleared before the troops and guns could again be moved forward.

For hours the fight is here maintained with unflinching and uniform gallantry on both sides. Again and again the Roundhead charges are renewed and repelled. But towards the afternoon Essex, profiting by the advantage gained through the operations of his right wing at Enborne, has crowned the plateau of the Wash; and is now on equal terms with his opponents.

The temporary repulse of the Parliamentary left in Skinner's Lane was possibly due somewhat to the series of brilliant charges just described over the level ground of the Common, excellent

---

* It would seem that the King took an active part in this battle. Sergt. Foster in his "True Relation" says, I am creditably informed by those who were this day in the King's army, that the King himself brought up a regiment of foot, and another of horse into the field, and gave fire to two pieces of ordnance, riding up and down all that day in a soldier's grey coat." In the 'Mercurius Aulicus' (the Royalist journal) of Sept. 21, 1643, it is related that "the Rebels espying from the Hill, that many stood bareheaded in a part of the field, supposed the King to be there, and made great shott at the place," but significantly adds, "The Lord covered the head of His Anointed."

† The Cornet or flag of the Earl of Essex was—"orange, on it a label (like the King's, that is 'With God and my Right') of silver, with this motto in roman letters, sable, 'VIRTVTIS COMES INVIDIA'; the lining of the motto or back, of gold; fringed with gold and silver, tasselled gold." (Prestwick's 'Respublica,' p. 24.) It is related that Essex was advised to leave off his *white hat*, because it rendered him so conspicuous an object to the enemy. No! replied the Earl, "It is not the hat, but the heart! the hat is not capable of either fear or honour!"

THE FIRST BATTLE OF NEWBURY. 33

for such a purpose. The Parliamentary centre touched the left wing at the point where the lane debouches on the flat; and naturally when the enemy, driven back into this close ground, had rallied on his supports, the hand-to-hand *melée* must have resulted in disorder to the horse and have choked the narrow road with bodies. In fact the temporary check sustained by the Parliamentary left led to the consequent speedy withdrawal of the centre, hastened too by the influence of Rupert's charges, and the battle on this side probably remained more or less stationary without marked advantage on either side until the advance of Essex's right wing brought greater numerical superiority on his side upon the level ground of the plateau.

The following letter extracted from the Rupert correspondence * more especially refers to the engagement near Cope Hall, and supports the view here taken. The letter having no signature, and being apparently a transcript, it is difficult to identify the author, but it seems to have been written by a leading officer of horse in the King's right wing, explanatory of his own part in the action:—
"The King's army being drawne up on a Heath neere Newbury, the enemy were discovered approaching ye town, Prince Rupert was pleased to command mee and Major Smith with a party through the town to face the enemy, afterwards His Highness commanded mee to advance with ye party to ye hill upon our left hand, from thence we sent out parties all night, which gave His Highness satisfactory intelligence, and when it was day, His Highness went with his own troope, a party of mosqueteers and my horse to take possession of a Hill [the hill in front of Skinner's Green Lane above Cope Hall], I drew ye party into a close † that contained a considerable part of the hill, then we discovered the enemy and there began the service. But before relief could come to the mosqueteers, they retreated, and I drew ye horse into the next close though not without losse both with great and small shot where wee stood, untill in which time my horse received a shott in his neere shoulder. But ye foot crying out for ye horse, I returned into ye first mentioned close and was very slowly followed by reason of the straitness of the passage, but when I thought I had men enough to doe ye service, I went to ye furthest part of ye said close wheere were neere about 1,000 of ye enemies foot drawne up in order and one piece of artillery, and as I was charging my horse was shott againe into ye breast and faltered with mee, for that, I being out of hopes to do other service than to lose myself, I gave orders to ye party in these very words in Major Smith's hearing,

---

* Add. MSS. 18980−2, Brit. Mus.

† A meadow in the position indicated by the writer of the above letter is known as "Jacob's Mead." Only a few weeks since, two cannon balls (6lb and 3lb) were found in removing a bank in this field, and are both in the author's possession.

F

—'Fall on, my Masters! for I must goe change my horse.' And in my coming I met with my Lord Byron. My distresse at that time compelled mee to desire him to lend mee a horse. I likewise desired ye same favour of Sir Lewis Kirke, but presently meeting with Sergeant-Major Daniel, major to ye Prince of Wales his regiment, hee lent mee a horse. That horse I changed for one of Capt. Sheldon's of His Highness Prince Maurice his regiment, which I conceived to be much better. When I was thus supplied I was going back to my charge, which I thought Major Smith would have had a care of in my absence, as I conceived in duty he ought, I being for that present disabled, but in my way back contrary to my expectation I found Captain Scot of Sir Arthur Aston's regiment and Capt. Panton of Lord Carnarvon's regiment,* and some other officers of ye party with neere about 40 men, I desired that wee might goe up ye Hill again, Capt. Panton answered mee that my Lord Lieut.-General [Earl of Brentford] commanded them to stay in that same place, whereupon I sent one to him to know his further commands. In the meantime came Sir Lewis Kirke to mee with commands from ye King to goe looke to ye passe by the river side which the enemy were then endeavouring to gaine [the road, now called Guyer's Lane, leading to the Kennet, where the river appears to have been fordable], but when I came to ye place I found Sir William Vavasour there with his brigade, which I conceived sufficiently secured that place. Whereupon I sent Capt. Scot to ye King to desire His Majesty that I might goe to some place where I might doe him better service, which His Majesty did not grant."

This view of the result of the fight about Cope Hall is fully borne out by a study of the various narratives of the battle and by an inspection of the ground. The Parliamentary left gaining the rounded hill by Skinner's Green Lane, before referred to, pushed their infantry forward beyond it, to still further check the attack of the Royalist right moving over the enclosed ground towards the guns. A small round-contoured hill just in front of the latter was gained by the rush above described; and this advance, reaching as it did the hedgerows of Dark Lane,† would have been pushed further but for the

---

* This officer became a Major-General in the King's service, and fell mortally wounded at Cropredy Bridge, 29 June, 1644.

† Byron's advance appears to have been over the ground between the boundary-line of the parishes of Newbury and Enborne (defined by a bank and hedge, and at the point shown on Plan passable for cavalry) and the old road called 'Dark Lane' which formerly ran from near Enborne Farm obliquely over the fields below the Wash to the Enborne-road, which it entered by Enborne-gate Farm, another road (Guyer's Lane) leading from this point to the Kennet. There was also a lane entering from the Skinner's Green road below 'Cope Hall' and joining the Wash-road. Most of these roads have been stopped, and it is now difficult to trace them. In removing the bank of 'Dark Lane' a few years ago, a 15-lb

action of the cavalry of the right wing, which, diverted from a direct advance by the character of the ground, now came upon the scene. In fact the Royalist right wing seems to have been roughly handled up to this time.

Byron, who gives his own account, without considering what the other fractions were doing, and naturally lays considerable stress on his share or part in the action of the right wing to which he was attached, says: "The commanded foot not being able to make good the place, my uncle Byron, who commanded the first tertia, instantly came up with part of the regiment of guards and Sir Michael Woodhouse's and my Lord Gerard's regiments of foot, commanded by his Lieut.-Col. Ned Villiers, but the service grew so hot, that in a very short time, of twelve ensigns that marched up with my Lord Gerard's regiment, eleven were brought off the field hurt, and Ned Villiers shot through the shoulder. Upon this a confusion was heard among the foot, calling, horse! horse! whereupon I advanced with those two regiments I had and commanded them to halt while I went to view the ground, and to see what way there was to that place where the enemy's foot was drawn up, which I found to be enclosed with a high quick hedge and no passage into it, but by a narrow gap through which but one horse at a time could go and that not without difficulty. My Lord of Falkland did me the honour to ride in my troop this day, and I would needs go along with him, the enemy had beat our foot out of the close, and was drawne up near the hedge; I went to view, and as I was giving orders for making the gapp wide enough, my horse was shott in the throat with a musquet bullet and his bit broken in his mouth so that I was forced to call for another horse, in the meanwhile my Lord Falkland (more gallantly than advisedly) spurred his horse through the gapp, where both he and his horse were immediately killed. The passage being then made somewhat wide, and I not having another horse, drew in my own troop first, giving orders for the rest to follow and charged the enemy, who entertained us with a great salvo of musquet shott, and discharged their two drakes upon us laden with case shott, which killed some and hurt many of my men, so that we were forced to wheel off and could not meet them at that charge.

---

cannon-ball was found imbedded in the soil. The correctness of the tradition that Falkland fell on the spot till recently indicated by a poplar tree in front of the farm-house known as 'Falkland Farm' is extremely doubtful: he certainly fell as the royal cavalry were advancing towards the body of the Parliamentarians, who were endeavouring to gain the heath, but at this early period of the fight Essex had not secured a footing on the Wash. Clarendon relates that "the enemy had lined the hedges on both sides with musqueteers from whence he [Falkland] was shot with a musquet in the lower part of the belly, and in the instant falling from his horse, his body was not found till next morning." ‡ The hedges on both sides of Dark Lane would perfectly accord in position with Byron's narrative and with Clarendon's description.

‡ Clarendon's Hist., vol. ii, 359.

I rallied my men together again, but not so soon but that the enemy had got away their field-pieces for fear of the worst, seeing us resolved not to give over, so I charged them a second time, Sir Thomas Aston being then come up with his regiment, we then beat them to the end of the close, where they faced us again, having the advantage of a hedge at their backs and poured in another volley of shott upon us, when Sir Thomas Aston's horse was killed under him, and withal kept us off so with their pikes we could not break them, but were forced to wheel off again, they in the meantime retreating into another little close and making haste to recover a lane which was very near unto it [Skinner's Green Lane], finding then they could not keep the ground, which before they could do, I rallied the horse again, and charged them a third time, and then utterly routed them, and had not left a man of them unkilled, but that the hedges were so high the horse could not pursue them, and besides, a great body of their own foot advanced toward the lane to relieve them. Our foot then drew up on the ground from whence we had beaten the enemy and kept it, and drew the horse back to the former station; for this service I lost near upon a hundred horse and men out of my regiment, whereof out of my own troop twenty-six. The enemy drew up fresh supplies to regain the ground again, but to my uncle's good conduct (who that day did extraordinary service) was entirely beaten off."

This road was a short distance in the rear of that Falkland Farm which is situated on the Wash,* and a tradition that the body on its recovery the next morning was first carried to the farm-house is no doubt founded upon fact. This farm-house and Yew-tree Cottage are said to have been the only buildings on the Wash at the time of the battle, and the former is still especially associated with several incidents of the fight in local traditions. The lanes at this period, as we have above-noticed, had high banks and hedges on either side, and formed a series of stout defences as well as serious obstacles to the movement of troops, being in many places equal to well constructed entrenchments. In 'Heath's Chronicle,' it is stated that "the left wing of the Parliament and the right wing of the King could not be engaged only in small parties by reason of the hedges." That this was the case is quite clear. The steep embankment forming the western boundary of the parish of Newbury would alone be an

---

* There is however another building bearing the name of Falkland Farm situated on the south of the En near Wash Mill; but its distance from the field of battle renders it exceedingly unlikely that it has any associations connected with the great fight. The name may have been given it and probably was, for purely fanciful reasons. There was an old cottage near this Farm some years since and in its garden was discovered a groat of the reign of Edward IV., so that the buildings here are probably ancient.

insurmountable barrier to the free action of large bodies either of horse or foot.

Lord Clarendon, in his 'Life,' written by himself, gives the following account of Lord Falkland's death. "In this battle of Newbury, the Chancellor of the Exchequer lost the joy and comfort of his life; which he lamented so passionately, that he could not for many days compose himself to any thoughts of business. His dear friend the Lord Falkland, hurried by his fate, in the morning of the battle, as he was naturally inquisitive after danger, put himself into the head of Sir John Byron's regiment, which he believed, was like to be in the hottest service, and was then appointed to charge a body of foot, and in that charge was shot with a musket bullet, so that he fell dead from his horse. The same day that the news came to Oxford of his death, which was the next day after he was killed, the Chancellor received a letter from him, written at the time when the army rose from Gloucester: but the messenger had been employed in other service, so that he came not to Oxford till that day; the letter was an answer to one the Chancellor had then sent to him, in which he had told him, how much he suffered in his reputation with all discreet men, by engaging himself unnecessarily in all places of danger: and that it was not the office of a privy counsellor and secretary of State to visit the trenches, as he usually did; and conjured him, out of the conscience of his duty to the King, and to free his friends from those continual uneasy apprehensions, not to engage his person to those dangers, which were not incumbent to him. His answer was, that the trenches were now at an end, there could be no more danger there. That his case was different from other men's, that he was so much taken notice of for an impatient desire of peace, that it was necessary he should likewise make it appear, that it was not out of fear of the utmost hazard of war: he said some melancholy things of the time; and concluded, that in few days, they should come to a battle, the issue whereof he hoped would put an end to the misery of the kingdom." *

The Royalist accounts of this part of the action are equally detailed and the 'Mercurius Aulicus' thus describes it.† "Many of their living have cause to remember how the little enclosed Hill commanding the town of Newbury, and the plaine, where His Majesty in person was drawne up (being the first place attempted by our foot by daybreak), was then prepossessed by a great body of their foot, till in their advance to it, ours beate them off into the hedgerows, under which shelter they much annoyed both our foot and horse, the right valiant L.-Col. Villiers and ten of his ensigns being hurt upon the ground the rebels

---

* Life of Edward, Earl of Clarendon, vol. i, pp. 164-5.
† October 14, 1643.

first stood on, yet though they lost the hill, they kept the hedges all the forenoon, till a fresh supply of neare 200 musqueteers advancing up a lane to surprise our pykes and colours by that gallant resolute charge made by Sir Thos. Aston with his own troope (through a double quick-set hedge), these poachers were dislodged, their fresh supply routed, and fled before him in such haste, that though his horse was shot in the entrance to the lane and drew him by the leg amongst them, they had not the civility to help him up, but let him walk away on foot leaving their pykes and colours to shift for themselves, and never after regained the place. But Prince Rupert himselfe drew down a fresh relief of foot and made good the lane against them, and about three of the clock two small pieces of ours being then drawne up to that hill, *which was the place of most concernment*, and was never quit by us till the King drew off all his foot in a body to Newbury field, nor ever after mann'd by them. This is the naked truth, which for three weeks together they have so loudly rail'd at, but shall never heare more of it, if now they are unsatisfied."

While these conflicts are going forward on the hill, the battle rages with fury on Enborne Heath, where Essex's right wing, heedless of the gallant charges of the royal cavalry, are making a strenuous effort to surmount the broken ground that the approach to the Wash everywhere presented. Excited nearly to frenzy by reports that their comrades are being worsted on the left and may be cut off from their support, they charge with an ardour which passionate zeal for their cause alone could give. The general officers Skippon, Stapleton, and Merrick expose themselves as fearlessly as the common soldiers, and the very domestics, workmen, and camp-followers rush to the field, and, animating each other to the highest pitch of fanatical excitement, fight as bravely as the bravest officers.

The Royalists, almost paralyzed by the prowess of the men, of whom till then "they had too cheap an estimation," are straining every nerve to keep at bay the foe they cannot overcome. Meteor-like, Rupert flashes from one point of the position to another, and is always to be seen in the thickest of the fight; but nothing can keep back his fierce assailants. On they come through gorse and brushwood, in face of a heavy cannonade from the Royalist guns on the heath,—through a storm of musquetry bullets flying amidst the darkened air—and in a few minutes they breast the western slope of the Wash:

"Now comes the brunt, the crisis of the day!"

Old Skippon who had coolly watched the progress of the advance, calls on his men to "charge!" an enthusiastic cheer answers the order! and with an impetuosity not to be resisted Stapleton's mailed cuirassiers cleave their way through the royal squadrons,

HENRY SPENCER, EARL OF SUNDERLAND.
From the portrait by WALKER.

and gallantly clear the ridge, the remainder of the troops pour up the ascent, the head of the royalist column is overwhelmed, and the battle virtually won! The Royalists' left flank being completely turned by this brilliant charge, the successful cooperation of the centre and finally of the left, as the Royalists are pushed back towards the town, completes the victory, and the soldiers of the Parliament are at length left masters of the hard-fought field, which, in the early morning, they had so defiantly promised their general to win.

A final effort was made by "The enemy," says Lord Digby, "On a passe by the river" (apparently Guyer's Lane); but Sir William Vavasour with the King's life-guard defeated it with heavy loss. The struggle was however practically at an end, though the ground was still stubbornly contested. It was no headlong flight down the northern slopes of the Wash to Newbury, but a dogged sullen retreat, in which the pursuer dared not press his unquestioned advantage by endeavouring to force the King beyond the line of the Kennet.

Night was well advanced before the last shots ceased; and then, the struggle ended, the wearied soldiers formed their hasty bivouacs. But the losses had been heavy and important on both sides. Here on the Heath, fell the brave young Lord Carnarvon, who, "emulating the noblest actions recorded in the annals of war," was struck down as he was returning from a successful attack. Also the gallant Sunderland, "a lord of great fortune, tender years, and an early judgement," who, putting himself in the King's troop as a volunteer, fell pierced by "a cannon bullet" while he was gathering up his bridle reins for the first charge. But equal courage, so Lord Byron asserts, was not shown by all of those engaged: he says, "What was done upon the Heath (where the main body of our horse and foot fought) I will not relate, because I was not an eye-witness of it, only this is generally confest, that had not our foot play'd the poultroons extremely that day, we in all probability had set a period to the war, our horse having behaved themselves with as much gallantry as could be * * * * My Lord Carnarvon (than whom no man acted a more honourable part in the war) and many other valiant men were here slaine."

Space will not permit a detailed recital of all the various turns of fortune experienced by the two armies throughout the latter part of the day; but the following extract from Robert Codrington's narrative, quoted by Mr. Forster in his 'Life of Cromwell,' and which in comparison with all accessible accounts of the battle, though somewhat tinctured by the feelings of a partisan, appears to be very superior in clearness to other statements, may be introduced at this point; as it admits of one or two of the localities referred to being defined.

"After six hours long fight, with the assistance of his horse

Essex gained those advantages which the enemy possessed in the morning, which were 'the Hill, the Hedges, and the River.' In the meantime, a party of the enemies' horse did wheel about, in a great body, and about three quarters of a mile below the Hill fell upon the rear of our army, where our carriages were placed,* to relieve which his Excellency sent a selected party from the hill to assist their friends who were deeply engaged in the fight; these forces marching down the hill, did meet a regiment of horse of the enemy's, who in their hats did wear branches of furze and broom, which our army did that day wear for distinction sake to be known by one another from their adversaries, and they cried out to our men, "Friends! Friends!" but being discovered to be enemies, our men gave fire upon them, and having some horse to second the execution, they did force them further from them. Our men being now marched to the bottom of the hill † they increased the courage of their friends, and after a sharp conflict, they forced the King's horse to fly with remarkable loss, having left the ground strewed with the carcasses of their horses and riders. In the meantime His Excellency having planted his ordnance on the top of the hill, did thunder against the enemy where he found their number to be thickest, and the King's ordnance being yet on the same hill did play with a like fury against the forces of His Excellency:— the cannon on each side did dispute with one another, as, if the battle was but new begun."‡

Night came on, but still the fight was continued by isolated parties, though it was now more immediately confined to the valley between Newbury and Enborne, which is about half-a-mile in length. "The glimmer of the matches § and the flashing of the fire-arms served to shew each other where the other lay;" and the contest raged in a desultory way till 11 o'clock or thereabouts, when the King's troops finding they had decidedly the worst of the conflict finally retired, and by day-break had quitted the ground of the previous day's action. The chief part of the horse crossed the river into the fields on the Speen side,

---

* Shown on the Plan.
† The fields on either side of the Enborne Road.
‡ By "*The Hill*," the plateau of the Wash was meant, by "*The Hedges*" those more especially crossing the fields between the Wash and the Kennet, and by "*The River*," the Kennet, now called the Old River; the canal being a modern work. It is evident Essex did not cross the river; for Vicars says, "during the whole day our soldiers could not get a drop of water to drink;" and Sergeant Foster in his 'Marching of the Trained-Bands,' adds, "we were in great distress of water or any accommodation to refresh our poor soldiers, our men walking up and down to seek for it." In one respect at least the country is little changed since then, for the furze still grows plentifully on many parts of the field, and the "bonny, bonny broom" yet blossoms on "Broom Hill."
§ The *Matchlock* had a long coil of twisted tow steeped in saltpetre attached to it; this was only lighted in time of action, a cock bringing it down to the touch-hole of the piece when it was to be discharged.

and quartered in detachments in the neighbouring villages; while the foot were drawn into the town.

Essex, at the close of this well-fought day, established himself upon the ground abandoned by the Royalists, and his troops bivouacked on the field of battle in a very cheerless state, being absolutely without food. The night was very damp and chilly, and not a drop of anything to drink was to be had, though the wounded were dreadfully tormented with thirst; and it is reported by a Parliamentary journal, that one officer offered ten shillings for a quart of water! The infantry rested on their pikes, the cavalry stretched themselves beside their horses, anticipating a bloodier and fiercer day on the morrow. The Parliamentary general, like Prince Rupert, was in the saddle all night, and as he rode over the heath while the moon shed an uncertain light on the wide scene of carnage, he "could not," says the 'Parliamentary Scout,' "understand his own happiness in the victory, and could hardly entertain it with a private joy." But the feelings of the man triumphed over those of the general, and the old veteran is stated to have prayed fervently that peace might once more shine upon the land.

Glancing critically at the conduct of the action, there is little doubt but that it was more or less of a running fight extending at the very close of the day over even the southern suburbs of Newbury. This is supported by the authority of Oldmixon and Whitelock, and also in 'The True Relation' of a parliamentary trooper. Bullets, spurs, portions of swords, &c. of the period, have been found in excavating for buildings in the upper or south-west side of the town, and the traces of the fight are widespread. "It was a kind of hedge fight," says a Cavalier, who was present, "for neither army was drawn out into the field; if it had, it would never have held from six in the morning, till ten at night. But they fought for advantages; sometimes one side had the better, sometimes the other. They fought twice through the town, in at one end and out of the other [!], and in the hedges and lanes with exceeding fury. The King lost the most men, his foot having suffered for want of succour from their horse, who on two several occasions could not come at them. But the Parliament's foot suffered also, and two regiments were entirely cut in pieces, but the King kept the field. * * * Essex had the pillage of the dead. * * * his camp rabble stript the dead bodies."*

This writer can scarcely be deemed, however, an impartial judge. Whether through an error in judgment or through party bias he certainly does not take a true view of the result of the action as this and the following extract both show:—

"At Newbury 1st fight, when we beat the enemy upon all

---

* 'Memoirs of a Cavalier' (Col. Andrew Newport), pp. 250—1.

disadvantage from the town's end to the top of the hill by the Heath, a wing of Essex, his horse moving gently towards us made us leave our execution of the enemy and retreat into the next field, where were several gaps to get to it, but not direct in any way, yet with the colours in my hand I jumpt over hedge and ditch, or I had died by a multitude of hands: we kept this field till midnight, and until intelligence came that Essex was marching away with a great part of his army, and that he had buried a great many of his great guns, by two o'clock in the afternoon; near unto this field, upon the Heath, lay a whole file of men six deep with their heads all struck off by one cannon shot of ours [!]: we pursued Essex in his retreat, took Reading without opposition, made it a garrison, and Sir Jacob Astley governor."* This endeavour to blind themselves to the true facts of the case is not singular in the correspondence of parties at that time.

The casualties of the two armies in this battle, it would be difficult to estimate with anything like exactness. In Heath's 'Chronicle' it is stated that the loss on both sides was between 5,000 and 6,000, and that the greatest loss, if there were any difference, was on the side of the Parliament. This engagement is represented by several writers as having been more obstinately contested than that at Edgehill, where 5,000 were slain; the estimate therefore in the 'Chronicle' is probably not exaggerated. M. de Larrey, the French historian, states that "8,000 men were killed on the spot, and nothing but the night could separate these furious Englishmen, who seem'd delighted to shed the blood of each other." Clarendon does not give the number of the slain, but mentions—"there were above 20 officers of the field and persons of honour and publick name slain upon the place, and more of the same quality hurt." Oldmixon (a iolent opponent of the Stuarts) relates that 2,000 Royalists were slain from the time of Essex's removal from Hungerford to the end of Newbury fight, and that the Parliamentary loss was only 500 !

On the Royalists' side the following names of officers killed are recorded.—The Earl of Carnarvon, the Earl of Sunderland, Lord Falkland, the Hon. Henry Bertie, and Sir Anthony Mansel. *Colonels.*—Edward St. John, Joseph Constable, Poole, Murray, Richard Platt, Pinchbeck, Wheatly, Eure, Slingsby, Thomas Morgan, and Stroud. *Captains.*—Robert Molineux (of the Wood, Lancashire), Wm. Symcocks (Captain in Lord Percy's troop), Francis Bartis, Thos. Singleton (of Stanyng, Lancashire), and Francis Clifton (of Westby in the same county). Captain Sheldon, of Broadway Court, Worcester, is said to have been slain in the battle; he served in Prince Maurice's regiment of horse. *Lieutenants.*—Henry Butler, George Collingwood, and Wm. Culcleth.

---

* Gwynne's Memoirs, ch. x, pp. 46, 47.

THE FIRST BATTLE OF NEWBURY.   43

Among the wounded were the Earl of Carlisle, the Earl of Peterborough, Lord Andover, Lord Chandos, Sir Charles Lucas, Sir John Russell, Sir Edward Sackville, Sir Edward Waldegrave, Major-General George Porter. *Colonels.*—George Lisle, Fielding, Thomas Dalton,* Gerard, Ivers, D'Arcy, Villiers, Howard, Spencer, Bartley. *Captains.*—Panton (fell 29 June, 1644, at Banbury), Thurston Andrews (died of his wounds at Oxford), and Mr. Progers (groom of the bed-chamber to the Prince of Wales), who attached himself to the King's interest during the war with the Parliament, with laudable fidelity.† The Royalist prisoners taken at Newbury and Cirencester, according to the 'Mercurius Britannicus,' numbered 500, including a colonel, a major of horse, and some other officers, who were confined in Windsor Castle. Among these was Lieut. Daniel Kingsmill, of Sydmonton.‡

On the Parliamentary side, the name of no officer of note is given as having fallen in this battle. *Colonels.*—Davies, Bamfield, Tucker, Mainwaring (of the London Brigade), Greaves, and White. *Captains.*—Hunt, Ware, Talbot, St. Barbe, and Massey are mentioned as being amongst the slain; and Captains Bolton, Mosse, Stoning, Juxon, and Willet died of their wounds a short time after the battle. Colonel Dalbier, Commissary-General Copley,§ Captains Hammond, Fleetwood, and Pym, and Cornet D'Oyley, are said to have been wounded.

After the Parliamentary Army had left Reading, the King having placed a force of horse and foot there, and established a garrison at Donnington Castle under Col. John Boys, retired with Prince Rupert and the remainder of his army to Oxford; where, says Clarendon, "there appeared nothing but dejection of mind, discontent, and secret mutiny in the army, anger and jealousy amongst the officers, every one accusing another of a want of courage and conduct in the action of the field, and they who were not of the army blaming them all for their several failings and gross neglects." Both Lord Byron and Lord Digby ascribe great *cowardice* to the King's foot; the latter says, "our foot having found a hillock on the heath, which sheltered them from the enemies' cannon, could not be drawne a foot from thence." The hillock referred to was no doubt "Bunker's Hill," which is situate as Lord Digby describes. In its immediate neighbourhood

---

* Col. Dalton, of Thurnham, Lancashire. An enthusiastic and gallant royalist, who raised a troop of horse for the King's service. He was severely wounded in this battle, and, dying at Andover, the 2nd November following, was buried in the Church of St. Mary in that town, as the parish register records.

† See Illustrations to Grammont's Memoirs, p. 381.

‡ See MS. Letter, No. 127, Addl. MSS., Mus. Brit., No. 18980.

§ The 'Mercurius Britannicus' (30 Nov. to 7 Dec. 1643) says:—"Commissary Copley, who lost as much bloud as would write a chronicle of that battle, is now well and abroad, and refreshed, to recruit his veines again with his enemies' bloud."

is "Coward's Mead!" Trundle Hill (*Trundle*, a kind of shot used at this period), King's Mead, War-end, Steel Hill, Ball Hill, and many other names within the area of the battle-field probably originated from some incident connected with the fight.

"Without doubt," says Clarendon, "the action was fought by the Earl of Essex with incomparable conduct and courage; in every part whereof, very much was to be imputed to his own personal virtue; and it may well be reckon'd among the most soldierly actions of this unhappy war."* Neither he nor his men imputed want of courage, however, to their adversaries; on the contrary they all acknowledged the devotion and bravery of the King's party; and the latter recognised the like of Essex and his soldiers. "All were Englishmen, adds Whitelock, "and pitty it was that such courage should be spent in the bloud of each other." †

Naturally excuses were made by the Royalists for their defeat. Lord George Digby asserted that they were short of powder, being disappointed of a supply of 100 barrels from Oxford. They spent, as it was, four score barrels during the action, or "a score more than had turned the fight at Edgehill." To this "foolish and knavish suggestion of want of powder" Lord Byron attributes the withdrawal of the Royalist army from the advantages "they had gained with the loss of so much good blood." Certain it is that, though the conflict was most obstinate, the King's infantry do not appear to have acted well in this battle; and the cavalry, which was by far the most effective branch of the service, bore the brunt of the actual fighting.

Many interesting anecdotes have been left of this battle, and though, like all such traditions, they may possibly be not strictly true, they were probably based on facts, and to that extent are therefore worth preserving.

It is said, for example, on the authority of the descendant of a man who resided at Enborne on a small farm which had been in the possession of his family for many generations,‡ that a party of Parliamentarians were regaling themselves in "Lushy Gully" (on the south side of Mr. R. H. Valpy's house), at Enborne, thinking that they were out of danger, when, to their great consternation, a cannon ball passed through the party, without doing any injury more than carrying away a roasted pig which they were eating.

---

* Clarendon's History, vol. ii. p. 349.

† Whitelock's Memorials, p. 71.

‡ Our informant was the late Mr. John Matthews, of Enborne, one of whose ancestors, it is said, was an officer of the Trained-bands and fought in this battle. A sword, rapier, and pair of pistol holsters, elaborately worked, reported to have formed part of his equipment on that memorable occasion, were in the possession of his descendant above-named till his death, which occurred a few years since, when these interesting relics, which are in excellent preservation, passed into the hands of Mrs. Hoath, of Burloy Lodge, East Woodhay, in whose possession they still remain.

Old books relating to the War have many anecdotes; Whitelock in his *Memorials* instances two which are noteworthy. He says, "A passage or two I shall here remember of extraordinary mettle and boldness of spirit. One is of Sir Philip Stapleton (though he would not acknowledge it), that he being with other Parliament Commanders in the head of a body of horse facing another body of the King's horse, before whom stood their commanders, and the chief of them was Prince Rupert. The Parliament Officer desiring to cope singly with the Prince, he rode from before his company up to the body of horse, before whom the Prince with divers other Commanders were, and had his pistol in his hand ready cockt and fitted. Coming up to them alone, he looked one and another of them in the face, and when he came to Prince Rupert, whom he knew, he fired his pistol in the Prince's face, but his armour defended him from any hurt, and having done this, he turned his horse about, and came gently off again without any hurt, though many pistols were fired at him.

"Another passage was of Sir Philip Stapleton's groom, a Yorkshire man, and stout, if not too rash. By this story, he was attending on his master in a charge, where the groom's mare was killed under him, but he came off on foot back again to his own company. To some of whom he complained that he had forgotten to take off his saddle and bridle from his mare, and to bring them away with him; and said that they were a new saddle and bridle, and that the cavaliers should not get so much by him, but he would go again and fetch them: his master and friends persuaded him not to adventure in so rash an act, the mare lying dead close to the enemy who would mall him, if he came so near them, and his master promised to give him another new saddle and bridle. But all this would not persuade the groom to leave his saddle and bridle to the cavaliers, but he went again to fetch them, and stayed to pull off the saddle and bridle, whilst hundreds of bullets flew about his ears, and brought them back with him, and had no hurt at all." *

Both parties seem to have displayed great solicitude for the decent interment of the dead left upon the field. Previous to his advance from Newbury, Essex issued the following order to the Rector (the Rev. Mr. Elke) and Churchwardens of the Parish of Enborne: "These are to will and require, and straightly command you forthwith in sight hereof, to bury all the dead bodies lying in and about Enborne and Newbury Wash, as you or any of you will answer the contrary at his peril. Dated one and twentieth September, 1643. ESSEX."

The King also issued the following warrant to the Mayor of Newbury (Mr. Gabriel Coxe), "Our will and command is that

---

* Whitelock's Memorials, p. 71.

you forthwith send into the town and villages adjacent and bring thence all the sick and hurt soldiers of the Earl of Essex's army; and, altho' they be rebels and deserve the punishment of traytors, yet out of our tender consideration upon them, being our subjects, our will and pleasure is that you carefully provide for their recovery as well as for those of our own army, and then send them unto Oxford. The one and twentieth day of September, 1643. RUPERT."

The dead bodies were principally buried in several tumuli on the Wash, some of which have become nearly obliterated. The largest mound, known in Borough perambulations as "Bumper's Hill," is situate midway between the parishes of Newbury and Enborne, the boundary line passing over its apex. In a plantation near the large barrow is a circular embankment with an outer ditch, at first sight presenting the appearance of an ancient earthwork; but it was no doubt prepared as an additional burial place for the slain, some of whom were probably buried round its margin. In the year 1855 when Wash Common was enclosed, the levelling of these receptacles of the dead was commenced for the purpose of making a road; but the desecration was stayed by the late Mr. Winterbottom, the owner of the land. The workmen, however, found indications of the bodies having been thrown in a heap and the earth cast over them, the floor of the mound being the natural surface. Many human bones, soldiers' buttons, buckles, and portions of accoutrements, bullets, and cannon balls were mixed with the soil which was removed. In addition to the bodies buried on the Wash, it is said, a number were thrown down a deep well, and others cast into ditches and pits; but it is evident from the Churchwardens' accounts for the parish of Newbury that many of those who were killed or mortally wounded were buried in the churchyard of St. Nicholas, as will appear from the following extract:—

	£	s.	d.
Paid for watching on the Tower ..	0	0	6
Ringing when King was in Town ..	0	5	0
Paid for burying dead Soldiers in the Churchyard and Wash	3	0	1
Paid for Shrouds	0	6	4
Burying Soldiers in the Church ..	3	4	4

Many cannon balls, chain, and case shot, swords, pike-heads, stirrup-irons, bridle-bits, and other relics of the fight have been found on Enborne Heath and the Wash. Mr. Lousley has in his collection an amulet of large beads picked up on the field; and many other articles, including a musqueteer's cap or helmet, two leathern water bottles (one silver-mounted), buckles, spurs, &c., are to be seen in the Museum at Newbury.* The 'Parliamentary

---

* See Plate.

Scout' also notices that "there were divers fine and rich crucifixes found about the dead, whom we pillaged, so that his Holiness has lost some blood as well as the Parliament."*

Several skeletons have been discovered from time to time in the fields below the Wash. Cannon and musquet balls have also been met with in Newbury; and probably the upper part of the town suffered considerably from stray shot.† The tower of the Church is also said to have sustained damage from the artillery.

On Friday morning, September 22nd, Essex marched from Theale to Reading, where a committee of the Lords and Commons met the victorious General, to compliment him on his great service and to learn the wants of his army.

The Earl remained two days at Reading and then moved on by way of Maidenhead to Windsor Castle. There the prisoners taken in the battle were left, and so cruelly treated, it was said, by the Governor, that three men dropped down dead in the streets on their release.

On Thursday, the 28th, Essex made a triumphal entry into London. The Lord Mayor (Pennington) and the Aldermen received him and his troops at Temple Bar, and they had many thousand welcomes from the people as they passed in martial order through the streets. The next day Essex was waited upon at Essex House by the Speaker and the members of both Houses of Parliament, who declared to him, that they came to congratulate him on his mighty success and to render the thanks of the kingdom for his incomparable conduct and courage, and had caused their acknowledgement to be entered in their Journals as a monument and record of his valour, and their gratitude.

The Earl used the occasion for presenting several colours captured from the enemy. On one of these, taken at Cirencester, was a representation of the Parliament-house with two traitors' heads upon it, with the motto *"Sicut extra sic intus"* (as without, so within), which being supposed to belong to Col. Spencer's regiment, that officer and his family were ordered to be exiled from the kingdom; but it appears after all not to have been the Colonel's ensign. A second colour bore the Harp and Crown Royal with the motto, "Lyrica Monarchica." Another had the figure of a melancholy virgin in whose face were depicted all the characters of distress and sorrow, with the figure of a cross, pulled down by violent hands, lying despised at her feet, with

---

* September 22nd to 29th, 1642.

† With the many petitions presented to the Parliament for redress, after the war, and preserved at the Public Record Office, is one from a farmer of the name of Daniel, who states he has a lease of a farm at Enborne at £60 per annum, and that in the first fight at Newbury the mounds and fences were utterly destroyed, the ground laid waste, and the farmer's house and outbuildings battered with shot—the damage being estimated at £100 or nearly £300 according to the present value of money.

the inscription "Meliora spero." A fourth represented an angel
bearing a flaming sword and treading on a dragon, with the motto
"Quis ut Deus." A fifth bore the French motto "Courage pour
la Cause." Lastly, in the Hall of the Chapel Royal, Whitehall,
is a silk flag bearing the motto "Constanter et fideliter," to
which the following account is appended; "This flag was taken
by Bernard Brocas, of Beaurepaire, from Cromwell's army,* at the
battle of Newbury, August 20th [September 20th], 1643. He
was taunted by the Royalist party with indifference to their
cause, on account of his love for a daughter of Lord Sandys, who
held the adjoining property [The Vyne], and was in Cromwell's
army, and stung by the imputation of cowardice, swore in the
next engagement to take a standard or die in the attempt. This
flag was found in his hand after the battle, and the standard-
bearer dead by his side."

The flags taken at Newbury were exhibited to public view,
the people thronging round these trophies, while the trained-
bands and auxiliaries, who had shared in the expedition, related
all the details. Everywhere, in domestic conversations, in sermons,
and in groups formed in the streets, the name of Essex was loudly
shouted or silently blessed.

Old Fuller, the author of 'The Worthies of England,' who
strenuously adhered to the Royal cause, quaintly remarks;—

"Both armies may be said to *beat* and be *beaten*, neither winning the
Day, but both the *Twi-light*. Hence it is said that both sides were so
sadly filled with their *supper* over night, neither next morning had any
stomach to *breakfast*, but keeping their stations, were rather contented
to *face* than willing to *fight* one another. * * * * Many here lost
their lives, as if Newbury were so named by a sad Prolepsis, fore-
signifying that that Town should afford a *new burying* place to many
slain in two bloody battles."†

That the battle was looked upon as grave and serious by
both sides is very evident. The loyal historian Sir Richard
Baker considers, for example, that "this was a harder bout then
that of Edgehill; so that neither part having any stomach to
renew the fight, they marched away one from the other, both the
King and Essex having first sent their warrants to Newbury and
Enborne for the Burial of the Dead Bodies. Essex his aym was
to relieve Gloucester, which he accordingly effected, though not

---

* The Parliamentary army is here spoken of as "Cromwell's Army," but at this time the future Protector held only a subordinate command, and was not engaged in this battle. The estate of the Brocas family at Beaurepaire, near Sherborne St. John, has long since passed into other hands, and the house has been modernized. The Vyne is an interesting old mansion, and was originally built by the first Lord Sandys in the early part of the 16th cent., but was greatly altered by Inigo Jones and his son-in-law Webb. In the private chapel, which Horace Walpole described "as the most heavenly chapel in the world," is an altar tomb, with an effigy of Challoner Chute, Speaker of the House of Commons in Richard Cromwell's Parliament.

† 'Worthies,' Lond., 1662, pp. 111, 112.

without some damage: for Colonel Hurrey with a good party of horse fell upon the rear of his army, commanded by Sir Philip Stapleton, whom in a narrow lane they charged so furiously, that they forced them to a run directly forward through their own foot, till at length getting into the field they faced about, and forced the King's party back again: many colours of the King's cornets were carried up to London, and much reputation was gained by this expedition to General Essex and the London Trained Bands; not that there had been wanting the height of gallantry and resolution (however Fortune fail'd) on the King's side." *

In fact the loss in officers and men was very heavy; and the "Weekly Account" of Sept. 28, 1643, bears vivid testimony to this fact. In it the writer says, "It was a lamentable spectacle the next morning to behold what heaps of bodies and diversities of slaughter in one field this tragedy had compiled, and that the consanguineous foes, whom the sun could never hope to see reconciled, should on his return, with cold arms be observed to embrace one another, and to mingle themselves in each other's blood, by the incestuous cruelty and union of death."

Of all those who fell on this memorable day no one was so missed as Falkland, none so frequently referred to at these and later times. Ward,† writing in 1757, a hundred years after the great fight, fully endorses the opinion as to the single heartedness of this, one of the earliest victims to the Civil War. He says:—

"Maintaining still his secretary's post,
Till he at once his life and office lost,
Resigning both at Newb'ry, in the field
Of battle, by a fatal bullet kill'd,
As boldly charging with undaunted force,
In the front rank of noble Byron's horse.
Falling among the valiant and the just,
Who dy'd that day an honour to their Trust."

When morning broke Essex drew up the remnant of his shattered forces on the Wash, and announced his willingness to renew the fight, "if the enemy had any stomach for the field," by the firing of artillery, but the challenge not being accepted, Essex, finding the way to London by Greenham open before him, proceeded on his march towards Reading without opposition.

From this, it is evident how complete his victory was. Had there been any power of renewing the engagement, doubtless the Royalists would gladly have availed themselves of it. But beaten back after an action which had lasted from dawn to dusk,

---

* 'Chronicle of the Kings of England,' by Sir Richard Baker, knight, 4th edit., London, 1664, p. 570.

† 'England's Reformation,' v. ii, p. 327.

H

their demoralization and fatigue must have been extreme. So
the stern Parliamentary call to battle passed unheeded. The
spirit of the King's army crushed by recent defeat had "little
stomach" to try again the fortunes of another day. The army
of Essex, prepared to fight again if necessary to obtain the right
of passage past the town of Newbury, had no longer any such
need. Re-forming his column of march from battle array, the
Earl resumed his movement eastward with no further fear of
immediate molestation.

The route taken by the Parliamentary troops was by Monkey
Lane,* Greenham Common, Brimpton, and Aldermaston. No
sooner had Essex and his men entered the narrow lane between
the latter village and Padworth † than Prince Rupert, who, with a
column of cavalry and 800 musqueteers had unperceived taken
up a position in his line of march, fell suddenly on the rear-
guard under Sir Philip Stapleton, throwing it into considerable
disorder. The horse galloped through the foot crying, panic
struck, "Away! away! every man for his life! you are all dead
men." But the foot soon rallied, and, spreading themselves along
the hedges on either side, poured in such telling volleys on
Rupert's wearied cavalry, that after a desperate struggle, in
which great courage was shown by both parties, the Royalists,
having no force to support them, were compelled to abandon the
attack, and fall back, losing (it is said) in this short and mur-
derous affair something like 300 men.‡ After this, the final
rencontre, Essex crossed the Kennet at Padworth,§ and pushed on
to Theale, where he arrived about ten o'clock and quartered
for the night.

The Field being clear of the enemy, the King's immediate care
was bestowed on the wounded, who were lying in frightful numbers all around, every neighbouring cottage, and the old farm
house at Enborne,‖ being crowded with those who had been able

---

* *Monkey Lane.* An ingenious origin has been assigned to this name—that it
was a favourite walk of the Monks at the neighbouring priory at Sandleford, and
hence was called "Monks' Lane," which has been corrupted into the present
unmeaning appellation. A Monks', or Abbot's Walk or Lane is frequently found
in the vicinity of monastic establishments.

† See Notes on this encounter in the Appendix.

‡ The *Mercurius Aulicus* states that the party sent in pursuit of Essex was
under the Earl of Northampton and Lord Wilmot, the Prince being the prime
leader, and computes his loss at 100. Oldmixon, following an earlier writer, gives
Hurry the credit of leading the horse under Rupert, and estimates the King's loss
at 80 men, and that of the Parliament at 8 ! The foot were under George Lisle.

§ *Padworth.* Near this place a small iron casket, of the time of Charles I, was
found some few years since. It is supposed to have been used for conveying the pay
of the troops, but was found empty ! The relic is in the possession of W. G. Mount,
Esq., President of the Newbury District Field Club.

‖ Near Enborne Lodge, and in the occupation of Mr. Wm. Heath It is still known
as "The Hospital," and is an old-fashioned gabled building, apparently little changed
since the time of the battle.

to crawl to a place of shelter. Nor was his Majesty's care limited to mere enquiry: for the "Parliamentary Scout"* of the time states that "It is reported that His Majesty desired to see the wounded, which, some say, having viewed, he went sadly away." The more sorely wounded were left upon the battle-field the whole night. The bodies of His Majesty's chief officers, many of whom there was reason to suppose had fallen, were first sought for, and, when discovered, it was found that they had been spoiled and stripped by Essex's camp followers. The King whose silence evinced his deep sorrow, ordered an escort of their own gallant troopers to attend the remains of their beloved leaders to the town, where they were respectfully deposited in the Town Hall (at that time standing in the centre of the Market-place), and covered with the ensigns of their loyalty, till the necessary preparations could be made for honourable interment.†

Lord Grey of Groby, Sir Philip Stapleton, Sir John Meyrick, Sir Samuel Luke, Captain Charles Pym, and several other officers were rewarded with the thanks of Parliament for their distinguished services at Newbury.

This battle was important in two ways. Politically it disheartened the Royalist party. From a military point of view it gave courage to the Parliamentarians, for it showed that the apprentices of London and the Roundhead horsemen were as dauntless as any of those who wore the Royalist badge, and could meet even the charge of Prince Rupert's cavaliers with coolness and stedfast valour. Essex did not aim at gaining the town of Newbury. His object was to push past the place and pursue his journey unmolested to London. This he accomplished, although he left the town in the King's hands. The Parliamentary organ 'Mercurius Britannicus'‡ ventured to boldly advance that "the towne of Newbery is a just witness who won the field"; but this is fully counteracted by the opinion held by the royalist journal 'Mercurius Aulicus' the following week that "It is your Moderator's § own towne, and is a very indifferent judge."

---

* September 22 to 29, 1643. † See Appendix.

‡ Friday, September 29, 1643. The *Mercurius Britannicus* was conducted by Marchmond Needham, who, educated at the Poor School at Burford, was one of the Choristers at All Souls College, Oxford, and B.A., 1637. During the Civil War he distinguished himself by his political pamphlets, first against the Parliament and afterwards against the King, so that at the Restoration it was with difficulty that he obtained his pardon.

§ Dr. Twisse, Prolocutor of the Assembly of Divines. The *Mercurius Aulicus* was written by John Birkenhead, born of poor parents in Cheshire, a Fellow of All Souls College, Oxford. He suffered much in His Majesty's cause, being frequently in prison, and deprived of all his preferments. Soon after the Restoration he was made LL.D. Elected a Burgess for Wilton, knighted by His Majesty, and made Master of the Faculties, one of the Masters of Requests, Fellow of the Royal Society, he died in 1679 without having, as it seems, made such returns as he might to those who befriended him in his necessities. See Walker's 'Sufferings of the Clergy,' pt. ii, p. 98.

There seems to be little to criticize in the conduct of the action on the Parliamentary side; certain it is that, despite the unquestionable valour of their opponents, they were able to carry out their object, that of marching on London. This point must be clearly kept in view. The destruction of the King's army, and the pursuit that should always follow a victory in order to reap the full results of the success, were not necessary here. The Earl wanted the right of way and he obtained it. Though the King's army still held Newbury, it had been definitely forced back into the town. The pursuit effected by Rupert was practically barren of results, and cannot be taken as a proof that the King could claim to have won the hard-fought field. If a few enthusiastic troopers could, as they did, follow the plume of the dashing cavalier, the rest of the army could not. The barren occupation of the battle-field, which can be the only grounds on which the Royalists could base their claim, was solely possible because Essex did not want it. The advance of the weak force by Guyer's Lane on the passage of the Kennet may be looked as a mere petty reconnaissance on that side, and could exercise no influence on the fortune of the day. To get hold of the river line and Newbury was not Essex's object, and no importance should be attached to this affair. The value of the reserves and their usefulness in checking the counter attack of the Royalist cavalry on the then exposed left flank of the left wing, resting as it was almost "en l'air," in the field, is clearly noticeable, and on this side the fight was ably and well conducted; but it is difficult to see why the attack of the right wing was not more vigorously pressed.

A more determined advance by Trundle Hill would have taken in flank and soon in reverse the line of Royalist guns, already fully engaged with the musketeers and artillery of the left wing from Skinner's Green. Moreover an advance in echellon from the right, that is gradually advancing that wing further than the other, without destroying connection and communication between them, would not merely have brought his force across the flank of the Royalist army, but have prevented altogether an advance of the King's right on the Kintbury road, which was always possible and might have been dangerous. The probable explanation is that the open nature of the ground rendered the advance on this flank difficult against troops that could display such bravery and tenacity as the cavaliers of the King.

Turning to the Royal forces there is less to criticize, the more so as the details of their dispositions are somewhat wanting. Their left wing seems to have been well posted, and to have effectually checked the advance of Essex's right; but it is a question whether the massing of all their artillery from the commencement so far back on the Wash was advisable. Evidently their chief wish was to block the way simply; and the King appeared desirous of offering a passive resistance, so that the artillery position as selected, resting as it did with both flanks on the slope, north and south of the narrow neck of the Wash, across which the entrenchment stretched and the main road ran, seems well chosen at first glance to fulfil the object, especially bearing in mind the short range of the field artillery of the period. But the left was liable to be taken in enfilade from Trundle Hill, and the right could be threatened from the cover of the hedge-rows of Dark Lane which approached to within musket shot of the King's guns.

Further the Royalist account states that they were much annoyed by the fire of the Parliamentary guns on the Round Hill, and it was owing to their position that the counter attack along the valley towards Newbury was mainly checked. It has been already pointed out that this side was for Essex that which was most vital to him.

It would have been wiser therefore for the Royalists to have prevented the occupation of the round spur above Cope Hall; and this need not have been done, as suggested by them, by the actual occupation of the ridge, but by holding with their foot the hedge-rows of Dark Lane, and placing their right wing artillery or a portion of them on the spur to the right rear of the lane, whence they could both cover the low valley towards the Kennet, and at the same time bring so powerful a fire on the "round hill" as to preclude the possibility of the guns of the attack coming into action. In fact that two batteries, one on the spur east of Dark Lane, the other at about the same position as the entrenchment actually occupied, with the left flank well "refused" or thrown back so as to meet the fire from Trundle Hill, would have made the occupation of the "round hill" impracticable. The right wing battery thus echelloned would have been protected from cavalry attack by the hedge-rows, and could have fired, over the heads of the musketeers there, on the opposing artillery when endeavouring to unlimber. Though not definitely stated, the piercing the Royal centre by Falkland Farm, which seems to have been Essex's main attack, must have been coupled by an advance of his right from Trundle Hill, and the greatest credit is due to the King's commander in having been able, as he did, to withdraw under these circumstances all his forces into Newbury without having, as is often the case, the two wings separated and driven in diverging directions from the field.

The charge of the Royalist cavalry under Falkland against the hedge-rows of Dark Lane was a daring and gallant action, but a useless waste of life. In all probability it would have been difficult even for a good horse and rider in the hunting field; how much more so with the weight of armour and the intense excitement of the charge.

The spirit lived (and let us hope it still survives) in the breasts of those who rode so gallantly to death up the Balaklava Valley against the Russian guns; but the French Marshal's remark that "c'est magnifique, mais ce n'est pas la guerre," is as true of the gallant cavaliers of Charles I., as it was of the fearless horsemen of Cardigan's light brigade.

APPENDIX.

APPENDIX I.
A LIST OF THOSE REGIMENTS OF TRAINED-BANDS AND AUXILIARIES OF THE CITY OF LONDON, WHICH WERE ENGAGED AT THE FIRST BATTLE OF NEWBURY.

Extracted from a MS.* by Richard Symonds (author of the "Diary of the Marches of the Royal Army"), entitled:—

"THE ENSIGNES† OF Yᵉ REGIMENTS IN Yᵉ CITTY OF LONDON
BOTH OF TRAYNED BANDS AND AUXILLARIES.
TOGEATHER Wᵀᴴ THE NEAREST NUMBER OF THEIR TRAYNED SOLDIERS,
AS THEY MARCHED INTO FINSBURY FIELDS, BEING THEIR LAST GENERALL
MUSTER.
TUESDAY, SEPTEMB. 26, 1643.
ANNO PESTIFFERÆ REBELLIONIS."

THE RED REGIMENT OF TRAYNED-BANDS.

This Regimᵗ· was not at yᵉ generall Muster in ffinsbury ffeilds.
Muskettes | Officers about
Pikes | The Totall
Came from Newbery on Thursday, Sep. 28, 1643.

Collonel Isaack Pennington, Vsurper Maior, 1643.
Colonels Captayne Richard Verner.
The limitts of this Regimᵗ·
    Cornhill, Lumbard-street, Fenchurch, the vpp. pt. of Grace Church Street, &c.

Lieut. Col. Robt. Dauies
    a Slop-maker for Seamen neare Billingsgate.

Sʳieant Maior Tho. Chamb'laine. O viol' a Merchant, liuing neare Lenden hall.

1. Capt. Thomas Player
    a hosyer and wholesaleman for narrow wares, liuing vpon new ffish street hill.

2. Capt. Chr. Whichcott, a merchant
    Colonel of the Greene Regimᵗ· of Auxiliaries about Cripplegate.

3. Capt. Wᵐ· Manby, clerke of Leathersellers hall.

4. Capt. Joseph Vaughan, displaced.

---

* Harl. MS. No. 986.
† The Ensigns or Colours of Regiments and Companies, given in the 'Diary,' are not reproduced here.

THE YELLOW REGIMENT OF TRAYNED-BANDS.

This Reg[t.] marched 2[d] into yo feild at yo generall Muster aforesaid and consisted of

    Muskets .. 506
    Pikes 448
    Officers about .. 070

    The Totall .. 1024

Collonel Thomas Adams, Alderman, he was not at Newbury.
Collonel's Captayne Edw. Clegatt.
Limitts of this Regim[t]
  pt. of Thames Street, beginning at St. Magnus Church and reacheth to Bread Street, Dowgate, Walbrooke, ffriday street and part of Watling Street, &c.

Lieut. Col. Francis West, A Silke man liuing in Bread street.
This West was Colonel of this Regim[t.] at Newbery. Capt. Edw. Stoning was his Capt.-leiut. there, and shott in the heele and dyed at Reading and buried [there].

S[r]ieant Maior W[m.] Vnderwood, a Tobacco Seller in Bucklers Bury. Capt. Rich. Hacket p[r]eeded this Vnderwood in this Regim[t.] but left them refusing there oath of Associacon and is now in his Ma[ties] Service.
Garlicke hill and Queene Hithe Company.

1. Capt. Edw. Bellamy
    a Vintner at the Rost on ffleetbridge.
    a ffishmonger in Thames Street neare the Bridge.
    Capt. Rich. Hacket was Capt. of this Company.

2. Capt. John Booker
    Register to y[e] Com'issioners of Banckrupt.
    Liuing in Wallbrooke.

3. Capt. Geo. Dipford, aly Merchant.
    a Linnen Drap' neare Bow Church in the Ch. yard.
    Cheape Side Company ag[t.] the Standard.
    St. Antsokins Bow-Lane, &c. Company.

4, Capt. William Coleson.
    he wth his Company carried the Statues in the Church of All-hallowes to y[e] Parliam.
    A Dyer liuing neare Dyers hall in Thames in Little All-hallowes p'ish. tenant to N.E.H.

THE BLEW REGIMENT OF TRAYNED-BANDS.

This Regim[t.] was not at this Muster but came from Newbery on Thursday, Septemb. 28, 1643.
It was the biggest Regim[t] of y[e] Trayned bands 1400 of them at Bramf. or Turnha' greene.

The limitts of this Regim[t.] is Colman Street, The Stocks Lothbury, Old Jewry, pt. of Cheape side.

Collonel John Warner Alderma'.

Collonels Captayne Thomas Juxon a Sugar baker liuing in St. Thomas Apostles, most violent, slayne at Newbery in this Manner, his horse was shott by a Can'on bullet in the forehead, being stun'd w[th] the blow, ran w[th] him violently right on, into his Ma[ties] Army where the horse fell downe dead, and he was mortally wounded and left dead, but the body of y[e] Army leauing the place left him too, and by that time he recouered his sences and was carried to London, and dyed w[th]in four dayes. His estate was neare Godalming in Surrey where he liued.

Lieu[t.] Col. Mathew ffoster.

Vintner at the Shipp behind the Exch. put out himselfe, but tooke the oath of Assoc. taken by the Capt. of the Citty for opposing all forces raysed w[th]out consent of P.

S[r]ieant Maior Owen Roe, a Mercer in Cheape side.

1. Capt. Mathew Sheppard. Merchant, a Sugar baker p'ner w[th] Juxon afores[d] in St. Thomas Apostles.
2. Capt. ffrancis Roe, brother to Owen Roe, one of these Roes liues in Colman street.
3. Capt. Robt. Mainwaring, of y[e] Custome hovse. Liuing in Aldermanbury.

Hath a Troope of horse besides and quitted this Capt.

THE RED REGIMENT OF AUXILIARIES.

Colonel Thomas Atkins
Alderman.
Colonels Captayne or Capt. Leftenant,
Geo. Mosse.

The limitts of this Regm[t.]
Aldgate, Marke Lane, Tower street, Billingsgate, &c.

Leuit. Colonel Randal Mainwaring
his shop is In Cheape side neare Ironmonger lane by Col. Towse. Was Colonel of the Red Reg. of Auxiliaries and wth them at Newbery.

Prisoners Removed out of Ely howse, 1643.
Mr. Wm. Ingoldsby, of Walton in Com' hertf. Cl:
Mr. Walt. ffarr Essex
Mr. John Scriuener, Com' Suff. Esqr.
Mr. Hen. Wilford Esq.
Mr. hopesill Tilder Jucate of Sandwich
Mr. Sam' Daniell of Bulmer in Essex Recusant
Mr. —— Tilyard } of Yarmouth.
Mr. Hall of Horney }

S[r]ieant Maior Tucker Carried the Prisoners out of Ely howse to the Ship, was slayne at Newbery, Sep: 1643, his head shott off. This Tucker went out Colonel of this Regim[t.] at Newbery.

I

1. Captayne Willm' Tomson.
   This Tomson was leiftenant Colonel of this Regmt· at Newberry.
2. Capt. Edw: Hooker.
3. Capt. Lawrence Bromfeild.
4. Capt. Richard Hunt:
   a Confoctionor in Bearebinder lane: slayne at Newbery quondam S'unnt to Capt. Ditchfeild.
   This Hunt was 3d· Capt. at Newbury.
The Ensigns or Colours of the Blue and Orange Regiments of the Auxiliaries are given by Symonds, without any names of officers.

Total of the Trained-Bands and Auxiliaries engaged at Newbury.

TRAYNED BANDS.

Red Reg: S'ppose it recruted 1000
Yellow Reg: Mustered 1024
Blew Reg: Suppose it recruted, and at most 1000

AUXILIARIES.

Red Reg.
Blew Reg. } Suppose they all 3 recruted } 3000
Orenge Reg. } and to consist of ....

NOTE.—Until the reign of Queen Anne, every "Company" in a Regiment carried a "Colour." Those used by the Trained Bands at this time were of the same colour as the name of the Regiment denotes: thus the Red Regiment bore a red flag. The devices on each were different in the several Regiments. The Colonel's Colour was perfectly plain; the Lieutenant-Colonel's had the red cross of St. George on a white ground in the first quarter; the remainder were similar, with the addition of a number of devices, such as a diamond, a trefoil, ball. or other such device, corresponding to the number of the Company. The Sergeant-Major [Major] had one such mark; the Senior Captain two, and so on. 'History of the Hon. Artillery Company,' by G A. Raikes; pp. 139, 140.

II. THE ATTACK ON ESSEX'S REAR THE DAY AFTER THE FIRST BATTLE OF NEWBURY.

It is difficult at times to reconcile local traditional history and names with the probable course of events gathered from other and more trustworthy sources. Now, near Theale is a narrow winding lane (leading *north* from the main Reading road) to which has been assigned the name of "Deadman's Lane," and this has been described by several writers as the spot where this encounter took place, and somewhat in verification of this tradition, a sword,* portions of horse-trappings, &c.,

---

* While inspecting the ground near Deadman's Lane a short time since, the writer was informed that in removing a bank in the immediate neighbourhood, a sword had been dug up, and this he was fortunately able to secure. The sword is a straight cut-and-thrust blade, much worn by repeated grinding; the fighting sword of a gentleman from its lightness and finish. The hilt is of the ordinary pattern of the 17th century. This relic is now in the hands of the Rev. A. Clutterbuck, rector of Eng efield, to whom it has been presented.

have been found in the adjacent fields; but a glance at a map will prove at once that this "affair" had nothing whatever to do with the pursuit after the battle of the 20th.

It is quite clear that, after having driven the King's forces into the town of Newbury and to some extent across the Kennet, the Earl of Essex would endeavour to keep that obstacle, the river, between him and the enemy as long as possible, and only cross it to gain the main road by Reading to London, which ran along the north bank of the Kennet, *i.e.* on the *enemy's side* of the river, when fairly beyond all danger of being disturbed by the King's troops from the direction of Shaw House.

It is well known that Essex after the battle advanced by Greenham Common *en route* for Reading and London, and it is evident he must have marched by the old winding roads through Aldermaston to the point of passage at Padworth and so by Theale. This line of march would leave Deadman's Lane on the left, and there would be no object whatever in going down it, unless the force had unaccountably lost its way. On this ground alone, therefore it is improbable that any fighting took place there on this occasion.

Further, Sergeant-Major Foster, of the trained-bands, says that when on the march towards Reading, Prince Rupert overtook the army "in the narrow lanes about 1½ mile from the village of Aldermaston," and after the skirmish they marched unmolested to Theale, where they arrived at 10 o'clock.

Again, the 'Mercurius Britannicus'* says:—"Whereupon we marched toward Reading (to gaine quarters to supply our want of victuals) and when we had marched 6 or 7 miles, the enemy's horse having got an advantageous passage, which our horse endeavouring to cleere, charged them, *and in a narrow lane neere Sir Humphrey Forster's house*, part of our foote were disordered neere into a route by our own horse, for relief of which Col. Middleton alights from his horse and draws out 60 musqueteers, which he valorously led up first to relieve a stout cannoneer of ours, who with three men made good his station where he had charge of three case of drakes, against all the enemy's horse, the King's horse were beaten off and 80 slain in the place with the loss of 10 of ours." The 'Mercurius Britannicus' is never very particular as to accuracy in numbers.

This is evidence enough that Deadman's Lane had nothing to do with the march on London, as the lane is 5 or 6 miles from the village of Aldermaston, which is definitely named.†

---

* From Tuesday the 19, September to Tuesday 26, September 1643.

† The following extract from the parish register of Aldermaston, made with the kind permission of the vicar, the Rev. J. B. Burne, tends to show that Essex and his men passed through that village, the soldier buried in the church-yard having most probably died on the march.

"1643 September 23, a Parliament souldier kill'd at Newbury."
There are also two antecedent entries (as follow)
"1643 May 13, a Parliament souldier being a German."
"1643 August 29, Wm. Hill, a Parliament souldier."

In moving the ground for the purpose of making a vault in Padworth Churchyard some years since, the remains of several male bodies were found promiscuously thrown into a large grave, which, from certain indications, were supposed to belong to soldiers who fell in some affray in the neighbourhood.

60   APPENDIX.

A probable explanation of the finding of the sword and other articles near Deadman's Lane, is that some other fight occurred here during Parliamentary times—such as appears by the following letters to have taken place the previous month, August 1643.

(No. 1). Letter from the Earl of Essex to Col. Goodwin.
Sir. Understanding from Col. Ven* that som hors heave nowe quartered at Veal 3 myls from Reading, I resolved to send som hors to visit them, which Collonel Dalbeere desired to perform, as much [as] I know I have sent you, by which you may perceive it was no great matter for a great body of hors to tack som hors of a brocken troupe that quartered themselves at Wikeham against orders, and if the enemy had not taken the payns to have carried the lieftenant away I had called him to a Marshall's Court.† I am, your attached friend, ESSEX.   Kingston, 13 Aug., 1643.   (Tanner MSS., Bibl. Bodl. v. 62-1, No. 254).

(No. 2). Letter from Col. Dalbier to the Earl of Essex.
"According to orders marcht from Kingston to the quarters of my regiment at Cobham, and gave orders for the several troops to march to Bagshot, where, with Capt. Pym's troop, I arrived about 7 o'clock: the troop consisted of 40 men, in all about 100 men, passed from Bagshot 10 at night with a guide who brought me to Swallowfield, where I took another guide who brought me to Burfield Bridge, which was a little after break of day, when, and no sooner, did I hear the enemy was got at Theale, which made me the greater diligence to get them unaware, which indeed we did, for we found them without guard onely ready to goe away, not knowing anything of our entering the town, there was some 5 or 6 kill'd and so many or more sorely hurt: 26 of horse brought to this Castle prisoners, among which is the Captain who commanded, Lieut., Cornet, Quarter-master, and some Corporals, the rest are troopers. My men hath gotten about 40 horses, but very poore, insomuch that in all the matter is no great value. I am both weary and sleepy, and my horses tyred, which makes me stay here this night. I shall, however, if it please God, come to your Excellency to relate the business more at large.   J. DULBIER."
Windsor, 13 Aug., 1643.   (Tanner MSS., Bibl. Bodl., v. 62-1; No. 235).

---

* Col. Venn, who before joining the army had been a silkman in Cheapside, was Governor of Windsor Castle, which was garrisoned for the Parliament soon after the breaking out of the war.   Prince Rupert made an unsuccessful attack upon it in the autumn of 1642.   The Castle continued in the hands of the Parliament during the whole war, and in 1648 became the prison of the unfortunate King, who, as Heath expresses it, kept his sorrowful and last Christmas here.   Col. Venn was one of the King's judges.

† The latter part of this letter evidently refers to other proceedings in Buckinghamshire, in which the Parliamentarians had the worst of it.

III. THE PRESENCE OF QUEEN HENRIETTA-MARIA AT THE BATTLE.

It has been stated by some writers that the Queen herself was present at the First Battle of Newbury, but this is not borne out by the following letters* written by Her Majesty, when at Oxford, to the Duke of Newcastle.

Harl. MS. 6988, fo. 157.
Oxford. ce 23, Sept.

Mon cousin ce porteur est demeure sy a propos quil vous portera la nouuelle de la victoyre que nous auons eue sur les rebelles de quoy je vous en voye la relation: et quoy que se n'aye pas estte vne totalle desfait neaumoins sest vne fort grande victoyre il est vray que nous y auons perdu quantite de honneste gens: qui y ont fait des merueilles je vous assure que nos gens que jay amene auec moy n'ont pas mal fait tellement que lon peut dire que nostre armee du north a ayde a la desfaite je suis sy lasse non pas de mestre batue, mais de en auoir ouy parler, que je finiray en disant que je suis constamant,
Vostre fidelle amie,
HENRIETTE MARIE R.
A Mon cousin le Marquis de Newcastel.

Harl. MS. 6988, fo. 158.
Oxford ce 7 Octobre.

Mon cousin jl y a sy longtamps que je nay reseu de vos nouvelles que je commance a croyre que vous nous croyes ysy tout morts: se que nous ne sommes pas; sest nous qui tueons le autres: nonobstant les grandes rejouisances faits a Londre. Il trouent que ils ont perdu leur armee: il y a beaucoup des fammes des citisiens de Londre qui vienent chercher leur maris a Newbery disant que Mr. desex leur a dit quils estoit la en garnison: du depuis le Roy: tout batu quil est a en voye vne garnison a reading et son exselance ne les a point ampeches tout les jours jl vient des forces du parlement trouuer le Roy: jl m'est ariue vn malheur au quel je crois vous prandres part: Watt Monteque est pris a rochester par le parlemant venant ysy auec l'ambassadeur de france: il a voulu saduanser devant et a estte recongnu et pris: je croy que lambassadeur ne veut point venir quil ne lait encore: jl y a vn chose que je desire sauoir de vous de vant que de la faire:

Marquis Hertford   *Groume*
174   a desire destre 15· 17· 27· 45.|
de stoule   *du King of England.*
22· 50 35. 62· 44· 7· 5· 8. 48. 35. 62. 23. 8. 66.| 5· 63· 189.|
quite
sela estant jl fault quil 52· 62· 27· 45· 8· 68.| destre.| 22. 35· 63.
Gouerneur   *de Prince Charles*
64· 8. 50. 40· 10· 63· 51·| 5· 7· 239. tellement que il en fault 55. 42·
Estre vn autre   *de P. Charles*
8. 48. 45· 50· 8. 62. 41. 17. 62. 45. 50. 8.| au pres 5· 8· 239. ce que

---

* One of these letters is partly written in cipher, as will be seen; and some deciphered words appear to have been intercalated in the original.

APPENDIX.

Queene   *vous*
260, ne veut pas sans premierement sauoir sy.   63. 35. 63· 48. |
               la rauoir
66· 4· 70 voules *23. 18. 50· 17. 62· 35· 27. 50.* | se que jay cru auec
            vous   *auez*   *pas*
lamploy que 64· 35· 63 48. | 17· 62· 8· 48. ne se pouroit 33· 17· 48.
accorder
17· 11 35· 50· 5· 8· 51. neanmoins: je atandray vostre responce: et sy
                                                                 deux
vous tombes days la mesme opinion que moy: jl y a 5· 8· 62· 48.
        Places
autres 33· 23· 17· 11· 8· 49· que je desire sauoir la quelle vous sera
plus agreable: nayant rien tant dans ma pancee que de vous faire voir
et a tout le monde lestime que je fais de vous: sest pour quoy mande a
moy franchement et comme a vne amie: comme je fais a sette heure a
                             Chambellan ou gentilhomme de la Chambre du lit
vous: se que vous desirez *11· 31· 17· 40· 13· 8· 23· 24· 18· 40· 5· 35·*
62· 27· 17· 41· 45· 28· 23· 31· 35· 42· 44· 7· 5· 8· 24· 17· 11· 31· 19·
43· 13· 50· 7· 5· 62· 24· 28· 45·   sy jauois voulu aler par seremonies
je vous lorois fait escrire par vn autre: mais sela est bon la ou jl nia
pas vne estime comme jay de vous: et comme se sy est escrit auec
franchise je demande vne responce de mes me: et que vous me croyes
comme je suis veritablement et constamment,
                              Vostre fidelle et bien bonne amie,
                                      HENRIETTE MARIE R.
A Mon cousin le Marquis de Newcastel.

The Marquis of Newcastle was at this time in the North, and a few days previously writes as below to Prince Rupert, congratulating him on his (questionable) success at Newbury:—
"May it please your Highness. God give you joy of your late great victory, which I am confident the rebels will never recover: so that upon the matter one may salute the King, King again, and only by your hand, Sir, * * * Your Highness's most faithful obliged servant,   W. NEWCASTLE.
Cottingham, 6 Oct., 1643.

IV. A CASE OF WITCH-MURDER AT NEWBURY.*

"A MOST
"CERTAIN STRANGE AND TRUE DISCOVERY OF A
" WITCH
" Being taken by some of the Parliamentary Forces, as she was sliding
"On a small planck board and sayling on it over the River at Newbery,
"Together with the strange and true manner of her death, with the
propheticall
"Words and Speeches she used at the same time.
Printed by John Hammond 1643.
[A very rough woodcut of the conventional "Witch" is printed with the title.]

"Many are in the belief that this silly sex of Woman can by no meanes attaine to that so vile and damned a practise of sorcery and Witchcraft in regard to their illeterateness and want of learning, which many Men of greate learning have become. Adam by temptation toucht and tasted the deceiving apple so some high learn'd and read, by the same Tempter that deceived him hath bin ensnared to contract with the Devil as for example in the instancing a few English, Bacon of Oxford, Vandermast of Hollande, Bungy of Germany, Fostus of the same place, Franciscus the English monke of Bery, Doctor Blackleach and divars, others that were tedious to relate of, but how weake Woman should attain unto it many are incredible of the same and many too are opposite of opinion gainst the same, that giving a possibility to their doubtings that the malice and inveterate malice of a woman entirely devoted to her revengefull wrath frequenting desolate and desart places and giving way unto their wicked temptation may have commune with that world roaring Lion and covenant and contract upon condition, the like hath in divars places and tymes been tried at the assises of Lancaster, Carlile, Buckingham and elsewhere, but to come to the intended relation of this Witch's and Sorceresse's doings as is manifestly and credibly related by Gentlemen, Commanders and Captaines of the Earle of Essex his Army.
"A part of the Army marching thro' Newbery some of the Souldiers being scattered by reason of theyre loytering by the way in gathering Nuts, Apples, Plummes, Black berries and the like, one of them by chance in climbing up a Tree being pursued by his fellows or Comrade in Waggish Merriment jesting one with another espied on the river being there adjacent a tall lean slender Woman as he supposed to his amasement and great terrour treading of the water with her foete with as much ease and firmnesse as if one should walk or trample on the earth, wherewith he softly calls and beck'ned to his fellows to behold it and with all possible speed that could be to obscure them from her sight, who as conveniently as they could they did observe, this could

---

* It is only for the sake of illustrating the thoughts and actions of the times referred to, that the f llowing account of a heartless and superstitious murder is here given, with the grossly illiterate form retained in which the brutality credulity, and ignorance of the day produced it as a catchpenny sheet for the vulgar.

be no little amasement unto them you may think to see a Woman dance upon the water, nor could all their sights be deluded, though perhaps one might, but arriving nearer to the Shore they could perceive there was a planck or deale overshadowed with a little shallow water that she stood upon which did beare her up, anon rode by some of the Commanders who were eye-witnesses as much as they and were as much astonished as they could be, still too and fro she fleeted on the water, the boord standing firm about upright, indeed I have both heerd and read of many that in tempests and on Rivers by casualty have become ship-wrack'd or cast overboord where catch'g empty Barrells, rudders, boords or plancks have made good shift by the assisting providence of God to get on shore, but not in this woman kind, when as little thinking who perceived her tricks, or that she did imagine that they were the last she should ever show, as we have heard the Swan sings before her death, at last having been sufficiently upon the water he that deceived her alway, did so then, blinding her that she could not see at her landing the ambush that was laid for her, coming upon the shore she gave the boord a push, which they plainly perceived and crossed the river, they searched after her, but could not find her she being landed. The Commanders beholding her gave orders to lay hold on her and bring her to them straight, the which some were feerfull, but some being more valorous than other some, boldly went to her and siesed upon her by the armes demanding what she was, but the woman no whit replying any words unto them they brought her to the Commanders to whom, tho' mightily she was urged she did reply as little, so consulting with themselves what should be done to her, it being so apparently appear'd she was a Witch, being lothe to let her goe and as loth to carry her with them, so they resolved with themselves to make a shot at her, and gave orders to a couple of their Souldiers that were approv'd good marksmen to charge and shoot her strait, which they purposed to doe, so setting her strait again a Mud Banke or wall two of the Souldiers according to their comand made ready when having taken aime, gave fire and shot at her, as thinking sure they had sped her, but with a deriding and loud laughter at them she caught theyre bullets in her hands and shewed them, which was stronger testimony than the water that she was the same that their imagination thought her so to be, so resolving with themselves if either fire or sword or halter were sufficient to make an end of her, one let his Carabine close to her breast, where discharging, the bullett back rebound'd like a ball and narrowly it missed his face that was the shooter, this so inraged the Gentlemen that one drew out his sword and manfully [!] ran at her with all the force his strength had power to make, but it prevayled no more than did the shot, the Woman still, tho' speechless, yet in a most contemptible way of scorn still laughing at them, which did the more exhauste their furie against her against her life, yet one amongst them had heerd that piercing the temples of the head it would prevayl against the strongest sorcery and quell the force of Witchcraft, which was allowyd for trial, the Woman hearing this knew that the Devil had left her and her power was gone, whereupon she began aloud to cry and roare, tearing her haire and making piteous moan, which in these words expressed were, And is it come to passe that I must dye indeed, why then his Excellencie the Earle of Essex shall be fortunate and win the field, after which no

APPENDIX. 65

more words could be got from her, wherewith they immediately discharged a Pistoll underneathe her eare at which she strait sunk downe and dyed, leaving her legacy of a detested carcasse to the wormes, her soule we ought not to judge of, though the evills of her wicked life and death can scape no censure. FINIS."

IV.*—THE DISCOVERY OF THE COFFIN AND REMAINS OF THE VAULT OF ROBERT DEVEREUX, THIRD EARL OF ESSEX, IN THE CHAPEL OF ST. JOHN THE BAPTIST IN WESTMINSTER ABBEY, JUNE, 1879.*

The only entry of this burial in the Register of Westminster Abbey says that the Earl of Essex was buried "in St. John Bap. Chapel in a vault on the right side of the Earl of Exeter's monument, 19 Oct. 1646." There is also a memorandum that a certain burial took place "neare y⁰ Earle of Essex."
Probably no monument to him has ever existed, for there is no note of one. The memorandum of 1685, quoted above, renders it very probable, however, that his gravestone then existed.
This obscurity has always been unsatisfactory; but no attempt to throw light on the subject has ever been made until the present year, when a descendant of the Devereux family proposed to Dean Stanley to have an examination in St. John the Baptist's Chapel.
The existence of a vault having been inferred from the memoranda, it was thought there would be but little difficulty in finding it; and, under the order of the Dean, the search was made early in June. It began in the ground south of the Exeter tomb, where there was found the wall of the vault built by Baron Hunsdon, now partly under the Exeter tomb; and southward was found the marble coffin of an Abbot of the fifteenth century. The south-west corner of the Chapel was found to be filled with coffins, laid side by side and in piles, without any sign of a vault.
As regards the Earl's burial all this labour was fruitless, and with a feeling of disappointment the search was hopelessly given up.
On returning to the Chapel the next day for the purpose of closing all up, there was seen the angle of a lead coffin, which lay low down in the earth, at the extreme south-west corner of the area. It appeared to be a coffin of more than usual importance from the form of the soldering of the sheet-lead. The earth above the coffin was cellular and loose, and so allowed the hand to pass through towards the place of the coffin-plate. This was done, and a loose plate was felt and brought out. On partially clearing off the corrosion, the name of Robert Devereux, Earl of Essex, was seen, and the discovery was achieved.

---

* From an account of the operations which led to this discovery, prepared by Mr. Henry Poole, Master Mason of Westminster Abbey. Inserted with the courteous approval of the Very Rev. A. P. Stanley, D.D., Dean of Westminster.

K

The coffin had the appearance of being one of a number of common burials, and without a vault; but its position at the very bottom induced further examination. Then it became evident that the coffin had been once enclosed in a beautifully wrought vault of stone, which had been, not many years afterwards, wholly demolished to give room for interments over the coffin and by the north side of it.

The coffin lay on the original stone floor of the vault, and it seemed never to have been disturbed. Besides the floor, there remained a part of the south wall, but all the other three walls and the arch over them had disappeared.

After the disheartening abandonment of the search on the previous day, the pleasure arising from its successful resumption may be conceived.

The brass inscription-plate of the coffin was now flattened and attached to a small slab of marble, and laid on its place on the coffin.

The Dean directed the coffin to be enclosed within a new vault of stone, utilizing what remained of the old vault, and finally, that on the top of the covering should be laid a slab of marble thus inscribed:—

"This vault, shattered by later interments, was opened for the purpose of ascertaining the grave of the Earl of Essex, in June, 1879, and was then restored."

The vault was formally and finally closed on the 19th June, in the presence of the Dean, Mr. Evelyn P. Shirley, of Lower Ettington, near Stratford-on-Avon, Mr. Knight Watson, secretary of the Royal Society of Antiquaries, and Mr. Doyne C. Bell, secretary to the Privy Purse.

From the nature of the fine white Purbeck marble gravestone which lay over the vault of the Earl, it is thought to be his original stone, once engraved with his inscription, and referred to in the memorandum of 1685. In 1710 was buried the wooden coffin which was found pressing on the Earl's coffin, and then, perhaps, the vault was demolished, and the Earl's inscription was smoothed out and superseded by that of "Mary Kendal." All this seemed to warrant the erasure of the inscription of that lady, and its renewal in smaller characters below the middle of the slab.

The upper part of the marble slab is now occupied by the inscription and the shield of arms of the Earl's coffin-plate, of which it is a fac-simile, but twice-and-a-half larger.

The vault of the Earl has been spoken of as one of excellent work. Its construction, shape, and finish are very much like those of the beautiful vault which King Henry VII. built for his Queen Elizabeth of York, under their magnificent tomb.

It may be well to note here that the entry quoted in the first sentence of this notice is erroneous The public prints of the day give the date of the funeral "on Monday 22nd, October," whereas the Abbey-Register says "October 19." Such errors are not infrequent in that Register.[*]

---

[*] On submitting the foregoing to Colonel Chester, the Editor of the Westminster Abbey Registers, he does not accept Mr. Poole's conclusion, but is inclined to maintain the accuracy of the entry in the Register. He points out that in the year 1646 the 22nd of October did not fall on Monday, but on Thursday; while the 19th was really Monday, and that, as the "public prints of the day" were certainly wrong either as to the day of the month or the week, the balance of proof is in favour of the Register.

COFFIN PLATE OF ROBERT DEVEREUX, EARL OF ESSEX.
Discovered in Westminster Abbey, 1879. See page 65.

APPENDIX. 67

V. BIOGRAPHICAL NOTICES OF OFFICERS AND OTHERS

MENTIONED IN CONNECTION WITH THE FIRST BATTLE OF NEWBURY.

§ 1. ROYALIST OFFICERS.

PATRICK RUTHVEN, EARL OF FORTH. Created an English peer with the title of the Earl of Brentford, 27 May, 1644; had been made Field-marshall by the King at Coventry, and succeeded Lord Lindsey as General-in-chief after the battle of Edgehill; engaged at both fights at Newbury; "an experienced commander and a man of naturall courage, and purely a soldier, and of a most loyall heart (which he had many occasions to shew, before the warr was ended, and which his Country-men remembred, for they used both him and his Widow with all extremity afterwards)." (Sir Philip Warwick's Memoirs, p. 229.) He had seen service in Sweden under Gustavus Adolphus, in Denmark, Russia, Livonia, Lithuania, Poland, and Prussia. In England alone the number of his wounds had equalled that of the battles in which he had exposed himself. At Edgehill, says Lloyd, he modelled the fight. He was at Brentford and Gloucester, was shot in both the fights at Newbury, at Cheriton, and near Banbury. He had been shot in the head, in both arms, the mouth, leg, and shoulder; and, as if all this had not been enough for his scars and his story, the catalogue was finished by a fall from his horse that broke his shoulder. He survived to wait upon Charles II. in exile; and, returning to his native country, was buried in 1651 at Dundee. (Mil. Mem. of Col. Jno. Birch, Cam. Soc., p. 99.)

PRINCE RUPERT. Prince Rupert came over from Holland to the assistance of the King his uncle about the time of the raising of the royal standard at Nottingham. He possessed in a high degree that kind of courage which is better to attack than defend, and is less adapted to the land-service than that of the sea, where precipitate valour is in its element. He seldom engaged but he gained the advantage, which he generally lost by pursuing it too far. He was better qualified to storm a citadel, or even mount a breach, than patiently sustain a siege; and would have furnished an excellent hand to a general of a cooler head. (Granger's Biog. Hist. v. i., p. 344.) Prince Rupert died, unmarried, at his house in Spring Gardens, 29 Nov., 1682, and was buried in Westminster Abbey.

SIR JOHN BYRON. Sir John Byron, K.B., M.P. for the town of Nottingham in the reign of James I., and for the county of Nottingham in that of Charles I. A faithful adherent of, and gallant officer under the latter King. Sir John commanded the corps of reserve at the battle of Edgehill; and the victory of Roundway Down, 5 July, 1643, wherein Sir William Waller was routed, was chiefly owing to his skill and valour, having at the head of his regiment charged Sir Arthur Haslrigg's cuirassiers, and after a sharp conflict, in which Sir Arthur received many wounds, compelled that impenetrable regiment (as Lord Clarendon writes) to fly. Sir John Byron having given such proofs of his courage, and his six brothers at that time following his loyal example, he was in consideration thereof advanced 24 October, 1643, shortly after the first engagement at Newbury, to the dignity of a Baron of the realm, by the title of Lord Byron, of Rochdale in the Co. Palatine of Lancaster, with limitation, in default of his own male issue, to each of his brothers. His Lordship married twice; but dying in 1652 issueless, the barony devolved upon his brother Richard. Lord Byron's letter to Clarendon, frequently quoted in the text, was written while in exile, and is dated "St. Germains, December 10, 1647."

LORD WILMOT. Henry, 2nd Viscount Wilmot in Ireland, was created, 29 June 1643, Lord Wilmot of Adderbury, co. Oxon, in the English Peerage. He was further advanced to the Earldom of Rochester, 13 Dec. 1652, He died at Dunkirk in 1659, and was succeeded by his only surviving son, John, the better (but not so favourably) known Earl of Rochester. Lord Wilmot "ordered the horse at Newbery first Battel (being Lieutenant-General under Prince Rupert) in so convenient and spacious a place (Downs have been pitched upon as the most commodious Scene of a Horse Engagement), advising them by no means to be drawn into any uneven and streight places; with so strict an eye upon all advantages and opportunities, and in such Ranks, that one Troop might be *in subsidiis* assistant to another, and no part stand naked or fail in the singleness of its own strength, but that one may second another from first to last, being aware of Livius' Charge upon *Cajus Sempronius (Pugnavit incaute inconsulteque non subsidiis firmata acie non equite apte locato)*." (Lloyd's Memoirs, pp. 465-6.)

EARL OF CAERNARVON. Robert Dormer, grandson to Robert Dormer created a baronet by K. James I., June 10, 1615, and Baron Dormer, of Wing, co. Bucks, the 30th of the same month in the same year, succeeded to the Barony on the death of his grandfather in 1616, and was created Viscount and Earl of Caernarvon by Charles I. in 1628. This gallant nobleman it would appear, like his noble compatriots Sunderland and Falkland, fell in the early part of the fight. Clarendon states that the Earl, having charged and routed a body of the enemy's horse, and coming carelessly back by some scattered troopers, was by one of them, who knew him, run through the body with a sword, of which he died within an hour; and describes him as being an honour to the cause he embraced, and his death a sensible weakness to the army. In Sir Roger Manley's 'History of the Rebellion,' his death is thus described:—"There was a little hill five hundred paces from the town, which the Cavaliers had possessed and fortified with guns. Essex perceiving it, and having no other way to pass, he himself with his own regiment and that of the general's guards attacks it fiercely, being as bravely received by the royalists, Stapleton with his own regiment and that of the general's guards, charging the Earl of Caernarvon was repulsed, but the Earl, pursuing too far, was killed by a shot in [at] the head of his own men; a person no less remarkable for his fortitude and fidelity to the King, than for the nobleness of his extraction." The context shows that Sir Roger refers to the Wash as the hill fortified with the King's artillery.* Lloyd, in his 'Memoirs,'

---

* The traditional spot where Lord Caernarvon fell is marked on the Plan.

ROBERT DORMER, EARL OF CARNARVON.

From a portrait by VANDYKE.

gives this account:—"The Earl receiving Sir Philip Stapleton with his regiment of horse and Essex his life guard with a brisk charge and pursuing them to the foot, when a private hand put an end to his life, and in breathing out his last he asked, 'whether the King was in safety?'" At the battle of Lansdown, two months before Newbury, it is recorded that of 2000 cavalry who entered the field and fought valiantly under Prince Maurice and Lord Caernarvon only 600 could be mustered when the sun went down! Eachard gives Charles II. the credit of saying "Lord Caernarvon was the finest gentleman he ever saw." In Defoe's 'Memoirs of a Cavalier' (Colonel Andrew Newport), which, though woven into a romantic story, is written with apparent fidelity of statement, it is said:—"The Earl of Caernarvon was brought into an inn at Newberry, where the King came to see him. He had just life enough to speak to his Majesty, and died in his presence. The King was exceedingly concerned for him and was observed to shed tears at the sight. We were indeed all of us troubled at the loss of so brave a gentleman, but the concern our royal master discovered moved us more than ordinary. Every body endeavoured to have the King out of the room, but he would not stir from the bed-side, till he saw all hopes of life gone." The body of the Earl was conveyed under guard to Oxford, and buried in the chapel of Jesus College. While on its way, the escort, it is said, was attacked by a body of Parliamentary horse, and the Earl's jewels and plate were taken. Lord Caernarvon had married Anne Sophia, daughter of Philip Herbert, 4th Earl of Pembroke and Montgomery (from whom the present Lord Carnarvon paternally descends), and left an only child Charles, his successor, who dying without male issue, the earldom became extinct, and the Barony of Dormer devolved on a distant kinsman, in whose posterity it remains.

EARL OF LINDSEY. Montague Bertie, 2nd Earl of Lindsey, K.G. This nobleman being with his gallant father at Edgehill, when his Lordship received his death-wound, voluntarily surrendered himself prisoner in order to be near and attend him. The Earl's second wife was Bridget, daughter of Edward Wray, Esq., by Lady Elizabeth Norreys his wife, only daughter and heir of Francis, Earl of Berkshire and Baron Norreys, of Rycote, and widow of Sir Edward Sackville, who was engaged at Newbury fight. By this Bridget the Earl had a son James, who became Lord Norreys in right of his mother, and was created Earl of Abingdon, also a daughter Mary, married to Charles Dormer, 2nd Earl of Caernarvon, and two other children. Lord Lindsey commanded the King's life-guards in several of the considerable battles that were fought in the course of the civil war, and was wounded in that of Naseby. His affectionate regard to his unhappy sovereign was conspicuous after the death of the latter; he attended his body to the grave, and paid his last duty to him with tears. After the Restoration he lived in retirement with dignity, and "approved himself an example of a better age." He died at Campden House, Kensington, the 25th July, 1666.

EARL OF NORTHAMPTON. James, 3rd Earl. This nobleman, while a commoner, and M.P. for the co. Warwick, having voted, in 1641, against the bill for attainting the Earl of Strafford, his name was amongst those called *Straffordians*, in the list posted up in the Old Palace Yard; and subsequently, with other members, he was expelled the House. He was afterwards distinguished with his gallant father (who fell at the battle of Hopton Heath) under the royal banner; and his lordship, on the magnificent entry of Charles II. into the city of London, 29 May, 1660, headed a band of two hundred gentlemen attired in grey and blue. The Earl married 1st Isabella daughter and co-heir of Richard, 3rd Earl of Dorset, by whom he had one surviving daughter, Alathea, who married Sir Edward Hungerford, Bart. On her death without issue in 1678, her great fortune devolved upon her cousin, John, 3rd Earl of Thanet. The Earl married 2ndly Mary, daughter and heir of Baptist Noel, Viscount Camden, by whom he had three sons and two daughters.

EARL OF NOTTINGHAM. Sir Charles Howard, 3rd Earl. He died 26 April, 1681, when the Earldom of Nottingham expired.

EARL OF CLEVELAND. Thomas Wentworth, Earl of Cleveland, and Lord Wentworth of Nettlestead, 1625. Lord Cleveland especially distinguished himself at the Second Battle of Newbury, where he was instrumental in saving the life of the King. On the death of the Earl, 25 March, 1667, the Earldom of Cleveland became extinct, but his grand-daughter Henrietta Maria succeeded to the Barony of Wentworth. She was the only child of his only son, Thomas, Lord Wentworth, who served his Majesty throughout the war, but died before his father, and was buried at Toddington, Beds., 7 March, 1664-5. As the Baroness Wentworth she is best remembered from her unhappy connection with the Duke of Monmouth. She died 23 April, 1686, when the title reverted to her aunt, her father's only sister, Lady Anne, wife of John, second Lord Lovelace; and at her death, 7 May, 1697, it passed to her grand-daughter Martha, wife of Sir Henry Johnson, and at her death, in July, 1745, without issue it reverted to Sir Edward Noel, 6th Bart., and at his death in 1774, passed to his son Thomas, at whose death in 1815, it fell into abeyance, which terminated, 12 Nov., 1856, in favour of Lady Byron, widow of the Poet, whose grandson, Ralph-Gordon-Noel Milbanke, is now 11th Baron Wentworth.

EARL OF HOLLAND. Henry Rich, Earl of Holland, captain of the King's guard, and general of the horse in the expedition to Scotland, was much in favour with James I. In the latter end of the reign of James, he was sent ambassador to France, where he negotiated the treaty of marriage between Charles and Henrietta Maria. His handsome person, gallant behaviour, and courtly address, are thought to have made an early impression upon the heart of that princess, of whom he is known to have been a distinguished favourite. His conduct was so various with respect to the King and Parliament that neither party had the least regard for him, if they did not look upon him as their enemy. Lord Holland with the Earls of Clare and Bedford had left the Parliament and joined the King, shortly before the battle of Newbury, Col. Blagne, the governor of Wallingford, receiving the converts at the castle, and forwarding them with an escort of honour to Oxford. The three Earls subsequently returned to the Parliament. In 1648 Lord Holland once more adopted the royal cause; and having received from the Prince of Wales (afterwards Charles II.) a commission as general, and the queen, who was in Paris, promising money, he joined with the Duke of Buckingham, his brother Lord Francis Villiers, and a few others of high rank, in a rash and feeble effort for the King at Kingston-on-Thames. Being surrounded by a superior body of the Parliament horse and foot, he fled with Col. Dalbier and about a hundred horse to St. Neots, where he was taken prisoner at an inn; he was then confined in Warwick Castle, and afterwards in the Tower. He was tried by the so-called "High Court of Justice," and, by the casting vote of the Speaker, sentenced to be executed. Lord Holland was beheaded at Palace Yard, 9th March, 1649, upon the same scaffold as the Duke of Hamilton and Lord Capel. The Duke of Buckingham managed to escape at Kingston, but his handsome and brave brother, the young Lord Francis Villiers, was killed. He behaved with signal courage, and, after his horse had been shot under him, stood with his back against a tree, defending himself till he sunk under his wounds. The initials of his name were inscribed on the tree, and remained until it was cut down in 1680. The names "King Charles' Road" and "Villiers' Path" at present alone commemorate the scene of this fight, which was one of the last struggles made for the King—then a prisoner in the Isle of Wight.

EARL OF BEDFORD. William, 5th Earl of Bedford, son of Francis, 4th Earl, elected a Knight of the Garter, 1672; and created 11 May, 1694, Marquis of Tavistock, and Duke of Bedford. His grace married Anne, daughter and sole heiress of Robert Carr, Earl of Somerset, by his too celebrated countess, Frances Howard, the divorced wife of Essex. "Francis, Earl of Bedford," says Pennant, "was so averse to the alliance, that he gave his son leave to choose a wife out of any family but that. Opposition usually stimulates desire: the young couple's affections were only increased. At length the King interposed, and sending the Duke of Lennox to urge the Earl to consent, the match was brought about. Somerset, now reduced to poverty, acted a generous part, selling his house at Chiswick, plate, jewels, and furniture, to raise a fortune for his daughter of £12,000, which the Earl of Bedford demanded, saying, that "since her affections were settled, he chose rather to undo himself, than make her unhappy." The lady proved worthy of the alliance. It is said that she was ignorant of her mother's dishonour, until informed of it by a pamphlet, which she accidentally found; and, it is added, she was so terribly struck with this knowledge of her parent's guilt, that she fell down in a fit, and was found senseless, with the book open before her. The duke had issue by this admirable woman, seven sons and three daughters, of whom the eldest surviving son was the celebrated William Lord Russell. See Burke's "Peerage and Baronetage," *sub. nom.* Sir John Russell, a younger brother of William, 5th Earl of Bedford, was also engaged in the First Battle of Newbury.

EARL OF CLARE. John Holles, second Earl, who succeeded his father on his death, 4 Oct., 1637. He married Elizabeth, eldest daughter and co-heir of Sir Horatio Vere, Lord Vere, of Tilbury. He lived in retirement during the Commonwealth. Lord Clarendon says of him:—"he was a man of honour and courage, and would have been an *excellent person* if his heart had not been set upon keeping and improving his estate; he was weary of the company he kept, and easily hearken'd to the Earl of Holland, in any consultation how to recover the King's authority, and to put an end to the war." The Earl died the 2nd and was buried 23rd January, 1665-6, at St. Mary's, Nottingham.

72   APPENDIX.

JOHN, LORD BELASYSE, second son of Thomas, first Viscount Falconberg, created Baron Belasyse, of Worlaby, co. Lincoln, 27 Jan., 1644-5. He was buried in the choir of the church of St. Giles's in the Fields, 14 Sept., 1689, and his loyalty to his King is perpetuated by the following inscription copied from the monument formerly existing in the old church. "This monument was erected, Anno 1670, in memory of the Honourable John, Lord Belasyse, Baron Worlaby, second son of Thomas, Lord Viscount Fauconberg, his wives and children. Who, for his loyalty, prudence, and courage was promoted to several commands of great trust, by their Majesties King Charles the First and Second, viz.:—Having raised six regiments of horse and foot in the late Civil Wars, he commanded a Tertia in His Majesty's Armies at the Battles of Edgehill, Newbury, and Naseby, the sieges of Reading and Bristol. Afterward being made Governor of York, and Commander-in-chief of all His Majesty's Forces in Yorkshire, he fought the battle of Selby with the Lord Fairfax. Then being Lieutenant-General of the Counties of Lincoln, Northampton, Derby, and Rutland, and Governor of Newark, he valiantly defended the garrison against the English and Scotch Armies, till His Majesty came in Person to the Scotch Quarters and commanded the surrender of it; at which time he also had the honour of being of the King's Horse Guards. In all which services, and during the wars and other achievements, he deported himself with eminent courage and conduct, and received many wounds, sustained three imprisonments in the Tower of London, and after the happy restoration of King Charles II. was made Lord Lieutenant of the East Riding of the County of York, Governor of Hull, General of His Majesty's Forces in Africa, Governor of Tangier, and Captain of His Majesty's Guard of Gentlemen-Pensioners." The remainder of the inscription referred to his marriages and issue. His third wife was Lady Ann Paulet, daughter of the Marquis of Winchester. (From Maitland's 'Hist. and Survey of London,' 1756, vol. ii. p. 1362.) This monument, which no longer exists, was possibly put up by Lord Belasyse in his life time, unless the date 1670, is a misreading for 1690. The former explanation is probably the correct one, as all the books give that date, and as the date of his death does not appear on the monument.

GEORGE, LORD DIGBY. Son and heir of John Digby, 1st Earl of Bristol, summoned to Parliament in his father's barony of Digby, June 9, 1641. At the Restoration he was made Knight of the Garter, and died in 1676. The title became extinct on the death of his only son in 1693.

LORD JERMYN. Henry Jermyn, created Baron Jermyn, 8 Sept., 1643, and Earl of St. Albans 27 April, 1660. He was master of the horse to Queen Henrietta, and one of the Privy Council to Charles II. In July, 1660, he was sent Ambassador to the Court of France, and in 1671 he was made Lord Chamberlain of His Majesty's household. He died unmarried, 2 January, 1683-4, when the Earldom became extinct, but the Barony, by limitation of the patent, devolved on his nephew.

LORD PERCY. Henry Percy, youngest son of Henry, 9th Earl of Northumberland, and brother of Algernon, 10th Earl. He was Governor of Jersey at the breaking out of the rebellion, but returned to England, raised a regiment of horse, and was constituted General of the Ordnance. He attended the King throughout the whole of the war; and was created Baron Percy of Alnwick, 28 June, 1643. He afterwards followed Charles II. into exile, and was appointed Lord Chamberlain of his Household. Died in Paris, unmarried, in April 1659. His brother Algernon took an active part against Charles I., but was entirely free from any participation in his death, and subsequently promoted the Restoration.

LORD CHANDOS. George Brydges, son of Grey, 5th Lord Chandos, by Lady Ann Stanley, daughter and co-heir of Ferdinando, 5th Earl of Derby, succeeded as 6th Lord Chandos, on the death of his father, 10 Aug., 1621, being then only a year old. He died at his house near Covent Garden (on the site of the present Chandos Street) 1 February, 1654-5, and was buried with his ancestors in the chapel of Sudeley. Leaving no male issue, the title passed to his brother William. "His Castle, at Sudeley near Winchcomb in Gloucestershire," says Lloyd, "being besieged by *Massie*, with 300 *musqueteers* and three *companies of dragons*, and two *sakers*, after a long siege, several assaults and batteries, when they were almost smothered by the smoke of hay and barns burned about the house, yielded *Jan*. 1642. A loss revenged by my Lord at *Newbury, Sept*. 20, 1643, when with the Earls of *Caernarvon* and *Northampton*, the *true* Heir of his father's valor, commanding His Majesties' Horse there, the King said, Let 'Chandois alone, his *errors are safe*.'" Lloyd's Memoirs, p. 366. It is related by the Rev. Alex. Jacob, chaplain to Henry, second Duke of Chandos, in his 'Complete English Peerage' that Charles I. was so sensible of the advantages that had accrued to his army during this battle by the example exhibited by Lord Chandos, as well as the personal service performed by this nobleman, that he offered to create him *Earl of Newbury;* but his lordship, who had espoused the King's cause from motives of honour and justice, refused that distinction till he should have deserved it more by having a principal share in the re-establishment of His Majesty upon the throne. Lord Chandos was immediately descended from Richard Brydges, of West Shefford, near Newbury, who was made a K.B. at the coronation of Queen Mary, and married Jane, daughter of Sir William Spencer, of Wormleighton, ancestor to the Duke of Marlborough and Earl Spencer. He died at the Manor house, West Shefford, in 1548. James, the first Duke of Chandos, purchased the Shaw Estate of the representatives of the Dolman family, and frequently resided at Shaw House, which figures so conspicuously in connection with the Second Battle of Newbury. His second duchess, but third wife, Lydia Catherine, died at Shaw House in 1750, and lies buried in Shaw Church.

LORD MOLYNEUX. Richard, 2nd Viscount, succeeded to the title on the death of his father in 1632. He actively supported the interests of Charles I., and with his brother Carlyll raised two regiments of horse and foot, with which they served during the course of the war. Lord Molineux was in the battle of Worcester. He died soon afterwards, leaving no issue by his wife Lady Frances Seymour, eldest daughter of William, Marquis of Hertford, and the honours devolved upon his brother Carlyll, 3rd Viscount, who was outlawed by Parliament for his exertions on behalf of the Charleses. The Viscountcy of Molyneux is now held with the Earldom of Sefton.

HON. HENRY BERTIE. Son of the 1st Earl of Lindsey, and brother to Montagu, 2nd Earl, who was also engaged at Newbury. This gallant young nobleman fell in the early part of the fight, and his body, like that of his comrade Falkland, was not found till next day. He is mentioned in a letter written by Prince Rupert to the Earl of Essex, printed further on (see FALKLAND).

SIR CHARLES LUCAS. Son of Thomas Lucas, Esq., next brother to John, who was afterwards the first Baron Lucas, of Shenfield, co. Essex. His family was one of the most distinguished in the kingdom for its valour and its sufferings in the royal cause. "He carryed 2000 horse to assist His Majesty, with whom we finde him eminent both for his directions and execution about the hill near *Newbery* and *Enborne Heath*, which he maintained with one regiment well disposed and lined with musqueteers, and a drake, with small shot against the gross of *Essex* his army, the leading-man of which he pistolled himself in the head of his troop, giving close fire himself, and commanding others to do the like." Lloyd's Memoirs, p. 475. Sir Charles was at the head of those loyalists, who, in 1648, shut themselves up in Colchester, and defended it against the army of Fairfax for three months. When the garrison yielded to the enemy, their ammunition was reduced to a barrel and a half of powder; and their provisions to two horses and one dog. Sir Charles Lucas met with cruel treatment for his resolute defence of this place. He, and his friend Sir George Lisle, were ordered to be shot to death the same day on which the Parliament army entered the town. He begged a day's respite to prepare for death, but his request was refused, and he was executed August 28th, 1648. He died with the courage of a soldier and a christian. His faithful servant, who was a sorrowful spectator of his death, with great earnestness begged the executioner of his master to dispatch him also, as his life was become "his torment." The bodies of the two friends, Lucas and Lisle, were interred in a vault in the north-aisle of St. Giles's Church, Colchester. At the Restoration a large flat marble slab was laid over their grave, at the expense of Lord Lucas, with the following inscription:—"Under this marble lie the bodies of the two most valiant cavaliers Sir Charles Lucas and Sir George Lisle, knights, who, for their eminent loyalty to their Sovereign, were, on the 28th August, 1648, by command of Sir Thomas Fairfax (the General of the Parliament Army) in cold blood barbarously murdered." In Lord de Grey's 'Memoir of Sir Charles Lucas,' a tradition is related that George Villiers, Duke of Buckingham, who married Fairfax's only daughter, applied to Charles II. to have this inscription erased. The King mentioned it to Lord Lucas (the brother of Sir Charles), who said that he would obey his Majesty's commands, if his Majesty would allow the following to be substituted: "Sir Charles Lucas and Sir George Lisle were barbarously murdered for their loyalty to King Charles the First, and King Charles the Second ordered the memorial of their loyalty to be erased." Thereupon the King ordered the inscription to be cut more deeply than before. Whitelock, in a few words, expresses the grief of heart the King suffered for the catastrophe of his two brave soldiers. He says, "At the sight of a gentleman in deep mourning for Sir Charles Lucas, the King wept." ('Memorials,' p. 330.)

SIR GEORGE LISLE. Son of Cave Lisle, of Compton Darvill, co. Somerset, had his military education in the Netherlands. He signalized himself upon many occasions in the Civil Wars; particularly at the last battle of Newbury, where, in the dusk of the evening, he led his men to the charge in his shirt, that his person might be more conspicuous. The King who was an eye-witness of his bravery, knighted him on the field of battle. In 1648 he rose for his Majesty in Essex, and was one of the royalists who so obstinately defended Colchester, and who died for their defence of it. This brave man having tenderly embraced the corpse of Sir Charles Lucas, his departed friend, immediately presented himself to the soldiers, who were ready for his execution. Thinking that they stood at too great a distance, he desired them to come nearer: one of them said "I warrant you, sir, we shall hit you;" he replied, with a smile, "Friends, I have been nearer you, when you have missed me." Executed August 28, 1648. Sir George commanded the "forlorn hope" of foot in the first battle of Newbury.

SIR EDWARD WALDEGRAVE. Son of Sir Edward Waldegrave, Bart., of Staninghall, Norfolk. He died at Oxford, and was buried at St. Mary's Church in that city, 8 Dec., 1644.

SIR BERNARD BROCAS. Of Beaurepaire, near Sherborne St. John, Hants. He was probably the son of Thomas Brocas (son of Sir Pexsall Brocas) by Elizabeth, daughter of Robert Wingfield, of Upton, co. Northampton, as no other of the name is mentioned in the pedigrees of the family at this period.

SIR LEWIS KIRKE. Second son of Gervase Kirke, gent,, Merchant of London, and of Dieppe, in France, and of Greenhill, in the parish of Norton, co. Derby, by Elizabeth, daughter of John Gowding (or Goudon) of Dieppe. He was born about 1600, and commanded one of the ships in the expedition to Newfoundland and Canada in 1626, under the chief command of his elder brother, Captain (afterwards Sir) David Kirke. He afterwards joined the Royal cause, and became a distinguished cavalier. He was knighted at Oxford, 23 April, 1643, and was subsequently Governor of Bridgnorth; at his death he was one of the Band of Gentleman-Pensioners. He survived the Restoration; and his Will, in which he described himself as of the Savoy Parish, co. Middlesex, dated 21 August 1663, was proved 7 October following, in the Prerogative Court of Canterbury, by his brother and nephew, both named John Kirke, father and son, to whom he left the reversion of his estate after the death of his wife. His widow, Dame Elizabeth, by whom he left no issue, did not long survive him, as she was buried at St. Giles' in the Fields, 20 Dec., 1663. Her maiden name was Haines, but she was a widow when she married Sir Lewis Kirke, and her first husband's name has not been ascertained. (Communicated by Col. Chester, LL.D.)

SIR HENRY SLINGSBY. Second but eldest surviving son of Sir Henry Slingsby of Knaresborough, co. York, Knight, and Dame Frances his wife, daughter of William Vavasour, of Weston in the same county. He was born 14 Jan. 1601, married 7 July, 1631, Barbara, daughter of Thomas Belasyse, first Viscount Falconberg, and in 1638 was created a Baronet of Nova Scotia. He raised 600 horse and foot at his own expense and marched at the head of them into the field to assist the King. He was in action throughout the Civil War; and, after the death of Charles was ever solicitous for the restoration of his son. He was long a prisoner at Hull, and was tried for contracting with some officers to deliver up one of the block-houses in that garrison for the service of Charles II. Cromwell, who was informed that the Royalists throughout the kingdom were intent upon a scheme to restore the King, was resolved to intimidate that party by sacrificing Sir Henry Slingsby and Dr. Hewit. They were brought before the High Court of Justice where Lisle presided; they denied the jurisdiction of the Court, but were condemned without any ceremony. Sir Henry Slingsby was a man of deeds rather than words. He said very little upon his trial, and as little upon the scaffold. He persisted in his loyalty and told the people that he died for being an honest man. Beheaded June 8, 1658. After his execution, the authorities permitted his remains to be removed by his friends, and they were buried in the Slingsby Chapel in Knaresborough Church. (See 'Diary of Sir Henry Slingsby,' edited by Rev. Daniel Parsons, London, 1836.)

SIR WILLIAM VAVASOUR. Son of Sir Thomas Vavasour, of Haslewood in the county of York. Commander-in-chief of the Gloucestershire forces, engaged at Marston Moor, 1644, where his brother Thomas was slain. Being disgusted with the miscarriage of that great battle, he left the King's service and went over to Hamburgh. Afterwards he joined the Swedish service, and was killed under the walls of Copenhagen, 1658 or 1659.

SIR THOMAS ASTON. Was created a Baronet by King Charles I., 25th July, 1628, and was subsequently in the Civil Wars a zealous supporter of the Royal cause. He died at Stafford from wounds received in the King's service, 24th May, 1645.

SIR ANTHONY MANSEL, Governor of Cardiff, son of Sir Francis Mansel, Bart., of Trimsaren, co. Caermarthen.

SIR EDWARD STRADLING. Of St. Donat's, Glamorganshire. This gentleman, who, like his father and uncles, was a zealous royalist, brought a troop of horse to the assistance of the King at Newbury, and after the loss of that day, retired to Oxford, where he died of consumption. Burke's 'Extinct Baronetage.'

SIR MICHAEL WODEHOUSE. Governor of Ludlow. He had been sometime page to the Marquis of Hamilton, had served in Ireland; whence returning early in 1643, he was preferred to be Sergeant-Major-General of the army of Prince Charles, and to the command of his life-guards. Webb's Civil War in Herefordshire, vol. i, p. 387.

SIR JACOB ASTLEY. This stout old commander, more especially referred to in the account of the Second Battle, was father of Sir Bernard Astley. He served in the Netherlands under Prince Maurice and his brother Henry, and afterwards under Christian IV. King of Denmark and Gustavus Adolphus, King of Sweden. He was wounded before Gloucester; and, for his signal services, he was created Baron of Reading, 20, Car. I. The title became extinct on the death of his grandson Jacob.

SIR JOHN FRECHVILLE. For the services rendered by Sir John Frechville to the royal cause, and on his petition to the King, a warrant was signed by Charles I. at Oxford, 25th March, 1644, for his creation as a peer by the style of Lord Frechville, of Staveley, Musard, and Fitz-Ralph. The preamble of the patent takes notice of the loyalty of the said Sir John Frechville, and his eminent services against the "rebels," at Kineton, Brentford, Marlborough, Newbury, and many other places, where he had received several wounds. Christian Frechville, daughter to John, Lord Frechville, married Charles, Lord St. John, eldest son to John, Marquis of Winchester and Earl of Wiltshire, 28 Feb., 1651, and departed this life 22 July, 1653, dying in childbed, The following lines in the hand-writing of Sir John Frechville were taken out of a Bible formerly in his possession:—

"Mownt, mownt my soul, adiewe vaine world, adiewe,
With all thy wealth, thy pleasure, and renowne;
What heights, what sweets, what glories doe I view,
Heaven, my sweet Jesus, an immortal crowne!"
under which was written:
"Ve misero patri superstiti"—
which may be translated;—
"Woe to the unhappy father who survives [his children]."

SIR JOHN HURRY, frequently styled "Urry" and "Hurrey," but always "Hurry" in his own signatures, was a Scotchman, who had previously served in Germany under Lord Forth. Col. Hurry deserted from the Parliamentary Army and rode up to the King shortly before the battle of Chalgrove-field, and gave the information which led to the successful attack on the Parliament's troops on that occasion, and to the death of Hampden, in which affair Hurry signally distinguished himself, and was allowed to convey the news to Oxford: for this he was knighted by the King, Col. Hurry's colours were azure or deep blue, with the Thistle of Scotland, as usually represented, leaved, &c., of gold, flowered, proper, around which in letters of gold, "✠ NEMO ME IMPUNE LACESSIT;" fringe argent and azure. The motto is that of the Order of St. Andrew, to whose badge, *The Thistle*, it has reference.

MAJ.-GEN. GEORGE PORTER. "Loyal bloud like *Harvies*, went round the *Porters* from the highest to the meanest, 26 of the name having eminently suffered for his Majesty." Lloyd's Memoirs, p. 657.

COL. ST. JOHN. Edward, third son of Sir John St. John, of Lydiard Tregoze, co. Wilts. Nephew of Sir Oliver St. John, Viscount Grandison. Sir John had three sons killed in the King's service, viz.—William his second son under Prince Rupert at the taking of Cirencester, Edward above mentioned at Newbury, and John his fifth son in the North.

COL. EDWARD VILLIERS. Youngest son of Sir Edward Villiers, kt., by Barbara, eldest daughter of Sir John St. John, of Lydiard Tregoze, co. Wilts, kt., and younger brother of the Viscount Grandison. He was knighted 7 April, 1680, and the following year, became Knight-Marshall of the Royal Household. He died in 1689, and was buried in Westminster Abbey, July 2. See 'Westminster Abbey Registers,' edited by Col. J. L. Chester, L.L.D., p. 223.

COL. WILL. LEGGE. Son of Edward Legge, vice-president of Munster. He eminently distinguished himself by his faithful attachment to the King and his son Charles II. He was engaged in both battles of Newbury, and it is said, that the night after the first action, Col. Legge being in attendance on the King in his bed-chamber, his Majesty presented him with a hanger (a short curved sword) with agate handle set in gold, which he had that day worn, and would have knighted him with it, had he consented. The hanger was kept in Col. Legge's family till the house at Blackheath was robbed in

1693. Col. Legge died in 1672 at his house in the Minories, London, granted him by Charles II., and was buried with great pomp in the adjoining Church of the Holy Trinity. He was the direct ancestor of the Earls of Dartmouth.

COLONEL DANIEL O'NEILL. Lieutenant-Colonel of Prince Rupert's regiment of horse; afterwards Groom of the Bedchamber to the King. "The Honourable Col. Oneal, the onely Protestant of his family; its a question whether gaining more honor by his hard service about *Gloucester*, and in both the *Newberries* with King *Charles* the First, or by his assiduous Negotiations and Messages posting from place to place (in *Holland*, where he was warned to the Countess of *Chesterfield*, in *France*, where he was welcome to the best *Cavaliers*, and *Germany*) for King *Charles* the Second, especially in the various Occasions, Opportunities, and Revolutions, 1659, at *Fontarabia, Scotland, Flanders, England*, &c., that made way for his Majesties' Restoration, who let him to farm the Post Office. He died 1664. Its more to be called an *Oneal*, than an Emperor in *Ireland*." Lloyd's Memoirs, pp. 664-5.

COLONEL MORGAN, of Weston in Lancashire, who raised a troop of horse for the King at his own charge: his estate was seized by the Parliament and bestowed on the son of 'King Pym.'

COLONEL THOMAS EURE. The evidence as to the identity of this officer is conflicting, but, he appears to have been the son of William, 6th Lord Eure.

COL. RICHARD PLATT. Among the State Papers, Dom. Series, Vol. lxxxiii. Pub. Record Off., is a petition from Veronica, widow of Col. Richard Platt, to King Charles II. for a portion of the sum allotted for such sufferers. Her husband, she says, spent a fair estate in raising troops for the late King, and was slain at the First Battle of Newbury, and she, a Venetian, is left in great necessity. Shortly after, a warrant authorises £100 to be paid the said Veronica Platt out of the Privy Seal Dormant.

There is also a petition, in the same series, from the widow of an artilleryman named Clarke, whom she describes as "gunner to the late King," and states he was slain at Newbury battle, that herself and children had been turned naked out of doors at Weymouth during the Protectorate, whipped out of the town, and her goods worth £300 taken by Col. Sydenham. Mrs. Clarke appears to have found a second martial husband, who, she mentions, "has been a prisoner amongst the Turks," and prays a Tidesman's place for him in the Custom House, and some reparation for her losses and sufferings.

COLONEL CHARLES GERARD. Son of Sir Charles Gerard, knt. of Halsall, co. Lancaster. He had been brought up from his youth in the profession of arms upon the usual scene of European warfare, the Netherlands; and joined His Majesty King Charles I. at Shrewsbury soon after he had raised the royal standard, and became eminently distinguished among the Cavaliers:—first, at Kineton or Edgehill, where he received some dangerous wounds, and soon after at the taking of Lichfield, the First Battle of Newbury, and the relief of Newark. General Gerard then accompanied Prince Rupert into Wales and acquired high reputation by his victories at Cardiff, Kidwelly, and Cærmarthen, and for his success in taking the Castle of Cardigan and other fortresses, and reducing the strong garrison of Haverfordwest, with the Castles of Picton and Carew. In consequence of such gallant

APPENDIX. 79

services, he was made by the King Lieutenant-General of his horse, and elevated to the peerage as Baron Gerard,* of Brandon, 8 Oct. 1645. His Lordship after the Restoration was created 21 July, 1679, Viscount Brandon and Earl of Macclesfield; but in the time of James II. he was committed, with the Earl of Stamford and Lord Delamere, to the Tower and condemned to death, but pardoned. He lived to see the Revolution, and in fact to witness, says Banks, "three singular occurrences in the annals of English history (he might have characterised them as the three *most* singular), 1st, the deposition and decapitation of King Charles I.; 2ndly, the Restoration of his son; and 3rdly, the Revolution and total expulsion of the royal family so recently restored." Besides his Lordship, there were of his family the following persons actively engaged upon the royal side in these unhappy conflicts:

His Brothers { Edward Gerard, a Col. of foot, wounded in the first battle of Newbury.
Sir Gilbert Gerard, slain near Ludlow.

His Uncles { Sir Gilbert Gerard, governor of Worcester.
Ratcliffe Gerard, Lt.-Col. to his brother.

This gentleman had three sons,
Ratcliffe. } All in the
John, put to death by Cromwell. } battle of
Gilbert created a baronet. } Kineton.

(Burke's Dormant and Extinct Peerage, pp. 229, 30.) Charles, Earl of Macclesfield died 9 Jan. 1693-4, and was buried in Westminster Abbey.

CAPTAIN THOMAS BAGEHOT. At the Restoration Captain Bagehot applied for re-admission to the place of Groom of the King's Chamber in ordinary, which he held under the late King; and recounts his services at Newbury. (State Papers, Dom. Series, vol. xxii.)

CAPTAIN BASIL WOODD. Son of Basil Woodd, LL.D., Chancellor of St. Asaph and Rochester, and High Commissioner. In a petition presented by Capt. Woodd, at the Restoration, he states:—"I have received several shots in my head, and one in my arm, which troubles mee many times. Several horses were shott under mee, one at Round-way-down, another at Newbury fight." Two other sons of Dr. Woodd served the King, one of whom fell at Preston; a daughter married the brave Col. Bowles who was killed in Alton Church, 1643. Basil Thomas Woodd, M.P., Conyngham Hall, Knaresborough, great-great-great grandson of Dr. Basil Woodd, has in his possession the Star of the Mantle of the Order of the Garter, traditionally held as the parting memorial given to Capt. Basil Woodd by Charles I. on the morning of his execution.

CAPTAIN CLIFTON. Francis Clifton, son of Sir Cuthbert Clifton, of Westby, Lancashire.

CAPTAIN NEWMAN. See note, p. 16.

---

* His Lordship was first created Earl of *Newberry*, but the title was changed to *Macclesfield*. [Col. Chester, LL D., the editor of the 'Westminster Abbey Registers,' says that he cannot find any authority for this statement made in 'Burke's Extinct Peerage.' Charles Fitzroy, natural son of Charles II. by the Duchess of Cleveland, was created *Baron of Newbury*, Duke of Southampton, &c. in 1675, four years before, and it does not seem likely that the title should have been duplicated. It is quite possible, however, that "Earl of Newbury" was the title first selected, and the alteration made before the patent passed the Great Seal.]

CAPTAIN GWYNNE. Was a retainer in the household of Charles I. before the commencement of the Civil War, and employed in training the children of that unfortunate monarch to military exercises. He naturally engaged in the royal service, and seems to have distinguished himself by his personal courage and activity. After the execution of the King, he followed the banner of his son (Charles II.) in the most difficult enterprises in which it was displayed. Gwynne was with Montrose in his last unhappy attempt. He afterwards served under the Duke of York in the fight before Dunkirk and other actions in Flanders. At the restoration he appears to have experienced his share of neglect with which Charles II. treated the old cavaliers.

HENRY SPENCER. First Earl of Sunderland, son of William 2nd Lord Spencer, of Wormleighton, by Penelope, eldest daughter of Henry Wriothesley, Earl of Southampton, was born in 1620. After a few days' visit at Oxford, Lord Sunderland joined the army as it was on the point of engaging at Newbury. The Earl having no command in the army attended upon the King's person under the obligation of honour, bringing, according to Lloyd, £15,000 and 1,200 men to his Majesty. He married the beautiful Lady Dorothea, daughter of the Earl of Leicester, by whom he had one son Robert, his successor, lineal ancestor to the Duke of Marlborough and Earl Spencer, and one daughter Dorothy, married to Sir George Savile, Bart., afterwards created Marquis of Halifax. The following letter was written by Lord Sunderland to his wife Lady Dorothea (Waller's Sacharissa) a few days before the battle of Newbury, in which he was killed:—"Since I wrote to you last from Sudley, we had some hopes one day to fight with my Lord Essex's army, we receiving certain intelligence of his being in a field convenient enough, called Ripple Field, towards which we advanced with all possible speed; upon which he retired with the body of his army to Tewkesbury, where, by the advantage of the bridge, he was able to make good his quarter, with 500 men, against 20,000. So that though we were at so near a distance as we could have been with him in two hours: his quarter being so strong, it was resolved on Thursday, that we seeing for the present he would not fight with us, we should endeavour to force him to it by cutting off his provisions; for which purpose, the best way was for the body of our army to go back to Evesholme, and for our horse to distress him: upon which I, and many others, resolved to come for a few days hither, there being no probability of fighting very suddenly, where we arrived late on Thursday night. As soon as I came, I went to your father's, where I found Alibone, with whose face I was better pleased than with any of the ladies here. This expression is so much a bolder thing than charging my Lord Essex, that should this letter miscarry and come to the knowledge of our dames, I should, by having my eyes scratched out, be cleared from coming away from the army for fear: where if I had stayed, it is odds I should not have lost more than one. Last night very good news came to Court, that we, yesterday morning, fell upon a horse quarter of the enemies, and cut off a regiment, and that my Lord of Newcastle hath killed, and taken prisoners, two whole regiments of horse and foot that issued out of Hull; which place he hath great hopes to take ere long. By the same messenger, last night, the King sent the Queen word that he would come hither on Monday or Tuesday; upon one of which days, if he alter his resolutions, I shall not fail to return to the army. I am afraid our sitting down before Gloucester has hindered us from making an end of the war this year which nothing could keep us from doing if we had a month's more time which we lost there, for we never were in a more prosperous condition. Before I go hence, I hope some body will come from you, howsoever, I shall have a letter here for you. I have taken the best care I can about my economical affairs; I am afraid I shall not be able to get you a better house, every body thinking me mad for speaking about it. Pray, bless Popet for me and tell her, I would have writ to her but that upon mature deliberation I found it to be uncivil to return an answer to a lady in another character than her own which I am not yet learned enough to do. I cannot by walking about my chamber call anything more to mind to set down here and really I have made you no small compliment in writing thus much for I have so great a cold that I do nothing but sneeze and mine eyes do nothing but water all the while I am in this posture of hanging down my head. I beseech you to present his service to my lady who is most passionately and perfectly yours." They never met again! The day after the battle, the body of the Earl was removed from Newbury, and subsequently interred in the family burial-place at Brington, Northamptonshire.

LORD FALKLAND. Lucius Cary, Viscount Falkland, born at Burford, about 1610. He was the eldest son of Sir Henry Cary, of Berkhampstead and Aldenham in Herts, and of Elizabeth, daughter and sole heiress of Sir Laurence Tanfield, Chief Baron of the Exchequer.* Sir Henry was raised to the peerage of Scotland, November 10, 1620, by the title of Viscount Falkland, and died in September, 1633, when his son Lucius inherited his title and estates. Lord Falkland's reputation for talents, genius, and general literature, by which he was distinguished, may be inferred from several addresses made to him on the occasion of his leaving England in the expedition against the Scots in 1639 with the Earl of Holland, particularly by the poets Waller, Cowley, Ben Jonson, and Suckling, neither of whom would have dared to satirize a man of his character by vain adulation and false praise. Cowley's poem commences with these lines:—

"Great is thy charge, O North; be wise and just;
England commits her Falkland to thy trust,
Return him safe; learning would rather choose
Her Bodley or her Vatican to lose.
All things that are but writ or printed there,
In his unbounded breast engraven are;
There all the sciences together meet,
And every art does all his kindred greet."

---

* In Burford Church is a stately monument to Sir Laurence Tanfield and his lady, with their effigies at full length in the habit of the period; and at their feet Lord Falkland their grandson, who fell at Newbury, is represented in armour, kneeling, with his back towards them; and his helmet was formerly suspended over the tomb. (See Gentleman's Mag. lxi. p. 896. The tour of the Captaine, Lieutenant and Ancient, Lansdown MS. No, 213.) It is said that when the Earl of Essex and his troops lay in Burford Church, June 6th, 1644, they took down the pennons and flags over Tanfield's monument and wore them for scarves. The Manor of Burford was sold by Lord Falkland to Speaker Lenthall in 1634.

And in Waller, we find this passage:—
"Ah! noble friend! with what impatience all
That know thy worth, and know how prodigal
Of thy great soul thou art (longing to twist
Bays with that ivy which so early kiss'd
Thy youthful temples), with what horror we
Think on the blind events of war and thee!
To fate exposing that all-knowing breast
Among the throng as cheaply as the rest."
He was chosen Member of Parliament for Newport, April 1640, and again in November of the same year. He distinguished himself by his speeches in Parliament on the subject of ship-money, episcopacy, &c. In January, 1641-2, Lord Falkland was sworn of the Privy Council, and became one of the principal Secretaries of State. He followed the King to York, and supported the Royal cause by his pen and his sword till his death. He fought at the battle of Edgehill, and attended the King at the siege of Gloucester. At the First Battle of Newbury, he served in the first rank of Lord Byron's regiment, and whilst charging the enemy he received a musket shot in the stomach, and fell dead from his horse. The body of Lord Falkland was not found till the day after the battle, when it was discovered, says 'Aubrey' "stript, trod upon, and mangled and could only be identified by one who waited upon him in his chamber, by a certain mole his Lordship had upon his neck." The same morning a letter had been sent to Essex by Rupert as follows:—
"We desire to know from the Earl of Essex, whether he have the Viscount Falkland, Capt. Burtue [Henry Bertie, brother to the Earl of Lindsey], and Sergt. Major Wilshire* prisoners, or whether he have their dead bodies, and if he have, that liberty may be granted to their servants to fetch them away.
Given under my hand at Newbury this 21 Sept. 1643.
RUPERT."
The body of Falkland having been recovered, it was placed across the back of one of the royal chargers, and mournfully escorted down the hill by a detachment of the King's own troop, and gently laid in the Town Hall. The following morning the corpse was removed to Oxford, thence next day to Great Tew, and interred the following day in the chancel of the parish church of St. Michael, as the register thus records:—
"THE 23RD DAY OF SEPTEMBER, A.D. 1643, THE
RIGHT HONOURABLE SIR LUCIUS CARY, KNIGHT,
LORD VISCOUNT OF FALKLAND,
AND LORD OF THE MANOR OF GREAT TEW,
WAS BURIED HERE."
No monument marks the spot, for fear, it is thought, of desecration during the Commonwealth. It must however have been known, as his wife and sons were buried at his side. Lady Lettice was buried at Great Tew, Feb. 27, 1646, leaving behind her a high reputation for virtue and piety.

---

* There were three or more Wilshires, Wilsheers, or Wiltshires, engaged in the Civil War, and it is difficult to determine the identity of the "Sergt.-Major Wilshire," mentioned in Prince Rupert's letter.

APPENDIX. 83

Another version, however, of the temporary disposal of the body of Falkland and the other Lords killed at Newbury is furnished by a MS. in the possession of F. D. Hibbert, Esq., of Chalfont House, Gerrard's Cross, entitled "John Saunders, His Book, 1712. The account of my travels with my Mistress." * From this the following is an extract:—"Augt. ye 1. She went in ye Alesbury coach, and I on ye outside, we din'd at yo Crown at Uxbridg, and went that night to Sr Richard Holford's house in Lincoln's Inn Fields, whar we ware welcomely receiv'd, but found my Lady in aweful condiscion. We stayed there till ye 11 of August, then my Mrs. went with Sr Richd. and Lady in their coach, and I on ye outside for Avebury, we sat out on Tuesday, and din'd that day at Mr. Bolding's at yo Crown at Slow, one mile from Winsor, I saw yo Castle as I past yc road. I lay that night at yo Bare, at Reading, which is a large town, and four churches in it, it is a good place for trade, ye river of Thames comes to it, it is .... miles from Slow. Ye 12 we din'd at Mr. Phillips at ye Bare in Spinumlands, in Nuberry parish, whare was ye great fight in ye sivil wars, four noble Dukes [Lords] thare killed and carried into that very house where I dined, it is .... miles from Reading. As I first [came] near Nuberry I see ye fields where many brave English men weare killed, and much blood was spilt there." This statement does not interfere with the accuracy of the tradition already referred to; for it is more than probable that the bodies of all the more important personages who fell during the battle were first received at the Town Hall for identification, and as a temporary measure, and were then individually transferred to other places previous to their final interment, or transmission to the places selected for that purpose. Falkland's body may well have been brought first to the official centre of the town, and then have been moved to the Bear Inn on the Oxford Road, where it was placed in a shell or coffin and prepared for its final removal.

It is not difficult to fix the position of the Bear Inn, and Mr. John Tanner's evidence on the point is amply sufficient to establish the fact. In a letter received from him, he states, "I have referred to the papers I wished to see and I find that my impression is correct, namely that the premises now occupied by Mr. Adnams, Mrs. Fidler, and Mr. Hunt (on both sides of the gateway) were the Bear Inn." These buildings are situated on the right hand side of London and Bath road at Speenhamland. Mr. Tanner then goes on to say, "In a deed dated 29th September, 1757, the premises now in the occupation of Messrs. Forster and Abel (which were then known as the Elephant Inn) are described as adjoining to the Chequers Inn on the West, and the *two* messuages or tenements *(formerly the Bear Inn)* on the East. These two messuages or tenements were in 1757 in the occupation of John Awbrey and Francis Sheppard, who were, I think, brewers. From Mr. Sheppard they have come down to Mr. E. J. Alderman the present owner.

"It is not many years since in making some alterations in the garden at the back, some skeletons and, I believe, cannon balls were dug up. I heard many years since that the Bear Inn was shut up for some time,

---

* Sarah, youngest daughter of Samuel Trotman, Esq., of Siston Court, Gloucestershire, and Bucknell, Oxon, died in 1684, the wife of the Rev. Dr. Hickes, rector of Whimple, Dorsetshire.

and probably never again opened as an Inn, in consequence of a murder supposed to have been committed, if I remember right in some altercation between the mistress and her cook; one or the other of them was thrown down stairs and killed."

Dr. Pordage, rector of Bradfield, a celebrated enthusiast, placed by Baxter at the head of the Behmenists, was tried at the Bear Inn, Speenhamland, in 1654, before the Commissioners of Berks, appointed by an Ordinance of the Lord Protector Cromwell and his council for ejecting "Scandalous, Ignorant, and Insufficient Ministers." The Commissioners at the first sitting consisted of Mr. Fettyplace, chairman, Mr. Samuel Wightwick, Mr. Samuel Dunch, Major Fincher, Major Allin, Mr. Evelyn, Mr. Angell Bell, Mr. Mills, Mr. Cox, and Mr. Stroude, with Mr. Woodbridge, rector of Newbury, Mr. Christopher Fowler, vicar of St Mary's, Reading, Mr. Hughes, Mr. John Tickell, of Abingdon, and other ministers as assistants. The Commissioners sat at the Bear Inn, Speenhamland, on Oct. 5th, Oct. 19th, and Nov. 2nd, 1654, and at the Bear Inn, Reading, on Nov. 22nd. and Dec. 7th. Sentence of ejectment was pronounced the day following the last sitting. The case is given *in extenso* in State Trials, vol. ii. pp. 217, 259.

The night previous to the battle, Lord Falkland slept at the house of a Mr. Head, in Cheap Street, yet standing, and occupied by Mr. Joplen, and early next morning, by his express wish, the sacrament was administered to him by Dr. Twiss, the then Rector of Newbury, in the presence of Mr. Head and his whole family, who attended at Lord Falkland's especial request. The apartment which tradition points out as being the scene of Falkland's last communion is still preserved, and contains a curious cupboard fitted into a recess, concealed by a panel. The cupboard is of mahogany, and the shell-like ornament at the top and the mouldings are gilt.

COPY OF LORD FALKLAND'S WILL, FROM THE PREROGATIVE
COURT OF CANTERBURY.

"SIR LUCIUS CARY, KNT., VISCOUNT OF FALKLAND, in perfect health and memory. My soul to God, my body to earth to be buried as my ex'trix shall think fit. All my personal estate to my dearly beloved wife, Lettice, Viscountess of Falkland, whom I appt. my ex'trix. She to have the education of my three sons, Lucius, Henry, and Lorenzo, and to bear the charges of educating my younger sons Henry and Lorenzo."

Dated 12 June, 18 Charles, 1642. (Signed) FALKLAND. Witnesses Robert Stanior, Thomas Hinton. Proved at Oxford, 20 October, 1643 by Lettice, Viscountess of Falkland.

Seal. Arms and crest of Cary, with a label of 3 points; no coronet.
The Will, all but the signatures "Falkland" and "Thomas Hinton," seems to be in Robt. Stanior's handwriting. With it is a copy altogether in one hand without seal and the signature written "Falkland." No notice of date or time of death. (See 'Herald and Genealogist,' vol. iii. p. 133.)

PARLIAMENTARIAN OFFICERS AND OTHERS.

EARL OF ESSEX. Robert Devereux, Earl of Essex, was only son of the unfortunate favourite of Queen Elizabeth, and inherited much of his father's popularity. He acquired, in the Low Countries, a great reputation as a soldier; a kind of merit that was despised by James I, and overlooked by Charles. His courage was great, his honour was inflexible; but he rather waited for, than sought opportunities of fighting; and knew better how to gain, than improve a victory. When he took the command of the Parliament Army, he was better qualified than any man in the kingdom for that post; but was soon eclipsed by a new race of soldiers, who, if not his superiors in the art of war, went far beyond him in spirit and enterprise. He died the fourteenth of September, 1646; and his death helped to open a way for the ambition of Cromwell. An account of the recent discovery of the burial place of the Earl appears on page 65.

LORD ROBARTES, OR ROBERTS. John, Lord Robartes, second baron of Truro, co. Cornwall, created Viscount Bodmin, and Earl of Radnor, 1679. "That which in the first place crownes all his actions, was the fierce and famous battell at Newberry, where this noble lord lead on the battell in his owne person, charging the maine body of the King's army with such resolution, as did inliven the London Brigade to second and relieve them suddenly: yet notwithstanding this noble champion stood to the fight, and lead up other souldiers,,and incouraged them, and so continued untill the enemy retreated with great losse of men and armes." Ricraft's 'Survey of England's Champions,' 1647. At the Restoration he was well received by Charles II., and appointed a Privy Councillor, Lord Privy Seal, and Viceroy of Ireland. He died at Chelsea in 1685. Dr. Calybute Downing, the famous Puritan divine, Rector of West Ilsley, near Newbury, was chaplain to Lord Robartes' regiment.

LORD GREY OF GROBY. Thomas Grey, son of Henry, second Lord Grey, created Earl of Stamford, 26 March, 1628. He was one of the King's judges, and his signature appears on the warrant of execution.

SIR JOHN MEYRICK. He had served in the royal army, and was knighted by the King, but he deserted to the Parliament, and was made Sergeant-Major-General by the Earl of Essex, and, afterwards, at the siege of Reading appointed General of the Ordnance, being superseded in his former office by the famous Skippon, by order of Parliament. Sir John Meyrick's Will was proved in 1659.

SIR PHILIP STAPLETON. Inherited "but a moderate estate in Yorkshire, and, according to the custom of that country, had spent his time in those delights which horses and dogs administer." A Member of the Long Parliament; joined in the prosecution of Strafford; opposed the self-denying ordinance, 1644. Withdrew beyond sea, and died at Calais as soon as he landed. "Was denied burial upon imagination that he had died of the plague." "Peacock's Army List," p. 25. His

Will was proved in 1647. Stapleton's cuirassiers were called "Essex's Life-Guard," and corresponded to Lord Bernard Stuart's cavalier troop.

SIR WILLIAM CONSTABLE. Son and heir of Sir Richard Constable, of Flamborough, co. York, Kt., by Anne, daughter and heiress of John Hussey, of Driffield. He was knighted by the Earl of Essex in Ireland, in 1599, and created a Baronet, 29 June, 1611. He had been Colonel of a Regiment of Foot, and some time Governor of Gloucester, and was one of the signers of the death-warrant of King Charles I. His will, dated 13 Dec., 1654, was proved 18 July, 1655, by his relict Dame Dorothy, who was the eldest daughter of Thomas, first Lord Fairfax. He left no issue, and the title became extinct. He was buried in Westminster Abbey; but, not only were his remains exhumed after the Restoration and thrown into the common pit in the church-yard, but his estates were especially excepted in the general pardon subsequently granted by King Charles II. His relict died 9 March, 1656, and was buried in the Church of St. Mary Bishophill, Senior, York. See Note to Burials, "Westminster Abbey Registers," edited by Col. J. L. Chester, LL.D., p. 148.

SIR WILLIAM BALFOUR. Of the family of Balfour of Pitcullo, co. Fife, Scotland, gentleman of the King's privy-chamber, and Lieutenant of the Tower of London. Though he had great obligations to the Court, he made no scruple of attaching himself to its most violent opponents. He was turned out of his office as Lieutenant of the Tower a little before the breaking out of the Civil War, and was succeeded by Col. Lunsford. At the battle of Edgehill, Sir William Balfour commanded the reserve, and greatly distinguished himself. He led also the right wing of horse at the Second Battle of Newbury. His Will was proved in 1661.

SIR SAMUEL LUKE. Governor of Newport-Pagnell in 1645. The supposed original of Butler's Hudibras, and author of the Journal of the Siege of Reading, printed in Coate's History of that town.

SIR ARTHUR GOODWIN. Of Wooburn, co. Bucks, the intimate friend and neighbour of John Hampden. Like him, he held a command under the Earl of Essex, and was quartered at Aylesbury in the first campaign. The following interesting letter addressed by Col. Goodwin to his only daughter, Jane, second wife of Philip, Lord Wharton (by whom she was mother of the famous Marquis, and grandmother of the more famous duke, who, soon dissipated the estate which she had brought into the family), conveys a faithful estimate of the patriot's character. "Deere Jenny. * * * Let me beg of you to send me a broad black ribbon to hang about my standard. * * * I am now here at Hampden in doing the last duty for the deceased owner of it, of whom every honest man hath a share in the loss, and therefore will labour in the service, for the loss of such a friend ; to my own particular, I have no cause of discontent, but rather to bless God he hath not according to my deserts bereft me of you and all the comforts allowed to me. All his thoughts and endeavours of his life was zealously for the cause of God's, which he continued in all his sickness even to his death,—for all I can learn, the last words he spoke was to me, though he died 6 or 7 hours after I came away, as in a sleepe, truly Jenny (and I know you may be easily persuaded to it), he was a gallant man, an honest man, an able man, and take all, I know not to any man living second. God now in mercy hath rewarded him. * * * ARTHUR GOODWIN. Hampden, 26 June, [1643]. To my daughter Lady Wharton at my Lord Wharton's house, Clerkenwell. Carte's MSS., Letters, Bibl. Bodl. v. 103, No. 40.

MAJOR-GENERAL SKIPPON. Philip Skippon was Sergeant-Major-General of the Parliament army, Major-general of the London militia, and governor of Bristol. After the passing of the "self-denying ordinance," he was preferred to the same post in the army that he held before; to which he was thought justly to be entitled in the ground of merit. He was president of the Council of War under the Earl of Essex, and both in the cabinet and the field approved himself an excellent soldier. He commanded the infantry at the battle of Naseby, where he exerted himself with his usual intrepidity. "Magnanimous Skippon," says May, "was grievously wounded, yet would not forsake the battle; but with all possible endeavours performed his part, till the victory was obtained." He was a zealous republican, and indeed went the greatest lengths with that party. His name frequently occurs as a member of the House of Commons in the Interregnum. He was also one of Cromwell's Council of State. He had £1,000 a year in lands of inheritance assigned him by the Parliament for his services. The Duke of Buckingham's estate at Blecheley in Buckinghamshire was given to him, in that nobleman's forfeiture; but at the Restoration it reverted to the real owner. Walker says, "he was heretofore waggoner to Sir Francis Vere;" but if he were a waggoner, which is extremely improbable, it adds much to the greatness of his character, to have been able to raise himself to such eminent posts in the army and the state, under every disadvantage of education. Note to Ricrafts's 'Survey of England's Champions,' 1647, pp. 81, 2. Skippon's colours were:—"From the dexter corner blue clouds and therefrom issuing a naked arm and hand proper, holding a sword proper, hilted or, before this, paleways, a book closed and clasped or; beneath these, on two lines in writing 'Ora et pugna. Juvat et juvabit, Jehovah;' fringed gold and argent." Prestwich's Respublica, p. 38. Skippon won the hearts of his soldiers by such speeches as these, "Come my boys, my brave boys! I will run the same hazard with you; remember the cause is for God: come my honest brave boys! let us pray heartily, and fight heartily, and God will bless us."

MAJOR-GENERAL DEANE. The well-known Parliamentary General-at-Sea. He was the eldest son of Edward Deane, of Pinnock, co. Gloucester, Esq., by his second wife, Ann Wase. (For an elaborate and admirable account of him and his career, consult his "Life," by the Rev. John Bathurst Deane, published in 1870.) He was killed during the naval engagement with the Dutch on the 2nd June, being only in his forty-second year. He married at the Temple Church, 21 May, 1647, Mary, daughter of John Grimsditch of Knottingley, York, Esq., who survived him, and married at St. Bartholomew the Great, London, 2 January, 1654-5, Colonel Edward Salmon, another well-known Parliamentarian. Colonel [he is described as 'Colonel' in the Register] Deane's remains were ignominiously exhumed after the Restoration, and, with those of others equally eminent in maintaining the honour of the British flag, thrown into a common pit in the churchyard. His will, dated 31 March, 1653, was proved

20 January, 1653-4, by his relict. He left two daughters, Mary and Hannah. The stupid stories propagated by his political enemies as to his vulgar origin and early career have been abundantly disproved by his recent biographer; and posterity is already doing justice to his memory. Note to Burial, 'Westminster Abbey Registers,' edited by Col. J. L. Chester, LL.D., pp. 146-7.

LIEUT.-GENERAL MIDDLETON. See Appendix to the Second Battle.

COLONEL SHEFFIELD. Younger son of the Earl of Mulgrave.

COLONEL JOHN MELDRUM. "There appear," says Col. Chester, in a note to the burial of Col. John Meldrum, in Westminster Abbey, "to have been two eminent military men of this name, both Scotchmen, and both named *John*, who are often confounded in contemporaneous history. *Sir* John Meldrum, who was knighted at Windsor 6 August 1622, was undoubtedly the one who took part in the memorable actions at Newark, Hull, Scarborough, etc., and received his death-wound at the last place. His will, dated 24 May, 1645, was proved 2 June, 1647." The Meldrum named in the list of Parliamentary Officers who fought at Newbury was no doubt *Colonel* John Meldrum, who is said to have been killed at Alresford, Hants. His name occurs in the List of the Parliamentary Army in 1642, as Lieutenant of the 2nd Troop of Horse, under the general command of William, Earl of Bedford, and he evidently obtained rapid promotion. As the Battle of Brandon (or Cheriton) Heath, near Alresford, took place on the 29th March, 1644, and his nuncupative will was made on the 8th of April following, it is probable he was mortally wounded on that day; or, the two dates may be identical, allowing for the difference between Old and New Style. The Will states that he was "very much wounded." It was proved 16 November, 1648, by his relict Jane, then a minor. His remains were included amongst those of other eminent Parliamentarians which were exhumed after the Restoration, and thrown into a common pit in St. Margaret's church-yard.

COLONEL NORTON. See Appendix to the Second Battle.

COLONEL DALBIER. Prominently mentioned in connection with the Siege of Donnington Castle.

CAPTAIN HUNT. An officer in one of the city regiments of trained-bands, slain in the First Battle of Newbury. The 'Mercurius Aulicus' of October 1, 1643, has the following notice of Captain Hunt.—"A confect. maker, in St. Mary, Woolnooth. This Hunt was the first that committed sacrilege in his own parish church (after John Pym's orders for defacing of churches), pulling down the cross from the steeple, the cross from the King's crown over the font, lopping off the hands and pulling out the eyes from the tombs and monuments, cutting off the cherumbim's wings placed upon the arches, and (which both Christian and Jew will abhore) blotting out the dreadful name of God as it stood over the commandments, in Hebrew, Greek, and Latin. In this Hunt's pockets were found his watch, his commission from the rebels, an assessment roll of his neigbours at Hackney parish, besides £16 in money, which the souldier had who stript off his Buff."

CAPTAIN FRANCIS ST. BARBE. He was fourth and youngest, but second surviving son of Henry St. Barbe, Esq., of Ashington, co. Somerset, and Broadlands, Hants. His name occurs in the list of killed in this engagement.

CAPTAIN HAMMOND. This was probably the same Captain Hammond

who was engaged in the Second Battle at Shaw, and the King's gaoler at Carisbroke Castle.

CAPTAIN CHARLES FLEETWOOD, afterwards the distinguished Parliamentary general, the son of Sir William Fleetwood, cupbearer to K. Charles I., and comptroller of Woodstock-park. On the breaking out of the war between King and Parliament, Young Fleetwood declared for the latter. He commanded a regiment of cavalry in 1644, and held the rank of Lieut.-General at the battle of Worcester, to the gaining of which, by Cromwell, he largely contributed. He married the Protector's daughter after the death of her first husband Ireton, and was appointed commander of the forces in Ireland in 1652. He strongly opposed Cromwell assuming the title of King in 1657; and was soon after superseded in Ireland by Henry Cromwell, the Protector's youngest son. On the death of Cromwell, he concurred in the appointment of Richard as his successor, but soon after joined in inducing him to resign, and thus paved the way for the Restoration. He died 4th October, 1692, and was buried in Bunhill Fields.

CAPTAIN CHARLES PYM. Son of "King Pym."

WILLIAM TWISSE, D.D., Rector of Newbury. The son of a clothier at Newbury, whose father had immigrated from Germany. He was born at Speenhamland about 1575, in a house said to have stood in the Lamb-and-Castle Yard. He was educated at Winchester and Oxford, became a fellow of New College, 11 March, 1597-8, and was presented to the living of Newbury in 1620 by the Prince of Wales, afterwards Charles I. Twisse was appointed Prolocutor of the Assembly of Divines under the Commonwealth; but on account of his age and infirmities he was soon unable to attend the sittings of the Assembly, and in a few months was taken ill, and laid upon his bed, where he lingered for about a year, and died July 20, 1646. His funeral in Westminster Abbey was attended by most of the members of the House of Commons and the whole of the Assembly of Divines, but his remains were included among those disinterred after the Restoration. His will, dated 9 September, 1645, with a codicil, 30 June, 1646, was proved 6 August in the latter year. He would seem not to have been so reduced in circumstances as the accounts of him usually represent, for, besides other not inconsiderable legacies, he bequeathed his manor of Ashampstead, Berks, to trustees for the benefit of his younger children. He left four sons and three daughters, but his wife (Frances, daughter of Barnabas Colnett, of Combley, Isle of Wight) had predeceased him. (See Note to Burial, 'Westminster Abbey Registers,' edited by Col. J. L. Chester, LL.D., p. 140.) There is a portrait of Dr. Twisse in the Vestry of Newbury Church, which appears, from the Churchwarden's accounts, to have been either painted by, or purchased of, one Richard Jerome, in 1647, a year after Twisse's death, at a cost of one pound fifteen shillings. The following is the entry in the Churchwarden's book:—

"1647.—Paid to Richard Jerome for Dr. Twisse his picture. 1. 15. 0."

Dr. Ward, the antiquary, mentions this picture as having been much damaged by cleaning, in 1745.

ROBERT CODRINGTON. The author of the account of the battle, originally printed in 1646, from which extracts have been taken, was second son of Robert Codrington, Esq., of Codrington, co. Gloucester. He was elected Demy of Magdalen Coll., Oxford, 29 July, 1619, when he was about 17 years of age, and took his M.A. degree in 1626. After that he travelled into several foreign lands, and at his return lived a gentleman's life, first in Norfolk, where he married, and finished his life in London, by the plague in the year 1665. He published many pieces of different taste in his life-time, and left several manuscripts prepared for the press. Though Codrington plainly declares himself a Parliamenteer, his history, so far as it goes, is the least exceptionable and the most comprehensive of any writings on the same subject, in those times; for, besides the character of his hero, the Earl of Essex, he gives us the general opinion, and the ground of the first part of the Civil War; and seems to relate the natural facts without aggravation. He always speaks of the King's Majesty with respect, ascribing the ill-conduct of his affairs and bad success, to the wickedness and heat of the counsels he received; and heartily wishing a good and lasting reconciliation and peace between the King and his Parliament. 'Life and death of Robert, Earl of Essex,' Harleian Miscell., vol. 1, pp. 211, 212.

VI.—EXTRACTS FROM THE CERTIFICATES OR RETURNS OF THOSE PERSONS WHO, PURSUANT TO AN ORDER OF THE HOUSE OF COMMONS, MADE THE PROTESTATION IN THE COUNTY OF BERKS, 30TH JULY, 1641.

This Protestation was reported and agreed to in the Commons, and ordered to be made by every member of that House, on the 3rd May, 1641. It was agreed to by the Lords, and ordered to be made by every Member of their House on the following day. Subsequently it was resolved that the Protestation is fit to be made by every one, and that that person soever who shall not make the same is unfit to bear office in the Church or Commonwealth, and that it is "A Shibboleth to discover a true Israelite."

The Protestation runs as follows:—I, A. B., do in the presence of Almighty God promise, vow, and protest to maintain and defend as far as lawfully I may with my Life, Power, and Estate, the true *Reformed Protestant Religion* expressed in the Doctrine of the *Church of England* against all Popery and Popish Innovations, within this Realm, contrary to the same Doctrine, and according to the duty of my allegiance to His Majesty's Royal Person, Honour, and Estate, as also the Power and Privileges of Parliaments, the lawful Rights and Liberties of the Subjects, and every Person that maketh this Protestation in whatsoever he shall do in the lawful Pursuance of the same; and to my power, and as far as lawfully I may I will oppose and by all good Ways and Means endeavour to bring to Condign Punishment all such as shall, either by Force, Practice, Counsels, Plots, Conspiracies,

APPENDIX. 91

or otherwise,do any thing to the contrary of any thing in this present Protestation contained, and further, that I will in all just and honourable ways endeavour to preserve the Union and Peace betwixt the Three Kingdoms of England, Scotland, and Ireland: and neither for Hope, Fear, nor other Respect, shall relinquish this Promise, Vow, and Protestation.—LORDS' JOURNAL, IV. 234.

The Extracts following are made from the original returns preserved at the House of Lords, by permission of Sir William Rose, K.C.B., Clerk of Parliaments.

BRIMPTON PARISH:—Mr. Thos. Bird (minister) and parishioners.

CHADDLEWORTH PARISH:—Thomas Nelson, Thomas Tipping, John Blagrave, and several members of the Bartholomew and Pocock families.

CHIEVELEY PARISH:—Richard Nixon (vicar), John Money, Laurence Money, Richd. Pocock, sen., Richd. Pocock, jun., Edward Aubery, sen., John Aubery, jun., John Dolman, jun.; Gyles Smith, and Peter Holdways, churchwardens; Edward Paty, and Richard Chaulk, Overseers; Stephen Butler, Constable.

COMPTON PARISH:—Richard Hasell, Minister, Richard Pottinger, sen., Richard Pottinger, jun., Robert Ffetiplace.

ENBORNE PARISH:—Edward Blandy, Mr. Wm. Elk, jun., George Mathews, John Mathews, William Lovelock, Bartholomew Hasell, Wm. Elk, Rector of Enborne; Mr. Philip Hedd and Edward Bromley, Churchwardens; Paul Hunt, High Constable. But Wm. Holmes, Sen. above 4 score years old and deaf and feeble; and John Holmes, jun., a simple young man and lame; and Wm. Plantin, 3 score and 12 or above, and infirm and decayed both inwardly and outwardly in mind and all other means, and Saml. Lyford, and John Warner, poore disabled men, and Francis Belcher, a yonge swageringe stranger who hath lately at Newtown married Margaret Nalder, and is now living with his wife at Enborne, have not made protestation.

FRILSHAM:—The Protestation taken in the public congregation and signed by Samuel Watkins, pastor there, Richd. Smallbone, Luke Hore, and members of the Fisher, Pocock, Nowbery, Chamberlain, and other families.

GREENHAM (a Tything of Thatcham). All most willingly took the Protestation, not one refusing. John Howes, John Warde, Thos. Barnes, James Osgood, Edward Kiggill, Thos. Collins, sen., Thos. Collins, jun., Wm. Hawkins, Jno. Degweede, Jno. Pocock, Joseph Hickman, John Hickman; Simon Ffarant, Curate; Thos. Osgood, constable; Thos. Knighton, churchwarden; Edward Green, overseer; Thos. Parker, tythingman.

HAMSTED-MARSHALL:—Thomas Slocock, Jo. Slocock, Ric. Slocock, and others. All the residents in the parish signed, except Wm. Bunn now four score, and Thos. Pary who is in Wiltshire and has not had warning, both are good protestants and would not refuse to sign the protestation. Saml. Paine, curate; John May and Thos. George, churchwardens. The names of Baker, Dore, Bartholomew, Harding, Lovegrove, Tubb, Holmes, Crooke, and Toms appear as residents in the parish at this time.

HAMPSTED-NORRIS:—Wm. Moore, vicar. Protestation signed by the Palmer, Dore, Bosely, Matthews, Abery, Goddard, Marriner, Kimber, and Howse families. The following refused, Henry Prince, Andrew Prince, Richard Brabrooke, Esq.

WEST ILSLEY:—John Head, minister, &c.
EASY ILSLEY:—Joseph Warner, minister, &c. Refusals—John Boulton, Henry Lipeat, recusants. Signed, Giles Pocock, Jo. Ambrose, churchwardens; Jas. Pottinger, constable.
INKPEN:—Richard Money the elder, Richard Money the younger, John Brickenden, rector; Wm. Kirke, Ffortunatus Hamling, churchwardens; Humphrey Banks and William Bayley are from home.
KINTBURY:—Sir John Dorrell, John Dorrell, Esq., Alex. Browne, John Gunter, Robert Elgar, John Elgar, Robt. Field, Wm. Hazell, Robt. Ffidler, Richd. Blandy. *Wallingtons* — Sir Jno. Kingsmill, Charles Gunter, Marmaduke Gunter. *Inglewood and Balsden*—Thos. Lowder, Thos. Webbe, Willm. Webbe, James Choke. *Tything of Holt*—Willm. Nalder, James Nalder,—Faithfull; Francis Allen, vicar; Edwd. Butcher, Robt. Field, churchwardens; Thos. Mountigue, Jas. Wiggins, overseers.
LECKHAMSTEAD:—Giles Hatt, Richd. Blagrave, Henry Blagrave. Signed also by parishioners of the name of Adnams, Head, Maskell, Selwood, Whistler, Wernham, Buckeridge, &c. Henry Greetham, clerke, Giles Spicer, constable, Richd. Hatt, overseer, John Spicer, Edwd. Averill, churchwardens.
MIDGHAM:—John Tull, absent, Thos. White, Thos. Bird, absent at court, Thos. Prior, curate, Thos. Tull, Richd. May, churchwardens.
NEWBURY:—Willm. Pearse, maior, Willm. Twisse, rector, Timothy Avery, gent., Richd. Tomlyne, Esq., Richd. Avery, gent., Richd. Waller, gent., Hugh Hawkins, gent., John Houghton, gent., John Cooke, gent., John Wheatly, curate, John Barksdale, gent., John Edmonds, Gabriell Cox, Richd. Holwell, Edd. Trenchard, Esq., Henry Trenchard, gent., Thos. Knight, Adam Head, John Hamblin, Joell Dance, Richd. Cox, John Bruce, Mr. Dunce, Esq., Philip Weston, Wm. Waller, Wm. Bew, John Merryman, gent., Nathaniel Hempsteed, Edwd. Blandy, Ed. Avery, James Purdue, Thos. Pearse, John Dibley, Francis Norris, Willm. Smart, John Waulter, Thos. Wilson, Joseph Gilmore, Alexdr. Gilmore, sen., Alexdr. Gilmore, jun., George Cowslade, Thos. Cowslade, Richd. Shaw, John Mundy, gent., Thos. Virtue, Thos. Sansum, Wm. Curteis, Joseph Nalder, W. Arundell, W. Nash, Mr, E. Lovelock, gent., Wm. Goddin, Richd. Bowyer, Thos. Jemmett, John Hoare, Thos. Somersby, Thos. Gray, &c., &c. No refusals to sign the Protestation in the parish of Newbury, Wm. Twisse, rector, Briant Linch, Ralph Kingham, church wardens. The Protestation taken before Humphrey Dolman and Roger Knight, two of His Majesty's Justices of the County of Berks, 1641.
PEASEMORE:—Edd. Lyford, rector, John Stampe, gent. Signed also by Dew, Bew, Drew, Tanner, Fisher, Aubery, Garlick, Hide, Caulcott, Hatt, Clark. Harding, and others.
SHAW-CUM-DONNINGTON:—Francis Rowland, sen., Francis Rowland, jun., Wm. Besley, Thos. Dolman, Richd. Money, John Blagrave, John Nalder, John Graye, Richd. Kinge, Wm. Portlucke, Mr. Griffin Doncastle, and Mr. Richard Smith, of Grange, John and Robt. Hastinges, Gyles Stampe, John Royston, rector, Roger Whatley and Wm. Snowswell, churchwardens, Thos. Shipton, John Norcroft, and John Challis, overseers of Poore.

LITTLE SHEFFORD:—John Prime, rector. With the exception of the Rector, none of the parishioners could sign their names, but all put their "mark."
GREAT SHEFFORD:—Jo. Nixon, rector. Geo. Browne, Esq., Elleanor Browne, his wife, Elleanor Browne his daughter—These desired a long time to consider which was refused. George Browne sone of Geo. Browne, aforesaid, and Morrice Jonathan, servant—would sign in all except the part against Popery. Anne Cooper, Anne Northover —professing themselves simple maidens requested time to consider on the part of religion. Elizbh. Wylder, Ursula Wylder, widow, daughter of said Elizabeth—absolutely refuse to sign the Protestation. John Arundell, constable and churchwarden.
SPEEN; — Thos. Castillian, Esq., Jo. Barker, and others, John Barker, minister.
WASING:—Thos. Walker or Walthen, rector,
WELFORD:—Hinton, Esq., and others, John Mundy, clerk.
WINTERBORNE DANVERS in the parish of Chieveley:—Henry Greetham, clerk, Laurence Head, Thomas Kimber, and others.

VII.—LIST OF THE SEQUESTRATORS OF THE ESTATES OF "DELINQUENTS, PAPISTS, SPYES, AND INTELLIGENCERS," FOR THE COUNTY OF BERKS; APPOINTED UNDER ORDINANCE OF THE LORDS AND COMMONS, APRIL 1, 1643:—

Sir Francis Pile, Bart. (1); Sir Francis Knollys, jun. Knt. (2); Peregrine Hobby (3); Henry Marten (4); Roger Knight (5); Henry Powl (6); Thomas Fettiplace (7), and Tanfield Vachell (8), Esquires. *

(1). SIR FRANCIS PILE, second bart. Sat for the County of Berks in the second Parliament of 1640, succeeding on the disablement of Mr. John Fettiplace in 1646. The first of the family who was created a baronet was Francis, of Compton-Beauchamp, who received that honour from Charles I, 12 Sept. 1628, for his services to the Crown. He married Elizabeth, daughter of Sir Francis Popham, of Littlecote, knt., and dying in 1635, he was succeeded by his eldest son, the member for the county above mentioned. The baronetcy became finally extinct 4 May, 1761, on the demise of the 6th baronet.
(2). SIR FRANCIS KNOLLYS, JUN, second son of the famous Sir Francis Knollys, K.G., Treasurer of Queen Elizabeth's household and captain of the Guard, who received from his royal mistress the grants of Whitley Park (the Abbot's park mentioned by Leland as being at the entrance to Reading town), and the manor or farm of Battle, which also belonged to Reading Abbey. Sir Francis resided at the Abbey-house of Reading at the period of the civil war. Captain

---
* This Committee sat at Reading Abbey.

Symonds, who was at Reading in 1644, described the dining-room at the Abbey-house as having the arms and initials of Queen Elizabeth, for whose reception it was probably fitted up. Sir Francis, jun., the sequestrator, sat for the county of Berks in the Parliaments of 1614-25, and for Reading in those of 1625-26-28-40 until his demise in 1645.

(3). PEREGRINE HOBY, son of Sir Edward Hoby, of Bisham, co. Berks, who received the honour of a visit from Queen Elizabeth at Bisham in 1592, who when Princess had spent part of three years here under the guardianship of Sir Thomas Hoby. Edward, the son of Peregrine, was created a baronet 12 July, 1666, a title which became extinct on the death of the Rev. Sir Philip Hoby, fifth baronet, June 29, 1766.

(4). HARRY MARTEN. The Regicide. Son of Sir Henry Marten, of Longworth, near Faringdon, Dean of Arches, Judge of the Prerogative court and of the High Court of Admiralty, who was esteemed the first civilian of the age. His "ungodly son," as Wood calls him, represented the county of Berks in the Parliaments of 1640-40, and was governor of Reading in 1642, but upon the approach of a party of the king's horse Marten quitted the town and fled with his garrison. After the Restoration, Marten surrendered on the Proclamation and was tried at the Old Bailey, he was found guilty, and petitioned for pardon, which he obtained on condition of perpetual imprisonment. He was first confined in the Tower, but soon removed to the Castle at Chepstow, where he was incarcerated twenty years. Marten was buried in the Church at Chepstow, and over his remains was placed a stone with the following inscription, the acrostic epitaph being written by himself.

"Here
Sep. 9, in the year of our Lord 1680,
Was buried a true Englishman,
Who in Berkshire was well known
To love his country's freedom, 'bove his own,
But living immured full twenty year,
Had time to write, as does appear,
HIS EPITAPH.
H ere or elsewhere (all's one to you, to me,)
E arth, air, or water, gripes my ghostless dust
N one knows how soon to be by fire set free
R eader, if you an oft tryed rule will trust,
Y ou'll gladly do and suffer what you must.

M y life was spent in serving you, and you,
A nd death's my pay (it seems) and welcome too;
R evenge destroying but itself, while I
T o birds of prey leave my old cage, and fly,
E xamples preach to th' eye, care then, (mine says)
N ot how you end, but how you spend your dayes."

(5). ROGER KNIGHT, of Greenham. See *Appendix*, "Second Battle."
(6). HENRY POWLE. Of the family of Powles of Shottesbroke. This Henry Powle was High Sheriff of the County of Berks, 8 Car. i, 1632. Mr. Powle's younger son Henry, sat for Windsor in the Convention Parliament of 1688, over which he presided as Speaker,

became Master of the Rolls, 13 March, 1689-90, and died 21 Nov., 1692. He married, in 1679, Frances, Countess Dowager of Dorset, relict of Richard Sackville, 5th Earl of Dorset.

(7). THOMAS FETTIPLACE, of Fernham, near Faringdon.

(8). TANFIELD VACHELL, of Coley House. M.P. for Reading in the Second Parliament of 1640, succeeding to that seat on the demise of Sir Francis Knollys, jun., knt. in 1645. King Charles was at Coley House in May, 1644, which at this time belonged to John Hampden in right of his second wife, Letitia, daughter of Sir Francis Knollys, brother to William, Earl of Banbury and widow of Sir Thomas Vachell. "Mr. Tanfield Vachell whom the King made Sheriff of Berks in 1643, and who left his service and went to Rebellion, whose house on the south side of the town newly built upon the old priory and now pull'd down, is cousin and heir to ye said Sir Thomas Vachell, his uncle. 'Tis reported in Reading an old story of Vachell, y^t would not suffer ye Abbot of Reading to carry the hay through his yard, ye Abbot after many messengers, sent a Monk, whom Vachell in fury kill'd, he was forced to fly, and his kin after adopted the motto, "It is better to suffer than revenge." (Symond's "Church Notes," Harl. MSS., 965, Mus. Brit.)

VII.*

THE COMMISSIONERS FOR RAISING MONEY AND FORCES WITHIN THE COUNTY OF BERKS, AND FOR MAINTENANCE OF GARRISONS WITHIN THE SAID COUNTY FOR USE OF PARLIAMENT, APPOINTED JUNE 27, 1644, were:—

William Lenthall, Speaker and Master of the Rolls (1); Sir Francis Knollys, knt., Sir Francis Pile, Bart., Sir Robert Pye, sen. (2); Sir Benjamin Rudyerd, knt. (3); Richard Whitehead, Edward Dunch (4); Henry Marten, Peregrine Hobby, Tanfield Vachell, Daniel Blagrave (5); Major-General Richard Browne (6); William Ball, John Packer, sen. (7); Robert Packer (8); and Cornelius Holland (9).

(1). WILLIAM LENTHALL, (the speaker of the Long Parliament), of Besilsleigh, co. Berks, who purchased this property of the Fettiplaces in 1634. The old mansion which was a magnificent structure, surrounded by a quadrangular court is now destroyed except a picturesque portion of the offices and the massive stone pillars of the gateway. Cromwell and other distinguished characters of the day were frequent guests at Besilsleigh. The elder branch of the Lenthalls became extinct at the decease of William Lenthall, a gentleman of the Privy Chamber to Charles II., M.P. for Wallingford in 1680. The family is now represented by Edm. Kyffin Lenthall, Esq., of Besilsleigh.

(2). SIR ROBERT PYE, SEN. Upon the breaking out of the Civil War he sided with the Parliamentarians, and, as Colonel of horse in General Fairfax's regiment, headed an assault on his own house at Faringdon, in which he was repulsed by the royalist governor Sir Marmaduke Rawdon. During the protectorate he enjoyed many high favours; he nevertheless joined in the attempt to restore Charles II., and was subsequently committed to the Tower for a breach of privilege in presenting a petition from the County of Berks, complaining of the want of a settled form of Government. Pye was released at the Restoration and appointed Equerry to King Charles II. He married a daughter of John Hampden. He lived with her upwards of 60 years, and died in 1714 within a week of her death. Sir Robert Pye's great-great-grandson was the poet-laureat Henry James Pye.

(3). SIR BENJAMIN RUDYERD, KNT., of West Woodhay, near Newbury, descended from the Rudyerds of Rudyerd, co. of Stafford; third son of James Rudyerd, Esq. of Hartley, co. Hants, by Margaret his wife, daughter, and heiress of Lawrence Kidwelly, of Winchfield, in the same county, esquire. Sir Benjamin was born on St. Stephen's day, 1572, and educated at the public school, Winchester, and St. John's College, Oxford. By the influence of his patron, Sir John Harrington, afterwards Lord Harrington, of Exton, preceptor to the accomplished but unfortunate Princess Elizabeth, Rudyerd soon obtained a favourable reception at the Court of King James I. and in the above-mentioned noble family, distinguished alike by their talents and piety, he, no doubt, received those lessons of moderation which so greatly distinguished his whole political career. From that family, too, he chose a partner in the joys and sorrows of his life, in the person of Elizabeth, one of the two daughters and co-heiresses of Sir Henry Harrington, next brother to John, first Lord Harrington of Exton. On the 9th March, 1617, Rudyerd was appointed to the then high and distinguished office of Surveyor of His Majesty's Court of Wards and Liveries, and on the 30th of the same month, King James honoured him with the degree of knighthood. Upon the differences arising between King Charles I. and Parliament, Sir Benjamin was one of the several members of both houses who did all they could to persuade the Parliament to an accommodation, and warned them of the miseries of a civil war. On the abolition of the Court of Wards and Liveries in 1647, £6,000 was voted to Rudyerd, and so great was the esteem of the House towards him, that they further voted him a part of the forfeited estates of the Marquis of Worcester as a reparation for the loss of his office, but notwithstanding these marks of favour, he was heartily disgusted with the disloyal attempts of the Independents, and he stood to his post to the last moment advocating moderation and deprecating destruction. In December, 1648, Rudyerd and other well affected members of the Parliament having been beaten on the 4th instant, question, "whether the King's answers to the propositions of both Houses were satisfactory," on the 6th, the question was varied by the King's friends, among whom Rudyerd stood prominently forward, in the hope of further averting the progress of the rebellion, and making a happy peace with the Sovereign, then a prisoner. It was now put in these terms,—that the answer of the King to the propositions of both Houses are a ground for the House to proceed upon for the settlement of the peace of the kingdom," which was carried by a majority of 129 to 83. Such an unexpected occurrence threw Cromwell and the Parliamentary generals into the greatest consternation, and the result was the well-known coup d'état, when all the obnoxious members were seized as they arrived at the House: one of the victims on this occasion was Rudyerd, then 76 years of age, who was thrown into prison with the rest. It appears Rudyerd did not remain in confinement any length of time, as the Journals of the House of Commons record his release from the Gate-house shortly afterwards, owing, it is said, to the influence of Mr. Prynne. Sir Benjamin then retired to his house at West Woodhay, built for him by Inigo Jones, and spent the remainder of his days in the quiet to which his mind must have been a stranger while engaged in the political struggles of the times. Sir Benjamin died at West Woodhay on the 31st May, 1658, aged 86 years; a few months only before the death of Cromwell. No stronger example of the sincerity of Rudyerd's religious sentiments can be adduced than the following beautiful hymn which he composed in his declining years:—

"O God! my God! what shall I give
To Thee in thanks? I am and live
In thee; and thou dost safe preserve
My health, my fame, my goods, my rent:
Thou mak'st me eat, whilst others starve,
And sing, whilst others do lament.
Such unto me thy blessings are
As though I were thy only care.

But oh! my God, thou art more kind,
When I look inward on my mind:
Thou fill'st my heart with humble joy,
With patience meek, and fervent love
(Which doth all other loves destroy),
With faith which nothing can remove,
And hope assur'd of Heaven's bliss:
This is my state, my grace is this."

Sir Benjamin was buried in the Church at West Woodhay, where in Ashmole's time there was "a neat black marble monument" to his memory, with an epitaph, written (according to the authority of Wood, "Athenæ Oxonienses," vol. iii.) by Sir Benjamin in his younger days. It is printed in Ashmole's "Collections," and in the "Hist. of Newbury," p. 289. The only son of Sir Benjamin married one of the five daughters and co-heirs of Sir Stephen Harvey, of Morton Murrell in the co. of Warwick (created Knight of the Bath at the coronation of King Charles I.); and by this connection Mr. Rudyerd was brother-in-law to the celebrated Speaker Lenthall. Mr. John Rudyerd, the ingenious designer of the Eddystone Light-house erected in 1708, and which stood until destroyed by fire in 1755, was a lineal descendant of Sir Benjamin.

(4.) EDMUND DUNCH. Member for Wallingford in the Parliaments of 1628-40, and for the County in the Parliaments of 1654-56. His return to the Long Parliament was declared void. Mr. Dunch, High Sheriff of the County, 9 Car. 1, 1632-3, was the son of Sir William Dunch, who married Mary, daughter of Sir Henry Cromwell, and aunt to the Protector. In 1658 he was created a baronet, and afterwards called to the Upper House by the title of Baron Burnell, of which he was divested at the Restoration, he died in 1678. The grandson of "Baron Burnell," and his namesake (Edmund Dunch) married a daughter and co-heiress of Col. Godfrey, by Arabella Churchill, sister to the great Duke of Marlborough; and on his demise without male issue in 1719, his family became extinct. The marriage just alluded to is note-worthy, as, the last Mrs. Dunch being half-sister to the children of James II., the blood of the Cromwells and Stuarts became thereby commingled.

(5.) DANIEL BLAGRAVE, of Southcote, one of the Regicides, was third son of Anthony Blagrave, Esq., and nephew of the eminent mathematician who built Southcote Manor-house. He represented the borough of Reading in Parliament; and, as a reward for his services to the Commonwealth, received the office of "Exigenter" in the Court of Common Pleas, worth annually at that time £500, and was made Master in Chancery. He was likewise Treasurer of Berkshire, and one of the County Committee, who were authorized to remove all "inefficient" ministers, in which office he distinguished himself by his vexatious persecution of the clergy. The emoluments of his office in the Common Pleas, it is supposed, enabled him to purchase the King's fee-farm-rent of the valuable Manor of Sonning and some other estates; and, having kept in with every form of government during the interregnum, he obtained a seat in the Convention Parliament of 1658. At the Restoration, finding the danger which threatened him, he fled the kingdom, and, retiring to Aachen in Germany, died in 1668 in an obscure condition. John Blagrave, nephew of the above and son of Anthony Blagrave, by Dorothy, daughter of Sir Thomas Dolman, of Shaw, was one of the gentlemen of Berks who had assisted in the Restoration, and qualified to be made a knight of the proposed Order of the Royal Oak. This family of the Blagraves of Bulmarsh Court and Southcote became extinct in the male line on the demise of John Blagrave, Esq., in 1787, and is now represented in the female line by J. H. Blagrave, Esq., of Calcot Park.

(6.) RICHARD BROWNE. Major-General of Oxfordshire, Berkshire, and Buckinghamshire, was an eminent citizen of London, a warm advocate for the presbytery, greatly distinguished himself in the field, and had no small influence in the Parliament. He attended the Earl of Essex when he first marched against the King; and had a considerable hand in defeating the Royalists near Worcester and at Edgehill. He took Arundel Castle by storm, and, seizing on Abingdon, bravely defended it against the whole force of the garrison at Oxford. In a sudden sally from Abingdon he surprised and took Bellasith House, which was strongly garrisoned by the royal party, and found in it a good supply of provision. He was one of the Commissioners deputed to receive the King from the Scots army; when, perceiving the great advantage His Majesty had in his disputes with their politicians and divines, and probably penetrating the designs of the Independents, he returned to his allegiance, and ever after inflexibly adhered to it.

He was much in favour with Charles II., whose Resident he was at Paris before the Restoration, and was soon after created a baronet, having before received the honour of knighthood. He had the command of the City Militia, and was Lord Mayor of London in 1660. His only daughter and heiress espoused John Evelyn* during her father's residence in France.

(7.) JOHN PACKER, of Donnington Castle. } See Appendix to the
(8). ROBERT PACKER his son. } Second Battle.
(9.) CORNELIUS HOLLAND, M.P. for Windsor. One of the King's judges. Once servant to Sir Harry Vane, by whom he was preferred to be Clerk of the Green Cloth to the King whose death-warrant he ultimately signed. Winstanley in his "Martyrology," and the author of a work entitled "The History of the King Killers," concur in representing this regicide as a man of great depravity. In "The Mystery of the Good Old Cause," it is stated that Holland made himself a farmer of the King's Feeding-grounds at Crestoe in Bucks, worth £1,800 or £2,000 per annum, at the rate of £20 a year, which he discounted. He possessed Somerset House a long time, where he and his family nested themselves. He was keeper of Richmond House which served for his country-retreat. He was also commissary for the garrison at Whitehall and the Mews; and he had an office in the Mint. It is supposed he gave £5,000 to each of his ten children!

VIII.—SHIP-MONEY.

"Ship-Money," a word, says Lord Clarendon, "of a lasting sound in the memory of this kingdom," indicates a project which in its progress made the dissensions between King and Parliament irreparable, and in its consequences led to the misery of eleven years of almost uninterrupted Civil War.

Schedules were prepared and sent to each Sheriff, containing the list of all the counties, cities, and corporate towns, and the proportions in which each was rated, to the end that each district and community might be made aware that the contribution was enforced impartially. These Schedules present a view of the comparative wealth and importance of those places, which is remarkable in the contrast it affords with their respective conditions in present times.

---

* Cowley in his "Garden," addressed to this worthy gentleman, compliments him upon his taste for horticulture and books, and his happy choice of a wife, who had, as he expresses it,
"The fairest garden in her looks,
And in her mind the choicest books."

DISTRIBUTION OF SHIPS, WITH THEIR TONNAGE, NUMBER OF MEN, AND CHARGE, AND THE SUMS SET ON THE CORPORATION TOWNS IN THE COUNTY of BERKS. (From Sir Peter Temple's MS. Papers—Stowe, given in the Appendix to Lord Nugent's "Life of Hampden.")

		TONS.	MEN.	CHARGE.
Berkshire County,	One Ship of	320	128	£4000
Town of Windsor				100
Borough of Newbury				100
Borough of Reading				220
Borough of Abingdon				100
Borough of Wallingford,				20

Portsmouth was assessed at £60; Bath £70; Preston £40; Stafford £30; and Liverpool £25! Such a disproportion to the present wealth of some of these places shows what great changes are wrought by the hand of Time!

PETITION OF THE GRAND JURY OF THE COUNTY OF BERKS AGAINST SHIP MONEY, &c.*

To the King's Most Excelent Matie.

The Humble Petition of your Maties most Loyall subjects the Grand Jury Impaneled 11 July, 1640, to serve at the generall assizes holden for the County of Berks, in the behalfe of themselves, and the rest of the Countie. Sheweth, That whereas your Petitioners have been of late yeares and still are much burthened with sundry grievances of divers natures deriving ther authority from y^r Maje but being directly contrary to y^r Maties Lawes established in this your kingdom, the chief of these presenting themselves in a schedule hereunto annexed, for redresse, whereof, as your petitioners hoped, your Matie was graciously pleased about the midle of Aprill to assemble the great Councell commonly called the High Court of Parliament, and about three weeks after to dissolve it, for want (as it seemes to your petitioners) of a goode agreemente betwixt the two houses. Neverthelesse since the said dissolution to express such a fatherly care of your Poor people, that y^r Matie has vouchsafed by a Printed declaration to invite them to the poureing out of their complaynts unto your Princely eare. It may therefore please your most Excellt. Matie to take the sayd particulers into your tender consideration, to give your Petitioners such ease therein, as in your Royall Wisdome shall be thought fitte. And whereby it may appeare to all your Maties Subjects, and especially to thos of y^r Maties most honorable Privy Councell, and your Officers and Ministers of Justis, that y^r Matie is resolved to continue unto them all their rights and Liberties which they desired by ther Petition of Right, and wer

---

* Addl. MSS., Brit. Mus., No. 204064, f. 9.

confirm'd by y^r Matie the 3rd yeare of your rayne. And your Petitioners as they are bound shall continue to preserve the length and happinesse of y^r Mat^ies sayd raigne by ther prayers and all other actions of zeal and duty.

A Schedule of such grievances as most oppresse the Countie.

1.—The Illegall and insupportable charge of Ship mony, now these 5 yeare Imposed as high as ever, though the subject was not able to pay the last year, being but a third.
2.—The new tax of coal and conduct mony, with the undermeanes used to enforce the payment of it by messengers from Counstable.
3.—The compellinge sume freemen by imprisonment and thretnings to take peoples mony, and others for feare of the like imprisonment do forsake ther houses and habitations hideing them selves in woods, whereby ther families are obliged to be maintayned by the parishes, and harvest work undon for want of Labourers.
4.—The Infinite number of monopolies upon every thing allmost the Countrymen must bye. Besides the easterne part of this Countie, wher your Mat^ies fforest of Windsor is, is particularly burthened with immeasurable inroades of the deare, which if they shall goe on soe for five years will leave neither foode nor roome for any creatures in the fforest.

With rigid execution of forest lawes in ther extremitye, with the exaction of the Imoderate fees by som officers under the Ld. Cheef Justis in Iyre. *

---

* Lord Falkland felt and spoke strongly upon the extra-judicial opinion the Judges had given at Charles' request, on the King's right to Ship-Money. "No meal undigested," he said, "can lie heavier upon the stomach than that unsaid would have lain upon my conscience." He complained that the judges, "the persons who should have been as dogs to defend the flock, have become the wolves to devour it;" that they had exceeded their functions, "being judges of law and not of necessity, that is, being judges and not philosophers or politicians;" that to justify the plea of necessity, they have "supposed mighty and eminent dangers in the most quiet and halcyon days, but a few contemptible pirates being our most formidable enemies;" they also, "supposing the supposed doings to be so sudden that it could not stay for a Parliament which required but a forty days' stay, allowed to the King the sole power in necessity, the sole judgment of necessity, and by that enabled him to take from us what he would, when he would, and how he would." He especially declaimed against the Chief Justice (at this time Lord Keeper) Finch, who importuned the other judges "as a most admirable solicitor, but a most abominable judge." * * * "He it was who gave away with his breath what our ancestors have purchased with so long expense of their time, their care, their treasures, and their bloods, and strove to make our grievances mortal and our slavery irreparable." * * * "He who hath already undone us by wholesale," and now as Chancellor "hath the power of undoing us by retail."—Cordery and Phillpott's "King and Commonwealth," p. 83.

IX.—STATE OF PUBLIC FEELING IN THE COUNTY IN 1643.

That the County of Berks was generally favourable to the Parliament may be inferred from the following extract of Members returned to the Long Parliament, compiled by Professor Masson, and introduced in his "Life of Milton."

(The Shire and four Boroughs)   No. of Members.
Parliamentarians   5
Royalists   2
So unstable as meanwhile
   to have changed sides   ..   1
Non-effective   2
                                                    10

The Royalist element in the County is indicated by the following list of those who faithfully attached themselves to the interest of the King, and had to compound for their estates, under the ordinance of Parliament, April 1st, 1643: extracted from Fellowe's "Historical Sketches of Charles I."

COUNTY OF BERKS.

			£	s.	d.
Appleyard, Charles	Wargrave		0003	10	00
Bunbury, Thomas	Reading	Dr.	0117	00	00
Braxton, Anthony	do		0100	00	00
Bishop, Richard	Collestley	Esq.	0385	00	00
Bricket, Thomas	Shenfield		0012	08	08
Chok, Francis *	Avington	Gent.	0572	00	00
Clifford, Richard	Shalbourne	Gent.	0145	10	00
Davy, John	Pangborne	Esq.	0382	10	00
Dicus, Hugh	Reading		0060	00	00
Fartham, John	do		0002	13	04
Foster, Sir Humphrey (over and above £500 paid the Committee in the Country)	Aldermaston		0500	00	00
Gwynn, William	Sunning-hill	Gent.	0112	15	00
Gardiner, Roger	Whitewalton		0015	13	04
Hide, Humphrey	Kennington	Esq.	0538	00	00
Hall, Thomas	Windsor	Gent.	0020	00	00
Hamlyn, Henry	Reading	Gent.	0033	06	08
Herbert, Edward	Bray	Gent.	0166	13	06
Langton, William	Stanwick	Esq.	0111	00	00
Langton, George	do	Gent.	0008	06	08

* Sir Francis Choke, of Avington, was Lieut.-Col. of Sir Faithful Fortescue's regiment raised for the King.

APPENDIX. 103

			£	s.	d.
Milton, Christopher *	Reading		0080	00	00
Masson, Robert	Hidden	Esq.	0522	00	00
Neville, Richd.	Billingbere	Esq.	0877	00	00
Peacock, John	Conmer	Gent.	0140	00	00
Porter, William	Marcott	Gent.	0681	00	00
Reeves, Thomas	Reading	Esq.	0160	00	00
Sawyer, Edward	Dudcot	Gent.	0091	00	00
Stonehouse, Sir Geo.	Radley	Bart.	1460	00	00
Stafford, Edward	Bradfield		0848	00	00
Thomas, John	New Windsor		0022	13	04
Tyle, Richd.	Marfield	Yeoman	0032	10	00
Worktop, Thomas	New Windsor	Gent.	0160	00	00

This list must not be supposed to specify the whole of the losses of the Berkshire Gentry on this occasion, as there is no doubt that those who were actively concerned forfeited their whole property, not being allowed to compound.

Among the Recusants in the neighbourhood who suffered severely for their religious principles were the Eystons of Hendred (a family who have now held property in the County for over 500 years), the Perkinses of Ufton Court, Brownes of Gt. Shefford, and the Dancastles of Well-House, and the Grange, in the parish of Shaw. The name of Gabriel Coxe who, while Mayor of Newbury, received the King at his house, occurs in the catalogue of persons reported to be Papists.

---

* Christopher Milton. This was the brother of the great poet, John Milton, Cromwell's Latin Secretary. "He entered as a student of the Middle Temple, of which House he became an ancient Bencher, and kept close to that study and profession all his life-time, except during the Civil Wars of England, when he adhered to the Royal cause, and became obnoxious to the Parliament by acting to the utmost of his power against them so long as he kept his station at Reading in Berkshire, and therefore, as soon as that town was taken by the Parliamentary forces, he was obliged to quit his house there and steer his course according to the motion of the King's army. When the war was ended, and his composition made through his brother's interest with the then prevailing powers, he returned to his profession." "Collection of the Works of Milton," 1738.—Bodleian Lib.

X.—AGREEMENT BETWEEN CHARLES I. AND THE COUNTY OF BERKS RESPECTING A CONTRIBUTION TO BE LEVIED FOR THE SUPPORT OF THE KING'S ARMY.

THE AGREEMENT MADE BETWEEN HIS MAJESTY AND THE KNIGHTS, GENTLEMEN, FREEHOLDERS, AND INHABITANTS OF THE COUNTY OF BERKS FOR THE BETTER PROVISION AND ORDERING OF HIS MAJESTIE'S ARMY, AND A DECLARATION OF HIS MAJESTY'S GRATIOUS ACCEPTANCE THEREOF, AND HIS ROYAL PROCLAMATION COMMANDING THE DUE OBSERVANCE THEREOF IN ALL PARTS.

Printed by His Majestie's command at Oxford, Oct. 19, by Leonard Lichfield, Printer to the University, 1643.

At a Councell of Warre Held the 13 October, 1643, His Majesty being present.

This day the High Sheriffe, Gentlemen, and Freeholders of the County of Berks did present to His Majesty their agreement, on the behalfe of all the inhabitants of that County, which was in this manner following:—

FIRST.—They doe agree to pay by way of Loane, during the space of a Moneth, a weekly contribution of 1000l. by the week, towards the maintenance of the King's army out of that County, to be proportionately laid upon all parts of the County (except the hundreds of Riplesmere, Bray, Cookham, Benhurst, and Wargrave, lying within the Furest division, which are left to His Majesty to dispose of), to beginne from the 29 September now last past, to be levyed and rated upon the Lands, Rents, Annuities, Parsonages, and Tythes, and Personal estates of the inhabitants of the whole County (except before excepted) in such manner, and according to such proportions, as by the ancient and usuall course of the severall parts of the County rates laid upon the County have been rated and levyed.

That the one halfe of the said 1000l. by the week shall be paid in mony, and the other halfe in provisions, and for the provisions they shall be of such sorts as the souldiers shall desire at the rates hereunder written, viz$^{t.}$

Oates to be rated at 20$^{d.}$ the Bushell.
Beanes and Pease at 3$^{d.}$ the Bushell.
Hay at 5$^{d.}$ the Todde.
Grasse for a horse at 3/- the Weeke.
Straw at 10/- the Load.

And so often those rates for a greater or lesser quantity. But it to be alwaies at the election of the parties paying, to pay the whole rate in mony if they so please.

APPENDIX. 105

That, if any losse or damage shall happen to any of the inhabitants either in their horses or other cattell or in any of their provisions or other goods by any of the King's souldiers, such losse or damage shall be repayed and recompensed to the party suffering out of the said weekly Loane.

That all the provisions to be delivered according to this agreement shall be delivered at the Towne of Abingdon on Friday in every week, or at such other places as shall bo mutually agreed upon, and the delivering to bee on such daies in every week, as shall bee likewise agreed upon, to the hands of the Collectors or Commissaries to be to that purpose appointed, who shall then also receive the mony to be paid according to this Agreement, and Books shall be kept wherein shall bee set what shall be paid in mony and what and how much in provisions, and from whom, and by whom the same is paid, that so the defaulters may also appeare, and be proceeded against accordingly for such their default.

That the Defalcations or Reparations to be made to any according to this Agreement shall be held good, and allowed of whensoever it shall be set downe and allowed under the hands of any three of the Commissioners named in the Commission for setling of this Contribution. And if the losse or dammage amount to more than the party damnified in his own particular should pay for the week, then the Reparation to be made up and repayed to the party grieved by the High Constable or Collector of that part of the County, upon warrant under the hands of any three of the said Commissioners allowing the same aforesaid, and if any Hundred, Parish, or particular Person, shall make default of payment, that Hundred, Parish, or Person, so making default shall be left to the care and discretion of the Commander of that part of the King's army next to the place where such default shall be, and for the supply of whom that part shall be allotted.

That no manner of free-quarter or billetting shall be taken by or for any Horse or Foot Souldiers, nor any Taxe, Charge, or Imposition whatsoever shall be laid upon or required from any inhabitant of this County, without present payment for the same in mony, as they shall agree by consent, except only for House room according to the quality of the person Billeted, and of the Person in whose House he is so Billeted, and except for fire and candle, such as the Master, Mistris or Dame of the Family use for themselves and their own family.

That no Women, Boyes, or Children following the army be admitted from henceforth to have House room, unlesse it be by consent, and by composition with the owner of the House for the same.

That the High Constables in every Hundred respectively be the immediate Collectors both of the Moneys and Provisions from the Inhabitants paying the same, and they to pay the same over to the High Sheriff of the County, or such as he shall appoint, at the times and places before mentioned, and they to pay or deliver the same to such officers of the army as shall be appointed to receive and distribute the same unto and amongst the Souldiers.

And because the said weekly summe of a 1000*l*. was formerly laid upon the whole county, whereof the five Hundreds above mentioned were parcell, It is now ordered that such summe of mony, parcell of the said 1000*l*., which the said five Hundreds should have borne and are now excepted as aforesaid, shall by the Rule of proportion bee rated and layed upon the rest of the County.

P

That these agreements be setled by order of the Councell of Warre, and entred with the Secretary of the Councell to the end that all Commanders, Officers, and Souldiers may take knowledge of and observe the same.

And it is further desired by the County, and on their behalfe, that the Lords and others, His Majesty's Commissioners, would by their order, as much as in them lyeth, confirme the same, and give life to the execution thereof, and that His Majesty by his Royal Proclamation will bee pleased to command the due execution and observation thereof, in all the parts thereof. And His Majesty having perused these agreements, and declared his gratious approbation thereof, now according to the request made on behalfe of the Country, the Lords and others His Majesty's Commissioners doe order—That they will be ready to give their best assistance that these agreements shall be duly observed, that they will constantly meet in the Audite-house there to receive the complaynts of the Country if there shall be cause, and as there shall be cause to recommend the Redresse of what shall be amisse in any part, either to the King's Majesty or the Councell of Warre, if the Lords themselves shall not have the meanes otherwise to redresse the same. And to the end that the County may have a convenient opportunity on all occasions to present their complaints when there shall be cause, they doe with one consent make choyce of William Hynton, Esquire, one of the gentlemen of His Majesty's Privy Chamber, and one of the Inhabitants amongst them, to performe the good office for them from time to time, which His Majesty doth very well approve.

All which His Majesty doth very well approve of, and doth command to be printed and published, in every Church and Chappellry of the County to the end that notice being generally taken thereof, all persons of all qualities, whom it doth or may concerne, may apply themselves to the performance thereof.

And further His Majesty being desirous that so good a worke may not perish in the execution which is the life of all good actions, doth by his Royal Proclamation declare—That he doubteth not, but the Inhabitants of this County will on their parts observe the same, and will continue it as long as the necessity shall continue, which His Majesty will, by all possible meanes he can, endeavour to shorten and ease, for he doth strictly charge and command, That on the part of the Souldiers, the same be duely observed. And that if any Souldier of what quality soever presume to broake those agreements or to offend contrary to the same, every such offender shall be severally proceeded against, according to the quality of his offence, that by the exemplary punishment of some, others may be warned and deterred from committing the like. His Majesty being resolved, as on the one side to punish those who will not be admonished according to the due course of justice, so on the other side, to reward those who have and shall deserve well by their good examples, according to their severall qualities and deservings, as soone as it shall please God to enable Him thereunto.

Given at His Majestie's Court at Oxford, the 17 day of October in the Nineteenth yeare of His Majesty's Raigne, 1643.

THE SECOND BATTLE AT NEWBURY,

OCTOBER 27TH, 1644.

THE Royal cause had not been at all prosperous in the Winter of 1643-4, and the Spring entered with no better prospect.

In May, 1644, the Parliamentary armies left London, and marched—the one, under Essex, to Windsor, and the other, under Waller, to Hartford Bridge, intending to beat up the gallant Marquis of Winchester at Basing. The King then withdrew his garrison from Reading, and proposed to make a stand at Abingdon; but, on Essex's approach, Abingdon was evacuated; and he garrisoned it for the Parliament, and threw troops into Newbury also, which a few weeks previously had been occupied by the King's forces; so that before the end of May the Parliament were the masters of all this part of Berkshire, except Donnington Castle.

In the Summer of 1644 the war swayed northward; and on the 2nd of July was fought the first momentous battle of the Civil War, that of Marston Moor.

Since this victory had secured the North for the Parliament, the main stress of the war had been in the Midlands and Southwest, where Essex and Waller, the two parliamentary generals, then were. After co-operating for some time against the King in the Midlands, those two generals had separated in June. Essex persisted in undertaking the expedition against Prince Maurice and his royalists in the South-west, which service the Parliament had designed for Waller. The latter remained in the Midlands, where a check sustained by him at Cropredy Bridge, on the borders of Oxfordshire, on June 29th (three days before the battle of Marston Moor), had enabled the King to follow Essex into the South-west, with the intention of joining his nephew Prince Maurice and crushing Essex by superior force.

Essex, instead of turning back to fight the King, as he wished, was urged by Lord Roberts (or Robartes), a man described by Clarendon as of an impetuous disposition and full of contradictions, to push into Cornwall,* in which extremely loyal County,

---

* During the Rebellion the mainstay of the throne was in the West and North, especially in Wales, Devon, and Cornwall. The famous Generals Grenville, Godolphin, Trevannion, and Slanning were called "the wheels of Charles's wain." They were, says Prince in his "Worthies of Devon," all slain at or near the same place, at the same time, and in the same cause.

the King and Prince Maurice having joined their forces, he found himself cooped up in August, in the most precarious condition. To send Waller to his comrade's relief, with a newly equipped army, was then the strenuous effort of the Parliament; and, as, to complicate matters, Prince Rupert was sure to move southward, it became a necessary part of their plan that Lord Manchester's army should come out of its quarters in the Eastern Counties, and follow Waller's route westward.* Colonel Middleton was also dispatched with a force of 3,000 or 4,000 horse and foot to harass the King's rear. He had orders to reduce, on his way, Donnington Castle, the residence of Mr. John Packer, which, on account of its commanding the great road by which the western trade was carried to London, had been garrisoned and fortified by order of the King shortly after the First Battle of Newbury, the previous year, and Colonel Boys appointed its governor. The following Commission† is without subscription, but undoubtedly refers to the appointment of this staunch supporter of the Royal Cause to the command of the fortress:—"Charles R. Trusty and well-beloved, we greet you well. Whereas we have thought fit, for the defence and security of this part of our County of Berks, to leave a sufficient number of soldiers in Donnington Castle, we have made choice of your foot and of the dragooners of Sir Robt. Howard. Wherefore our will and pleasure is that you forthwith repair with the said forces unto the said Castle, there to continue and keep the same for our use, and to command all the officers and soldiers therein as you shall find fit for our service. And for your so doing, these shall be your sufficient warrant. Given under our sign-manual at our Court at Newbury this 22nd Sept. 1643." As to the supplies, it is recorded that "Donnington Castle hath three Hundreds out of which he (the Governour) weekly receives contribucion, vizt., Kimbry [Kintbury] Eagle 20 parishes, Faire-Crosse 14 parishes, and Compton 8 parishes, besides Newbery is in too. These found him beds and weekely payment for the building the workes, which cost about £1,000. Faire-Crosse Hundred paid about £60 per weeke."‡ The main element of defence of this little fortress was its massive gate-house, with barbican and portcullis, and the extensive series of earthworks constructed by Boys, and thickly planted with his heaviest guns. The remainder of the structure with its subordinate towers and curtain-walls had, as Camden says, "windows on all sides, very lightsome," and was unable to offer much resistance to an artillery attack at near distance. It was more especially owing to the

---

* See "Manchester's Quarrel with Cromwell." Camden Soc., pp. lviii. lix.
† Warburton's "Prince Rupert," vol. ii. p. 314.
‡ Symond's "Diary," p. 144.

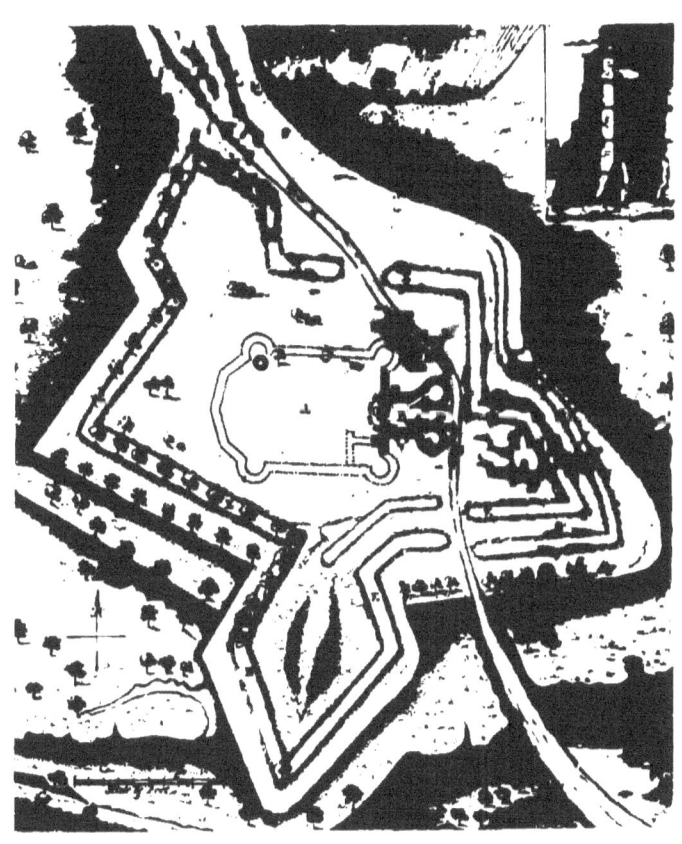

DONNINGTON CASTLE.

OUTWORKS OF DEFENCE.

marvellous prowess of Sir John and his brave little band that the old castle held out so well as it did.

The operations of Middleton before Donnington Castle are mentioned in the following terms in "The True Informer" from Saturday, Aug. 10th, to Saturday, Aug. 17th, 1644. "On Monday, July 29th, Lt.-Genl. Middleton came before Donnington Castle with between 3,000 and 4,000 horse and foot. At their entrance into Newbury they took divers of the stragglers of Donnington Castle, and on Wednesday morning drew up both horse and foot against the Castle, and without summons fell on a barn,* wherein the Governor of the Castle had placed some musquetiers, which our guards gained, beat the enemy, and took divers of them prisoners, after which the General sent a summons to the Governor, in these words;—'Sir, I demand you to render me Donnington Castle for the use of the King and Parliament. If you please to entertain a present treaty you shall have honourable terms. My desire to spare blood makes me propose this. I desire your answer. JOHN MIDDLETON.' 'Sir,' answered Boys, 'I am instructed by His Majesty's express commands, and have not yet learned to obey any other than my Sovereign. To spare blood, do as you please, but myself and those who are with me are fully resolved to venture ours in maintaining what we are entrusted with, which is the answer of JOHN BOYS. Donnington Castle, July 31, 1644.' After this answer received, the said Lieutenant-General drew up his foot with scaling ladders and other provisions, dividing themselves into three several places, at last the enemy fired the barne, whereupon our soldiers who were in it came forth, and the rest, in regard that they had not great pieces to batter the Castle, retreated with the loss of 6 common soldiers and a Lieutenant, concerning whom the Governor of the Castle (considering he had gott a great prize, though he lost three persons) sent a Drum to the Lt.-Genl. with this message. 'For Lt.-Generall Middleton. Sir, Christian charity requires me to give you notice that I have many bodies of yours, which I cannot accommodate with Christian burial, as likewise many of your wounded men which I know not how to dispose of. This I thought good to give you notice of, that you might take some course for them accordingly. Your Servant, JOHN BOYS. Donnington Castle, July 31, 1644.' To which message the Lt.-Generall sent this answer—'I conceive no inherient holinesse to be in any place or buriall, for all earth is fit for that use. In that you say you have no accommodation for our wounded men, who are your prisoners, if you please to exchange them, quality for quality, I shall take it a curtesie done to, Sir, Your Servant, JNO. MIDDLETON.'" On the following

---

* The Barn belonging to Donnington Castle is still represented by a portion standing in the Castle Farm.

Monday morning, the Castle being recommended by the Parliament to Major-General Brown, Governor of Abingdon and Commander of the Forces of the Associated Counties of Oxon, Berks, and Bucks, Middleton proceeded to join Essex in the West; but on his way he was met and routed by Sir Francis Doddington and Sir William Courtney, and compelled to retreat to Sherborne in Dorsetshire, where he fell upon a party of the King's horse, and, putting them to flight, repaired his credit by their overthrow.

The Earl of Manchester with his army arrived at Huntingdon on the 8th of September. By that time, however, the fate of Essex in Cornwall had been decided. Before relief could reach him he had been obliged to make his own escape by sea to Plymouth, on his way to London, leaving the mounted troops, under Sir William Balfour, to cut their way eastward as they could, and his foot, under Major-General Skippon, to negotiate terms of surrender, which were agreed to on September 1st. The news of Essex's defeat reached Manchester at Huntingdon, whence, on the 8th of September, he wrote to the Derby-House Committee,* expressing his condolence over the sad event,—"The Lord's arm," he adds, "is not shortened, though we be much weakened. I trust he will give us a happy recovery. I shall with all speed I can march in observance of your former orders." Manchester was now instructed to march westward for Abingdon with all possible expedition, and to send advertisement of his progress as he advanced.

The activity and firmness of the Parliament at first caused the King to slacken his movements. He addressed a pacific message to the Houses; and, for three weeks, contented himself with appearing before Plymouth, Lyme, and Portsmouth, which did not surrender. Towards the end of September, however, he learnt that Montrose, who had long since promised him civil war in Scotland, had at last succeeded, and was already obtaining one triumph after another. In a fortnight he had gained two battles (at Tippermuir, Sept. 1, and at Dee Bridge, Sept. 12), occupied Perth, taken Aberdeen by storm, raised most of the northern clans, and spread fear to the very gates of Edinburgh. On hearing these news, Charles flattered himself that the disaster of Marston Moor was repaired, that Parliament would soon find in the North a powerful adversary, and that he himself might without fear proceed to follow up his successes in the South. He resolved to march upon London; and, to give his expedition a popular and decisive appearance, a proclamation, sent forth in every direction at the moment of his departure, invited all his subjects of the South

---

* The Derby-House Committee consisted, for the English Parliament, of seven selected Peers and fourteen selected Commoners. Essex, Manchester, Waller, and Cromwell were of the English part of this Committee. Derby House, Cannon Row, Westminster, being the meeting-place of the Committee, it received the name of the "Derby-House Committee."

and East to rise in arms, choose officers for themselves, and, joining him on his way, march with him to summon the Parliament at length to accept peace.*

Prince Rupert on the 3rd of October had left the King for Bristol; and the latter promised not to engage until the Prince returned to him with reinforcements of Langdale's and Gerrard's troops. On the 11th, however, the pressing necessities of his four gallant garrisons at Basing, Donnington, Portland, and Banbury, induced him to put his army in motion; and on that day he thus writes to his Nephew from Blandford:—

THE KING TO PRINCE RUPERT.

"Nephew, [In cipher.]
I am advertised by a dispatch from Secretary Nicholas that the Governors of Basing, Banbury, and Donnington Castle, must accommodate in case they be not relieved within a few days. The importance of which place and consequently [illegible] hath made me resolve to begin my march on Tuesday towards Salisbury, where, Prince Rupert may rely upon it, the King of England shall be, God willing, on Wednesday next, where I will desire Prince Rupert to come with what strength of horse and foot you can, and the two demi-cannons, many of my men being unarmed. I have sent to Bristol for musquets which I desire Rupert to speed to me. I desire to hear daily from you, and particularly when you will be with me, and which way you will march, and how strong you can come to

Your loving Uncle and most faithful friend,
Blandford, 11th Oct. 1644.   CHARLES R."†

If everything had happened as the King imagined, he might have arrived in London before the Parliament's forces could have joined to form a new army; but his troops, instead of increasing on their march, as Charles had supposed, daily diminished: their pay was long in arrear; the men were half-starved, and in want of shoes and stockings; sickness had disabled many; desertions were numerous; and he was obliged to make frequent halts in towns, to wait for money and other necessaries, which he found would not be supplied when he had gone.‡ Owing to

---

* The proclamation is dated from Chard, September 30, 1644. Rushworth, vol. ii, 3, 715. Guizot's "Hist. Eng. Reform.," p. 244.
† Warburton's "Prince Rupert," vol. iii, pp. 26—27.
‡ The King's army about this time consisted of 5,500 foot and 4,000 horse. Clarendon, vol. ii. p. 541. The royalist forces, being supported by voluntary contributions, were poorly paid; whereas the pay of the Parliament was very good, especially that for the officers; but soon after the breaking out of the War an ordinance was passed, wherein it was enacted that all officers of the Earl of Essex's army, whose pay amounted to 10s. a day and upwards, should only receive half their pay, the other half being postponed until the troubles should be over. Horses at this time were valued at about £4; they had been as cheap as 30s. and 50s. Oats were 1/6 a bushel, and 12/- a quarter; peas and beans 2/- a bushel. Hay 5d. the tod; and grass-feed 2/6 a week. In 1655 wheat was 33/- and malt 20/- a quarter.

these delays, the King did not reach Salisbury till the 15th of October, six weeks after the surrender of the Parliamentarians at Lostwithiel; and, instead of proceeding toward London, as was at first intended, he decided to direct his march to Oxford, relieving his distressed garrisons on the way. Before this could be accomplished, however, he had to meet the combined army of the Parliament at Newbury.

While the King was advancing from Cornwall, news had come to Oxford that the gallant old Marquis of Winchester—
"He who in impious times untainted stood,
And midst rebellion durst be just and good,"
was so hard pressed at Basing that he must surrender in ten days if no relief came. Sir Arthur Aston, the governor at Oxford, declared, that the dangers of the relief were more than any soldier who understood command would expose himself to, and that he could not suffer any of the small garrison under his charge to be hazarded in the attempt; but Colonel Gage, who had lately come from the English regiment in Flanders, a worthier servant than whom the King did not possess, offered to take the command, and hoped to give a good account of it, if the Lords then at Oxford would enlist their servants, and raise a good troop or two of horse. Col. Hawkins' regiment, having opportunely come into Oxford, was raised to 400 by volunteers, and, with 250 horse, was placed under Gage's command. With this small force he threaded his way through bye roads to Wallingford and Aldermaston, and thence to Basing, where, on the 14th of September, he attacked and beat off the besiegers, levied arms and provisions in Basingstoke and the neighbouring villages, relieved the garrison, and then, though the whole country was up, came back to Oxford on the sixth day with 100 prisoners.* It was agreed in all sides that a more soldierly action had not been performed during the war. Col. Gage was knighted for this and other gallant services, in the Presence Chamber, at Christ-Church, Oxford, Nov. 2, 1644; but the brave Colonel did not long enjoy his distinction, being slain at Culham Bridge, near Abingdon, the following January.

On the King's arrival at Salisbury (15 Oct.), he was informed that the Parliament had made preparations to intercept his march; that Waller with his troops lay at Andover; that Manchester had advanced as far as Reading with 5,000 horse and foot and 24 pieces of ordnance; and that the London Trained Bands, consisting of the red and blue regiments of the City of

---

* In the year 1839, in digging a grave in the nave of Ewhurst Church, on the Basingstoke road, near Kingsclere, the remains of two soldiers, with portions of military ornaments, were found at a shallow depth. These interments had the appearance of having been hastily conducted; and were supposed to have been the bodies of officers slain in a skirmish in the neighbourhood during the operations before Basing.

THE SECOND BATTLE OF NEWBURY. 113

London, the red regiment of Westminster, the yellow regiments of Southwark and the Tower-Hamlets, making in all about 5,000 men, commanded by Sir James Harrington, were beginning their march to join him. The Earl of Essex's army, newly organized and equipped, was near Portsmouth, as well as those troops returning from the West under Colonel Middleton; and these were expecting orders to join the other forces.

If the King had utilized this information, and hastened his march to Oxford, he might have brought this year's campaign to a conclusion, which was the more reasonable, because he had received letters from Prince Rupert, in which he stated that it was impossible for him to bring up his troops so soon as the King expected. Had such a determination been formed, Donnington Castle and Banbury might both at a seasonable time have been relieved. But misfortune always attended the movements of the unhappy Monarch. He was too easily led. John Milton thus describes the King's fatal peculiarity:— "Whether with his enemies or friends, in the Court or Camp, he was always in the hands of another; now of his Wife, then of the Bishops; now of the Peers, then of the Soldiery; and lastly of his enemies: for the most part, too, he followed the worse counsel, and most always of the worser men." ("Iconoclastes.") In this instance Lord Goring who did not wish Prince Rupert to join in these operations, urgently advised the King to march against Waller, who was, at that time, with about 3,000 horse and foot, at Andover, and at some little distance from the bulk of the Parliament's forces. A Council of War was held, and the King at last yielded; the ostensible object being to cut off Waller before he could effect a junction with Essex and Manchester, and thus the more readily to advance the relief of Basing and Donnington Castle.

The cannon which the royalists had taken from Essex in Cornwall had been left at Exeter. The larger guns then with the forces were ordered to be sent to the garrison at Langford House, near Salisbury; the remainder of the artillery and baggage-waggons were placed at Wilton House. The Royal army was drawn up in Clarendon Park, and guards were posted at all the entrances to the City of Salisbury, to prevent information of the King's purpose being spread about. This succeeded so well that the royalists reached within four miles of Andover before Waller had any notion of their movements. On the enemy's approach he drew out his whole force, as though disposed to fight; on perceiving the King's strength, however, he drew back into the town, leaving a body of cavalry to make good his retreat; but the King's troops charged furiously, and effected a complete rout, pursuing the Parliamentarians through the town of Andover, giving no quarter. Waller, nevertheless,made good his retreat to Basingstoke. "It was a greate mercy of God," says Sir W.

Q

Waller in his "Recollections," "when the King came upon me with his whole army at Andover, and I had nothing but a mere body of horse and dragooners with me, I made a faire retreate to Basingstoke."

This affair is thus recorded by Capt. Symonds, who was then with the King's Army, "Friday, 18 Oct., 1644. His Majestie, &c. left Sarum and marched towards Andevor, Generall Goringe raysed a forlorne of horse, consisting of about 200 gentlemen, who were spare commanders of horse, beate them out of Andevor, took Carr, a Scot colonell, and another captain, a Scott, that died, who a little before his death rose from under the table, saying he would not dye like a dog under a table, but sate downe upon a chayre, and ymediatly dyed of his wounds. Tooke about 80 prisoners, followed the chase of them two miles, who all ran in great confusion. Had not night come so soone, it might have been made an end of Waller's army, for our intention was to engage them, but they disappointed our hopes by their heeles." *

On the 14th of October, Lieut.-General Oliver Cromwell, who had been in the neighbourhood of Banbury, and present at the latter part of the siege with a detachment of horse, joined at Reading the army of the Earl of Manchester, who for more than a fortnight had been lying idle there, finding excuse after excuse for not marching further west. On the 16th, the Earl, after a consultation with Waller, marched from Reading to Basingstoke; and on the 21st his forces, united with those of Essex and Waller, near Basing, consisted of about 11,000 foot and 8,000 horse and dragoons.† Such a force, both in respect of numbers and composition, had not as yet been formed under one leader since the commencement of the war. To the chief command of this army, magnificent for the period, the Earl of Manchester, in the absence of the Earl of Essex, was nominated. Cromwell retained as before the rank of General of Horse. The whole, wound up to the highest pitch of enthusiasm, prepared to advance against the King.

The Derby-House Committee had by this time sent two of their number, namely the Scottish representative, Sir Archibald Johnston, of Warriston, and the English, Mr. John Crewe, to see that all possible advantages should be taken against the enemy, and to prevent any contention between the chief officers as to the command, and other matters. These two civilians met Manchester at Basingstoke.

At this time a difference of opinion existed in the Parliamentary camp as to the best course of action. Cromwell and

---

* Symonds' "Diary," p. 141.

† "That after this conjunction, wee being at Basing, neare 11,000 foote and about 8,000 horse and dragoones, and the King with not above 10,000 horse and foote." Cromwell's evidence from the "Information against the Earl of Manchester;" Public Record Office.

some of the other generals urged a direct interception of the royal army; but Manchester, who seemed disposed to give the King every chance, resolved to march back to Reading, with the object (as he states in his defence) of making the attack from the north, or left bank of the Kennet. Cromwell's evidence partly bears out this view:—"On Tuesday, 22nd Oct., it being agreed (as we thought) to march towards him [the King] or to interpose betwixt him and Redding, about Aldermaston Heath, and our horse marching before to the heath, our foot struck down to Swallowfield, and thence next day to Redding, as if we had declined to fight, and thus making fower days march from Basingstoke to Newbery (which might have been little more than one t'other way), wee gave the King opportunity to have got cleare to Oxford (if hee would) without fighting; and, staying there, he had thereby time to fortify himself against our approaches to Newberry.*

The Earl of Manchester further states in his "Narrative of the Campaign:" "For the subsistence of the armies at Basingstoke it was concluded to march to Redding, and so come uppon the other side of the Kennet uppon the enemy, and to forse the King to fight, notwithstanding the enemy being in their strengthe. My Lord of Essex beeing in Redding leaft sicke."

Nor were the Royalists at all clear as to the strength and intentions of the Parliamentarians, as the following extract from a letter to Prince Rupert from Lord Digby shews:—"Wee may promise ourselves a very happy conclusion of this summer's warre, for now we know the worst of the Rebells forces. Essex, Manchester, and Waller, and the Trained Bands newly come out of London, were all joyned yesterday, and by all intelligence of those who hath seen them at their rendezvous do not muster in all [cypher] foot and [......] horse, of which the only considerable ones are Cromwell's. His Majesty, over and above what your Highness knows of, hath [here the forces are enumerated in cypher]. It seems the Rebells begin to apprehend themselves too weake to encounter us, for our intelligence this morning is that they have retreated to Reading. Believe it is for their feares, and the distractions in London are soe great, in all probabilitie it will be fatall to them. Yours, &c., GEO. DIGBYE. Newbery, 23 Oct. 1644."†

The easy success of the King's army in the affair with Waller at Andover so raised the spirits of his troops that they were eager to engage the combined forces of the Parliament; but, as Clarendon sagely remarks, "The King did not wisely seek the opportunity." It was, however, resolved to attempt the relief of

---

* Cromwell's Evidence, from the "Information against the Earl of Manchester." State Papers; Public Record Office.
† Addl. MSS. Brit. Mus., No. 18980.

the closely besieged garrisons of Donnington Castle, Basing, and Banbury before going into quarters at Oxford for the winter; and, for this purpose, orders were dispatched for the guns and baggage, which had been left at Langford and Wilton, to be at once sent forward.

On Saturday the 19th of October, the King advanced from Andover to Whitchurch, where he was to remain until his General Lord Brentford, who was behind, and the Earl of Cleveland, who had been detained with the siege of Portland, should come up with the remainder of his force. On Sunday, a party of horse was dispatched to relieve Donnington Castle; and returned the next morning. On Monday night, Oct. 21, 1644, a spy in the service in the Parliament returned to the camp with the following intelligence:—"His Majesty's army was in Whitchurch all Sunday night; and that town was full of soldiers, both horse and foot, but their train of artillery was not there, only some few wagons belonging to Officers. That their train stood on Andover downes, within two miles of Whitchurch or thereabouts. The King was last night [Sunday] at Whitchurch, but by some reported to be at Winchester, and by others at Andover. The last night, about 8 of the clock, went out about 4000 horse out of Whitchurch to give an alarm, and returned this morning about break of day. [This was the party which was sent to relieve Donnington Castle.] Yesterday it was ordered that the train should be drawn up to Whitchurch Downes, but was hindered by the wet weather, and so staid two miles short. And that this day [Monday] the rendezvous was to be kept upon Sevenborough [Seven Barrows]: the drums beat up at Whitchurch at break of day. This day about 8 o'clock there stood at Whitclear [? Whitway or Highclere] a great body of horse, as he conceiveth to be 2,000, on this side Sevenborough. That about 12 o'clock there were going to Kingsclere some empty carts, accompanied with some troops of horse, which carts be supposed were to carry provisions that were summoned to be brought to Donnington Castle. [These apparently were the empty carts returning from the Castle.] That it is generally reported the King quarters at Donnington the next night. Carriages were warned at Bawgus [Baughurst] and the parishes adjacent, to appear this morning at Whitchurch. From Newbury, that great provisions of victuals are made, and all towns adjoining, for the army, which is expected there this night. That a great party from Oxford and Wallingford is to be there to meet the King's forces this night." *

On Monday, the 21st October, the whole army moved on to Kingsclere, which, being mid-way between Basing and Newbury, was considered a suitable position from which to attempt the

* "The Parliamentary Scout," 24 to 31 Oct. 1644.

relief of the former place. This position having been found too much exposed for an army threatened by an enemy so much superior in cavalry, the embarrassed royalists, after a night's halt, proceeded on their march to Newbury; a general rendezvous being appointed on Red Heath, on the south side of the town, the head-quarters of the horse being in the town of Newbury, with an advanced post on the Lambourn at Welford.* On the King's arrival at the camp on Red Heath, he was welcomed by the brave Governor of Donnington Castle, Col. Boys, who received the honour of knighthood from his Majesty for his valiant defence of Donnington, and was made Colonel of the regiment which he had before commanded as Lieut.-Col. to Earl Rivers, who was nominally the chief governor of the Castle.

A messenger having brought to the King at Newbury intelligence of the exhausted condition of the garrison at Banbury, Lord Northampton was dispatched on Thursday, 24th Oct., from the camp with 1500 horse for the relief of Banbury Castle, which for thirteen weeks had been gallantly defended by the Earl's brother, Sir William Compton. That night he quartered at Farnborough, and the next day near Woodstock, where the Earl was joined by Col. Gage with a regiment of foot and some horse from Oxford. Thence the united force advanced to Banbury, routed Col. Fiennes, and raised the siege. Thus the relief of Banbury was successfully accomplished. The very day after this service had been so well performed, however, Col. Sir John Hurry, who has been previously mentioned as a renegade, seized the opportunity to consummate a second act of treachery. Under pretence of retiring to the Continent, he obtained leave to withdraw from the royal army (in which it is probable he considered his services not sufficiently valued); and, availing himself of his pass, hastened to the Earl of Manchester's army and betrayed the unprovided condition and diminished numbers of the King. The immediate consequence of this intelligence was the Second Battle of Newbury.

Returning to Donnington Castle.—After the departure of Middleton, Colonel Horton (Lt.-Col. of Lord Wharton's regiment), who is described as Adjutant-General to Major-General Brown, was left to blockade the castle. Having effectually guarded all the avenues leading to the stout little stronghold, so that no succour could get to its relief, he summoned Boys to surrender, but met with defiance. Accordingly, having received reinforcements from Abingdon, Windsor, and Reading, he commenced to lay close siege to the Castle, and raised a battery "at the foot of the hill towards Newbury."† In a twelve days' cannonade he

---

* "The manor belonging to Mr. Hinton *jure uxoris;* a faire habitacion, com. Berks." Symonds' 'Diary,' p. 143.
† Traces of this battery can still be discerned iA the meadows on the south side of the road leading from Donnington to Speen. It is shown on the Plan.

beat down three of the south towers and part of the curtain-wall. Having received another contingent, Horton then summoned the Castle a second time, in the following terms:—"Sir, We have formerly testified our clemency in tendring you quarter upon your surrender of the Castle for the use of the King and Parliament, and now again we, being desirous (notwithstanding our increase of powers) to manifest our mercy, do hereby once for all freely offer yourself and men free quarter in case you yield the Castle, for the use aforesaid, before Wednesday next at 10 of the clock in the forenoon, and further we here testifie (in the presence of God) that if this our favour be not accepted and the Castle surrendered, there shall be no active man amongst you have his life, if God shall ever please to yield them to our mercy. Yours, JEREMY HORTON." To which Col. Boys replied:—"Sir, Neither your new addition of forces, nor your high threatning language, shall deter me, or the rest of these honest men with me, from our loyalty to our sovereign, but we do resolve to maintain this place to the uttermost of our powers, and for the matter of quarter, yours may expect the like on Wednesday or sooner if you please. This is the answer of, Sir, Your servant, JNO. BOYS."

Upon this second denial, Manchester himself came to Newbury on Friday, October 4th, and, getting another refusal, resolved to storm the castle on Wednesday, October 9th; but his men not being willing for the work, the proposed assault was abandoned, and Manchester returned to Reading, giving orders, however, for the siege to be continued. This was conducted with ordnance of a fairly heavy calibre. Symonds, in his "Diary," thus refers to the garrison at this time:—"The men within the Castle were the Earl of Rivers' regiment, about 200 [foot] and 25 horse, 4 peices of cannon. The enemy made a great open battery, with their hundreds of 36lb bullets, *toto* a 500 and odd bullets, most of them 36lb., some 6lb, some 12lb." Doubtless there were other guns used by besiegers and the besieged; and it may be interesting here to give some particulars as to the capacity of the Artillery at this period,* thus—

	Bore.	Weight.	Weight of Shot.	Point-blank range.	Extreme range.
	In.	Lbs.	Lbs.	Paces.	Paces.
Cannon Royal	8½	8000	66	800	1930
Culverin	5½	4500	17½	200	2500
Demi-culverin	4	3400	9½	200	2500
Saker	4	—	7	170	1700
Minion	3¼	1000	4	150	1500
Drakes	Carried a ball from 4 to 6 lb., and were used as light field-artillery.				

* See Monson's "Tracts," p. 342.

EDWARD MONTAGU, EARL OF MANCHESTER.

There were also guns termed "Basilisks" after that mythic creature; they were 48-pounders. Such a one is called "a warning piece" in Vicars' account of the siege of Bristol. "Falcons" with 6lb. shots, and "Falconets" with 3, 2, and 1lb.; "Peteraroes" for throwing stones, &c.

The day after Manchester's departure the besiegers removed their guns "to the other side of the Castle," that is, to Snelsmore Heath. Here the trenches constructed by the Parliamentarians are still very distinctly traceable, as shown on the Plan. The line of fire from this position was somewhat oblique; and this to some extent accounts for the preservation of the towers of the Gate-house. An attempt was made to approach the walls by saps;* but, this being perceived by Boys, the garrison made a sortie, and beat the enemy out of their trenches, killing the chief in command of the party and many soldiers: and they brought away the "cannon-baskets," with a large quantity of arms and ammunition. Though much disheartened, the Parliament-men went on with their approaches, and continued bombarding the Castle until Friday, 18th October; and then, hearing of the advance of the King's army, they drew off their ordnance and retired. In nineteen days (12 at Speen and 7 at Snelsmore) they had spent over 1000 rounds on the impregnable little castle with very little hurt to its defenders. Horton and his men retired towards Abingdon, and the Windsor force to Newbury; while Manchester's detachment fell back on Reading. The "Mercurius Aulicus" of Oct. 15th, 1644, contains some curious information as to the siege and defence of the Castle. The following is an extract:—" Such was Col. Horton's great mercy that the day before the Governor and his men were to dye (in case they did not surrender) they sent Master Fogge, Horton's Chaplain, with a letter which Fogge had procured from Mistris Fleetwood, in Newbury, to her husband, Dr. Fleetwood,† Chaplain to Earl Rivers' regiment (to whom Col. Boys is Lt.-Col.), and this letter Fogge brought to Dr. Fleetwood in the Castle, wherein Mistris Fleetwood wrote—' that if the Castle did refuse Col. Horton's mercy, they were all lost men,' and therefore desired her husband and the rest to prepare themselves (and indeed so

---

* Saps, that is, trenches made under cover from the fire of the enemy's place, behind a mantelet or stuffed gabion. Mantelets on wheels were used during the Civil War.

† Dr. James Fleetwood, son of Sir George Fleetwood, was made D.D., in 1642, at Oxford by the King's special command for the good services he had done him at the battle of Edgehill. Upon the Restoration he was the first person that was sworn Chaplain-in-Ordinary to Charles II.; when he was also made Provost of King's College, Rector of Anstey in Hertfordshire, and of Denham in Bucks. In 1675, he was consecrated Bishop of Worcester. He died in 1683, in the eighty-first year of his age.

There was a James Fleetwood, S.T.P., Rector of Shaw, near Newbury, shortly after the Restoration, which liviug he resigned in March 1660-61. It is highly probable that this is the person referred to in the "Mercurius Aulicus."

they did, to shew themselves gallant men). This letter, you must know, the poor gentlewoman was forced to write to her husband, tho' Fogge had the wording of it, and to make the pageantry more complete, Col. Horton pretends a great unwillingness to let any such letter passe into the Castle, and therefore sends this note to Fogge, on purpose also to be communicated:—'Mr. Fogge, At the earnest sute of Mrs. Fleetwood I am instructed to permit the passage of this letter into the Castle by your hands, hereby requiring you to testifie to all therein (if the Governor will permit it) that if they please to come forth before tomorrow at 9 o'clock in the forenoon they may have faire quarter, otherwise according to my solemn vow they may expect no favour. JEREMY HORTON.' This poor preaching was easily discerned by Col. Boys, who read it and scorned it." The "Mercurius Aulicus" adds, that "Manchester also gave orders to an unfortunate brother of Col. Boys (who was a Captain in Manchester's army) to write to the Governor, to assure him that, if he would surrender the Castle, he should not only have all honourable conditions, but freely be admitted to his house, and possess his estate quietly, in Kent;* and, if he would come forth and capitulate, he should do it safely; if not, [to demand] that his brother might be permitted to come to him into the castle, to inform him further of his Lordship's intention. To whom the Governor made answer;—That neither the Earl of Manchester and all his forces should deter him from his fidelity and loyalty to his Sovereign, neither would he entertain any manner of parley concerning the delivery up of the place, which he was resolved to maintain to his last drop of blood."

A letter, written by Chaplain Fogge, † respecting the siege, is given in the "London Post" of Oct. 23rd, 1644. It is to this effect:—"Sir, These are to certifie to you that Sir Miles Hobart's regiment is here at Newbery, where we had almost

---

* Sir John Boy's estate was at Bonnington in Kent: it was seized and sequestrated by the Parliament.

† When Prince Rupert took Bolton, and put so many to the sword, the Rev. Robert Fogge had a narrow escape. Having set his man to wait with two horses at a certain place, he determined, if the town was taken, to ride for his life; but when he came thither, the man and his horses were gone. He happened, however, to meet with another horse; or else he would have been killed, for the Prince had a particular aim at him. In the war-time he married his second wife, who proved to be a papist. Her sons were in the King's service, and much enraged against their father-in-law. One of them sent him a challenge. He took his sword under his coat and met him, and so humbled the young man that he was glad to be reconciled. Fogge died at Nantwich in April, 1676, aged 80. (Palmer's "Nonconformists' Memorial," vol. ii, p. 604.) Fogge's son Rowland subscribed to the Declaration in 1665, and ultimately became Dean of Chester. One of the Rev. Mr. Fogge's family, a certain Captain Fogge, directed the plundering of St. George's Chapel, Windsor. The numerous gold vessels, which the munificence and piety of successive Sovereigns and Knights-of-the-Garter had here consecrated to religious uses, were said to have been exquisitely wrought and to have weighed 3580 ounces.

brought Donnington Castle down to the ground by the active endeavours of General-Adjutant Colonell Horton. But Lieut.-Gen. Brown called him and his force away, and the gunnes are taken off and carried to Reading, and here is only one regiment and some of Col. Montague's, and 2 or 3 troops of horse; yet we keep them in the Castle, and if we might have gunnes and furniture, I would undertake we could have the Castle in a week. * * * The town of Newbery and the country adjacent cry out they must fall if we go and let the Castle stand. I wish the Committee were well informed concerning it. I dare say it is a place of such consequence as they would not lose the opportunity to gayne it, considering it is sore battered, and one breach in it that many may enter abreast. Truely two or three fire-balls or granadoes shot into it would make it ours. The Lord guide the state and be with you and us all.* Yr humble servt., R. F." [Robert Fogge].

Before proceeding further, it will be necessary to give an outline of the position of the royal army on the morning of Saturday, the 26th of October. The Royalist strength is said by the "True Informer" of Oct. 26, to have been about 13,000, "whereof 7000 foot are most of them very poore for want of cloaths, which is provided for them, but are not used for fear they should run away, or should be lost in battle." The King despised his late antagonist, Waller; and, having little apprehension of an attack, was ignorant of the strength of the enemy gathering around him. He remained quietly at Newbury, resolving to await the Earl of Northampton's return from Banbury, in order to relieve Basing. But the Earl's absence together with that of the troops under Prince Rupert, who was detained at Bristol endeavouring to raise a sufficient force to come to the King's assistance frustrated this plan. Upon the near approach of the Parliamentary army, the King, finding it too late to attempt a retreat to Oxford, was compelled to fight, contrary to his promise and inclination. He determined, however, as in the former action, to act only on the defensive. On Friday, 25th October, he therefore drew his army into "the fields between Donnington Castle and Newbury," thinking it wisest to await an attack, and to try the issue of a general action, on ground of his own selection; his judgment in this instance being seconded by an intimate knowledge of a locality where the year before he had met the same enemy. It is not difficult to fix the position occupied by the Royal army at this time. (See Plan.) The fields above-mentioned were the scene of the principal part of the fighting after the Royalists were subsequently driven from Speen Hill. They extend on the West to the old highway from

---

* This letter is given in Col. Columb's admirable little book, "Donnington Castle; a Royalist Story," p. 141.

R

Hungerford, now called "the Backway," on the North to the River Lamborne, and on the South to the hamlet of Speenhamland. The general appearance of the neighbourhood has been much changed since the period of the Battle. In maps of the seventeenth century the old gabled houses in the Broadway appear quite in the fields. A house still standing in the present London Road is said to have been the Manor-house; and in the old maps an avenue of trees is shown leading up to it from the direction of the Marsh. A range of buildings near, erected on the site of the Lamb-and-Castle Yard, marks the traditional birth-place of the famous Dr. Twisse. Newbury Marsh, opposite, is quite open to the old London Road, which, going somewhat northward, passed Shaw brick-kiln, and joined the old, or lower road to Thatcham. The original road from Shaw House to Newbury, it is said, ran to to the west of the present fish-pond, and entered Speenhamland near the block of houses which once formed a well-known coaching Inn,the " King's Arms."

In the last week of October, the Royalists occupied a formidable position in and about the town of Newbury, protected on one flank by the River Kennet, and in some degree covered by the guns of Donnington Castle on the other. They strengthened their front with breastworks and entrenchments, and occupied in force several houses and gardens, which extended conveniently beyond the town. One house in particular (Shaw House), the residence of Sir Thomas Dolman, stood in a most convenient situation, a little in advance of the chief breastwork. In addition to this, there was a row of smaller houses * to the east of the present Rectory, which were turned to the best advantage for the purposes of defence. All these, as well as the gardens of Shaw House, which they strengthened by thick embankments, were filled with troops, under the command of Sir Richard Page. At every window, battlement, and parapet, musquet and pike were ready for service; all the hedges and ditches swarmed with skirmishers; and every convenient mound was surmounted with one or more pieces of artillery. Sir Jacob Astley and Lt.-Col. Lisle kept the passage of the Lamborne at Shaw. Sir Thomas Hooper and Sir John Brown were placed with a strong body of horse and foot in the fields by the little hill on which the Water-tower now stands; around it a work was cast up, and they occupied this as well as the hedges and lane (Long Lane), and the old orchard above it. Colonel Thelwall, with his Reading brigade, held the gardens, and formed the reserve. Sir Bernard Astley's troops lay around an entrenched house in the park at Shaw, "between Shaw and Newbury."† Every house in the

---

* These houses, called the " Hop Gardens," were removed some years ago, and several cannon balls were found imbedded in the roofs.

† This entrenched house formerly stood at the south-east ar gle of Shaw Park: but was pulled down many years since. Considerable remains of the earthworks still exist in its vicinity, and are marked on the Plan.

village of Shaw was occupied and fortified by the Royalists. In one respect alone, however, and that a very essential point, their line on this side was weak. A hill (Clay Hill and the adjacent elevated ground), little more than a musquet-shot in their front, offered to an assailant every facility for the secure and undiscovered formation of columns of attack; and the result of the coming action proved that against that solitary defect in his position, all the other advantages possessed by the King could not avail.

Prince Maurice, with his brigade of Cornish horse and two brigades of foot and artillery, was posted in the village of Speen below Speen Hill. On the heath above Speen Hill hastily constructed works had been thrown up by the Royalists; and here were stationed part of the Cornish foot and the Duke of York's regiment, commanded by Sir Wm. St. Leger, with five pieces of artillery. The ground on which the King's left thus rested is evident enough at the present day, though the name of "Speen Hill" has been in later times wrongly applied to the well-known suburb between Newbury and the village of Speen. Speen Hill proper, the eminence referred to in the various narratives of the Battle, is the hill rising from the village of Speen towards Benham Park. The heath above Speen Hill, a portion of which remains still uncultivated, at that time extended over the now enclosed fields for some distance; on the west it skirted the Roman road from Speen to Cirencester by way of Wickham and Baydon, and on the south the present Bath Road. Sir Edward Walker thus refers to it—"At the entrance of the Heath, between two hedges we cast up a work which cleared the Heath and all the fields to the North even to the river [Lamborne]; to the South, within the hedge, there was one narrow field, and from thence a perpendicular descent into a Marish [Speen Moor] between that and the River Kennet. This was our position, wherein, had the traverse been finished and made down to the Marish, altho' we were inferior in number, yet we should have sufficiently provided to have withstood their force."* Mid-way between Newbury and Speen, Sir Humphrey Bennett's brigade of horse was drawn up. Lastly †

---

* Sir Edward Walker's "Hist. Discourses," p. 111.

† Sir Humphrey Bennet's Brigade of Horse consisted of the undermentioned Regiments. Symonds's Notes, Harl. MSS, No. 986.
  1. Reg. Col. ...... Bennet, High-Sheriff of South^{n.} had 9 troops in the field, almost full, but [only] 2 colo^{rs.} [colours].
     Lieut.-Col. ...... Verney, son to Sir Edm. V., who was slayne at Edghill.
     Sr. Major Richard Aldworth.
     Capt. Mr. Robt. Smyth, brother to Colonel Smyth, who was taken prisoner, wth Sr Alex. Denton, at Hilsden Howse, Com. Buck.
  2. Reg. Sr. Geo. Vaughan, Colonel, }
     Sr. Robt. Welsh, Lieut.-Colonel, } 80.
     but [only] 2 Troopes. }

the King, with the main body of the horse and artillery, was stationed in the fields between Donnington Castle and Newbury; and this was nearly the centre of his position.

Strong guards were placed on the south of the town, and detachments of horse guarded the outlying passages of the Lamborne at Bagnor and Boxford to check any advance upon the fords. Owing however to the want of a sufficient strength of cavalry, diminished by the loss of three of his best regiments which had been despatched to Banbury, the King was at this time overmatched in his favourite and usually most serviceable arm. He also had no effective reserve to support the scattered infantry, and was thus deprived both of the power of checking hostile reconnoitring parties and of obtaining intelligence of his opponent's movements.

It will be well here to give in more detail the circumstances that affected the relative position of the two armies at this time, and led to the important results of their active opposition.

The Parliamentarians, after a tedious and circuitous march, had returned to Reading, where Essex (who on Tuesday night, Oct. 22, with the Earl of Manchester, lay at Sir John Backhouse's, at Swallowfield) remained alone, despondent and inactive. Informed of this, Parliament charged a joint-committee to wait on him, and renew the assurance of its trusting affection. Essex thanked the Committee, but did not join the army, feeling that since the relief of Gloucester the day of his triumphs was over.*

Manchester, with Waller and Cromwell, again set out to meet the King, and by the 23rd of October had advanced as far as Aldermaston. There they quartered in Sir Humphrey Forster's park † until Thursday evening, when they crossed the Kennet at Padworth, and next morning (Friday 25th) halted on

---

* Whitelock's Memorials, p. 103.

† Sir Humphrey Forster's estates were sequestrated by the Parliament; and on his proposition to compound, Sir Humphrey pleads that his estate lies in the King's quarters, and is subject to every motion and change of the war, and hath been equally possessed by both sides, whereupon all the stock is taken away, the walls of the park and the fences broken, and damage done by the soldiers to the value of £8000: that his children have been in want and himself hath subsisted ever since by borrowing. That he has a family of 9 children, and his eldest son, who has been a Captain in the Parliamentary service, has a considerable amount of pay not yet paid to him. Sir Humphrey concludes by stating that he has voluntarily taken the covenant, and found six men for the defence of Reading. (State Papers; Dom. Series, Pub. Rec. Office.) In a petition to the Parliament from Lady Anne, wife of Sir Humphrey Forster, dated April 17, 1645, she states that, on account of Sir Humphrey's harsh treatment, she has long lived at a distance from him, and that when he became a delinquent the Committee for sequestrations made several orders for petitioner's maintenance out of his estates, and on the 21st March last, after full hearing, ordered that she should enjoy the fifth part of his goods and estates. She prays that in the ordinance for clearing him of his delinquency a special proviso may be inserted, securing her a fifth part of his estate, as formerly ordered, or that some other provision may be made for her maintenance. The proviso was ordered to be inserted. (The Lords' Journal, VII, pp. 384 and 420.)

Bucklebury Heath, having with them three days' provisions. At mid-day they appeared in the fields between Thatcham and Shaw, on the east side of Newbury, where some sharp encounters soon ensued between advanced parties of the Parliamentary horse and the cavalry outposts of the Royalists, but without serious loss on either side. On the following day the two Parliamentary Commissioners wrote from Thatcham to the Derby-House Committee to the following effect. "My Lords and Gentlemen. Yesterday upon Bucklebury Heath wee received your letter, which gave us hope that the army will shortly receive the provisions which you have sent. The newes of Newcastle came very seasonably to us, which much encouraged the souldiers, and so affected them that many of the regiments went presently of their own accord to solemn prayer. The army about an hower before night came within a myle and within view of the enemy, who was drawne forth in a body in a place of advantage neere Newbery. Our dragoones and theirs fired upon one another for two howers, twenty of our horses were killed, but not one of our men lost. A captain of our horse, who came up in the vann, was shott in the thigh, six o'clock in the evening. It was resolved last night that the field should be viewed by the chiefe officers early this morning. It will be an advantage to us to set upon his army on this side Newbery, because wee shall be betwixt the enemy and our provisions; and to fall upon him on the other side, because we shall be betwixt the enemy and Prince Rupert, who is dayly expected with additional forces, the ground not having been viewed they could determine nothing herein. Being informed by those that came from London that they met many souldiers going homewards, wee renew our desire that some exemplary punishment may be inflicted upon them. Wee remaine, your Lops. humble servants, W. JHONSTON, JO. CREWE. Wee have had a faire night (blessed be God), and hope for a faire day."* During the night of the 25th the detached parties of the King's troops were withdrawn; and the enemy were left in the advantageous possession of the heights above Shaw House.

The site of the Parliamentary Camp was on an extensive tract of elevated table-land, stretching from Clay Hill for a considerable distance towards Ashmore Green and Cold-Ash Common. It is now called, from the gravelly character of the land, "The Stones." Skirting this plateau on the west, is an escarpment, which forms a continuous natural rampart, in some places so well defined as to have the appearance of an artificial work. The meadows below the southern edge are now known as "Runaways." Donnington Castle stands out boldly in front of the camping ground. On Clay Hill, near "Red Field," is still to be seen part of an

---

* Letter-book, Derby-Ho. Com., No. 57; Public-Record Office.

extensive entrenchment or breastwork, which helped to defend the Parliamentary front. It is about 12 feet wide, by 8 feet deep, and originally extended along that face of the hill which has since been to a great extent removed in the process of digging clay. The ditch has been partially filled in; and the workmen in removing the earth have found many cannon-balls, bullets, and other relics of warfare, including scores of the well-known tobacco-pipes of the Caroline period. Wood-ashes have also been found in heaps beneath the surface in many parts of the higher ground, indicating the remains of the camp-fires around which the soldiers of the Parliament bivouacked.

When it was known in London that the two armies were at last in the presence of each other, the shops were closed, the people rushed to the churches, and a solemn fast was ordained, to seek the blessing of the Lord on the coming battle.*

The King in the absence of Prince Rupert, again led his own army, assisted by his nephew Prince Maurice, the old Earl of Brentford acting as Lieutenant-General, and Lord Goring being in command of the horse. Amongst his Majesty's more prominent supporters present in the engagement were:—The Duke of Richmond and Lennox, the Earls of Cleveland, Lindsey, Newport, Berkshire, Rivers; Lords Hopton, Capel, Colepepper, Bellasis, Digby, Herbert, Bernard Stuart; Sir Jacob Astley, Sir Bernard Astley, Sir Wm. Bronkard, Sir Wm. Ashburnham, Sir Edward Walker, Sir Wm. St. Leger, Sir Anthony St. Leger, Sir John Campsfield, Sir Richard Page, Sir John Owen, Sir Thomas Hooper, Sir George Lisle, Sir John Brown, Sir John Grenville, Sir Humphrey Benett, Sir Henry Gage, Sir Richard Lane, Sir Thomas Bassett, Sir Joseph Wagstaffe, Sir Charles Lloyd; Colonels Gerard, Markham, Leke, Topping, Thornhill, Thelwall, Legge, Fielding, Hamilton, Bovel.

The Parliament on this occasion was represented by many of its most eminent and foremost leaders. Among those whose names have been more prominently handed down to us as associated with this action and its concurrent incidents may be mentioned the following:—The Earl of Manchester, Sir William Waller, Sir William Balfour, Sir Arthur Hesilrige, Sir James Harrington, Sir John Hurry (who has now changed sides) Major-General Crawford, Major-General Skippon, Major-General Holbourne, Lieut.-General Oliver Cromwell, Lieut.-General Middleton, Lieut.-General Ludlow, and Colonels Bartley, Norton, Ingoldsby, Birch, Hooper, Jones.

The early morning of Saturday, 26 October, was devoted by the Parliamentarians to the pushing of a reconnaisance. This the Royalists endeavoured to interrupt by sending out clouds of musketeers to skirmish. Both parties kept up a smart can-

---

* Rushworth, Historical Collections, II. 3, 719—720.

nonade: the Parliamentarians from a battery which they had established on the summit of Clay Hill; the Cavaliers from the lower ground in the vicinity of the town. For some time the firing produced little effect on either side, but towards evening the Royalists brought two of their guns round to the south of the River Lamborne, at Woodspeen; and these they so planted as to enfilade the enemy's line as far as a bend on Red Field exposed it. A regiment of cavalry in particular, commanded by Col. Ludlow, which was on the slopes towards the Lamborne suffered severely, and was compelled to shift its ground. Ludlow's cousin Gabriel Ludlow, who had distinguished himself at Wardour Castle, here received his death-wound.

This incident on Red Field is thus related by Ludlow:*—"My Regiment being that day on the Guard, received the greatest Damage; amongst others my Cousin Gabriel Ludlow, who was a Cornet therein, and who had behaved himself so well in the Defence of Warder-Castle, was killed: He died not immediately after he was shot; so that having caused him to be removed out of the reach of their Guns, and procured a Chirurgeon to search his wounds, he found his Belly broken, and Bowels torn, his Hip-bone broken all to shivers, and the Bullet lodged in it; notwithstanding which he recovered some sense, tho the Chirurgeon refused to dress him, looking on him as a dead Man. This Accident troubled me exceedingly; he being one who had expressed great Affection to me, and of whom I had great hopes that he would be useful to the Publick. In this condition he desired me to kiss him, and I not presently doing it, thinking he had talked lightly, he pressed me again to do him that favour; whereby observing him to be sensible, I kissed him: and soon after having recommended his Mother, Brothers, and Sisters to my Care, he died."

Finding the King so strongly placed, protected by Donnington Castle, the Kennet, and the Lamborne, the Parliamentary generals held a Council of War on Red Field. It was then resolved to divide their force into two columns. Waller and Cromwell, with all the horse and foot which had lately been under the leadership of Essex, and four regiments of Trained Bands, under Skippon (one regiment had been left in garrison at Reading), were to make a flank march, and attack the Royalists' position on Speen Hill; while Manchester and Crawford with about 3000 foot, and a body of 1500 or 1800 horse under Ludlow, made a demonstration from the hill at Shaw. It was further agreed, that, as soon as the latter body should, by hearing the discharge of cannon, understand that their comrades at Speen Hill were engaged, Manchester should force the passage at Shaw; and thus, if both sides succeeded, they would completely encompass the King and

---

* Memoirs of Ludlow, vol. i, pp. 129-130.

have him at their mercy. The attention of the enemy was meanwhile to be diverted from the main body of the Parliamentarians while making the flank march, by continuous attacks on their position at Shaw, until the signal was given from the Speen side for the main blow to be struck.

These matters are thus referred to in the documents of the period. In Cromwell's "Evidence"* it is stated that "On Saturday, October 26, when we came up to Redhill Feild, within shot of Shawe, and found the passes of the river soe possest against us, it was agreed that the Lord-General's and the City foote, with the greatest part of the horse, should march about by Boxford and attempt to breake in upon the enemy on that side by Speene, and that his Lordship, with his owne foote and about 1500 horse, should stay behind at Shawe side, and fall on there at the same instant that he should perceive the other part to fall on at Speene (which was already in his viewe)."

The news of a body of Parliamentarians being on their march to Speen Hill appears to have been brought to Lord Digby at Newbury on the Sunday morning;† but, owing to the numerical weakness of his army, it was not possible for the King (who had from the first determined to stand on the defensive), to dispatch at that time a force to oppose Waller's march, and at the same time to keep Manchester (whose numbers had been over-estimated) in check at Shaw. It seems, however, somewhat surprising that notice was not given to the Royalists at Speen of Waller's march. Clarendon states that they were taken unawares. The King had, indeed, sent a body of troops, about 500 in number, under Sir John Douglas, to guard the pass of the River Lamborne at Boxford; where they made but a feeble resistance when the enemy appeared in such superior numbers.

Acting on the decision of the Council of War, on Saturday evening the right wing of the Army of the Parliament, under Waller and Cromwell, began their march towards Speen Hill, the route taken being apparently by the old Bucklebury road, and Cold-Ash, to the Hermitage road, thence by Prior's Court and through the village of Chieveley to North Heath, where they halted for the night.‡ Early next morning (Sunday) they were on the move; and, marching as rapidly as the heavy and hilly

---

* From the Information against the Earl of Manchester; State Papers, Public Record Office.

† In an original letter from Lord Digby to Prince Rupert, dated Newbury, 27 Oct., Addl. MSS., Brit. Mus., No. 18980. So also "They learn'd in the morning (Sunday) our greatest force was a-marching towards Spen Hill." "Narrative of the Earl of Manchester's Campaign;" State Papers; Publ. Rec. Off.

‡ "On Saturday the greater part of the Parliamentary forces retired to *Chieveley*, and quartered there that night in the open fields." Oldmixon, 'History of the Stuarts,' VI., p. 262.

roads would admit, by Winterbourne* church and woods, they passed the village of Boxford. Fording the River Lamborne at the latter place, as already noticed, they met with only slight opposition from the Royalist outpost here stationed to defend the passage. Crossing the Newbury-and-Wantage road, they proceeded by High-street Lane to Wickham Heath, which they gained at the cross-roads.

There is sufficient evidence in a letter from the two Parliamentary Commissioners, addressed to the Derby-House Committee,† to support this opinion as to the route taken. They state that "Yesterday the forces which went from Thatcham towards Newberry, by way of Wickam Heath and were there drawne up set upon a worke and breastworke, well-guarded with ordnance, horse, and foote, which commanded all the wayes which lead to that side of the field betwixt Newberry and Dennington Castle, where the King's army was drawne up."

They "passed the river," says Clarendon, "which was not well defended by the officer appointed to guard it, with horse and foot;" * * * But having thus got the river, they marched in good order, with very good bodies of foot winged with horse, towards the Heath." ‡

"About which time the Earl of Essex's forces [those recently under his command], all Waller's, and part of Manchester's horse, pursued their design of falling on the quarter at Speen, of which we had notice from Dennington, from whence their motion was discovered. And had Sir John Douglas actively opposed them (who was the day before sent with 300 horse and 200 foot beyond Dennington Castle to that end), they could not so easily have passed the river."§

The distance from North Heath to Speen Hill (the "Heath") is about 7 or 8 miles as traversed by the Parliamentarians: and this, considering the bad roads, was a fair four hours' march for such a large body of troops, who were not allowed to proceed altogether unmolested; for upon the high ground, they had been perceived by the garrison at Donnington Castle, and Sir John Boys had despatched a small body of horse to intercept them. These made a sharp attack on their rear; but, soon recovering from this slight interference, the Parliamentary Generals pushed on, and shortly approached the outworks of the Royalists; but it was nearly one o'clock before the artillery and the rear came up, and nearly three o'clock in the afternoon before the army was deployed for battle.

---

* "While the Cannon play'd from the Hill [Clay Hill] they drew the rest of their army through Winterbourne towards Boxford to have girt in His Majesty." "Mercurius Aulicus," Monday, 28 Oct., 1644.
† "Letter-Book, Derby-Ho. Com., No. 59, Pub. Rec. Off.
‡ Clarendon's Hist. II., p. 547.
§ Sir Edward Walker's "Hist. Discourses," p. 111.

Leaving Waller and Cromwell arranging the preliminaries of battle on Speen Hill, we will return for a moment to Manchester's force left on the hills at Shaw. As soon as it was daylight, on Sunday morning, which at this season (27th October) would be about seven o'clock, Manchester commenced the attack on the royalist post at Shaw, by despatching a body of 400 musqueteers to assault the entrenched position at the south-east angle of Shaw Park, crossing the Lamborne by a temporary bridge thrown over the river at the foot of Clay Hill the previous night.* They advanced at a quick pace over the meadows at what is now the back of Shaw Crescent, and favoured by the unevenness of the ground, and the haze of the early autumnal morning, were almost unperceived until they surprised the guard at the works covering the passage of the river and the house at Shaw. Without a moment's hesitation the Parliamentarians furiously assailed and mastered the party at the breastworks; but, their impetuosity carrying them too far, they were checked by a charge from the royal cavalry under Sir George Lisle and Sir Bernard Astley near Shaw House; and, being without adequate support, they were driven back with great loss. To add to their discomfiture in attempting to regain the temporary bridge and retreat on their main body, they came into collision with a reserve of their own men, who were tardily coming to their support; and in the mêlée many fell by the swords of the pursuing cavaliers, and numbers were drowned in the river in endeavouring to reach the opposite bank. In this the first onset about 40 prisoners and 100 stand of arms were taken by the royalists. This affair is thus alluded to by the contemporaries.— "My Lord of Manchester * * * commanded a party of 400 musqueteers to falle over the little river which passes by Dunington Castle, over a bridge, which most dextrously hee commanded the night before, to prepare for the diversion of the King's forces from goeing to Spen Hill, where they learned in the morneing our greatest force was a marching, which accordingly was done, and if those who weare commanded had not exceeded theire commission, [they] would have had greate victory; and as it was they tooke two workes from the enemy wherein they tooke a captayne and severall prisoners, and advanced too farr without order, and weare repulsed, to the greate greife of the Earle of Manchester."† "Sunday. as soone as day, they put over a tertia of foot over a bridge they made in the night, intending to surprize one of our guards. But that guard

---

* Near the Lamborne, as indicated on the Plan, where the Parliamentarians crossed the river in this attack, several skeletons were found some years ago. In Redfield, also, on the removal of a bank, about 40 years since, three skeletons were discovered lying side by side.

† "Narrative of the Earl of Manchester's compaign;" State Papers; Publ. Rec. Off.

retreated to the next; and joyned, fell upon them, being nothing considerable in number, made their two bodyes retreat, killed some, tooke about 40 prisoners and a 100 armes: then they lay quiet till 3 afternoone, onely our cannon and theirs playd."*
Again :—"Sunday, October 27. Some of Manchester's Forces and London Trained Bands† crossed the River Kennet [Lamborne] between the Hill and Newbury, and did some Execution on those who kept the Pass against them. But Sir Bernard Astley, coming to Rescue, forceth the other over the River."‡

After the unsuccessful attempt to pierce the Royalist line at Shaw, no further effort, with any vigour, was made by Manchester until the pre-concerted signal informed him that Waller's force had fallen on at Speen Hill. The interval until four o'clock was occupied by warm skirmishes between the two parties, accompanied by an active interchange of artillery fire. Manchester, busy with his preparations for advancing in force, rode to and fro, and spiritedly addressed his men, while his Chaplain, Simeon Ashe,§ offered up fervent prayers for their success.

The right wing of the Parliament Army, having successfully accomplished their flank march, are now on this Sunday morning, whilst the bells of the neighbouring churches are sounding for divine worship, preparing for the contest. Waller is in chief command; Sir William Balfour is to lead the right wing of horse; Lieut.-General Cromwell the left; Major-General Skippon, the foot. Their men are being rapidly placed in position on the high ground between the Wickham Road and Stockcross, overlooking on their right the Kennet Valley and the scene of their triumph the preceding year. At the same time, the Royal trumpets ring out "To arms!" The scattered troopers, many of whom, in fancied security, are engaged in foraging for their horses, gallop back to their comrades; but before their ranks are well formed a shout of revenge "for the business in Cornwall"‖ is heard along the Parliamentary line, the red, white, and blue colours are unfurled,¶ and the "forlorn hope" of 800 musqueteers

---

* Symonds's "Diary," p. 145.
† The greater part of the Trained Bands were with the right wing.
‡ Baker's "Chronicle," p. 579.
§ Simeon Ashe, Manchester's Chaplain, was author of "A True Relation," &c. Dr. Calamy speaks of him as a man of great sanctity, who went seasonably to heaven at the very time he was cast out of the church. He was buried on the eve of St. Bartholomew's day, 1662. Simeon fell under the obloquy of the Cromwellians: and he had a considerable share in the restoration of Charles II, whom he went to congratulate at Breda.
‖ It is said that the Cornishmen behaved with great inhumanity to the Parliament Soldiers who fell into their hands on the surrender of Lord Essex in Cornwall.
¶ "Col. Aldridge, blew colours with lyons rampant or. Col. Davies, white colours. Citty, London." Symonds's "Diary," p. 66. Col. Ingoldsby's colours were "gules, a scroll in three folds, its parts making two C's conjoined and endorsed, on which these words 'Pro Deo et Republica,' fringed sable with gules and argent." Prestwick's "Respublica," p. 36.

rush on with wild impatience. These were veterans who had lately served under their brave old leader Essex, and were now led by Lieut.-Col. Lloyd, with Hurry for his Major (nephew of the notorious renegade Colonel); they were supported by Colonel Aldridge's brigade, consisting of his own, Davies's, Fortescue's, and Ingoldsby's regiments. Essex's old regiment comes up as a support on the right (where the Trained Bands had already fallen on): sending in a hasty volley on the enemy and urged on by the excitement which prevails, they rush pellmell into the Royalists' entrenchments. A desperate fight succeeds; the blood of the Cavaliers is up; and, fighting hand to hand, they slaughter their assailants in heaps, as they mount the bank, and the ditch is filled with the dead and dying. Major Hurry, bravely leading the "forlorn-hope" (his colonel having already been struck down), falls mortally wounded. The gallant Col. Gawler, who has done good service for the Parliament in many a bloody field, drops lifeless from his horse, pierced by a royalist bullet. For a moment the enemy is repulsed; but determined to carry a position so necessary in effecting a junction with Manchester, he renews the attack. An hour's hard fighting succeeds; and then bringing all their energy to bear on this point, in the midst of a storm of shot from the gallant defenders, and from the guns at Donnington Castle,* the Parliamentary soldiers again come to the charge. Forward! is the word; and, despite the desperate resistance of the brave but outnumbered Royalists, they bear onward with a determination nothing can withstand. The King's troops at last give way. The Parliamentarian spurs are striking deep! And now again a stirring cheer rises from their ranks, and making a dash at the guns they had lost in Cornwall, now deserted by their late captors, who are flying at headlong speed down the hill, they clap their hats on the touch-holes, and embrace them with tears of joy.† The forces of Prince Maurice down in the village of Speen, unable to stand against the overwhelming numbers of the Parliament, stay the tide for a time, but at length yield to superior force, and, driven from their position to join in the retreat with the remnant from the Heath, they fall back discomfited on their horse and artillery in the fields "between Speen and Newbury," under the shelter of the Castle, and hastily endeavour to reform their broken ranks.

The Royalists are cleared from off the Heath. The guns ‡ lost at Lostwithiel, thus regained, are limbered up and sent to the rear,

---

* Letter from the Two Commissioners to the Derby-Ho. Committee, 27 Oct., 1644.

† Ludlow's "Memoirs," p. 130.

‡ "We tooke 9 good brass pieces, six of them being sakers, which we left behind in Cornwall." (Skippon's Letter to the Derby-Ho. Committee.) The other three guns were with Prince Maurice.

SIR WILLIAM WALLER.
From a portrait by CORNELIUS JANSEN.

together with those of Prince Maurice, which had been planted at the foot of tho hill. Waller now launches his cavalry in pursuit of the retreating enemy, and avenges in merciless slaughter the cause of the Parliament. Well might the Commissioners write "Wee desire to give God the glory of this victory, it being His worke and upon His day;"[*] while Waller exclaimed, like the Fifth Harry, in the fulness of his gratitude,

"O God, thy arm was here!
And not to us, but to Thy name alone,
Ascribe we all."

Great was the panic among the Cavaliers at this moment. They "threw down their arms, and ran away, crying 'Devils! Devils! They fight like Devils!' For ours gave no quarter to any they knew to be of the Cornish."[†] Following up this advantage, while Waller throws himself on the Royalists' rear in their retreat from Speen Hill, Sir William Balfour, with the right wing of horse, sweeps round under the hill, on the south side of Speen Church, skirting the Kennet, and, having gained "the large field" between Speen and Newbury, where the King, with the Prince of Wales and many of his attendants at that time stood, falls suddenly on the cavalry near the King, charging them at once in front and flank, first with a heavy fire of carbines, then at the sword's point. It is reported that—"His Majesty was in the interim in the midst of the field, with his son Prince Charles and divers of his council and servants where by his presence he did much encourage those that stood, and rallied those that were deserting the field; though a whole brigade of our horse, being stopped by his Majesty as they came down a lane from Speene, and by him commanded again into the field, very basely forsook him and ran into Newbery, out of which they were speedily forced by our guards then placed at the Bridge."[‡] The King at this time appears to have been in the fields not far from the backway to Speen, down which his deserting troopers fled. In an interesting letter,[§] of earlier date (March 1, 1623), from the Mayor and certain inhabitants of Newbury to the Council of the Prince of Wales, afterwards K. Charles I., assistance is sought towards repairing the bridge at Newbury, which had suddenly toppled over into the river on the preceding 8th of February. This shows that the river was bridged in the town at that period, and not passed by a ford, as has been represented.

It is evident that for a short time the King and his retinue were in imminent danger; for at the first shock, a whole

---

[*] Letter from the Two Commissioners to Derby-Ho. Committee, 28, Oct., 1644.
[†] Vicar's "Parl. Chron." Lond., 1644.
[‡] Sir E. Walker's "Hist. Discourses," p. 112.
[§] This letter is among the Tanner MSS., Bodleian Lib., No. 314, fol. 214.

brigade of Royalist horse, outnumbered to a great degree, and already demoralized by increasing panic, reeled and wavered, and at length, giving ground to the advancing host, clapped spurs to their horses, and fled in disorder towards the town. The King, desperate at the sight, dashed forward sword in hand, and vainly endeavoured to arrest their flight; but the authority of command was gone, and he found himself surrounded by the enemy. At the crisis Sir John Campsfield,* with two troops of the Queen's regiment, gallantly galloped forward to the support of his royal master. Sir Bernard Stuart and his life-guards gathered round the King; and rapidly wheeling round, to get more ground, with the troopers of Sir John they rushed valiantly against the eager enemy. A deadly strife ensued; many a horse ran riderless over the fields; the Parliament men were dispersed; and the King was rescued. The brave cavaliers, however, too ardent in their enthusiasm, always led away by the same fault, pushed on too far. The calm old Skippon, not less cool than daring, permitted them to continue the pursuit until their impetuosity carried them within a few yards of his infantry, when, at a signal, the musqueteers and pikemen furiously assailed them, and they were forced to retire through his ranks, exposed to a galling fire.

At this moment Lieut.-General Cromwell, with the left wing of horse, well in hand, came upon the scene, and made for Sir Humphrey Benett's cavalry brigade, stationed on the south-west side of Speen Fields towards Newbury, which was without doubt the weakest point in the Royal line. In ten minutes Sir Humphrey's steel-clad troopers, panic-struck at so vigorous a charge, and taken at a disadvantage, were completely overpowered, and had well nigh been annihilated had not Lord Bernard Stuart and his guards secured their retreat on Shaw. Cromwell now advanced "towards the north side of the field," in the direction of Donnington; but he was met by Lord Goring, with the Earl of Cleveland's brigade, who charged with telling effect on the leading squadrons, and forced them to retire over a hedge. Goring's troopers lept the obstacle in pursuit, but Skippon, once more rallying his battalions, drove him back in turn, routed and dispersed, with considerable loss. The gallant old Earl of Cleveland, at the head of his regiment, allowed his courage to carry him too far ahead of his men; and, his horse falling under him, he was taken prisoner.†

---

* The motto in Sir John Campsfield's banner was from the 101st Psalm,— "Fiat pax in virtute tua."—Estreune's "Mottos and Devices."

† "Drawing up (with General Goring) his brigade, at the east side of Spiene, in the Second Newberry fight, to secure the King's guards, in much danger, with such old English valor (telling his men they must now charge home), that he scattered the enemy, till too far engaged and overpowered he was taken prisoner, as the King himself was like to be." Lloyd's "Memoirs," p. 570.

"The Knight is left alone, his steel-cap cleft in twain,
His good buff jerkin crimson'd o'er with many a gory stain:
Yet still he waves his banner, and cries amid the rout,
'For Church and King, fair gentlemen! spur on, and fight it out!'"—*Praed*.

The battle on the Speen side of the Royalist position had now raged three or four hours; the sun had set, and the night was fast closing in, yet the contest was continued in broken order, but for the most part with unabated spirit. At last all formation was lost; and it would be tedious, if not impossible, to continue the narration of what had now become mere skirmishes in the dark, friend and foe commingled. The fighting gradually ceased. Both parties occupied themselves in drawing together their scattered forces.

Cromwell states in his Evidence against the Earl of Manchester * that "Wee on the other side [Speen], haveing gayned most of the hedges toward Newberry feild, did cease and drawe our men together to avoyd confusion in the darke by that scattered way of fighting."

The darkness of the night, until the moon rose, was advantageous to the dispirited royalists, many of whom escaped under its cover who would otherwise have been killed or taken prisoners. As there was considerable rivalry between the leaders in this battle, discrepancies in the various accounts of the action are very marked. Thus, Manchester, whose hostility to the future Protector was well known, gave it as his opinion before the House of Lords † that "On that day there was no service at all performed by Cromwell." But this is not at all likely; and personal dislike must have warped the Earl's mind. Oliver was not a man to stand idle when any fighting was to be done; and in the despatch of the Two Commissioners he is expressly mentioned as having done great service,—an assertion far more likely to be true than that of his comrade in the fight.

We turn now to the course of the action at Shaw. About four o'clock, ‡ Manchester heard the distant firing on Speen Hill, and beheld from the eminence with joy and thankfulness the hasty, disorderly retreat of the enemy towards Newbury. Animated with this encouraging sight, says his Chaplain, Simeon Ashe, the Earl prepared to descend to the more difficult work of forcing the strong position at Dolman's house.

For the purpose of carrying this important post, Manchester divided his force into two columns, to assault the house at two

---

* State Papers; Publ. Rec. Off.
† November 28, 1644; also in the "Narrative."
‡ Cromwell, in his charge against Manchester, says, that the Earl would not allow his men to fall on until half-an-hour after sunset: but this differs from other accounts of the battle, whether Royalist or Parliamentarian, which state that Manchester made his attack not later than 4 p.m.

different points; the right to attack on the north-east side by the garden; and the left, which was somewhat the larger body, to attempt it lower down at the foot of the little hill by the village of Shaw. (See the Plan.)

Suddenly, under cover of an active cannonade along their whole line, a dark and terrible mass of steel-clad men moved down from behind the protecting eminence of Clay Hill.

"Compactly move the blocks of spears,
" In 'back,' and 'breast,' and steel cap bright;
"And on each flank,
" In eight-deep rank,
"With lighted match, the musqueteers."*

The "battle-march" of the Puritan warriors was a solemn psalm pealing from their fierce array.† The royalist guns thundered a refrain. Preserving the greatest order, the Parliament men steadily descended the steep hill-side to meet again, for the second time that day, their equally brave, and no less devoted antagonists.

The eager and excited soldiers of the Parliament, who felt that they had been too long held back, brooked no further suspense. The foremost lines of the right column immediately advanced on the garden side of Shaw House. The Royalists had all the advantages of position; every accessible point being well protected in all directions, both by cannon and musquetry; and, full of confidence, they received the enemy with a tremendous volley, poured in from behind the hedges of Long Lane.‡ Though for the moment amazed and staggered, Manchester's men withdrew not an inch; and the first shock was no sooner overcome, than they rushed boldly forward, to be again driven back. Again and again were they led on, and as often repulsed; but, seconded by a strong body of Ludlow's cavalry, they once more fell on, and this time with some effect. The cavaliers sent another and telling volley from behind their breastwork on the little hill where the Water-tower§ now stands; but, nothing daunted, the Parliamentarians advanced, and drove out the foremost musqueteers from their cover. They now received a check; for Sir John Brown, with the Prince of Wales's regiment, caused terrible havoc in their ranks, the Royalist fire being maintained with great coolness. Still the assailants pressed on; pike met pike, sword clashed with sword; the one party en-

---

* "Donnington Castle," by Col. Columb, R.A., p. 157.
† Clarendon's "Hist." iv. p. 548.
‡ Several cannon-balls have been found in the banks of Long Lane.
§ The ground around the Water-tower has the appearance of having been artificially raised for defence, particularly on the eastern side of the mound. To the north-east of the road to Donnington from Long Lane, also, there are evident indications of entrenchments. The ramparts now faced with stone, are still well defined in the gardens of Shaw House.

deavouring to gain the hedges and entrenchments, the other resolutely opposing them. Many fell at the foot of this hillock; but not one put a foot on it, except as a prisoner. Again reinforced with a fresh body of horse, this gallant band returned to the charge, and almost reached the garden-wall,* while others penetrated even to the lawn in front of the house. Sir John Brown, for a time compelled to give way, prudently fell back on the reserve in the garden. Meanwhile Sir Richard Page, with his leather guns, and 400 musqueteers in the dry moat, delivered a biting fire.† Ludlow's cavalry recoiled, wheeled about, and retreated, followed by Sir John Brown; and many a brave trooper fell, never more to draw sword again in cause of Parliament.‡ The foot, however, soon rallying, advanced towards Thelwall's reserve, who brought his men boldly forward. Without waiting to return their fire, the Parliament men rushed in upon the Cavaliers and gallantly fought to the death. Even by their enemy's admission they struggled heroically; but the odds were against them, for they were able to do little against an enemy sheltered by walls and earth-works. Thus, though twice reinforced, and bravely led forward, twice they were repulsed; and, abandoning all hope of penetrating this well defended place, they gradually retired out of fire, to Clay Hill, leaving one of Crawfurd's colours and two "drakes" in the hands of the successful defenders of the royal stronghold.

Simultaneous with the attack on the garden, Manchester's left column made a vigorous assault, by the village of Shaw, on the north side of the Lamborne, towards the front of Shaw-house; but Sir George Lisle stripped to his shirt, and therefore (says "Mercurius Aulicus") mistaken for a witch § by the Parliamen-

---

* There was formerly a sunken road in front of this wall, with a raised bank on each side. When the roadway was diverted some years ago, and the present wooden fence erected, several human skeletons were met with; and a 6lb cannonball was found firmly imbedded in the brickwork On the Lawn in front of Shaw House are four iron guns, about 5ft. 9in. long, with 3½ inches bore. Such as these were called "Minions;" and they were probably left by the Parliamentarians, as memorials, when the house was given up to its owner, Sir Thos. Dolman.

† See Capt. Gwyn's "Mil. Mem." ch. xiii. The portable leather gun was made of the toughest leather, and bound with metallic hoops. A strong horse could carry two of them through miry roads. They could be discharged only 7 or 8 times. Col. Wemys is commonly supposed to have been the inventor; but the original inventor was Gustavus Adolphus, who employed them at the battle of Leipsic, Sept. 7, 1631. See "Mil. Mem. of Col. John Birch," Camd. Soc., 87, 88.

‡ Ludlow's "Memoirs," p. 131.

§ "At the last Newb'ry Battle, in the sight
Of Majesty, he led the Foot to fight,
Strip'd to his Shirt, that others might descry
His Actions, and Example take thereby;
From whence the frighted Rebels gave it out,
That a white Witch was seen to fly about
The Royal Army, scowring to and fro,
Where'er the Contest did the hottest grow."
'Hist. Grand Rebell.' By Henry Ward. Vol. ii, p. 432.

tary soldiers, burst at once, with his fiery cavalry, into the very heart of Manchester's infantry, and scattered them "like spray before some storm-driven ship." No pause was made,—no mercy shown by the excited troopers,—the whole mass was swept up Clay Hill,* pursued by the enraged cavaliers, who hewed down the fugitives by scores. It is said that they only escaped total destruction through the devoted heroism of Ludlow's men, who sacrificed themselves by moving forward to cover the retreat. So great was the execution that Clarendon states 500 men were left dead on one little spot of ground. †

The moon was now up. Manchester had received a reinforcement of horse, expected earlier in the day; and he resolved to make another and final effort. However skilful and daring the attempt, it was foiled by the pluck of the Royalists, who stood their ground, and again compelled their assailants to retire.

Though, at first sight, a matter of surprise that Shaw House should have suffered so little, considering that a series of violent attacks were made on it by the Parliamentarians, this seems easy of explanation. Firstly, only the eastern end of the House is turned towards Clay Hill, on the slope of which the enemy's guns must have been posted. Next, between the latter point and the building rises a hillock, on which the Water-tower now stands, and this very materially sheltered the house from view and injury. Thirdly, there were no heavy siege-guns brought against it, as at Donnington Castle. Further, it was concealed by trees, in most cases stout enough to stop shot from light field-guns, and was surrounded by high fences and a thick rampart. Thus we need not wonder that it escaped unscathed.‡

These important fights, at Speen and Shaw, constituted the last great action between the two parties here. Whatever its ultimate results may have been, at first each army seems to have fancied itself worsted. The Parliamentarians had been repulsed, and had suffered severely at Shaw; but their right wing at Speen had been completely successful. The King, on the other hand, who had been a witness of his ill fortune on the Speen side, and unaware that at Shaw the tide of war had turned in his favour, considered his position no longer tenable, and determined to act at once on the resolution he had taken in the morning, in anticipation of an unfavourable issue, namely, to retreat on Wallingford. Orders were accordingly dispatched to Prince Maurice, Lord Goring, Lord Hopton, Sir Jacob Astley, and the

---

* Walker's "Hist. Disc." p. 113.
† Clarendon's "Hist." II. p. 548.
‡ A shot-hole in a shutter in one of the eastern rooms of the House is registered by a brass plate as having been made by a bullet when the King was standing close by. When this could have occurred is difficult to determine.

other commanders, to draw off their men to Snelsmore Heath.*
Battalion after battalion began silently to quit its ground, and
march in the direction of the rendezvous; while the guns and
heavy stores were conveyed by a circuitous route to Donnington
Castle. Charles, at the earnest entreaty of his friends, who
perceived the utter frustration of all his hopes, now thought of
providing for his own safety; and, having sent for his guard, amid
a troop of fugitive horsemen made good his escape to Donnington
Castle, deciding to proceed to Bath, where he might by his
presence hasten the Welsh and Northern forces which his nephew
Prince Rupert was then getting together for his assistance.
After half-an-hour spent in the Castle with Sir John Boys, in
whose care he left his wounded, baggage, artillery, and ammunition, the King, with the young Prince of Wales, the Duke of
Richmond, the Earls of Lindsey, Berkshire, and Newport, Lord
Capel, and others, and accompanied by a guard of about 300 horse,
hurried from the scene of his overthrow, and by about four
o'clock in the afternoon of the next day reached Bath (having
ridden over fifty miles, as Symonds says, "sans rest"),† where he
met Prince Rupert, and informed him of the sad disaster.

The retreat of the army was ably conducted by Prince Maurice;
and, notwithstanding the great superiority of the enemy in
cavalry, he got to Wallingford by way of Compton without
hindrance the next day, and then quietly went on to Oxford.
The Parliamentarians, who remained on the ground all night,
awoke in the morning to find the King was gone! Waller and
Manchester appear to have been entirely ignorant of each other's
success or failure until the next day. Simeon Ash says,—"The
next morning, as soon as we had in the field, near the bodies
both of friends and foes which lay in the field, made our
addresses to God both by praise and prayer according to the
present affecting providences, we march'd over the river [Lam-
borne] to Newbury; and all this time we neither met with, nor
heard of our friends at Speen."‡

Thus finished the Second Battle of Newbury; but the losses
on both sides, in killed, wounded, and prisoners were heavy.
Sir Edward Walker § gives the following list of the "hurt and
wounded" on the Royalist side:—King's Life-guard, 29 common
soldiers; Prince of Wales's Regiment, 69 common soldiers,
2 Captains, 2 Lieutenants, 1 Ensign, 1 "Sarjant;" Sir Jacob

---

* Snelsmore Heath formerly extended over the whole of the now-enclosed
fields between Donnington Castle and the present Common. At the time of the
Civil War there were one or two cottages standing between the Common and the
Castle, which Sir John Boys burnt to prevent their being occupied by the enemy.

† Symonds's Diary, p. 146.

‡ "A True Relation," &c.

§ Harl. MSS., No. 6804; 92.

Astley's Regiment, 16 common soldiers; Col. Bellasis' Regiment, 25; Col. Bowles' Regt., 23; Col. Dalton's Regt., 22; Col. Owen's Regt., 14; Col. Harford's Regt. 18; Col. Dyve's Regt., 14; Col. Blagg's [Blague's], 6 common soldiers: in Sir Gilbert Gerrard's "Tertia," "9 officers slain," 22 "shott;" 100 "soldiers slain," 116 "shott," "41 sicke and unable to march:" in Lord Harbert's 5 "Readgements," 2 Captains, 1 Ensign, 45 common soldiers, "11 sicke men; my Ld. Harbert hath taken care to send these into Bristol:" in Lord Grandison's Regt., "5 common soldiers, 2 sicke men, 11 men killed:" in Col. Charles Garard's Regt., the Lieut.-Col., 2 Captains, 2 Lieutenants, 9 Ensigns, 7 "Sarjants," 78 common soldiers. The following summary of the casualities attending the action of October 27th, on the King's side, is given in Sir E. Walker's MS. here referred to—of Col. Sands' [Sandys'] Regt., 26; of Lord River's Regt., ...; of the Lord-General's Regt., 74; Soldiers hurt and not able to march, 351; of Col. Chas. Garard's Regt., 78; altogether 529, and 59 Officers hurt, total 588.

It is difficult from the above account, to summarize the number of those actually killed and of those only wounded; but the King's loss was evidently much greater than some of the royalist writers represent; for each party sought to reduce its own loss and augment that of its opponent. Sir Edward Walker, in his "Discourses," says there were not above 100 common soldiers slain; and Clarendon follows him; Sir Roger Manley, a zealous champion in the royal cause, goes so far as to say "3000 men were slain on the King's side;" while Whitelock, the Parliamentary writer, reduces the number to 200 slain and 300 prisoners. The following royalists are mentioned as having been killed in this engagement:—Sir William St. Leger, M.P., son and heir of Sir William St. Leger, a Privy Councillor, and Lord-President of Munster in 1629; Lt.-Cols. Leke, Houghton, Topping, and Jones (killed on the little hill where the Water-tower now is at Shaw); Majors Trevellian and Knyvett; Captains Whittingham, Catelyn, Walpole, Philpot, and Mildmay (eldest son of Sir Humphrey Mildmay); also Mr. Barksdale, a volunteer. This loyal gentleman was a member of an old Newbury family, one of whom (Mr. Thomas Barksdale) gave an acre of land to the Parish of Speen, the rent thereof to pay for a sermon at Speen Church every Easter-Tuesday. Of the wounded were—the Earl of Brentford, shot in the head; Sir John Grenville, Sir John Campsfield, Sir Edward Waldegrave, Lt.-Col. Page (shot in both thighs and in the arm); Major Alford, shot in the thigh; Capt. Wells, wounded severely, fell into the hands of the enemy, and died in prison; Mr. Stephen Knight, "chief clerk of the Avery" to King Charles. In his petition for restoration to the office, shortly after the return of Charles II., Mr. Knight pleads that he was severely wounded at Newbury in the last battle, and subsequently plundered of all he possessed, and that his family were turned out into the streets.

That the prisoners captured by the Parliamentary Army were numerous, appears in the contemporary papers.* It seems that many of the persons here enumerated belonged to the neighbourhood, and their descendants still reside in the locality. Some five or six hundred "stragglers" were subsequently taken prisoners by the Parliamentarians when they entered Newbury. Of these the "Weekly Account," in the succeeding week (from Oct. 31 to Nov. 4, 1644), reports—"The Letters from Sir William Waller confirm the taking of a great store of arms and many prisoners since the late victory near Newbury; but most of the men, being poore country-fellows (that were forst [forced], and offered to take the covenant not to fight any more against the Parliament), they were left to their election, whether they would fight for the Parliament, or depart to their own dwellings, upon which many of them made choice of the Parliament's service."

Of Lord Cleveland's Brigade, were—Lord Cleveland, Captain Philpot,† Lieut. Harper, Lieut. Roane, Cornet Whealand, Quarerm$^r\cdot$ Ironmonger, Quarterm$^r\cdot$ Campion, Quarterm$^r\cdot$ Nicholas, Mr. John Percy, and 38 Troopers of the same Brigade.

Of Sir John Astley's Brigade—11 officers and troopers.

Of Lord Hopton's Brigade—Capt. Elmes, Quarterm$^r\cdot$ Simon Court, and Henry Dimmock, Hugh Pope, and Edward Phillips, "Gentlemen of Armes," besides divers troopers.

The following were also taken prisoners—Colonel Philpot, Capt. Mildmay,‡ Capt. Nevet [Kynvett],‡ Mr. Richard Nishton, Mr. John Curtis, Mr. Edward Archer, and " divers other Gentlemen of Armes and Reformadoes,‖ of these many of them are officers, the rest gentlemen;"—Mr. John Champion, Mr. George Edmons, Mr. Henry Leonard, Mr. John Edges, Mr. John Goare, Mr. John Williams, Mr. William Bartholomew, Mr. James Lovelock, Mr. Henry Atkins, Mr. Thos. Poply [Pofley?], Mr. Thos. Holden, Mr. James Fant [Plant?] Mr. William Dormer, Mr. Thos. Plant, Mr. John Aldred, Mr. John Petty, Mr. Michael Francklin, Mr. James Champion, Mr. John Farnaby, Mr. Robert Hill, Mr. Henry Coard [Court?], Mr. Peter Holway [Holloway?], Mr. Thos. Compton, Mr. George Huntley, Mr. Richd. Thebon. Mr. Cornelius Owen, Mr. Thos. Greenfield, Mr. Richd. Painter, Mr. John Hobbs, Mr. Edmond Coard, Mr. John Davis, Mr. Wm. Halen [Allen?], Mr. Edwd. James, Mr. Joseph Hitchcocke, Mr. Robt. Kinder [Kimber?], Mr. Daniel Stout, Mr. William Wood, Mr. John Hill, Mr. Wm. Banister, Mr. Richd. Cornewell, Mr.

---
* "Perfect Occurrences of Parliament," from 25 Oct. to 1st Nov. 1644.
† Died of his wounds.
‡ Both died of wounds.
‖ "Reformadoes" were officers who, having lost their men, were continued on whole or half-pay.

Thomas Turke, Mr. Wm. Eiles [Eyles?], Mr. Peter Smith, Mr. Richard Whiston, Mr. Daniel Dongway, and Mr. Henry Vincent. On the side of the Parliament, the estimates of the losses likewise vary most considerably, Sir Roger Manley leads off with 2500 as the number actually killed. Clarendon, comes next with 1000; and Carte gives the same. On the other hand, the Parliamentary Commissioners, in their report to the Derby-House Committee, dated from Newbury, the day after the battle, state, " Major Skippon guesseth that the number slaine, on both sides, [*i.e.* of the Parliamentary forces engaged at Speen and Shaw] were between two and three hundred." Little reliance can be placed on these statements, which were made for party-purposes. The average of these figures would give about 1000, which is probably a fair calculation.

Very few names of Parliamentary Officers who fell in this battle have been handed down to us. Col. Gawler, Major Hurry, Captains Willet, Talbot, and Charles D'Oyley, of the Earl of Essex's Life-Guards, were killed at Speen (the latter, it is said, by the hand of Sir Humphrey Benett); and Cols. Norton, Bartley, and Lloyd are mentioned as wounded.

In an original letter, containing a brief account of this battle, from Col. Norton to his friend Richard Major of Hursley, the Colonel says—"We killed some men of note, and lost some, amongst wch was Lieut.-Col. Knight, sonne to John Knight, who was to me much lamented by my L^d. Man[che]ster and many others, and died wth ye reputac'on of as gallant a man as any in all y^o army and as much beloved; truly I am sorry for himselfe, and not lesse for poor John Knight's sake; but as he lived to be a good christian soe he died like a good souldier. Many we had wounded; amongst ye number I receaved a faier admonition (by musquet-shott in my legge) for medling where I had noe charge, but I thanke God, my bone was to hard for ye bullett, and I hope I shall be upon both legges againe ere it be long. I could not helpe it; for I thought there was need when engaged myselfe to lead up Col. Ludlowe's Regiment, his horse having broken his bridle, soe y^t he was faine to quit." [Here the remaining part of the sentence, probably with some others, is lost, the paper having failed at the fold.]

Endorsed:—"Coll. Norton, 29 Octob., 1644. Newbery battaile." ("Maijor* Letters and Papers," British Museum.)

Sir Wm. Waller, it seems, had a narrow escape in this engagement. To this he thus refers in his note-book,† in which he was in the habit of making daily jottings :—" At the second

---

* Dorothy, daughter of Mr. Richard Major, married Richard Cromwell, the Protector's eldest son. When the old house at Hursley was pulled down some time in the last century, a seal was found, supposed to have been the identical seal of the Commonwealth, which the Protector took from the Parliament.

† Sir W. Waller's "Recoll.," C. 45 *a*; Brit. Mus.

Newbery fight, when I fell on with my troopes by way of Speene Field and were there mingled with the enemy, I had a great deliv'rance, for one of the adverse party coming behind me, and being ready to fire his pistoll in my reines, in that instant one of my life-guard killed him, or otherwise in all probability he would have killed me.

O God, the Lord, the strength of my salvation, thou hast covered my head in the day of Battle!

The Angell of the Lord encampeth round about them that feare his worde, and delivereth them."

The greater number of the slain found a grave near where they fell, while many of those who died of their wounds in the town of Newbury were buried in St. Nicholas' church-yard. The Churchwarden's accounts from 23 Aug., 1644 to 20 Sept., 1645, contain the following list of payments in connection with these interments:—

Given at Vestry, 20 Sept. 1645. Account passed by William Nash, Mayor.

Paid for a shroud for a Soldier, carrying him to Church	0	0	8
Carrying Soldier and cleaning the Church	0	5	0
Carrying Soldier and making a great grave	0	4	0
Carrying a Soldier to Burying	0	1	4
Shroud for a Soldier	0	3	4
Carrying and Burying 3 Soldiers	0	3	0
Coffin for a Lieutenant	0	7	0
For Carrying, Burying Soldier	0	1	2
For Carrying another Soldier to Burying	0	1	0
Burying 2 Soldiers more	0	2	0
Burying 6 Soldiers more	0	5	6
Shrouds for Soldiers	0	3	6
Carrying a Soldier and Burying	0	1	0
Digging Graves for Soldiers	0	4	0
Burying 3 Soldiers more	0	4	6
Ditto 4 ditto	0	6	6
Digging Graves	0	2	2
Burying 2 Soldiers	0	3	5
Ditto 2 ditto	0	3	0
Burying a Soldier	0	1	6
Digging 19 Graves and cleaning the Church	0	4	0
Burying a Soldier	0	1	6
Ditto ditto	0	1	6

Heavy as these losses were, they did not prevent the speedy resumption of hostilities. Though the battle had been somewhat indecisive, inasmuch as the King had escaped, by way of Donnington to Oxford, Manchester soon steps to reap the full fruits of the battle, which he claimed as a victory. Early on Monday morning, the 28th October, when the Parliamentarians found that the King was really gone, a Council of War was called at Speen. It is asserted that Cromwell, on that occasion, not doubting as to the state in which affairs stood, repeatedly requested leave to push on with his cavalry and overtake the retreating royalists; but he was peremptorily restrained by the General-in-chief; and, as Cromwell brought a charge to this effect against Manchester in the House of Commons, the statement is probably true. But however this may be, after much time had been wasted in an angry discussion, Manchester reluctantly consented that Waller, Cromwell, and Hesilrige, with the horse (about 6000 strong), which had been engaged on the Speen side of the battle, should march in pursuit. With this force the Parliamentary Generals reached Blewbury, without firing a shot; and then finding that the enemy had got clear over the river at Wallingford many hours before, it was judged both hazardous and useless to pursue further; and the troops were accordingly quartered in Blewbury, Hagborne, Chilton, Harwell, and the neighbouring villages. Meanwhile a letter having been sent by Manchester from Newbury, desiring the return of the force, the three Generals came back to Newbury, where they had an interview with the Earl. They then pressed earnestly to have the whole army marched speedily into quarters beyond Oxford (about Witney, Burford, and Woodstock), where the King's troops had already begun to rally. That being denied, they requested that two or three thousand of the foot then quartered in Newbury should march to join the horse at Blewbury. Manchester could not, however, be persuaded to stir until the Saturday following (November 2nd), on which day he started with a portion of his infantry, and in two days managed to get as far as Harwell, which same distance, Cromwell says, the Earl on his return "dispatcht in one." Arriving at Harwell, Manchester refused to proceed further until he had received instructions from the Committee in London; his excuse being the badness of the roads and other impediments. The two commissioners, Lord Warriston and Mr. Crew, proceeded from Harwell to London to represent matters in person to the Derby-house Committee: but on Tuesday (November 5th), the day before the directions of the Committee were received, Manchester appointed a rendezvous for the next morning on Compton Downs four or five miles back towards Newbury. The whole body of horse under Cromwell on Tuesday night lay on Chilton plain, and the following day moved to Compton, and joined Manchester, who had by this time, much to his satisfaction, received orders from London not to divide his army, but to march back to Newbury and endeavour to take Donnington Castle. Siege-pieces and ammunition were dispatched to him for that purpose. Consequently the entire force retraced their steps, reaching Newbury on the 7th of November. From Cromwell's statement to the Commons, it appears that he commended these Berkshire Downs as a suitable position "for lying in the King's way" with his returning army, and indeed this locality narrowly escaped being the scene of a bloody conflict between the two armies; for no sooner had Cromwell quitted Chilton Plain, than the royal forces took up their quarters on the same spot on the Downs where their enemies had encamped the preceding day. But as this is somewhat anticipating the course of events, it will be necessary to return to the proceedings of the King after his retreat to Bath.

When the King met Rupert at Bath, the Prince had with him about 400 horse and 600 foot, making, with the King's own troop and followers, about 1300 men. With this strength Charles and his nephew marched out of Bath on Wednesday, 30th of October, and quartered that night at Sherston near Malmesbury; next day they reached Cirencester, where the King received a letter from Sir Jacob Astley (created Baron Astley of Reading a few days after, at Oxford), informing him of the good condition of his army, with advice to his Majesty to advance speedily, and, with the additional forces then at his command, to march again to Newbury, disengage his cannon, and offer the enemy battle. From Cirencester the King marched to Burford, and by the way he met the Earl of Northampton, with those regiments which had relieved Banbury; and he also received the intelligence that General Gerrard and Sir Marmaduke Langdale, with a force of 4000 horse and foot, would encamp that night at Stow-on-the-Wold. Whereupon, to give more ease to the troops, and to make preparations for his march to Newbury, the King left his force at Burford, and hastened, with his guards and attendants, to Oxford, which he entered on the 1st of November, being received with great joy and acclamation, after his long absence of five months, during which time he had passed through and overcome many difficulties.

Meanwhile, between the action on the 27th October and the King's return to Oxford, the Parliament's forces entered Newbury; and, with a strong body of horse and foot, surrounded Donnington Castle. They again summoned the indomitable Boys to surrender, assuring him this time, that, if he did not instantly comply, they would not leave one stone upon another. "If so, I am not bound to repair it," was the Governor's scornful reply. Being urged a second and a third time, with the offer that he should be permitted to march out with all the arms, ammunition, and stores deposited in the Castle,—"Carry away," he said, "the Castle walls themselves, if you can; but, with God's help, I am resolved to keep the ground they stand on, till I have orders from the King, my master, to quit it, or will die upon the spot." An assault was consequently determined on, but the officer who who led the storming party having fallen at their head, and great differences prevailing among the Generals, nothing further was at that time done. The Royalist journal, "Mercurius Aulicus," for Sunday, Nov. 17, 1644, gives the following account of some affairs as then reported;—"The Rebells sped so ill at downright fighting that they now practise a new way of murther, for we are certainly advised from Donnington Castle, that when the Rebells close besieged the place, they hyred a souldier to poyson their Well on the north side of the Castle, which lay without the workes, between the Rebell's trenches and the workes. This souldier having informed the rebells that the Well was most necessary for the support of that garrison received his twenty shillings (for that was all this poor Rebell demanded), and in the night time conveyed the poyson down the Well, but next morning the commander (toucht it seems with the horror of the fact) sent a Drum with a letter to Sir John Boys to give notice what was done. The Governor returned thanks to their Commander, and at first fit opportunity drew 40 musqueteers out of the Castle, and in the face of the rebells cleaned the Well, taking out the bag of poyson, and digging it deeper. After which time we kept the Well in despight of the Rebells, and to make tryall whether or no the Well was truely poysoned, we tryed the experiment upon a Horse, which having drunk of it, swell'd and dyed within 24 hours." This Well has recently been discovered on the north-west side of the Castle, about 400 yards from the buildings. By the nature of the ground it is screened from the observation of an enemy posted on Snelsmore Common; so that the garrison could obtain water thence without exposure or difficulty.

At this time the Earl of Brentford, who had been wounded on the 27th, sought temporary shelter in the Castle, where his Lady attended him; and the Parliamentarians, hearing he was there, sent Col. Hurry to his old general, with large offers, if he would give up the place, or induce Boys to do so,—a proposal rejected with indignation. This will be the last mention of the shifting Colonel, Sir John Hurry, who ended his life in the King's service. He was taken prisoner with Montrose, and was executed with him and about 40 more of the Marquis's followers, at Edinburgh, May 21, 1650. On the 30th Oct., three days after the battle, Lord Brentford, having somewhat recovered from his wounds, obtained a guide to direct him by cross-roads to Bath, where he was anxious to rejoin the King and inform him of the safe retreat of the army to Wallingford. But he was pursued by a party of the enemy's horse, led by Col. Birch, and his Lady was taken prisoner. The general, however, managed to escape, owing as Skippon in his dispatch states, to one of their party unadvisedly sounding a trumpet near where he was reposing himself.*

---

* This episode is related in a most interesting document recently printed by the Camden Society, entitled "A Military Memoir of Col. John Birch." That portion referring to the capture of Lady Brentford, is given in the APPENDIX.

As soon as the King came to Christ-Church, Oxford, he conferred the dignity of Knighthood on Colonel Gage, who, in his Majesty's absence, had done well both in defence of that city, and in the relief of Basing and Banbury. Charles also gratefully thanked the members of his Council, who had managed his affairs since his departure. This having been done, the succeeding days were employed in making preparations to take the field; a new train of artillery was expeditiously formed, and the whole army put into good serviceable condition.

On Wednesday, the 6th of November, the royal army was drawn out on Bullington Green, near Oxford, and inspected by the King, who found he had a force of 6000 foot and 5000 horse, with which again to try his fortune at Newbury. Prince Rupert consented without reluctance to supersede Lord Brentford as Commander of the King's forces; whilst the old General was solaced with the post of Lord-Chamberlain to the Prince of Wales.

On Thursday the King marched with his troops to Wallingford, and the day following, Friday, 8th November, the army encamped on Ilsley Downs, while His Majesty quartered with Bishop Goodman at West-Ilsley Rectory.*

On Saturday morning the King marched from Ilsley towards Newbury; and the succeeding events of the day are thus stated in detail by Sir Edward Walker:†—On Saturday "our army marched in battalia, expecting some opposition. The van was led by his Highness Prince Rupert and General Gerrard. In this order we marched, and got possession of the heath on the backside of Dennington Castle,‡ from which a small force of the rebels might have kept us, the entrance into it being steep and the way very narrow,§ and then we must have gone about and fallen in by way of Speene.‖ On that heath the army was drawn up about twelve of the clock, and every one prepared to fight. Thence in good order we marched by Dennington Castle, passing

---

* Dr. Goodman then held the Rectory of West Ilsley, *in commendam*, with the See of Gloucester, of which he was deprived by Archbishop Laud in 1640 for refusing to subscribe to the Canons; but was restored upon his submission. He was sequestrated by the Committee of Plundered Ministers, for his tithes of West Ilsley. In a petition to the Protector Cromwell, the Bishop says that his "great losses were such as he thinks no man suffered more," and complains that a Mr. Humphrey Newbery, who was appointed by the Committee to officiate the Cure, came with a body of soldiers to West Ilsley and forcibly took possession of his Living. Dr. Goodman ultimately became a Roman Catholic, and died in that faith Jany. 9, 1655. Dr. Goodman is said to have been concerned in the noble design of bringing the New River Water into London. See Walker's "Sufferings of the Clergy," Pt. II, p. 33. The old Rectory-house at West Ilsley, an interesting Elizabethan building, was taken down about 35 years since.

† "Hist. Discourses," pp. 118, 119.

‡ Snelsmore Common. The King's route was by Chievely and North-heath.

§ Bussock Hill.

‖ Through Winterbourne.

the river at a mill, and two fords below it* without any opposition, and thence drew into the large field between Speene and Newbery, where the army was set in order. The rebels in the interim drew a great body of horse and foot into the other field towards Shaw, having made breastworks and batteries on the backside of Newbery towards both these fields,† resolving to keep the town, which was the reason they gave us so easie a passage to the heath behind Donnington. About three in the afternoon we advanced within reach of their cannon, which they discharged amongst us without doing any hurt. Then a body of our horse charged another of theirs in the lower field ‡ and routed them, pursuing them almost to their breastworks; when the rebel musquetiers placed in the lane between the two fields§ gave fire on our horse and caused them to retreat (though without disorder). In the interim we could discover a great body of their horse on the hill on the south side of Newbury || almost at a stand whether to come down or retire. The armys being now on the point of being engaged, His Majesty advised with his Council what was fittest to be done, who considering that he had already effected what he came for thither, which was to relieve Dennington (provisions being put in in the interim) that it was in his power to draw off his ordnance and ammunition thence; and that he had sufficiently regained the opinion and honour of the day, by passing his army over the river in the face of theirs, and offering them battel if they durst draw out, and withal considering how dangerous it might prove to force them to fight, having the advantages of breastworks and batteries and a town at their backs, it was unanimously concluded that we should draw off and attempt them no further. And to let them know that we did it not out of any apprehension, Prince Rupert sent a Trumpet [a "Drum" or "Trumpet" was equivalent to a flag of truce], to give them notice of our intentions, so that, if it had been their will, they might have fallen on our rear. But they suffered us quietly to pass with drums beating and trumpets sounding the same ways we came over the river. His Majesty lay that night

---

* Donnington Mill. The fords over the Mill-stream and the Lamborne. This mill was probably a dependency of the Castle in mediæval times.

† These breastworks and batteries were in the Marsh, then open to the fields above-described, at the back of Speenhamland. The remains of the earthworks still existing in the Marsh are shown on the Plan. They were but "sorry works," as Skippon describes them.

‡ The "lower field" is that nearest to Shaw Avenue.

§ The "lane between the two fields" was the old road to Oxford, which followed about the same line as the modern highway from Newbury.

|| The body of horse seen on the hill on the south side of Newbury was that under Cromwell, in the meadows below the Wash, on the left of the Wash Road from the town. Manchester accuses Cromwell of not coming up with this body of cavalry until after the King had marched away; but Cromwell retorts that Manchester was "most ready to finde the danger or infeisibility of draweing out to interpose."

in Donnington Castle, and all the army about him. In this action we lost one Captain of horse * and about fourteen Foot slain by their cannon in the retreat; and I believe the rebels lost twice that number."

Some traces of this skirmish were discovered in the year 1869, when two skeletons were found in the garden of the premises belonging to Mr. J. H. Money, in Speenhamland. The skeletons were both perfect, and lay side by side, one on its back and the other on its face, and both in the direction east and west, about two-and-a-half feet below the surface. A piece of clothing, like a soldier's coat-trimming, and some brass buttons and portions of accoutrements were found with the remains; also a gold ornament, somewhat like a fastening, a spur, and the bowl of a 17th-century tobacco-pipe. Scores of such pipes have been picked up in the neighbouring fields. There is little doubt that these were two troopers, most probably officers, "brothers in arms," who fell in the above mentioned skirmish, which took place over this very ground on Nov. 9th, 1644. Some fifty years ago a skeleton, having a large gash in the skull, was discovered, with a sword by its side, not far from the same spot; and more recently another skeleton was exhumed in the rear of the adjoining premises occupied by Mr. Adnams.

A correspondent of a London Diurnal † communicates the following intelligence from the Parliamentary army, in connection with the return of the King to Donnington Castle:—"Friday, Nov. 8.—This day the King designed a partie of 6 or 7000 horse and foot to relieve Dennington Castle and to fetch away such things out of the Castle as were most materiall, vizt.—

1. The King's Crown, which His Majesty wore on some high dayes, and had carried and brought back from Exeter.
2. The Great Seale, and other Seales which the Lord-keeper had left also in the said Castle.
3. The King's writings and divers Writs of great consequence, which were also carried in thither.
4. Divers Jewells, much gould, silver, and other treasure, which was also in the said Castle.
5. That they should endeavour to bring away what artillery and ammunition they could.
6. To carry relief with them to the Castle.

"This party was at Wallingford, from whence they were to march to Dennington, and the Castle of Dennington doth so command all the fields between the Castle and Newbery, that it is not safe for our army to march out there; yet some guards of

---

* Capt. Fitzmaurice, of the Prince of Wales' regiment.
† " Perfect Passages of each Dayc's Proceedings in Parliament," Nov. 6 to Nov. 13, 1644.

horse were still out and the enemy from the Castle play'd this day very fast, many cannon-bullets falling in Newbery.

"Saturday, Nov. 9.—This day there came intelligence that the night before the enemy in Dennington Castle had not only made shot with their cannon gainst Newbery, but made many flourishes, and at night made a great fire at the top of the Castle, so that the Earl of Manchester, Sir Wm. Waller, Lt.-Genl. Cromwell, and Sir William Balfour (to whom the charge of the armies for the present is committed) began to suspect the enemy coming that way, and so special care was taken for securing our armies in their quarters that night, lest the enemy should come on a sudden, that therefore their outguards should be ready, which was performed with a great deal of paines, care, and discretion, but more especially to oppose the enemy between Kingsclere and Dennington Castle, if they came, which was their direct way from Wallingford, and no other was probable.

"Tuesday, Nov. 12.—Besides that spoken of in the instructions to the King's forces, there was left in Dennington Castle about 18 small pieces of artillery carried into the Castle, besides 5 or 6 great pieces of ordnance that were planted on the works below, and good store of ammunition, some say 60 cart-loads, besides 30 cart-loads they took with them, what of this was carried away they will not tell us. But about 5 o'clock in the afternoon they retreated with what they had taken out of the Castle, and what they brought in is best known to themselves, but what they did was in a short time, and the great pieces lie still upon their works."

To return to our narrative, on Sunday morning, the 10th of November, the King's troops were drawn up in marching order on the heath adjoining Donnington Castle, with so many of the guns which had been left with the garrison after the retreat on the 27th October, as they could conveniently take with them, attached to their train. All being in readiness, the King bade farewell to the gallant governor Sir John Boys, and looked, it may be imagined, with tearful eye on the shot-wrecked walls of Donnington, which had been maintained in his cause with such fidelity, and which was to himself so full of stirring memories of disaster and defeat, but never of dishonour. The trumpets gave a parting blast, answered by a hearty cheer from Boys' merry men on the Castle walls, as the King, accompanied by Prince Rupert and his retinue, led the vanguard over the heath. Soon, however, the sound of drums and trumpets died away, and the little company of heroes at the Castle were once more left alone.

From Snelsmore Heath the army marched to Winterbourne,*

---

* The Winterbourne estate at that time belonged to the Head family, one of whom was Lord Falkland's host at Newbury.

where the troops were halted, it is said, to give thanks to God
for their great success; the King, Prince Rupert, and the chief
officers of his staff, attending divine service in the parish church.
The route was then by Boxford and Shefford to Lamborne; and
here the King took up his residence with Mr. Garrard;* the
main body of the foot being quartered in the town, and the horse
at Wantage and the intermediate villages. This is referred to in
the following terms by a Parliamentary scout:—"Monday, 11
November 1644. The last night the King's head-quarters were
at Wantage and Lamborne; and a part of the horse took off all
the provision they could meet as they went along by Peesemoure
and other villages, and intended to quarter this night at Auburn
and Ramsbury; and wee heare they intend to relieve Basing.
That all the foot which lay at Lamborne marcht away this
morning towards Auborne, where they had a rendezvous, and
intended to quarter there that night, but there came a sudden
allarm that the Parliament horse were coming after them, that
they gave a comand that they should march to Marlbrough,
and in the afternoone they march'd out of Wantage, having 2500
horse and many stragling foot. They report that a party of their
foot was to winter at Marlbrough, the rest to go to Winchester.
The King is reported this night to bee at the army againe."†

The Parliament Generals, upon the intelligence that the King
was quietly marching away, rode to the top of Clay Hill, "to
looke uppon the departing enemy," and then called the inevit-
able Council of War, which resulted in the customary wrangle,
and in the usual inaction. But one of their officers, whose
name is not recorded, determined to have one slash at the
King before he was out of their reach; and, having got a few
horse together, started in pursuit. His advance, however, having
been noticed by Rupert, the Prince unobserved placed a body of
his cavalry in a barn by the road-side, and let the pursuers pass;
but the moment they reached the King's lines, the ambushed
troopers came out from their hiding place and took the Parliament men "front and rear," so that, as Symonds records, 15 of

---

* The principal residence of the Berkshire Garrards was at Kingwood, about
one mile from Lamborne, on the road to Marlborough by way of Ramsbury, and
occupied a beautiful position on an eminence overlooking the Lamborne Valley.
The old house (where a room in the east wing was long shown as "The King's
Chamber") was taken down many years ago. The Mansion must have been of
considerable extent, judging from traces of the foundations; and the remaining
stabling attests its having been of the Elizabethan character. The line of the
avenue, leading from the high-road, and crossing the park, is still defined by a
few trees here and there; and many other vestiges of former importance can be
discerned. Queen Henrietta Maria was also at Kingwood, April 18th, 1644,
on her journey from Oxford to Bristol. There are several memorials of the
Garrards in Lamborne Church. The arms of the Garrards of Lamborne were
azure, a chevron engrailed ermine.

† Sir Samuel Luke's Letter-book; Egerton MSS.

them were killed and more taken prisoners. This was the only effort made to oppose or harass the King's march.

From Lamborne, the Lords Capel, Hopton, and Culpepper, with other officers, were sent on to Marlborough to provide quarters for the army, and to levy contributions on the inhabitants of the district for the support of the King's forces.

On Tuesday, 12th November, which turned out (says Symonds) "a miserable wett windy day," the army moved on from Lamborne to Marlborough, the King quartering in the house of Lord Seymour* at the Castle. The army was encamped on the Downs at Fyfield, about two miles distant.

The King remained five days at Marlborough, during which time he personally superintended the fortifications of the place; and he found that the fierce threats of his officers of the Commisariat department had so strongly impressed the terrified inhabitants of the district, that not only were the wants of the troops amply provided for, but a sufficient quantity of food and forage was left to supply some of his necessitous garrisons. The greater part of the hay and corn which the neighbourhood had just harvested was sent off, with a body of cavalry, to Worcester; and arrangements were made for re-victualling the garrisons at Donnington Castle and Basing.

The following warrant will show the manner in which these supplies were procured:—

"To the High Constables of Ramsbury Hund. and to each of them: "These are in His Majestie's name to command you or either of you to charge, provide, and send in, out of your Hundred to my quarters at Andrew Goddard's House at Ogborne St. Andrew, near Marlbury, for the use of his Majestie, two and twenty hundred weight of bread, twelve hundred weight of cheese, three fat Beefs, tenn fatt Muttons, fower dosens of poultrie, forty bushells of oates, twenty bushells of beanns and pease, also you are straitly charg'd to bringe in eight able and sufficient Teems with Carts for His Majestie's necessary service. Charging you and every one of you and every petty constable in your hundred not to presume the least neglect in the due and speedy execution hereof in every particular, and that all the said provisions and carts be brought in by three o'clock in the afternoone next Sunday, as you tender the good of His Majestie's service, your owne persons and estates. Given under my hand this 14th day of November, 1644. WM. MORGAN, Commissary.

---

* Francis, Lord Seymour, was brother to the Marquis of Hertford, afterwards Duke of Somerset. It was this Lord Seymour who built the house at Marlborough, afterwards known as the "Castle Inn," and which subsequently constituted the nucleus of the present famous School-house. The plans and elevations of this house were furnished by Inigo Jones, who was of the same political party as the Seymours, and then at the height of his fame as an architect. Ramsbury Manor-house also is said to have been built from designs by Inigo Jones; but this was the work of his pupil and nephew John Webb. The King quartered at Ramsbury Manor in April, 1644; where also Cromwell visited Lord Pembroke 12 July, 1649.

"You or either of you are required to be there present, with a return of the names of those who shall refuse to perform what is chardged upon them." *

Another warrant, dated at Marlborough, empowers the officers to seize all such "Physick and Chirurgery" in that town as shall be necessary for the use of the army, the owners to be paid out of the contributions from the district.

At a Council of War held at Marlborough on Saturday, the 16th November, it was decided that the relief-party to be sent to Basing should consist of 1000 horse, each trooper carrying before him a bag of corn or other provisions, and should march so as to reach there by a given time (communicated to the garrison), then each should throw down his sack, and make good his retreat as best he could. To effect this design, Hungerford was thought the most fitting place in which to quarter the army, and whence to dispatch the enterprize. Its conduct was entrusted to Sir Henry Gage, who had had such good success on a former occasion. Accordingly the troops marched back to Hungerford, where they arrived the same evening. †

The next day (Sunday) Sir Francis Doddington came to the King, out of the West, with a newly raised body of 500 horse.

While the King was at Marlborough, the Parliamentarians, hearing of his intention as regards Basing, left Newbury with the greater part of their force, with the view (as Cromwell states in his "Charge against Manchester") of proceeding to Kingsclere, "for a more direct interposicion in the King's way to Basing, and that there we might fight with him upon the downes, if he came that way; and lye ready (if he should bend towardes Newberry) to repossesse it before him; and on those grounds onely and to that end was our remove agreed to in full Councell:" "But," adds Cromwell, "being thus got out, and upon our way to Kingscleare, having intelligence that the King was coming by Hungerford towardes Newberry, his Lordship [Manchester] would then neither go on to Kingscleare, nor return into Newberry, but upon new pretences (without the Councell of Warre) turn'd his course to Aldermarston (which was five miles homewards from Newberry, and seaven miles nearer home then Kingscleare). And, though Kingscleare was the knowne direct roade to Basing, yet he pretended to turn to Aldermarston with intent to goe directly to Basing, and that he would fight the King there which way soever he should come, if he attempted to releive it. This gave some satisfaction for present, but from Aldermarston his Lord-

---

* Sir E. Walker's papers, Harl. MSS., 6802; 295. Many other interesting papers relating to the doings of the King's army at Marlborough will be found in the same collection.

† The King's quarters, while at Hungerford, were at the Bear Inn. It was at this same hostelry, that William, Prince of Orange received James II.'s Commissioners in Dec. 1688.

ship would not be got to Basing (makeing excuses), but with much adoo being got out next day to Mortimer Heath, he would not be perswaded to goe on any further, alledging that many of his soldiers were run to Redding, and more would goe thither (being got so neare it); that (when he pretended for Basing) drawcing the army to Aldermarston (which was cleare out of the way) he brought the soldiers soe neare Redding that they would be running thither, and then made their running thither an occasion to avoyde going to Basing at all, and at last to drawe all to Redding."

Manchester, in his Defence, says—"So, uppon our intelligence of the King's remove from Marlbarrow, it was supposed hee was marching to Basing, to relcive it with his army, wee conceived it fitting to march that day to Oldermeiston, where wee continued uppon the feilds, and, if the enemy went to Bascing, to endevour to intercept him; and so at Oldermeiston, at a councell of warr, where the question was only, whether it was councellable to fight or not, and concluded by all, no man speaking so much against fighting as Cromwell, and so unanimously consenting not to fight, but to endeavour to hinder the releife of Bascing, or to withdrawe the forces, which weare lying before Bascing, and so to keepe our armies intire, dividing ourselves, the foote at Redding and Henly, and our horse all about Fernham, Okingham, Windsor, Maydenhead, and Stwins" [Staines].

No sooner had the Parliamentarians left Newbury than the Governor of Donnington Castle, exasperated with the inhabitants for their refusal to afford succour to his garrison in any way, made a sally into the town "on the Lord's day," with the intention of seizing the Mayor and some of the principal inhabitants, and carrying them prisoners to the Castle, and demanding a ransom for their release. This design Sir John Boys nearly accomplished before an alarm was given, and a party of Parliamentary horse quartered in the town came to the rescue. A Parliamentary Journal * affirms that the party from the Castle went to the Mayor of the Town and pulled him out of his house, which they plundered, and that they "abused his whole family most shamefully;" and that they then went to the houses of eight or nine more chief persons in the place, dragged them also out of their dwellings, "abused their wives, children, and servants," and carried away great plunder; and that the gentlemen themselves were actually conveyed prisoners to Donnington Castle.

To return, however,—the Parliamentarians having withdrawn from Basing, Sir Henry Gage's expedition for its relief was satisfactorily accomplished; and Sir George Lisle, with 1000 men, took an ample supply of provisions to Sir John Boys at Donning-

---

* "Perfect Passages of each Day's Proceedings in Parliament," Wednesday, Nov. 20, 1644.

ton Castle, and brought back "without let or hindrance" the rest of the spare and military stores, which had been left behind a few days previously. Both Donnington Castle and Basing having now been well cared for, the King decided to return to Oxford, with the intention, if practicable, of surprising the Parliament's garrison at Abingdon on his way.

On Tuesday, the 19th November, which was the King's birthday, the army marched from Hungerford to Great Shefford, his Majesty lodging for the night at the old Manor-house. In his "Diary" (p. 153), Capt. Symonds writes—"Tuesday, 19 November His Majestie lay at Gt. Shefford in the old Manor-House of Mr. Browne, Esq., co. Berks; a parke belonging to it. This day a soljer hang'd for plunder, but the rope broke." A portion of the old Manor-House is still standing, and the meadows surrounding are still called the "Home Park." In the chancel of the adjoining Church is a monument to Sir George Browne, Knight of the Bath, who died in 1678. His younger brother John was created a baronet 19th May, 1665. This title became extinct in 1774, on the demise, without issue, of the 5th Baronet, Sir John Browne. This family was a younger branch of the Brownes, Viscounts Montague. Among the Sequestration and Composition Papers in the British Museum Library (Addl. MSS., No. 5508), is the following statement—"Mr. Browne, of Shefforde, being proved a papist and in armes, his estate, worth £200 p. anum, was let at Micheallmas last at £70 to Mr. Browne's baley, and £1000 profered for his stock, and secueritie for the munies, was sould to his baly for £400 p."

In his "Diary," on the same day (Nov. 19), Captain Symonds also inserts the following notes—

"Lord B. [Lord Bernard Stuart] and troope at Little Fawley, the neate and faire habitacion of the Lady Moore, wife to Sir Henry. —Painted over the porch at Lady Moore's howse—*
"Argent, a moor-cock sable [Moore]. Motto—Regi et legi.
"The same; impaling, argent, a saltire engrailed gules, a chief azure, "TWITTYE." Suum cuiquo pulchrum.
"Champion all this part of Berks.†
"He that built this howse was Sergeant Moore,‡ temp. D. Egerton, Canc.: Sir Henry was his son. Nothing but Moore's coate in the church of Fawley."§

---

* A great portion of this Mansion still exists, and is occupied as a farm-house. The arms over the porch are gone; and the Church has been rebuilt.

† "Champion" *i.e.* champion land; land not inclosed; downs and open fields.

‡ The celebrated lawyer Sir Francis Moore, who was born at East Ilsley in 1558, died Nov. 20, 1621, and was buried at Great Fawley. Sir Francis married Anne, heiress of William Twitty, Esq., of Boreham in Essex, by whom he had five sons and five daughters. Henry the eldest, referred to by Symonds, was created a baronet in 1627, and died in 1635, when his son, of the same name, succeeded to the title and estates. The Baronetcy became extinct on the demise of Sir Thomas, 6th Baronet, without issue, 10th April, 1807.

§ Symonds's "Diary," p. 154.

On Wednesday, Nov. 20th, the King marched to Wantage, passing the night at the house of Sir George Wilmot at Charlton; and on Thursday he went on to Faringdon, lodging while at Faringdon with his garrison at Sir Robert Pye's house, near the Church. After remaining here a day, the King quitted the army, and, accompanied by his guard, proceeded to Oxford, to which city he made a safe and happy return on Saturday the 23rd November.

No sooner had the King left the army than Prince Rupert, strong in the power of his own will, determined to make an attack on the garrison at Abingdon; but the vigilant and able governor Brown was not to be easily caught; and the Prince, having lost several of his men, was glad to get back again to Faringdon, little satisfied with the result of his expedition. The King's army were then put into their winter cantonments, and Rupert joined the King at Oxford.

The Parliamentary historian, Oldmixon, the bitter opponent of the Stuarts, with creditable candour, thus speaks of the King's admirable conduct in this campaign. "If the same courage and conduct had been shewn by the King in so good a cause as that of King William at the Boyne, his fame and his memory would have been equally glorious and immortal."

The disappointment in Parliament, and in London generally, at the result of the Second Battle at Newbury was extreme. The day after the news arrived of the engagement between the two armies the monthly fast took place as usual (Oct 30, 1644), as if there were no subject for rejoicing. Disagreeable rumours began to circulate: the victory, it was said, might have been far more decisive; but discord had reigned amongst the generals, who had suffered the King to retreat without impediment, almost in the very face of the army, on a bright moonlight night, when the least movement might have prevented it. It was much worse when the news came that the King had just reappeared in the neighbourhood of Newbury,—that he had, without interruption, removed his artillery from Donnington Castle,—and had even offered to renew the battle, without the Parliamentary army quitting its inaction. The clamour became general, and the House of Commons ordered an enquiry. Cromwell had only waited for this opportunity, to break out:—" It is to the Earl of Manchester," he said, "all the blame is to be imputed, ever since the battle of Marston Moor; he is afraid to conquer, afraid of a great and decisive success; but now, when the King was last near Newbury, nothing would have been more easy than entirely to destroy his army. I went to the General; I showed him evidently how this could be done; I desired his leave to make the attack with my own brigade; other officers urged this with me, but he obstinately refused; saying only, that if we were entirely to overthrow the King's army, the King would still be King, and always have another army to keep up the war; while we, if we were beaten, should no longer be any thing but rebels and traitors, execrated and forfeited by the law." These last words greatly moved Parliament, who could not endure that any should suggest a doubt as to the legality of their resistance. Next day, in the Upper House, Manchester answered this attack; explained his conduct and his words; and in turn accused Cromwell of insubordination, of falsehood, even of treachery; for on the day of the battle (he said) neither he nor his regiment appeared at the post assigned them. Cromwell did not reply to this charge; but renewed his own accusations more violently than before.

It would be foreign to the design of this Memoir to devote much space to the elucidation of the notorious quarrel between Manchester and Cromwell, which has been so largely treated of by recent writers. This great leading incident in the history of our Civil War, observes Professor Masson,* "brought to the surface and into direct antagonism principles of the very greatest significance in reference to the management of the war; and the triumph of the movement-party on that occasion led directly to the ruin of the royal cause." Indeed, it enabled Cromwell, by the exercise of extraordinary finesse, to bring forward and successfully carry through the Commons the "Self-denying Ordinance," which enacted—

"That during the time of this War no member of either House shall have or execute any office or command, military or civil, granted or conferred by both or either of the Houses of Parliament, or any authority derived from both or either of the Houses, and that an Ordinance be brought in accordingly."

The Ordinance was rejected by the Lords. The Commons had found another way of effecting their great purpose of army reform, by requiring the Committee of both kingdoms to report at once on "The New Model of the Army," which they had been instructed to devise. This had been done on the 9th January, 1645; and by the 28th it had passed the Commons; and on February 15th, "The New Model Ordinance" became law. It was no longer of any use for the Lords to stand out against "The Self-denying Ordinance." That Ordinance, in fact, was already realized in the fabric of the "New Model;" and, accordingly, having been reintroduced into the Commons in a modified form, and having passed that House, it received the assent of the Lords on April 3rd, 1645. On the preceding day, the Earls of Essex and Manchester had simplified matters by formally resigning their military commands. The commander-

---

* Historical Preface to the "Quarrel between the Earl of Manchester and Oliver Cromwell."—Camden Soc., 1875.

in-chief of the New Model Army was to be Sir Thomas Fairfax, and the Major-General, or third in command, was to be Philip Skippon. The place of Lieutenant-General, or second in command, was at first left vacant, but Cromwell's name, exempted by special vote from the operation of the "Self-denying Ordinance," was soon inserted into the "New Model Army," in the post of Lieutenant-General, which had been purposely kept open for him. Thence, through successive stages, followed the rest of his career, ending in his Protectorship of the United Commonwealth of England, Scotland, and Ireland, with their Colonies and Dominions.

Professor Masson further remarks that the accurate student of English history will note that the termination of this famous quarrel between Cromwell and Manchester coincides in time with another great event, distinct from the new modelling of the army and the Self-Denying Ordinance, namely the Establishment of the Presbyterian system in England, the first definite votes for which, in the two Houses, were made in January, 1644-5.

It is worthy of record that the new model army, on their first march, came to Newbury. On the 30th April, Fairfax marched from Windsor to Reading; and on the 2nd May quartered in the town of Newbury, where a meeting took place between the General and Cromwell.* Fairfax then went on his way to Taunton; but, being recalled, with orders to invest Oxford, the army again returned to Newbury on the 14th; where they remained, "to refresh," three days. Within a few weeks (14th June) came the crowning defeat of the King at Naseby.

The end of this phase of the Great War was rapidly approaching; and a brief reference to the later history of Donnington Castle, as a royal garrison, which is related in a most interesting and hitherto unpublished narrative (given in the Appendix), will be sufficient to precede the closing scene.

The Parliament during the spring and summer of 1645 had too important work on hand to be able to pay much attention to Donnington Castle; but in the autumn of that year it was determined to set about the siege in earnest. Cromwell strongly urged the House to curb the predatory excursions of Sir John Boys and the Governors of Wallingford and Faringdon, which so injuriously interfered with the trade between London and the West; and, for that purpose, he advised "a strong quarter" being made at Newbury. Late in October Cromwell and Col. Dalbier were near that town, after the taking of Basing House (14th Oct., 1645). The Parliament had ordered that Donnington Castle should be taken; and had sent letters to the three Committees in Oxfordshire, Berks, and Bucks to join forces for this purpose. Cromwell seems to have weighed the chances of

* Sprigg's "Anglia Rediviva."

an assault, and to have decided against it, declining such a "knotty piece of service;" for he marched into Devonshire to join Fairfax, leaving Dalbier to invest the Castle, which he did in November. Boys still held out until March, in which month he made his last sally, and took 50 of Dalbier's men prisoners. This exploit and other incidents of the last days of the siege are thus described in the "Weekly Account," under date of Thursday, 26th March, 1646. "From Dennington we have received intelligence that Col. Dalbeer, drawing up close to the Castle to break the ground and intrench our men, the enemy at our beginning to break the ground sallied forth, took 50 prisoners, two colors, and some of the spades and pickaxes, but this retarded not the work, for since that time he hath shot divers granadoes into the Castle, fired the Barn and some other Outhouses, and done some execution on the main Fabrick, which hath brought the enemy to stoop and send out to desire a parley, which being refused the Governor hath sent to Oxford desiring to be satisfied in time whether he may expect reliefe, for otherwise he must be forced to a render on such conditions he could get, which his long standing out will in no way advance." The following week, Tuesday, March 31st, the correspondent of the same journal thus proceeds to inform its readers of the progress of events:—"I have already told you what execution Col. Dalbeer hath done against Dennington Castle, and of the Governour's sending to Oxford, I shall in this place give you the sequill; for it is this day certified that upon the messenger's going to Oxford Sir John Boys (Governor of the Castle) received not only assurance that he could expect no relief from Oxford, but further that there was a great defeat given to Sir Jacob Astley, which till now he seemed ignorant of. Hereupon the Governor stooping to play on such conditions as before he seemed to reject, a treaty was hearkned unto, and we understand this day by Mr. Packer's son, whose inheritance it is (and come from thence this day) that Col. Dalbeere is to have the possession thereof tomorrow at nine of of the clocke. * * There are in the Castle about 200 common souldiers, divers pieces of Ordnance, and good store of Baggage."

The "Moderate Intelligencer," of the same date, informs its readers that "This day came the news of the Accord of Dennington Castle, which they are to surrender tomorrow; the granadoes made such work that the souldiers within knew not where to secure themselves, divers leaping over their works and craving quarter; the house will be preserved for that universally well spoken of gentleman and owner Mr. Packer."

Boys, who was cooped up within the fortress, ignorant of the state of affairs without, and finding the old walls coming down about his ears, upon the return of the King's messenger with instructions to deliver up the Castle, surrendered it into the hands of Col. Dalbier on the following conditions:—

ARTICLES AGREED UPON, MONDAY, THE 30TH MARCH, 1646,
FOR THE SURRENDRING OF DENNINGTON CASTLE.*

1. It is agreed upon, that Sir John Boys, knight, Governour of Dennington Castle aforesaid, shall march according to the Articles insuing agreed upon (that is to say) upon Wednesday morning next, being the first day of April, by 6 of the clock, the Governour, with all his Officers, Gentlemen, and Souldiers, are then to march out with Cullers flying and Drums beating, the Governour with 4 horses and arms, and every Field Officer with 2, and every Capt. 1, the Lieut.-Col. of horse with two horses and arms, and the other officers and reformado officers of horse with 1 horse and arms apiece, 100 of the foot soldiers to march with their arms two miles, and the rest to march without, towards Wallingford, and then 50 to lay down their arms, and the other 50 to march with Cullers flying, drums beating, light matches, Bullets in their mouth, and Bandeliers fil'd with powder.

2. That if any officer or souldier in this Garrison hath been in the Parliament service, shall receive the equall benefit comprised in these articles.

3. That what officer or souldier late of this garrison shall desire to go beyond sea, shall have a Passe to go to London, or to what place they shall desire, within the Parliament's quarters, to procure the same accordingly.

4. That all Officers and Souldiers, late of this Garrison, who desire to go to their own Mansions or place of residence and several dwellings, have a free passe to do so, without being molested or pressed to any oath, provided that they be engaged never to take up arms against the Parliament.

5. That there shall be a safe conduct granted to Wallingford accordingly.

6. That there shall be two Carts with teams, provided by the time appointed, the one to carry Sir John's baggage, the other to carry the Officers'.

7. That the Governor, Officers, and Souldiers, late of Dennington Castle aforesaid, shall at the time deliver up the Castle aforesaid to Col. Dulbier for the use of the Parliament, with all the Ordnance, Arms, Ammunition, and Provision therein (except what is before expressed), without embezzling the arms or ammunition, or demolishing the works.

8. That the prisoners now in Dennington Castle shall upon the signing of these articles be delivered forth and set at liberty.

9. That the wounded Souldiers of the Castle shall have liberty to be left in Newbury or elsewhere the Governour pleases, and to have present passes, that after their recovery they may go to their severall mansions or dwellings without interruption or molestation.

Signed	COLL. MARTIN, MAJOR RYNES, MAJOR COLLINGWOOD	For COL. DULBIER.
	MAJOR BENNET, CAPT. OSBORN, CAPT. GREGORY,	For SIR JOHN BOYS.

---

* "Perfect Occurrences of Both Houses of Parliament and Martiall Affairs, beginning Friday, the 27 March, and ending Friday, 3 April, 1646."

SIR JOHN BOYS.
From an original portrait.

THE SECOND BATTLE OF NEWBURY.

The field which tradition points out as that in which Dalbier was encamped, and where the treaty for the surrender of the Castle was negotiated, is still called "Dalbier's Meadow." It lies on the eastern side of the Castle, and near the gardens and park of Donnington-Castle House.*

Colonel Dalbier, having been left out of the Parliament's New Model Army, left their service and joined the King's side, to avenge the affront. He was engaged with Lord Holland in the rising at Kingston-on-Thames in 1648, almost the last struggle for the royal cause, when Lord Francis Villiers was killed. The Earl of Holland, with Dalbier, a few other officers, and about 100 troopers, managed to escape; but, being pursued, they were forced to engage near St.-Noots, when Dalbier and young Kenelm Digby fell mortally wounded, while the Earl (according to Clarendon) gave himself up without resistance. Mr. Petit Andrews, in his reply to Mores' "Berkshire Queries," 1759, mentions that "the country people have a foolish notion that Dalbier was invulnerable, and that cannon-balls were seen to bound from his body!"

The honourable and exceptional terms given to the gallant and faithful custodian of the Castle, Sir John Boys, bear witness that his unshaken loyalty to his King was acknowledged and admired by those who by the chances of war were his enemies; and perhaps it would be impossible to find a brighter page in the whole history of these Civil Commotions than that which records the deeds of daring and devotion of this brave Cavalier.

---

* "Hist. of Newbury," p. 67.

APPENDIX.

I.—THE KING'S MARCH TO NEWBURY.

OCTOBER, 1644.

(From the "Iter Carolinum.")

Friday, 18 Oct. to Andover. The White Hart. (Dinner in the field.) 1 night; 15 miles.
Saturday, 19 Oct. to Whitchurch. Mr. Brooke's.* (Dinner on the field.) 2 nights; 7 miles.
Monday, 21 Oct. to Kingsclere. Mr. Towers'.† (Dinner at Whitchurch.) 1 night; 5 miles.
Tuesday, 22 Oct. to Newbury. Master Dunce's ‡ night's residence. (Dinner at Kingsclere.) 5 nights; 6 miles.
Monday, 21 October. His Majestie, &c. left Whitchurch, the general rendesvouz (sic) upon the Downe near Kingsmill's howse. §

---

* Whitchurch. The King when at Whitchurch quartered at "The Priory," the house of Mr. Thomas Brooke, a staunch royalist, whose family had long resided at Whitchurch. There are several of their memorials in the Church. Thomas Brooke was lay impropriator of the Rectory; but, being proved a "Delinquent" by the Parliament, his estates were sequestrated, and the Minister of his appointment expelled. The inhabitants of Whitchurch petitioned the Committee for Compositions, sitting at Goldsmiths' Hall, to grant an increase of stipend, out of Mr. Brooke's estate, to the "Orthodox" minister, Mr. Bellchamber, whose income was only £14 a year, a quarter of malt, and a quarter of wheat. The Committee accordingly voted £50 a year for this purpose. The petition, which is preserved at the Record Office, is signed by Will. Pointer, Robt. Mills, Richd. Holloway, Will. Rolph, Will. Webb, Dan. Clarke, and others.

† Kingsclere. The residence of Mr. Towers was at Frobury Park, about one mile from Kingsclere. Part of the old mansion at Frobury is now occupied as a farm-house, on the south side of which are the remains of the ancient chapel. A portion of the stone pulpit was in the building within the last fifty years; and at the present time the base of the font, which appears to be of local stone, does duty as a horse-block in the farm-yard. The house is partly surrounded by a moat, which probably also served as a fish-stew. Foundations have been met with in various parts of the grounds, showing that a building of considerable extent once existed here. Traces of a carriage-drive to the mansion from the Ecchinswell-and-Newbury road are discernible; the chief approach was, as at present, from the Kingsclere road on the south. In the "Lay Subsidy Rolls," Pub. Record Office, $\frac{175}{550}$, 17 Car. I. 1641, Robert Towers is described as "of Frobury, Gent.," and assessed as owner. This was most probably the gentleman who received the King. The property is now life-hold, and reverts to Lord Bolton.

‡ See Appendix II.

§ At Sydmonton. Henry, second son of Sir Henry Kingsmill, of Sydmonton, was slain when fighting gallantly for the King at Edgehill, and was buried in the Churchyard of Radway. In Jago's Poem of "Edgehill," there is a print of this monument; but only the mutilated remains of the effigy now exist, and these are preserved in the tower of Radway New Church. In the Kingsmill Chapel, Kingsclere Church, there is a fine alabaster altar-tomb, with effigies of Sir Henry and Lady Bridget Kingsmill.

APPENDIX. 163

(From Symonds's "Diary.")

Tuesday, 22 Oct. The general rendesvouz (sic) was upon Red Heath, neare Newbery.† His Majestie knighted Sir John Boys upon the hill, the Governor of Dennyngton Castle that was so much battered, and so often sett upon by all their forces at severall times. The King lay at Mr. Duns his howse in Newbery: the troope at Welford, the Manor belonging to Mr. Hinton, *jure uxoris,* a faire habitacion, com. Berks.

II.—THE KING'S STAY IN NEWBURY.

The late Mr. C. E. Long, M.A., the able editor of Symonds' Diary, has suggested that the name of the King's host at Newbury during the few days he was here before the Second Battle, and which is written by Symonds "Duns," and in the 'Iter Carolinum' "Dunce," may have been intended for "Dunch"; but no record has been found of any branch of this extremely anti-royalist family having resided in Newbury. In the "Protestation Returns," given at page 92, the name of — Dunce, * Esq., of Newbury, appears written exactly as spelt by the careful compiler of the "Iter Carolinum," Garter-King-at-Arms, who adds "a night's residence." We are told by "The True Informer" for the week ending Oct. 26th, that "His Majesty lay Wednesday night at Newbury, at one Mr. Weston's house, where he was on Thursday morning, it not being possible for him to get to Oxford, by reason of the great floods." If we can believe "Mercurius Aulicus," we are spared a deal of unnecessary investigation in endeavouring to identify the house where the King stayed, for that paper tells us *it was demolished!* The following is the version given by the Royalist chronicler—" Tuesday, Oct. 29, 1644, next morning after His Majesty's army was drawn off from Newbury, the Rebells very eagerly entered the town, where they quickly manifested their strength was much abated, but their malice as high as ever, for the first enquiry they made was for the house where His Majesty himself had lodged, and no sooner found it out, but instantly (like perfect Rebells) they layd the house flat with the ground, and if that was not sufficient to speake them the worst of Rebells, they took that very Bed whereon they guessed His Sacred Majesty had lyen, hacked the bed-poasts with their swords, cut and slasht the bedding, and scattered the pieces up and down the streets, evidencing themselves

---

* In the "Subsidy Rolls," Pub. Record Office, the name is spelt "Daunce," and also in a petition from the inhabitants of Newbury, 1625-6, in respect to the town's purchasing the manorial rights of the Crown. In Blewbury Church is a monument to the wife of Sir John Daunce, and daughter of Thos. Latton of Chilton, near Ilsley. The name has gradually been reduced to "Dance."

the most perjur'd, bloody, malitious covenanters, that sweare they fight for His Majestie's Person and Honour! and yet are wild because they cannot murther him, from whose mercies God Almighty still preserve him."

From the above accounts it appears quite clear that the King slept at Mr Dunce's house on Tuesday night, and at Mr. Weston's on Wednesday night. (The latter was Mayor of Newbury the following year, 1645, and also in 1652.) In the "History of Newbury" (p. 47), it is stated that a certain Mr. Hoar, a wealthy clothier,* who appears, from local records, to have been a person of good position in the town, gave up his house, on the west side of Chepe Street, for the residence of the King. The house was on the spot now occupied by the residence of Mr. E. P. Plenty, of the Eagle Iron-works.

When the army, however, was drawn out from the town and quartered at Shaw, Donnington, and Speen, the King probably took up his residence at Shaw House, placed at his disposal by Sir Thomas Dolman, then a youth, scarcely of age,—"which place," says Richard Blome in his "Britannia," published in 1673, "had the good fortune in the time of the late war to receive His Majesty and His Majesty now reigning" (Charles II., then Prince of Wales). At Shaw House a brass plate is inserted in the wainscot of a room on the east side of the mansion, to commemorate an attempt made to shoot the King while dressing at the window. It was probably placed here by the zealous antiquary, Mr. Petit Andrews, F.S.A., author of a "Continuation of Henry's History of England," who was born at Shaw in 1737, and contributed much valuable local information to Mores' "Collections towards a Parochial History of England." The brass plate is thus inscribed — "The Hole in the Wainscot, which appears through the aperture of this plate, was occasioned by a ball discharged from the musquet of a Parliamentary Soldier at King Charles the First, while he sate dressing himself in this Projection. The ball was found and preserved during many years, but is now lost. This regicidal attempt seems to have been made on Oct. 26 or 27, A.D. 1644."

Then follows an extract from Blome, a portion of which is given above, and a quotation from Ludlow's "Memoires," vol. i. pp. 129 and 131.

On another plate on the opposite side of the window, a second record of the event is placed in a frame, in the centre of which is a medallion portrait of Charles I., with this inscription—

"HANC JUXTA FENESTRAM
REX CAROLUS PRIMUS
INSTANTE OBSIDIONE
SCLOPPOPETRÆ ICTUS TANTUM NON
TRAJECTUS FUIT
DIE OCTOB. XXVII, MDCXLIV."

The above tradition of the bullet is probably not to be wholly disregarded, although the reference to a "siege" of the house is a mistake.

---

* The "Diary or Exact Journal," Oct. 24 to 31, 1644, certifies that the King lodged "in a Cloathier's house," but does not mention the name of its owner.

APPENDIX. 165

III.—RED HEATH AND RED HILL.

Many opinions have been given as to the locale of this Heath and Hill, mentioned by Sir Edward Walker, Symonds, and other writers as the spot where the King's army held their rendezvous on their arrival in the neighbourhood of Newbury, Tuesday, 22nd October, 1644; and where Col. Boys received the honour of knighthood from the King. Some have placed it on Greenham Common, others at Snelsmore; but the view now advanced is that the camping-ground was more probably on the Wash and adjacent Heath, where we still find the names of Red Heath and Red Hill (marked on the Plan).

It appears that the Royalists were surprised to find the Parliamentarians in such close proximity on Tuesday, 22nd October, on which day their whole army, according to Cromwell (a most exact narrator of the campaign), was in the neighbourhood of Aldermaston, on the way from Basingstoke, with the intention (as he thought) of intercepting the King by a direct advance towards Newbury. The Earl of Manchester, however, much to Cromwell's chagrin, who objected to such a retrograde movement, marched the next day to Reading, giving the Royalists an idea that they retreated to avoid coming to an engagement (see above, p. 115). When it was found that the enemy followed so closely on their track, the divergence from the direct route to Newbury from Kingsclere, and the holding-back of the main body of the King's army on Red Heath, may have been advised as a precautionary measure, in case the enemy should attack with his vastly superior force on the east side of Newbury; the King's position on the south of the town (which was occupied by a body of his horse) having the advantage of the River Kennet as a barrier to a surprise. Sir Edward Walker * mentions that "the King caused his army to be so quartered as to do but little duty, and yet to be secure from the rebels, who (it was thought) would not attempt us in that place, and whence his army could not conveniently remove till he had done his endeavours for the relief of Basing, and that the Earl of Northampton, with that additional strength he took with him to Banbury, was returned."

Again, a Parliamentary Journal of the 26th Oct.† tell us:—"The King's forces have pulled up Thatcham bridge [over the Kennet between Thatcham and Greenham Common] to prevent our forces, if they can, following after them. Our Pioneers are laying the Bridge again, because the waters are too high to pass over the fords," intimating that the King's forces were on the south side of the Kennet. The "Parliamentary Scout," of the same date, is more explicit on the subject—"We are informed (it reports) that this day at night our armies were very near the King's; that we had declined the way of the Bridge, by which we should have entered on the south side of the King's powers, and that we had gone up by the Rivulet [the Lamborne] which runs by Donnington Castle, and had forded it above . . . and were got upon the north between Oxford and the King" [the hill before Shaw].

---

* Histor. Discourses, p. 110.
† "Perfect Passages in Parliament," Oct. 26, 1644.

Another Diurnal* says—"The west was open to the King to bring in provisions: that he pulled up some bridges about Thatcham to hinder the advance of the Parliamentary forces, by reason of which it was considered His Majesty had resolved to retreat westwards." On the evening of the 27th October, a Spy informed the Scout-Master General [Sir Samuel Luke], that the King's army had arrived at Newbury on Tuesday, and were "quartered on the heath," the King and his chief officers lodging in the town, and that this day, about sun-setting, a party of horse left the camp to march to the relief of Banbury.†

The most precise delineator, however, of this disputed rendezvous is Capt. Gwynne, who, in his "Memoirs," ch. xi, says—"The second Newbury fight we drew upon the same ground the enemy fought us upon the first battle," in which the Captain was also engaged. Gwynne mentions, in the next chapter, that the King marched with his army from the camp "faire and orderly through the towne into the spacious Spinham-lands," clearly indicating that the troops advanced from the south side of Newbury. Further on, in ch. xv., Gwynne adds—"And the Messenger that came to the King at Newbury, and brought him intelligence that Banbury was besieged, might as well at the same instant told him that on the other side of the town were three armies [that] waylaid him, then perhaps he had thought fit to keep on the same side of the town he was on, and plant some of his great guns against the town's end and the river-side, and let the enemy which pursued him fall upon his cannons' mouth (if they liked it) rather than he did fall upon theirs, and if the King did approve of so doing, then he could easily march away that night and send to his army at Oxford and to the Earl of Northampton to come and meet him where he thought convenient."

From Kingsclere to Red Heath or Common the whole district was at that time one continuous heath, traversed by tracks and roads well enough adapted for the passage of an army, and enabling them to avoid the danger of marching through an enclosed country by narrow roads. There is apparently no reason why Greenham Common, had it been the rendezvous, should not have been correctly described, as even in "Domesday Book" it is called "Greneham;" and in all seventeenth-century maps and documents contemporary with the war it is properly designated; and, indeed, had the King's army been encamped here, their position could readily have been observed by the Parliamentarians on the corresponding heights at Shaw. The existence of the names "Red Heath" and "Red Hill" in the neighbourhood of the Wash certainly makes this locality more compatible with the narratives than other sites devoid of these distinctive appellations.

Cromwell, in his narrative, describes the field adjoining Clay Hill as "Red Hill field," and this has induced a consideration as to the site of the King's camp on the 22nd Oct. being on that side of the town; but this view does not prove tenable; for on the near approach of the Parliamentarians on Friday, this hill was occupied by a detachment of horse under Prince Maurice, but not in any strength.

---

* "Diary or Exact Journal," Oct. 24 to 31, 1644.
† Sir Samuel Luke's Letter-Book, Egerton MSS.

APPENDIX. 167

IV.—ACCOUNT OF THE SECOND BATTLE OF NEWBURY.

From a MS. belonging to the Earl de la Warr, in the "Fourth Report of the Historical MSS. Commission," p. 297.

"Oct. 30, 1644. CHAS. MURRY to SIR JOHN BERKELEY.

"About three in the afternoon Waller and Essex came with a resolution to carry all clear before them, which they had not much failed of, if they had known how ill our horse and some of Prince Maurice's foot behaved. The truth is, they had beaten our foot from the pase [pass], and routed most of our horse before ever they ...... them; but Lord Barrard [Bernard Stuart] that knows not how to retreat, charged so handsomely that he beat them back before they could see the disaster we were in; it was dark, they could not pursue. Amongst us was nothing known but utter ruin and loss of all, so that the King was advised, with his son and some lords and three troops (having but one way to pass to go away) which my Lord Bar. commands, to get away and join Prince Rupert; so the King got to Dennington Castle by 9 at night, and thence took guides that brought him safe next day by night to Bath. It seems that after the King had gone, the army rallied and marched that night to Wallingford, and found that we lost not above 200 or 300 men, and six cannons lost at the Hill toward Hungerford: for at the other pass and at a house which Geo. Lile maintained we beat them sufficiently at the same instant that the rebels were so successful at the other end. No man could have done action of more courage or resolution than he did that day; he killed above 500 and took two cannons." (2½pp.)

V.—NEWBURY CHURCH AS A PRISON AND HOSPITAL.

At the time of the War, Newbury Church was used both as a prison and a hospital. There is a most interesting petition among the State Papers, in the Public Record Office, from John Bonwak, a distinguished sufferer in the Royal cause, and prisoner at Newbury. Shortly after the Restoration he sued for some compensation. The signatures attached to his petition are by men of note and name. He alleges that he had been Clerk of Rygate, and at the time of his petition was Rector of Newdigate. He asks for letters mandatory to the University of Cambridge for his D.D. degree. He had left Christ's College, Cambridge (as many other University men did) in 1643, and entered the army to fight for the King. After the Second Battle, he says, he was stripped, imprisoned, and almost starved to death in Newbury Church. Thence he marched barefoot to London House, and was there again imprisoned. He escaped, and ventured his life for the Restoration. Attached to his petition, as testimony, is the *clarum et venerabile nomen* of Jeremy Taylor, also that of Lord Mordaunt and eight others, who testify that, rather than comply with the ruling powers, he had refused several good livings, and, with his wife and six children, had remained on one of £20 per annum.

VI.—BOXFORD.

There is no parochial record at Boxford of any local incidents connected with the military operations which took place in the immediate neighbourhood during the years 1643-4-5; but in the Register for the succeeding year there is the following entry— "Thomas Adams, souldier of Cap. Pym's troope was buryed April yᵉ 5, 1646." In one of the later Parish Books the following curious memorandum is made:—

"Thomas Dore declar'd in ye presence of us whose names are hereunto subscribed, that he remember'd in the Oliverian rump times, when subjects rebell'd and did wht seem'd right in their own eyes, that William and Ralph Coxhead pull'd down and carry'd away ye very well turn'd decent rails fixed and placed across the rising upper part of the Chancel to separate the Communion Table, and that they were carry'd by the above-named persons to one Edwd. Pokes (Schoolmaster), who then lived on Westbrooke side, who with his scholars triumph'd and rejoiced with those Puritans over this sacrilegious spoil and broke in pieces and burnt the same. Attested and declar'd in the presence of Anthony Tassell, rector, and Lucy Tassell, April 11, 1721." *

There is a tradition preserved in the village that the Parliamentary soldiers, on more than one occasion, stabled their horses in the church.

In this Church there is a monument, of neat design, to the Rev. Jas. Anderson, rector of the parish, who died in 1672. It has the appearance of marble, but it is made of clunch or hard chalk. The inscription describes Mr. Anderton as "a determined defender of the orthodox faith, even among the Robels." This clergyman figures conspicuously in the "Life of Oliver Sansom," the Berkshire Quaker, with whom he had a long religious controversy.

---

* However much such excesses as were practised at this period are to be lamented, it must be borne in mind that the destroyers were acting in many instances against their will, and in strict accordance with an ordinance which had passed the Houses of Lords and Commons, and which enacted that all altars and tables of stone, with candlesticks, basons, &c., should be taken away and demolished; and also that all communion-tables should be removed from the east end to the body of all churches and chapels; all rails before any altar or communion-table, likewise, to be taken away, and the chancel levelled; all crucifixes, crosses, images in and upon all and every church or churchyard to be destroyed; and none of the like "superstitious ornaments" to be allowed in any church, chapel, or other place throughout the land. The execution of this order was delegated to the Churchwardens of each parish, with severe penalties in case of default. Exception only was made to the monument of any King, Prince, or Nobleman, "which hath not been commonly reputed to be taken for a saint." Complaints having been made to the Parliament of laxity in performing this Order of the House, a second Ordinance was issued to the Committee of each County, peremptorily enforcing the execution of the decree. See "Journals of House of Commons, Aug. 27, 1643, and Aug. 19, 1645."

VII.—BUCKLEBURY.

The Register of this Parish (remarkably perfect from the first year in which such records were appointed to be kept, 1538) contains the following interesting entries, which have been courteously communicated by the Vicar, the Rev. T. Watts.

"1644, April 20. Wm. Basset being slaine by a souldier was buried.
" „ April 29. Richd. Buxie a soldier of the Kinge was slaine by a Parliament souldier at Chappell Row and buried.
" 1645, Oct. 29. Mr. Richard Warde a Lieutenant for the Parliament was slaine and buried.
" Dec. 9. Henry Hall being slaine was buried."

The famous Guy Carleton was Vicar of this parish during the troublous times of the Civil War. Walker gives the following account of him:—"He was of a good and ancient family in Cumberland, and educated at Queen's College in Oxford, where he became successively *Poor Child, Taberder, Fellow*, and *Proctor*. Upon the breaking out of the Rebellion he faithfully adhered to his Majesty's interest, and did him considerable service. He was first driven from his rich living in the North; afterwards, coming into Berkshire, he was patronized by Mr. Gravets of Hartley Court, who presented him to the living of Bucklebury, in the right of his Guard Sir Henry Winchcombe, from whence also he was driven by the Tryers. After which he was likewise seized and imprisoned in Lambeth House, whither his wife secretly conveyed him a cord, by the help of which he let himself down through a window towards the Thames; but, the cord not reaching to the ground, he was forced to drop from it, and in the fall dislocated one of his bones, but a boat being provided for him, he was soon carried off, and lay concealed during the cure, to pay for which his poor wife was forced to sell her very bed. After his recovery he fled beyond the seas to his Majesty; in the meantime one of his daughters was maintained by Mrs. Gravets; and his wife and two other daughters were supported in London, partly by some charities, and partly by their own labour. Mr. Carleton returned with his Majesty from beyond the seas, became one of his Chaplains, D.D., Dean of Carlisle, Prebendary of Durham, and in 1671 was advanced to the Bishopric of Bristol, and in 1678 translated from thence to Chichester. He died in the year 1685." Walker's "Sufferings of the Clergy," pt. ii. p. 214.

VIII.—THE LICENSE OF WAR.

The following letter, from one of their own officers, will convey some idea of the excesses committed by the Parliamentary soldiers in this neighbourhood, and of the grievous evils attendant on a state of civil warfare, such indeed as were also attributed with perhaps equal truth by the Parliamentary party to the Royalist soldiers.

From Col. Wm. Ball to Speaker Lenthall; dated from Reading, March 1, 1645.

"Sir, I have been 10 days at Reading upon the command of the House for the ordering of the recruits for the army, and find the employment very troublesome; yet the service succeeding indifferently well answereth my paines and expectations; but that which exceedingly affects me is the continual clamour of the soldiers at Newberry and country people thereabout, the soldiers having almost starved the people where they quarter, and are half-starved themselves for want of pay, and are become very desperate, raging about the country, breaking and robbing houses and passengers, and driving away sheep and other cattell before the owners' faces. Every day bringeth more instances of these outrages. I shall mention only two amongst others the country people are now relating unto me. Some of the soldiers were driving away the sheep of Andrew Pottinger, of Wolhampton, a freeholder of £60 per annum, a very considerable man for the Parliament, having a wife and 6 young children, who endeavouring to secure his sheep, the soldiers struck him on the head so that he became presently speechless, and dead within four hours, to the great grief and sorrow of the neighbourhood. Another party of nyne soldiers, armed with muskets, came yesterday to the house of Mr. Illsley, of Beenham, and broke open his door, to the great affright of his wife, he being absent, and hearing of it, got together his neighbours and so beat the soldiers that they were all wounded and not able to return to their quarters. I will give many more instances were it necessary, but this I thought fitt to discover unto you, that the soldiers and country people are all grown desperate, and continue one against the other that we are like to have little other than killing and robbery, if there be not a speedy supply of money for the soldiers. I beseech you to take the opportunity to acquaint the House with the condition of these parts, which under the most terrible time of the enemy was nothing so badd. I am sorry, I have such a badd subject, and shall therefore conclude, craving leave to subscribe myself, Sir, your humble servant, WILL. BALL."* (Tanner MSS., Bodl. Libr., vol. 60-2, No. 491).

Another case of outrage and pillage, in this instance countenanced by the Parliamentary officers, occurred at the house of the unfortunate Sir Humphrey Forster at Aldermaston:—"While Sir Humphrey, Sir Richard Kingsmill, his lady, and some other friends, consisting of Mr. Francis Smith, Mr. John Wright, Mr. Thos. Grove, Mr. James Weare, Mr. John Awberry, and Mr. John Young, were quietly sitting at dinner, a party of 60 or 80 Parliamentary troopers, headed by three officers, with swords drawn and pistols cocked, burst into the room, to the great terror of the company, having previously dangerously wounded the butler at the door, and demanded that all the apartments in the house should be showed them. This was readily granted by

---

* This was not the Capt, Ball, a famous Royalist freebooter, stationed at Reading in 1644, whom Sir Jacob Astley complains of to Prince Rupert in a letter given in Warburton's "Prince Rupert," vol. ii, p. 358-9.

the affrighted Sir Humphrey, who was in terror of his life, one of the troopers telling him that the wounds his man had received ought to have been in his (Sir Humphrey's) heart. After examining the house, and taking every valuable article they thought worth their attention, these servants of the Parliament broke open the stable doors, while others searched the Park, and succeeded in carrying off eight valuable horses, which they fully equipped with saddles, bridles, &c. To prevent any alarm being given, four of the troopers were quartered in the house for the night. Capt. Waldron, Lieut. Seymour, and the other officer were all old offenders, having being previously bound over for robbery and other barbarities committed in the County of Wilts." (Tanner MSS., Bodl. Libr. vol. $\frac{57}{1}$, No. 199.)

The "Mercurius Aulicus," the chief Oxford paper, of Thursday, Nov. 14, 1644, referring to the inhumanity of the Parliamentarians, recites the following instances of "the bloudy disposition of the Rebells, as well to their own creatures as His Majesty's good subjects." But such tales as these must be taken *cum grano salis*, no story being too foul or too false to be refused a place in the Journals and pamphlets issued almost daily by both parties. "We have it most certainly advertised that the day after the last Newbury fight when His Majesty's army was drawn off, the good Earle of Manchester went into Mr. Doleman's house at Shaw (near Newbury), where he found some wounded souldiers. Colonell George Lisle (who so gallantly commanded those Guards the day before) left a note in the house, wherein he certified that certaine hurt men (some whereof were His Majesty's souldiers, the rest were prisoners, whom the Colonell tooke in the last fight), which could not at present be removed from that place, without hazzard of the poor men's lives. Therefore desired all gentlemen, officers, and souldiers, whom it might concerne, to afford them protection and assistance, as he had done, for as much as the poore men were unable to help themselves. But the Lord Kimbolton [Manchester] and his Rebells, no sooner entered the house, but most barbarously they knockt these poore wretches' braines out, not merely his Majesty's souldiers, but their owne men also (for the bloody fit was now upon them), lifting up boards, breaking down wainscot, and pulling out the very barres of the windowes, pretending that His Majesty was concealed in that house, else (said they) the Popish Malignants would never have fought so desperately to maintaine it. Therefore they vowed to find him (the poore men's bloud not dry upon their hands), else they would put the Maister of the House to death. In conclusion (having left that house) they did all mischief imaginable to the owner of it (Mr. Doleman), leaving him not so much as cloaths to put on, nor anything else either in or about his house.

"Nor was their behaviour much better to their well-wishers thereabouts, for when that Faction, out of their zeal, brought them divers carriages loaden with provisions, these grateful Rebells took from them both their horses and carts in requital of the curtesie. And to make their accompt just, they took a farewell survey of their deare Society at Newbury, and for a Farewell plundered the town most equally, leaving them to contemplate the Reward of Rebellion, which is to be used worse by those for whose sake they have been most seditious."

The following day, "Mercurius Aulicus" has another little incident to relate:—A royalist soldier (a Welchman*), having been taken prisoner, and finding no way of escape, promised to take up arms for the Parliament. On perceiving the Parliamentary army preparing to leave Newbury, and being at that time sentinel outside the prison, where some 30 royalist soldiers were confined, he gave the prisoners his lighted match and a horn of gunpowder, for them to put into the lock, and blow open the door. This was so well done that the Welchman and the 30 other soldiers all came safe to His Majesty's army. "Had the Rebells thus escaped," adds 'Aulicus,' "they would surely have said it was a miracle."

The Anti-Royalist Journal, "Mercurius Britannicus," repudiates the "slander" against the Earl of Manchester "about the Shaw-house business;" and as to the breaking down of the wainscot, &c. in search for the King, satirically asks, "Has his ill-success in the late battle made a great king so little as to escape into a mouse-hole?"

The following anecdote will show to what peril property was exposed, which had to pass the western road:—In May, 1645, a party of west-country clothiers obtained from the Royalist Governor of Devizes a pass for London, and entered into a bond to pay him more than £400 excise on the cloth they were to convey to London. As they approached Newbury, Sir John Boys sallied out on them and demanded the full amount in the King's name. No expostulations could save the poor clothiers, they were forced to raise the money in Newbury, and after some days started on their expedition. They had not gone far before some Royalist troopers from Wallingford Castle pounced upom them, seized their teams, baggage and all, and took them into the castle, where the Governor, Col. Blague, not only forcibly detained their goods, but suffered his troopers to search their pockets. The end of it all was that, after much vexation and delay, the carriers obtained their final discharge by consenting to pay an additional £10 on every pack of cloth, or leaving an equivalent in value. (Waylen's "Hist. Marlborough," pp. 221—2.).

Notwithstanding what has been above stated with regard to the lawlessness of both the Royalist and the opposing forces, there is favourable evidence in another direction, in the following letter from a gentleman named Anthony Vaux, dated "Newburie, Nov. 4, 1642," to a friend in London. Giving an account of the proceedings of his Majesty's army in Berks, the letter shows that, at least in the early days of the war, there was little demoralization among the soldiers of the Royalist army.

"Rt. Worthy Sir. Cannot but be obliged unto you for your continuall favours unto me and my son Robert at Lincoln's Inn. I have understood by your letter the forwardnesse of the City of London, and the strength of men, ordnance, and other implements of engines in all places for the resisting of His Majesty's forces. I confess possession is IX points of the Law, so their managing the City with strength is a sure ground of resistance, but I believe to little purpose; for on Tuesday, I rid to Oxford and through the roads of His Majesty's

---

* There was a strong contingent of Welchmen in the King's service engaged at Newbury.

army, which exceeds the number of your relation; and having spent the day in the city, I came late to my house at Newburie, and there was no injury offered me by the way, or had forcibly taken from me the value of a point, though it hath been related that neither horsemen or footmen, waggon or carrier can travell about but the soldiers make them their prey. I assure you they are kept in good order without doing pillage as is related."

The writer further adds that while at Oxford he saw at least 50 burials, and "in an hour's respite" as many more, which he concludes were some of those slain at the late fight (Edgehill). At his Inn, "the Catherine Wheel," he chanced upon Secretary Nicholas, with whom he drank part of a pint of wine, and learnt the King's intentions, which he relates. He mentions that Reading has been pillaged of at least 5000 yards of cloth; and that divers troops of horse and foot are billeted at Thatcham, besides great store at Newbury. Reference is also made to the issuing of the King's warrant for plate and money, for food and sustenance for the troops, which is being brought to His Majesty in abundance, the treasure being conveyed upon wheels, and the money coined while travelling. It is a most excellent invention, he says, of Leniell, his Majesty's engraver, who, it was thought, was cut off at the last fight at Kineton (Edgehill).

IX.—THE CAPTURE OF LADY FORTH, COUNTESS OF BRENTFORD.

Extracted from "Memoirs of some Actions in which Collonel John Birch was engaged, written by [Roe] his Secretary."*

[The text where printed in italic type denotes corrections made in the MS. by Col. Birch. The original reading is given in the lettered foot-notes.]

* * * * * * * * *

"And the next day neere the evening, the Lord gave a great victory [the action at Newbury on the 27th Oct.], though the evill prosecution of it vexed you more then the other cheered you. However, with a few other gentlemen that were there with you, *and suche as you could gather up*, the pursuite was followed by you.a And after noone you being well wearied in the twoe nights and dayes (before) you dismissed your partie, and yourselfe wayted on by Maior Ashley, your regiment quartermaster, at that time, my selfe, returned late at night towards Newberry, where the head quarters were. And rideing easily 2 miles short of Newberry in the way from Hungerford, my

---

* "Military Memoir of Col. John Birch," edited by the Rev. T. W. Webb, M.A., F.R.A.S. Printed for the Camden Society, 1873.

a "vnto Hungerford and 4 or 5 miles beyond" cancelled.

selfe being before you, I heard a noise of horse and coaches comeing down the way towards vs.*b* Wherevpon I giveing you notice, you stood a little, and presently affirmed it was the enimy; for we had neither horse nor coaches at the head quarters. And they comeing on ffast, you had noe more time, but only to vtter these words, " What ever you see me doe, lett the like bee don by you." This was about *eight c* of the clocke at night, the 30th day of October, 1644, the moone shineing pretty light: and instantly therevpon you turnd your horse in a broad cart way into the feilds on your right hand *out of the comon road to Hungerford*. And instantly after vs about three pikes length they come into the feild the same way; and comeing on fast some of them were got vp even with us; but your fare being towards the west, and the moone being in the east-south-east, your face was soe shadowed thereby that they could not easily discover you; but as, as I suppose, takeing you to bee of their owne company, passed on with their whole partie, consisting of 96 mounted men, three coaches and a coach-wagon, with 30 led horses, as you presently tould your quarter-master, saying you had connted them, which I was at that time in too great a feare to doe. And soe soone as the last of this company was done, you turned backe your horse and wee likewise: and haveing gon backe about 40 paces, you mett on(e) of their company, to whome clapping your pistoll you bid him hold his peace, and turne backe with you, else hee was a dead man; which hee did; and carricing him backe into the lane hee confessed hee was one belonged to the King's Lord Generall, the Earle of Forth, whoe then past by; and those with him are his guard; and in the coaches his ladie and some other ladies, and the coach wagon was full of his bagadge, hee being come out of Dorington Castle into which hee was forced to fly the night before in the battaile. Vpon this relation you instantly turned for vs and said, 'I knowe not in what way God will bring it about; but I am very confident that all these coaches, horses and men will bee mine: nay they *are* mine. Come, therefore; letts vse the meanes.' And vpon that rid sharply with your prisoner towards Newberry; and comeing there gave this account to the Lord Manchester of what you had seen, and what danger you had escaped, desireing of him a partie of horse, and you would give him a good account of that company. But hee haveing long watched was soe extreame heavy with sleepe, you could not have one ready word from him. Wherevpon you thought of another course, and that was, to goe to the houses where souldiers lay, and see if you could gett vp a partie by your perswasion, and for hopes of prize, which you failed not to promise them, as was after-wards well performed. By thiz meanes you gott vp 47 resolved horse, *whereof foure weare trumpeters;* and away you marched; and vpon the way Lieftennant Caltroop asked you how many you judged the enimy

---

b "the comeing downe" cancelled. The "Mercurius Aulicus" of 4 Nov., 1644, states that Lord Forth escaped from the Castle during a dense fog, which had prevailed for some time. The route he took would appear to have been from the Castle to the village of Bagnor, where two fords were crossed, and the Lamborne Road reached; thence to Stockcross and into the Bath Road by Gravel Hill. Here it is doubtless, that the horses and coaches were heard "coming down." Distances given in those days, when there was a want of accurate information generally, are not to be relied on.

c "eight" altered to "10."

to be: to which you replyed, 'They are 30;' and then turned to your quartermaster and said 'If my heart faile mee not, noe bodies else shall for the number;' and soe went on, your selfe being still a distance before to discover any noyse, and likewise to finde the way they were gon; which you did at every turneing with your bare hands, feelling in the darke which way the coach wheeles turned; it being now about 2 of the clocke and somewhat darke. Thus wee went on about 16 miles; yourselfe still before; and being at a turneing and feeling which way the wheeles had gon, one standing neere by you, at a gate, as you after informed vs, vsed these words 'What rouge is that there?' for then it was neere breake of the day and very darke. You doubting, as indeed it was, that the wyly generall might have left a reareguard, and hee might bee a centry, and you had better goe to him: possibly you might make good the gate till wee come vp (whoe weare eleven score yards behind) rather then lett him and his ffellowes come out vpon you; which assuredly they would doe, if they were souldiers. There vpon you takeing out yur rapier and holding the point of it downeward vnder your rocket, went to the gate to him with your horse as hee was then in your hand; your pretence buing to aske him the way: but another *coming out to*^{d} him clapt his face over the gate close to you, and though darke yet discovered you, and pulling out his sword, with *an oathe,*^{e} not to be named, as you were informed vs, said you were a Roundhead: but you being more readye then he believed, made such a hole in his skinn as brought a groane from him. The other starting, but not seeing the danger, you said with soe loud a voice, that wee heard, whoe were then *a good way*^{f} short, 'What's the matter, gentlemen, doe you mean to abuse a man travelling on his way?' and with that more of them coming to the gate and endeavoring to fforce it, you made it good with your rapier, vntill instantly the trumpet (whoe had charge what to doe some hours before) comeing up, and finding you engaged, sounded a charge. Wherevpon the partie rushing upon that rearegaurd, being twelve, were quickly dispatched; and from some of them that were then alive, you did learne that the Earle of Forth was then refreshing himselfe in that village : which soe sone as you herd, you guest, as indeed it was, that the enimy would take the alarum and drawe into a body, and then the busines might be hazarded. And therevpon, instantly, the lane being pretty broad, and day appearing at the very instant, God was soe good as to direct the timeing of that busines, you *ordered the former devision being neare* g thirty prime men and horse to *go on with you,*^{h} the rest of the partie being almost tired were to march on 3 score paces after, and one trumpeter with them sounding a march; and soe to continue till they had ffurther order from you. In this posture marching a good trott, the first partie, where your selfe was, entring into a little *comon* ^{i} in the midle of the village, there, close by you, was the Lord Ruthven draweing his men together, and at that very instant the trumpets that were behinde sounded a march and you cried aloud, "Gentlemen, letts not stay for the body of horse but fall on them instantly;" which at a high trott

---

d standing by.   *e* another (!).   *f* 40 paces.   *g* drew out.
    h for a forlorne; and.   *i* towne.

was done and they presently routed, haveing not draune 40 togcther. This was noe sooner done, but, musket shot distance, as many more, whoe had then taken the alarum, were then gott together. Some of your partie seeing them said, 'Looke, Sir, backe yonder is a partie more.' You replied, 'The same are rallied againe, down with them:' and imediatly vpon a full gallop you chargod them. During theis 2 charges all the coaches and wagon were runne away.*j* This busines being pretty well over, and all that were in those twoo parties fallen or taken, with the generall's armes in his trumpet; *k* none escaped but the Earl himselfe, Collonel Feilding, and three more, who by reason of the goodness of their horse, after they had mett with some blowes, leapt of the comon into the closes, you being between them and the lanes end, by which meanes they escaped. Your selfe presently, and about *twelue l* more whoe were able, pursued after the coaches, and haveing gon at a great speed four *or five* miles you were close at them in a village, where God was wonderfully seen for you. For a *considerable part* of the Queen's regiment of horse quarterd then there, who could time enough to the flight: which you discovering *by seeing souldiers stir hastily about*, presently cried to the people as you were vpon a hard speed after the coaches, 'Gentlemen, lay out quarters in this towne presently for my Lord Manchester's regiment of horse:' and further called loud to your quartermaster, whoe then was most gallantly as hee had been all the morneing at your backe, sayeing, 'Quartermaster, in the next village let Sir William Waller's regiment quarter.' Vpon this and hearcing the trumpets, whoe were then farre behinde, *sound*, all the *souldiers* there, three times the number of your partie, runn away; and before our faces, some ridd out back wayes: most footed it into the woods; and you had an opertunity to ffall on the partie with the coaches, whoe never offered to strike, but cried for mercy; not one man of them escaped; coaches and coach wagon and all the ladies taken, with 57 men brought prisoners; and of their whole partie but the 5 aforesaid oscaped. Of horses of theirs, and those tooke from the Queen's regiment flieing as aforesaid you brought away 107, besides twenty one horse that were on the coaches and wagon. And now being 20 miles from Newberry, and in the enemies country, yet it pleased God soe to bless you that you brought safe away that day all the prisoners to your quarters neere Nuberry; although your partie was soo small that you were forced some times to put one man to gaurd 3 prisoners. This mercy of God, though I doubt not but you have it in perfect memory, yet his hand being soe plainely discovered in it, I could not omitt it, and hope the time you spend in reading of it will not seem long."

NOTE.—It is impossible to speak with certainty as to the place where the carriages were captured; but, from the distance stated, Marlborough would seem to be the town referred to; for it is about 20 miles from Newbury, and at that time was occupied by a body of the King's troops. It is also related in one of the Diurnals, that no sooner had the King passed through Marlborough in his flight from Donnington Castle, than a small company of the enemy came dashing through the town, enquiring which route the King had taken. The woods mentioned in the narrative probably indicate the Forest, through which the Bath Road passed, as at present.

---

j "and a partie with them," cancelled.
k i.e. the flag attached to the trumpet.   *l* 20.

Now although this adventure has been thus minutely recited, and Birch, by revision and correction, assented to every item, and claimed to himself the credit of the whole, yet it is curious to find a competitor starting up with an opposite claim, and appropriating to himself the origin and management of the exploit. A Lieutenant-Colonel Thorp, vindicating his character from some aspersions in the "Mercurius Aulicus," brought out in the ensuing spring a very different version; and his account introduces us to the obscure names of some others of the party. His case is thus stated:—"At the last fight at Newbury he was commanded upon the guard betwixt Newbeury and Dennington Castle after the fight; he then receiving intelligence from Col. Burch, drew some fourty men and horse from the guard; so he desired Col. Burch to go along with him; there were under his command, officers as followeth: Cap. Draper, Cap.-Lieutenant Evans, Cornet Mathews, Cap. Draper's Cornet; the intelligence was, that my Lord Ruthin, the King's Generall, his Lady, and divers more with him [had escaped]. So they pursued them some eight miles, where they tooke the General's lady, and some prisoners of quality with her, three coaches, and about fifty horse and men, a wagon with much goods in it; so Lieutenant-Col. Thorpe sent the lady and the prisoners towards Newbury, with Col. Burch and some of the troopers; the said Lieutenant-Col. pursued the Generall some nine miles further, and rid in view of him the most of that way, but he having but some two men with him, and his horse being weary, he returned back to Newbury, where he and the rest of the party divided the spoile. This was done without the losse of a man. This is the true relation of this piece of service." "Kingdom's Weekly Intelligencer," April 8, 1645. Note by the late Rev. John Webb, M.A., F.S.A., to the "Military Memoir of Colonel John Birch," p. 187.

X.—DONNINGTON CASTLE.

"CAPT. KNIGHT'S RELATION OF THE SIEGE OF DENINGTON." *

"Wee are Come to December 1645, and Dulbere wth Cromwell hauinge Surprissed that farmhousse garrisson of Bassinge, the s^d Dulbere wth too Reagiments of horsse and thre of foote marches into Newbery, of whose Advance S^{r.} Jo. Boys beinge advertissed fires Denington towne and other Ajatiente villages,† as was comanded by the Lds. and

---

* Clarendon State Papers, No. 2062; Bodleian Library.

† The Commons' Journal, 9th April, 1646, has the following entry:—"The humble petition of the poor inhabitants of Dennington in the county of Berks; shewing that their houses, stables, barns, and divers other buildings, together with their goods and houschold stuff, were burnt and consumed by command of Sir John Boys, governor of Dennington Castle, amounting to the sum of Five thousand, two hundred and eighty-three pounds and eighteen shillings,

Counsell at Oxford. hope is of A noble facultie. his matie and the Lds. at Oxford conceauod good hopes as expectinge A brave Resistaunce to be made by these men who in A former seege hade done soe gallautly, and of the noble gouerner S. Jo. Boys, A psone Examplarye for vallore and fidillitie. Dulbere being thuse prevented of his quarters of Denington towne, wch was wthin halfe A mile of the Castell, and also of other Ajatiente Villages and howses, loges his partie of foote in Newbery, and quarters his horsse in the Ajationte villages, soe yt Denington Castell may bee sd to bee now bloked, but not beseged, for yt Dayllie the Castillians made sallyes, broughte in contribution and such prisoners as Reffused to paye, and the Cuntrye peoplle, as to a marte, dayely brought in all sorts of provissions, soe faire A corrispondancy the Gouerner Sr. Jo. Boys keepte wth the peoplle of the Cuntrye yt hee was of them generally beloued, and treuley he Allwayes gave them A better price for thire Comodities then they could haue fownde att any of the Ajationte marketts, and treully soe good A Justiser was Sr. John yt England had not A beter Regullated guarrisson, nor better beloued of the Countrye then was this of Denington. Sr. Jo. and his, not to Seame Remisse or necligente, are studiouse to make all necessary pvissions [provisions] to preserve the place, and Consideringe Colonell Browne hade in the former seage made his battery one the northe side of the Castell, and yt from a place called the Queen's oake * the Castell might bee easilly stormed, beinge A leuell [level] and the Castell one all other pte standinge vppon A hill, hee thirefore made A mounte vppon the sd leuell some (200) paces of the Castell, trenche And pallasads it, the walls beinge heigh, Canone pffe [proof], and the tope made of greatte thicknes and stronge, as couered over wth brickes and Earth proped wth greate beames and layed over with packes of wall [wool] to prevente the execution of morter Granadas.

"The winter beinge very Rude and viollente Dulbere Could not laye A Closse seage to the Castell, nor well bloke it vppe now that the Ajationte villages and howsses were burned, and that Castell Cittuate vpon A Hill and the Cuntrye About it very blitte [? bleak], hee thire fore keeps hime selfe wthin the towne of Newberye. No guarrisson of

---

to the utter undoing of the petitioners, their wives, and many children; they consisting of two-and-thirty families, was this day read.

"The Articles upon which Denaington Castle was surrendered was likewise read.

"The House called upon a report, in the hands of Mr. Lisle. And

"It is ordered that the debate concerning Sir John Bois, and the articles for rendition of Dennington Castle, be taken into consideration next after the said report."

More momentous affairs than the question of the poor sufferers at Donnington having subsequently occupied the attention of the House, this seems to have been the only notice taken of the matter. An ancestor of the writer was churchwarden of the parish at the time; and in that capacity, and also as owner of property destroyed, he signed the petition. The baptism of his daughter Alice is the second entry in the parish-register of 1646; the earlier records were lost during the war.

* The memorable oaks mentioned by Evelyn, in his "Discourse on Forest Trees," as growing in Dennington Park, near Newbury, appear to have stood between the Castle and the little homestead on the north side, belonging to the Castle Farm, precisely in the spot mentioned by Capt. Knight. There are still two or three very fine oaks in this field.

his Maties was better maned then this of Denington, for besides the ordinary guaruisson Souldery, thire are Come to Sr. Jo. 140 men that marche of [off] from Winchester to Wodstocke, and are now com to Donington. Dulbere Acts littill, only att times to Ayere his souldery, drawes of of his hoolle [whole] to face the Castell. Nor is Sr. Jo. Boys Jdlle [idle] but Consults for the holding out the seage, and consideringe ye scarcittie of·horsmeate sendes Away All the superfluitie of his horsse for Wallingford, only keepinge a sellecte nomber of 40, and such gallants they were yt ye Enimie neuer faced the Castell wth theire horsse wthout some losse. Maior Stuard [Major Stuart] who then commanded the Rebells horsse in chiffe, A man of Action and of A turbillente spirite and greate Creuillte [to] All Royalliste, vsed more then Emullitarye [emulatory = emulative] offitiousnes to prejuduce the guaruison, in fine soe Ressollute A man hee was yt hee is Reported to pistoll suche of his troopers as turned taylle. An excellente discipline, for its most pbable A valliante leadere makes daring and bowld soulders, where on the Contrary no good Service is to be Expected from a Cowardly Comander, and sertainty stuard Comand As stoute A Regiment as was in ye Rebells service, besids hee was A justice and well Advised soulder, hee toke vpp his quarter at Kings Clere, thireby keepte his Regiamente in view, and too secure his quarters made turne pikes att the streets and bloked all the Avenaes,—the Kentish Reagimente beinge the other yt wayted vppon Dulbere ware not soe surcomspecte but toke vppe A more larger quarter—loging att Burclere and other Ajatiente Villages. Sr. Jo. Boys yt may in soe mannare be sd to bee A man that tackes Reste in Action, getts information of the quarteringe of the Enemies horsse and findinge An Impossibillitie to deall wth Stuarte Resoulves to attempte some dissigne vppon his Cuntreymen the Kentish Reagiamente [Sir Jo. Boys was a Kentish-man] and knowinge yt hee hade not horsse Suffitiente to beate vpp theire quarterres sends out a partie of 100 foote whoe passinge hegge and diche in the deade of the nighte felle vppon ptie [party] of the Kentish men's quarters, and besides prissoners brought Awaye About 80 horsse Armes and good pillage, nor doese Sir Jo. lette dallebere to snorte wth out feere in his hotte beed at Newbery, but gives hime alsoe soe stronge An Allarme that the greatist pte of his men Rane out of the towne, and hime selfe wth the Rest, drew out of the towne, standinge all the Reste of the night in Armes. Maior Stuard stormes att this disgrace of the Kentish Regiamente, and for a braueada the next daye faces the Castell, and to puocke [provoke] Sr. Jo. to Sallye sends out a Comanded ptie from the Reste of his maine bodie, Sr. Jo. sends out a partie of his Castillians, who seinge they might well charge the Enemie being A good distance from their maine bodie and wth all secureed by A good partie of muscitteres layd in Ambuscada to secure thire Retreate, falles vppon this partie of the Enemie and Routts them, killes many and taikes sume prissoners. Stuarte Advanced to the Rescue, but by the orderly Retreate of the Castillians and or partie of foote, Stuarte was frustrate of his intention, soe hauevinge tacken soe poore A Reuenge Returned to his quarters wth shame, the Kentish Regimente Attributs the blame of their losse to their landlords as fauores of the Cauallores [this presumably refers to the Kentish regiment being principally composed of landlords and their tenants], Remoues thire quarteres to Wodhaye [Woodhay], and for securitie Croudes them selues vppe in some fewe howsses. S^r. Jo. is Advertised where they are and howe loged, drawes out A partie of 120 ffoote whoe puided [provided] wth sleeges [hammers] and hachatts for the breaking vpp of doores and hauinge hande granades to through [throw] in att windoes Amongste them, passed heage and diche and in the deade of the night, falles vppon the Rebelles in foure howsse, Repartinge them selve, as S^r. Jo. Commanded, in to 4 parties, 30 in A Companye, in fine or [our] partie breake vpp thire doors vppon them, tocke 26 officers and souldery, and mitte haue taken many more if they would, but vaulloinge [valuing] their horses more then the men they brought of betwixte 80 and 90 horsse, Armes, and plunder. S^r. Jo. neaded not at this time to haue Alaremed dulbere in Newberye for the Rest of the Kentish Reagimente in a greate Confusion Rane to the heade quarters and soe Allaramed Dulbere y^t hee drew out of the towne and stoode all nighte in armes, in fine, Aftere this Dulbere changed his Course, for now hee sleepte all daye and wachte all night. The Kentish Reagemente hauinge now loste (200) or more of thire horsse were acquesed by Dulbere of slothe and Negligence, and hime selfe Receaued A like checke from the p'liamente, soe y^t to preuent the like disgrace hee keeps A stronge gaurd of horsse daye and nighte betwixte Denington and Newbery. It were tediouse to Recounte all the passages and scirmishes passed betwixte the Castillians and Rebels, the wholle seage beinge spente in suche like actions and beatinge vpp of quartteres. The Kentish Reagiamente drawes them selues in to Bolsome howsse, A place duble motted [moated], but S^r. Jo. Boys would not leauve them soe, and to that purpose, Communycates his Ressollution wth Colonell Blake [Blague] of Wallingforde, who joynes with S^r. Jo. sends A partie of 150 horsse wth whome Sir John Joynes his, and besides 120 foote with firelokes and other materialles fitte for beatinge vppe of quarteres, thease togeather stte out of Denington Castell, and Comes to balsome howsse, the Enimies quarter.* A place Able to haue wth stoode any parttie y^t had not brought Canone wth them, but whether these presuminge one the strengthe of the place thought S^r. Jo. woulde not have attempted to beate them vpp in a place of y^t strength, or how: Securitie distroyed them, for as they Coke shure slepte wth out keepinge guard or sentenells the Royallists come vnexpectedly vppon them, broke vpp thire gatts, and surprissed them. This laste action totally brake the Kentish Rigemente who

---

* The old Manor-house of Balsdon, Balston, or Balsome, near Kintbury, situate in a picturesque and secluded spot, is surrounded by a double moat, as described by Capt. Knight. The house, having become ruinous, was taken down many years since; but the inner moat, which encompassed it, is nearly entire and filled with water. The position of the draw-bridge is marked by the spot on the south side, where the moat has been filled up to form a passage to the garden. The outer moat has been partly levelled; but its direction is distinctly traceable. The Manor of Balsdon was anciently in the family of Polhampton; at a later period in that of the Darells. The Loders were of Balsdon Park in 1667; and it was most probably in their hands at the time of Sir John Boys' exploit. Sir John Darell in 1644 resided at Barton Court. An interesting account of Balsdon Manor is given in the 1st Vol. of the Newbury Field Club Transactions, pp. 132-4.

APPENDIX. 181

were once 4 or 500 horsse. in sume maior Stuarte has preserued his Regiments wth· littell losse to his no little glorye, who in his owne psone [person] vpon a scirmish vnfortunatley shotte that brauo gent. liustenante Colonell Smith,* liustenante Colonell to Sr· humphery Benette, where of he shorttley deyed.
"Sr· Jo. Boys to Revenge Smythe's deathe inquires out Stuart's Rendesuves, And hauinge intelligence yt hee [was at] Knights howsse of Greenhame† to a greatte Supper, to whose dafter [daughter] he

---

* This Lt.-Col. Smith was buried in the chancel of Newbury Church, as appears by the following entry from the Churchwardens' Accounts, given at the Vestry on 20 Sept., 1645.
"Received of Dr. Barker, for Burying Colonel Smith in the Chancel 0 13 4."
Dr. Barker, who was an eminent physician residing at Newbury in the 17th cent., was probably the Colonel's medical attendant. He is described as "the first physician in the country," in a petition to Mr. Secretary Williamson from a Mr. Dobson, of Newbury, dated 1666, requesting the Secretary's influence with the newly restored King, in order that a daughter of a neighbour of his, "a gentlewoman of good stock, whose husband was loyal to the late King," might be privately touched for the King's evil. Dr. Barker was nephew to Sir Christopher Barker, Garter-King-at-Arms, who, by virtue of his office, made the grant of Arms to John Winchcombe, eldest son of Jack of Newbury, which is given *in extenso* in the "Hist. of Newbury," pp. 149, 150.

† Greenham Manor-house, the supposed scene of this tragic occurrence, formerly stood close to the old chapel which has been recently taken down. Part of the site of the house is now occupied by the modern church John Knight, of Newbury, by his will, bearing date 1550, leaves to Elizabeth his wife, the parsonage of Greenham and Crokeham and the free chapel of Crokeham. In 1643, Roger Knight, of Greenham, was one of the Sequestrators of Delinquents' estates for the county of Berks; and in Thatcham Church there was formerly a memorial for Roger Knight, Esq., of Greenham who died in 1653, aged 69. Among the Ashmolean MSS. in the Bodleian Library there is a very curious letter from Mr. Roger Knight, junior, of Greenham, probably a son of the above mentioned, to the Astrologer Lilly, affording a remarkable instance of credulity and imposture. Mr. Roger, finding himself involved in a troublesome "affaire du cœur," desires Lilly's judgment in the matter. He thus minutely describes his birth, personal appearance, and temperament, for the Astrologer's guidance:—" I was borne 3 weeks before my time, on the 16 Aug., 1619, neare Newbury, but what hour I cannot tell. I am very tall of stature, but stoop a little at the shoulders. I am leane, having a thin flaxon hair, of a longish visage, and a pale complexion, gray eyed, haveing some impediment in my upper lippe, which hath a small mole on the right side thereof, also on the right side of my forehead another little mole. I am of melancholly disposition, having been all the time of my life in an unsettled condition." He here mentions that his father had propounded a match for him, and describes his ladye love's horoscope and astrological characteristics, and asks Lilly whether he had better make any attempt to again bring about the business, his first essay having failed; if so, what time of year would be best suited to renew his court; and he naively wishes to know if he may rely on the Astrologer's promise that he shall "be settled" by November. In conclusion, Roger, to be prepared for the worst, requests to be informed, "in case none of the things prophesied should come to pass," whether there is any probability for him to travel "beyond sea," which he much desires. An answer was to be sent by the Bristol post, addressed Mr. Roger Knight, junior, Greenhame, neare Newberry, to be left with the postmaster at Speenhamland. Mr. Roger adds, that he shall be glad to know if questions can be solved by letter, as there were divers persons of his acquaintance in the neighbourhood of Newbury, "who have had experience," and desire to employ the Astrologer's art, but cannot make the journey to London. Roger encloses an 11s. piece for Mr. Lilly's "present paines." This letter is dated "Sept. 8, at halfe an hour after 4 in the afternoon," but the year is not given. As reference is made to previous visits to the Seer in 1647 and 48, it was probably written Sept., 1649, at which time Roger would be 30 years old. (Ashmolean MSS. 423, 130. Bibl. Bodl.) Mr. Roger

was a servante [suitor], the sd Sr. John sendes out a partie of (60) ffoote, who came vpon them soe sudently betwexte 7 and 8 of the cloke [clock] in the yeavininge [evening] in marche, that they fowned the doores oppen and stuarte att super setting by the side of his mrs. [mistress], the man would take no quarter [and] was shotte deade in the place, many prissoners were taken wch not worthe the nomingnatinge J letto passe, in sume, this was the last beatinge vppe of quarters. †

" Wee are now come to the moneth of Aprill, ‡ and Dulbier takes the feller [field] faces the Castell, and the same night falles a digeinge vnder the maye poolle § wthin 15 score [? paces] of the Castell, Sr. John could

---

Knight, junior, appears to have overcome his "unsettled condition," as in 1673 he is described, in Blome's " Brittannia," as residing at his paternal estate at Groenham; but the sequel to his love story is not recorded.

Lilly,* in relating his astrological career, mentions that he was well acquainted with the "Speculator" of John à Windsor, a scrivener, sometime living in Newbury. This Windsor, he says, was club-fisted, wrote with a pen betwixt both his hands, and was much given to debauchery, so that at some times the Dæmons would not appear to the "Speculator"; he would then suffumigate: sometimes, to vex the spirits, he would curse them, and fumigate with contraries. Upon Windsor's examination before Sir Henry Wallop, knt. he said that he once visited Dr. Dee, in Mortlake, and out of a book, which lay in the window he copied out that call which he used when he invoked.—It was that which near the beginning of it hath these words.

"*Per virtutem illorum qui invocant nomen tuum,
Hermeli, mitte nobis tres Angelos*," &c.

Windsor, Lilly adds, "had many good parts, but was a very lewd person. My master, Wright, knew him well, and having dealings in those parts (Newbury) made use of him as a scrivener."

† The following incident in connection with the siege of the Castle, is related in "Perfect Occurrences of Both Houses of Parliament and Martial Affairs," for the week ending 13th March 1645-6. "A partee of Dolbier's men, surprised 9 of Donnington men [of the Castle garrison] in Bagnoll [Bagnor] drinking, amongst whom some Officers, Colonel Boise the Governour hearing of it, sent out a partee, who set fire on four or five houses in Bagnoll [Bagnor] to be revenged for the losse of his men."

‡ This relation was probably written from memory and the events occurring in March, 1645-6, are, from some fault in the recollection, said to have taken place the following month.

§ *The maye poolle.* There is no traditional spot where a Maypole stood in the village of Donnington; nor does there seem to be a suitable site for one. But orthographical errors are common with old writers; the same word is not unfrequently spelt several ways in the same page. Now in the grounds of Donnington Castle, about 300 yards from it, just within the park gates, and precisely at the point indicated by Capt. Knight, at the angle of Dalbier's approaches, which extend as far as "Dalbier s field," and are in some places still distinct in outline, there stands a venerable and solitary Maple tree, measuring at five feet from the ground 7 feet 7 inches in circumference; and, from the gnarled and twisted appearance of its trunk, it has been of very slow growth. This is probably the tree referred to, then standing amidst the din of arms and the alarms of war, under whose shade was planted that fatal "mortar peece" which gave wings to the destruction of that "little bulwark of loyalty," the Castle, the shells from it having such terrible effect on its walls. There are several clusters of maples near by; but probably then as now, this one particular tree seems to have been a noticeable object. The details of the relation agree with this suggestion that the word "maple" has been misspelt, as the distance of the works from the Castle is stated to have been "15 score" [? paces], and the intrenchments are easily approachable by a sunken road from the village of Donnington.

* "Hist. of his Life and Times," p. 145.

not degeste such Ruffe pceedings of the Enemie, Commands a sallie wth horsse and foote at heighe nowne, the Enemie leyinge carelesly in thire trenches, not suspectinge a sallye, for y^t they sawe the gatte shute and the brige drawne* but in this they were very much deceaved for S^r. John had A privatte Sallye portte made w^thin the bulworke trenche and pallissathes filed vpp wth earthe, wch now hee clered and through it passed his horsse and foote vndiscovered, this partie was Comanded by Capt. Donne who soe sodenley ffell vppon the Enemy that they beate them out of thire works, killed Aboue 80 personse vpon the place, brought Awaye Above (60) prissoners (4) Collores and many hundred Armes. Dulbere stricked [? stricken] wth this losse marches wth all his forces, horsse and ffoote to Regaine his trenches wch he deed w^tbout disputte, and the nexte daye plants A morter pece, and the same daye shootte 17 vppon the Castell, An oold weake Rotten howse y^t wth this one dayes worke was well ney all shattered to peces, however Dulbere knew he hade to deall with A braue Enemie and hime selfe hauinge Received soe many Rubes from the Castillians was in disgrace with the Pliamt Assayes to gaine S^r. Jo. and the garuison by treatey, and to that purpose writts S^r. John that the L. Hopton hade giuen vpp his Armey in the weste to Generall Fairefex, the L. Astley was latly Routed att Stowe of the owlde weste [Stow on the Wold], Chester surrendered, and y^t hee could expecte no Reeliffe, thire fore hee Advised hime to yealde betimes, whilles hee may be able to give hime Conditions, and y^t this Advice peeded from hime of mere loue as to hime selfe and soo many gallant men wth him, to whome hee bore much honor and love, finally that this was done ag^t most of the wills of his officers. S^r. Jo. called A Councell of Warre, Comunycatts Dulbere's l're [letter] wth his officers, in sume the Resoulte of this Councell was not to beleve Dulbere vppon his beare worde, but if it were soo y^t the s^d Dulbere should be moued to grante passes to too gent. of the Castell to gooe to Oxforde to the Kinge, to Acquainte hime wth the Condition of the Castell, and to knowe his mat^ies Reassollution, in fine, this Dulbere Curtiously granted, and Capt. Osborne and Capt. Done, † too noble gent. were sente to his mat^ic to Oxford, who sente to S^r. Jo. Boys that hee should gette the beste Conditions hee could for him selfe and his, and y^t if possiblely hee could, he should marche of to Oxford and bringe of All the Artillery of the Castell wth hime.

---

* The gate here referred to appears to have been the palisaded gate closing the passage through the earthworks; and the bridge was likely to have been opposite to the existing entrance, because that was most sheltered from the enemy's artillery, and the bridge was probably constructed to cross the ditch of the field-work that surrounded the battered building.

† In addition to these two gallant officers, the name of another of Sir John Boys' associates in defence of the Castle is preserved to us,—Mr. Robert Stradling, of the ancient family of the Stradlings of St. Donats, Glamorganshire. In a petition to the Bishop of London, at the Restoration, for assistance with Secretary Nicholas to obtain the place of messenger to the Queen, he states that, for his services at Donnington Castle and elsewhere, the King (Charles II.) had ordered that he should be put first on the list; and he annexes certificates by Sir John Boys and others in his favour. The Petitioner went with the Countess of Derby to join the King on his arrival in Scotland ; but he had been ill and had suffered much by imprisonment, loss of estate, &c. Public Record Office; (State Papers), Vol xlv, p. 382.

Vppon the Returne of those gent. a ply [parley] was holde with Dulbere where in the Conclusion was to surrender the Castell.
"The Castellians were to marche Awaye to Wallingeforde wth bagge and baggage, musketts chargd and primed, mache in Coke, bullate in mouthe, drumes beatinge, and Collurers ffleyinge. Every man taken wth hime as much amunishion as hee could Carye. As honourable Conditions as Could be given. In fine, thus was Denington Castell surrendered."

It appears that, after the surrender of the Castle, and withdrawal of the garrison, the forces of the Parliament, in whose custody it was placed, dismantled the fortress, and carried away a quantity of lead, timber, and other goods and materials belonging to Mr. Packer; and that he obtained an order from the House of Lords to search in Newbury and other places for the property unjustly disposed of. The execution of this Order gave rise to serious affrays in Newbury and Basingstoke between Mr. Philip Packer, son of Mr. John Packer, the owner, and a certain Ensign Robins, who had appropriated some of the lead. An account thereof is set forth at large in the Lords' Journals. The following deposition, made by Mr. Philip Packer, introduces the name of our old friend, Mr. Gabriel Coxe; and as the incidents narrated are illustrative of the period, their insertion in full may be excused.

"Philip Packer, of the Middle Temple, gentleman, maketh oath that while he was in Newbury, in county of Berks, to seize upon such lead as he could there discover to have been brought from Donnington Castle, and having seized divers parcels in Newbury by virtue of an order of the Hon. House of Peers, one Robins, an ensign in the Farnham regiment (and under Capt. Bruer as this deponent is informed), came to Mr. Coxe's (where this deponent lodged in Newbury) on Saturday night, 25 April, with one Lieutenant Brooks of the same regiment, and finding this deponent sitting at the table after supper, about 9 at night, said to this deponent, 'Sir, you have taken away my lead.' This Deponent replied, Sir, 'tis more than I know.' The ensign, with his sword undrawn in one hand and a pistol in the other, presented the pistol to this deponent's breast, and swore by God he would have his blood or his lead, and bad him, 'if he was a gentleman to give him presently satisfaction with his hand, or else he would post him upon the gallows as a slave and a base fellow.' This deponent bad him be advised what he did, for it was in disobedience of an Order of Parliament, and before them he would give him satisfaction, but conceived it was not to be demanded by the sword (or to that effect). He swore he would not depart the House till he had satisfaction, and that he would have his life or his lead. Mr. Coxe desired him to depart his house and to express satisfaction in another place, which he would not do, but still demanded satisfaction for the lead, and would have drawn this deponent out of the house to have given satisfaction, and swore he would break open the place where this deponent had laid the lead. But would not depart the house till Mrs. Coxe, the gentlewoman of the house, was in so great fright with his rude and insolent carriage that it was justly feared she would suffer much in her health, thereupon, with great threatenings, he left the house. And further this deponent saith that on Monday in the afternoon, April 27, the said Ensign met this Deponent in Basingstoke, and told him he was not now in Newbury, and that he had a sword on, and so followed him into the Bell Yard, where this deponent went, and laying hands on his horse and bridle, bad this deponent come down and give him satisfaction for the lead he stole, and drew his sword and struck the Deponent upon his arm, whereupon the Deponent drew his sword for his defence, and presently there came in two troopers under Capt. Terry, of Surry, whom the Ensign, as this Deponent believeth, called thither, being of his intimate acquaintance, who did abet him and would not suffer this Deponent to go or send for any of the magistrates. This Deponent shewed them the order of the Lords, which they said was not sufficient being subscribed only by John Browne, and no Lords' hands to it. He told them that he had done what he did by that Order, and what they did was in disobedience to it, so till this Deponent had given satisfaction under his Hand they would not give him liberty to go out of the place. All which or words to the same effect this Deponent affirmeth to be true.

"Jur. 20 Maai, 1646.   PHILIP PACKER."
"Thomas Heath."

Gabriel Coxe, of Newbury, gentleman, made oath and corroborated Packer's statement. Philip Packer further made oath and said that Barnard Reives, of Basingstoke, grocer, confessed to the Deponent that he had in his possession three tons of lead which belonged to Donnington Castle, but refused to deliver the same without a sum of money to be paid him at the delivery.

XI.—DEPOSITIONS OF WITNESSES AT THE TRIAL OF KING CHARLES I., AS TO THE PRESENCE OF THE KING AT THE TWO BATTLES OF NEWBURY.*

Gyles Gryce, of *Wellington*, in *Shropshire*, Gent., sworn and examined, deposeth, That he saw the King in the Head of the Army at the second Fight near Newbury.

John Vinson, of *Damorham*, in the County of *Wilts*, Gent., sworn and examined, saith, That he did see the King at the first Newbury Fight, about the month of September, 1643, in the Head of his Army, where this Deponent did see many slain on both Sides. This Deponent also saith, That he did see the King at the second battle at Newbury, about the month of November, 1644, where the King was at the Head of his Army in complete armour, with his sword drawn; and this Deponent did then see the King lead up Col. Thomas Howard's Regiment of Horse, and did hear him make a Speech to the Soldiers, in the Head of that Regiment, to this effect—that is to say, *That the*

---

* "The Journal of the Trial of K. Charles I." State Trials, vol. i, pp. 1031, 32.

said Regiment should stand to him that Day, for that his Crown lay upon the Point of the Sword; and if he lost that Day, he lost his Honour and his Crown for ever;—And that this Deponent did see many slain on both sides at that Battle.

George Seeley, of *London*, *Cordwainer*, sworn and examined, saith, That he did see the King at the head of a Brigade of Horse, at the Siege of Gloucester, and did also see the King at the first Fight at *Newbury*, about the month of September, 1643, where the King was at the head of a Regiment of Horse; and that there were many slain at that Fight on both sides. This Deponent also saith, That he did see the King at the second Fight at *Newbury*, which was about November, 1644, where the King was in the middle of his Army.

John Moore, of the City of *Cork* in *Ireland*, Gent., sworn and examined, saith, That at the last Fight at *Newbury*, about the month of November, 1644, he this Deponent did see the King in the middle of the Horse, with his sword drawn; and that he did see abundance of Men at that Fight slain upon the ground, on both sides.

Thomas Ives, of *Boyset*, in the County of *Northampton*, Husbandman, sworn and examined, saith, That he did see the King in his Army at the first Fight in *Newbury*, in Berkshire, in the month of September, 1643, and that he did see many slain at that Fight; he, this Deponent, and others, with a Party of Horse, being commanded to face the Parliament's Forces, whilst the Foot did fetch off the dead.

James Crosby, of *Dublin* in *Ireland*, Barber, sworn and examined, saith, That at the first fight at *Newbury*, about the time of Barley-Harvest, 1643, he this Deponent, did see the King riding from *Newbury.Town*, accompanied with divers Lords and Gentlemen, towards the Place where his Forces were then fighting with the Parliament's Army.

Samuel Burden, of *Lyneham*, in the county of *Wilts*, Gent., sworn and examined, saith, That in or about the month of November, 1644, he did see the King at the last Fight at *Newbury*, riding up and down the Field from Regiment to Regiment, whilst his Army was there fighting with the Parliament's forces; and that this Deponent did see many men slain at that Battle on both sides.

Michael Potts, of *Sharpereton*, in the county of *Northumberland*, Vintner, sworn and examined, deposeth, That he, this Deponent, saw the King in the Head of the Army in the Fields about a mile and a half from *Newbury-Town*, upon the Heath, the Day before the Fight was, it being about Harvest-tide in the year 1643. And he further saith, That he saw the King on the day after, when the Fight was, standing near a great Piece of Ordnance in the Fields. And he further saith, That he saw the King in the second *Newbury* Fight in the Head of his Army, being after or about Michaelmas 1644. And he further saith, That he saw a great many men slain at both the said Battles.

XII.—BIOGRAPHICAL NOTICES OF SOME OF THE OFFICERS AND OTHERS,

MENTIONED IN CONNECTION WITH THE SECOND BATTLE OF NEWBURY.

A.—ROYALIST OFFICERS.

PRINCE MAURICE. Third son of the King of Bohemia, entered into the service of Charles I. about the same time with his brother. He was not of so active and fierce a nature as Rupert; but knew better how to pursue any advantages gained over the enemy. It is said that he wanted a deal of his brother's fire, and Rupert a great deal of Maurice's phlegm. He laid siege to several places in the West, and took Exeter and Dartmouth. His most signal exploit was the victory at Lansdown. The Prince perished in a hurricane off the West Indies in 1654.

DUKE OF RICHMOND. James Stuart, eldest son of Esme, third Duke of Lennox, and Catherine, daughter and heir of Sir Gervase Clifton, was born in Blackfriars, London, April 6th, 1612. After the death of his father he was placed by his mother under the especial care and protection of Charles I., to whom he was nearly related. He was appointed Lord Steward, Warden of the Cinque Ports, and Privy Councillor; and created Duke of Richmond in 1641. He married Mary, only daughter of George Villiers, first Duke of Buckingham, who had been previously contracted in childhood to Charles, eldest son of Philip, Earl of Pembroke. He was sent to travel in France, Italy, and Spain, for the benefit of his education, and from the time of his return to England, at about twenty-one years of age, he never was absent from the King's person, but shared in all his councils, and attended him in every change of fortune till the secret flight from Oxford, when the King left behind him all the members of his household and of his Privy Council. The Duke resumed his post after this event whenever he was permitted to do so by those into whose hands the King had fallen, and he even accompanied him finally a short distance from Newport on the road to Hurst Castle; then, forced to take leave, he was never again allowed to see the King alive. He obtained permission, with three others, to attend his funeral; and was one of the four who are said to have offered their own lives to save that of their master. He died 30th March, and was buried in Westminster Abbey 18th April 1655. He was succeeded by his only son Esme, who died in his minority in Paris. His only daughter married Richard Butler, Earl of Arran, second son of the Duke of Ormonde.

LORD BERNARD STUART. The youngest of five sons of Esme, Duke of Lennox, all of whom served in the royal army, and brother to James, first Duke of Richmond. He was slain at Rowton Heath, about two miles from Chester, Sept. 26th, 1645. His brothers, Lord D'Aubigny and the Lord John Stuart, both fell in the King's service. It is stated by Lord Clarendon and others, that Lord Bernard Stuart was created

Baron Stuart of Newbury and Earl of Lichfield, in consideration of his gallant behaviour near the latter city. It was intended that these titles should have been conferred on Lord Bernard, but he died before the Patent passed the Great Seal; hence he never was Earl of Lichfield or Baron Stuart of Newbury, because it was the Great Seal only that would have entitled him to bear those titles He died simply Lord Bernard Stuart. Charles Stuart, only son of George, Lord D'Aubigny (who was slain at the battle of Edgehill), and nephew of Lord Bernard Stuart, was created (10 Dec., 1645) Baron Stuart of Newbury, Berks, and Earl of Lichfield, and succeeded his cousin Esme, 10 Aug., 1660, as third Duke of Richmond, and sixth of Lennox. He died at Elsinore, while ambassador to Denmark, 12 Dec., 1672, without surviving issue; and his titles became extinct. There is no doubt, says Col. Chester, LL.D., editor of the "Westminster Abbey Registers," who has obligingly answered an enquiry of mine on the subject, that the titles of Earl of Lichfield and Baron Stuart of Newbury, were conferred on Lord Charles Stuart, in consideration of the services of his Uncles, and especially to perpetuate the titles which were intended to have been conferred on his uncle Bernard.

EARL OF NEWPORT. Mountjoy Blount was a natural son of Charles Blount, Earl of Devonshire, by Penelope, daughter of Walter Devereux, first Earl of Essex, and divorced wife of Robert, Lord Rich. He was created Lord Mountjoy of Mountjoy Fort by James I., and Baron Mountjoy of Thurveston, co. Derby, and Earl of Newport by Charles I. He was Master of the Ordnance, and one of the Council for War in the royal army. He died at Oxford and was buried in Christ Church Cathedral 15 Feb. 1665-6. The title became extinct in 1681, on the death of his youngest son Henry, third Earl.

EARL OF BERKSHIRE. Sir Thomas Howard, second son of Thomas, first Earl of Suffolk, by his second wife, Catherine, eldest daughter and co-heir of Sir Henry Knevet of Charlton, Wilts, Kt., and widow of Richard Rich, Esq. He was created, 22 Jan., 1621-2, Baron Howard of Charlton, and Viscount Andover, installed K. G., 13 Dec., 1625, and advanced to the Earldom of Berkshire, 7 Feb. 1625-6. He died 16 July, 1669, aged about ninety. His grand-daughter Frances, daughter of Thomas, third Earl of Berkshire, married Sir Henry Winchcombe, Bart., of Bucklebury, ancestor of the present Winchcombe-Henry-Howard Hartley, Esq., of Bucklebury, Berks, and Sodbury Manor, Gloucestershire.

EARL RIVERS. John Savage, eldest son of Thomas, first Viscount Savage, by Lady Elizabeth D'Arcy, daughter and co-heir of Thomas, first Earl Rivers, succeeded his maternal grandfather as second Earl Rivers in 1639. He died 10 Oct. 1654. The title became extinct on the death, in 1728, of John fifth Earl, who was a Roman-Catholic priest.

LORD CAPEL. Arthur Capell, born A.D. 1603, son of Sir Henry Capell and Theodosia Montagu, sister to Lord Montagu of Boughton. Sir Henry died in the lifetime of his father, and Arthur Capell succeeded to his grandfather Sir Arthur Capell's estates. In November, 1626, he married Elizabeth Morrison. In April, 1640, he was chosen Member of Parliament for the County of Hertford, and again for the ensuing Parliament in November, 1640. On the 7th August, 1641, he was created Lord Capell of Hadham. At the breaking-out of the Civil War he raised a troop of horse in defence of the King. He was appointed one of the Prince of Wales's Council during the campaign in the West, and accompanied him to Jersey. In March, 1646-7, he returned to England, and again took up arms for the King; and, together with Lord Norwich, Sir Charles Lucas, and Sir George Lisle, defended Colchester against the attacks of Lord Fairfax. After more than eleven weeks' siege they were obliged to surrender. Lord Capell was subsequently tried by a high court of justice, erected for the purpose of trying Lord Norwich, Lord Capell, and others. Lord Capell was sentenced to death, and with exemplary firmness died on the scaffold, March 9th, 1648-9. "He was a man," says Lord Clarendon, "that, whoever shall after him deserve best of the English nation, he can never think himself undervalued when we shall hear that his courage, virtue, and fidelity is laid in the balance with, and compared to, that of the Lord Capell."

LORD HOPTON. Ralph Hopton, son of Robert Hopton, of Witham, Somerset, was created Baron Hopton of Stratton, September 4th, 1643. Lord Hopton, a nobleman of admirable accomplishments of body and mind, was trained up in the good school of war of the Low Counties. After exerting himself in the House of Commons, for the royal cause, he retired into the West; where, in a few months, he raised a considerable army, and strengthened no less than forty garrisons. He was so great a master of discipline, that his army moved as one man, and was in every respect different from those licentious and tumultuous rabbles, of which there were many instances in the Civil War, more resembling herds of banditti, than well appointed armies. His victory at Stratton, May 16th, 1643, which was one of the most signal in the course of that war, is an astonishing instance of what determined valour can effect. He will knew how to improve it, and it was only an earnest of several others. After he had done as much as courage, conduct, and activity could do, he, was forced for want of supplies to retire before Fairfax, and approved himself a great a general in his retreat, as he had done before in his victories. He died at Bruges in September, 1652.

LORD COLEPEPER. John, Lord Colepeper, was descended from a branch of the very ancient Kentish family of Colepeper settled at Bay Hall, near Pepenbury. He was the son of a knight of the same name, living at Wigsell in Sussex; and he spent some years in foreign parts, doing good service as a soldier, and was reported to be of great courage, but of a rough nature; his hot temper leading him too frequently into quarrels and duels. When he married he settled in the County of his ancestors, where he soon became popular amongst his neighbours; and, in consequence of the knowledge of business which he exhibited, and the ability with which he conducted it, he was frequently deputed by them to the council-board, and at length was knighted, and elected Member for Kent in the Long Parliament. The King, sensible of his value, admitted him to his privy council, and in January 6, 1642, made him Chancellor of the Exchequer. During that eventful year, with the assistance of Lord Falkland and Edward Hyde, though sometimes disconcerted by the King's hasty measures, he did what he could to serve his Majesty. He acquired great influence, but his counsels were not always very wise or temperate. To his advice is attributed the King's consent to pass the Bill for removing the Bishops from the House of Peers, the transference of the court from Windsor to York, and the attempt to obtain possession of Hull. On January 28, 1643, he was promoted to the Mastership of the Rolls, an office for which his previous education had in no degree prepared him. He took it as adding to his dignity and profit, without regard to its duties. As a counsellor, he was used on the most private occasions, and was added to the junto which, as a cabinet-council, managed the King's affairs; as a soldier, he was ever by the King's side, and took part in all his battles with the most distinguished bravery. In reward for these services, the King, on October 21, 1644, created him a peer, by the title of Lord Colepeper, of Thoresway in Lincolnshire, and named him one of the Council of the Duke of York. He died July 11, 1660, and was buried in the church of Hollingbourn in Kent, in which and the neighbouring parish the family property, including Leeds Castle, was situate. By his first wife, Philippa, daughter of Sir George Snelling, knt., he had one son, who died young. His second wife, who was his cousin, Judith, daughter of Sir Thomas Colepeper, of Hollingbourn, knight, brought him four sons, the three elder of whom enjoyed the title in succession, which then, for want of male issue, became extinct in 1725.

LORD GORING. George, Lord Goring, was the son of George Goring, Earl of Norwich, and Lady Mary Nevile. In consequence of the numerous debts he had contracted at home he went abroad in 1663, entered foreign service, and distinguished himself in the Low Countries, receiving a wound at the siege of Breda, which lamed him for life. In 1641, he was made governor of Portsmouth, and betrayed to the Parliament the intentions of the King to bring the army to London; and he continued greatly in favour with the popular party until 1642, when he declared for the King. In 1644 he superseded Lord Wilmot in the command of the Horse, and served in the West, where the want of discipline in his troops, and the licentiousness of his own conduct, materially injured the cause he had espoused. He suddenly quitted the country in 1644, and never returned. His habits of intoxication continued to the end of his life, and he died at Madrid, in 1662, having embraced the Roman-Catholic faith, and, it has been stated by some writers, having entered the Order of Dominican Friars. He married Lettice, daughter of Richard, Earl of Cork, but had no children. The Earl of Norwich survived his son George, and died January 1662-3, when he was succeeded by his son Charles, at whose death without issue, in 1670-1, the title became extinct.

SIR JOHN BOYS. During the Protectorate, Sir John Boys was imprisoned for some time in Dover Castle, for tendering (with several other Royalists) an address, or declaration, for a free Parliament; but he lived to see the Restoration; and then he petitioned Charles II. for the appointment of Receiver of Customs at Dover. The original petition, which describes Sir John Boys, as "one of yor Maties gent. of yor Privy Chamber in Ordinary," is preserved among the State Papers in the Public Record Office, and is endorsed "Done." Sir John died at his old house at Bonnington in Kent, in 1664. The following inscription, on a black marble slab over his grave, in the aisle of a chapel in the north chancel of the parish church of Goodnestone-next-Wingham, Kent, has been kindly copied by the Vicar, the Rev. M. T. Spencer. "Underneath rests S^r· John Boys, late of Bonington,

Kt., whose military praises will flourish in our Annales as laurells and palmes to overspread his grave. Dun[gan]non in Ireland may remaine a solemne mourner of his funerall, and Dunington Castle in England a noble monument of his fame, the former for the losse of its expert governor the latter for the honour of its g[alla]nt defender. To crown such eminent loyalty and [va]lour ye King royally added to his antient scutchon a crown. Leaving no other heires male than man[l]y deeds to keepe up his name his inheritance decended to his three daughters Jane, Lucy, Anne. In his [5]8th yeare, being discharged from this militant state below he was entertained as we hope in that triumphant state above, Octob. 8th, 1664." Above the inscription are the arms of Sir John Boys (or, a griffin segreant sable, on a canton azure, a crown imperial or). Stephen Tucker, Esq., Somerset Herald, has not been able to find any record at the Heralds' College as to the Royal augmentation. The crown was not an uncommon augmentation to the arms of Royalists in those days; and the omission of any enrolment may be due to the troubled state of the times. The pedigree of Sir John Boys at the Heralds' College is signed by his father (Edward Boys) in 1619; there being eight antecedent generations to the gallant Royalist. "John" (son of Edward) is there said to have been aged 14 years and upwards. In Dring's Catalogue of Lords, Knights, and Gentlemen who compounded for their estates, Sir John Boys, of Bonnington, Kent, is set down as having paid £0312 10. 0.

SIR BERNARD ASTLEY. Son of Sir Jacob Astley. An eminently good commander in his Majesty's army. After admirable service in six fights and eight sieges, he died of wounds received in a brave sally out of Bristol, Sept. 4th, 1645. Lloyd's "Memoires," p. 644. Sir Bernard Astley especially signalized his courage at the Second Battle of Newbury.

SIR WILLIAM BROUNCKER, frequently written BRONKARD. Sir Wm. Brouncker, kt., born 1585, was eldest son of Sir Henry Brouncker, Lord President of Munster. He became a Gentleman of the Privy Chamber to K. Chas. I., and was Vice-Chamberlain to K. Chas. II., when Prince of Wales. He was created Viscount Brouncker in the Irish Peerage 12 Sep. 1645, and dying shortly after, was buried in Christ Church Cathedral, Oxford 20 November in that year. The title became extinct in 1687-8, on the death of his youngest son Henry, third Viscount.

SIR WILLIAM ASHBURNHAM. There is no record of this gentleman having been knighted, although he is spoken of in a contemporary MS. referring to these transactions, as "*Sir* William Ashburnham," and is so described in the list of royalist officers at page 126. He was the second son of Sir John Ashburnham, of Ashburnham, Sussex, M.P. in 1640, who, with other loyal members, was expelled the House for his fidelity to the crown. He subsequently took an active and distinguished part during the civil wars, was maj.-gen. in the royal army, and col.-gen. (1644) of co. Dorset. After the Restoration, he was appointed Cofferer to the King. He married Jane, third daughter of John, first Lord Butler of Bramfield, and widow of James Ley, first Earl of Marlborough, but died without issue in 1679.

SIR WILLIAM ST. LEGER. He was knighted in his father's life-time; served in the Parliament of 1639 for Kilmallock; commanded a regiment in the war with the Irish; and, after it ceased, went, in

November 1643, to Bristol, to assist the King in England. With Col. Myn, he took over 1000 foot and some horse; and did great service in harassing the garrison of Gloucester. He fell in the Second Action at Newbury, 27 October, 1644; and not having been married, his brother succeeded to his estate. His descendant, Arthur St. Leger, was created by patent, 23 June 1703, Baron Kilmadow and Viscount Doneraile. Sir Anthony St. Leger, commanded Prince Rupert's Life Guard at the Second Battle of Newbury.

SIR JOHN OWEN. Of Klinenney, co. Caernarvon. He was wounded at the taking of Bristol in 1643. Tried by the High Court of Justice, with the Duke of Hamilton and Lord Capel, he was sentenced to death, but subsequently pardoned. He is said to have served in 7 battles, 9 sieges, and 32 minor actions.

SIR THOMAS HOOPER. Lieutenant-Colonel of Dragoons. Knighted for taking General Wemys (General of Sir William Waller's Artillery) at Cropredy Bridge. Symonds's "Diary," p. 2.

SIR RICHARD PAGE. Knighted at Leicester, 2 June 1645, after it was taken by storm. He had been "first on the escalade" at this memorable siege, which was one of the best fought and defended actions of the war.

SIR THOMAS BASSET, or BASSETT. General of the Ordnance to Prince Maurice. He was, with his brother Francis (a Cornish man, governor of St. Michael's Mount), knighted at Crediton, co. Devon, about 30 July, 1644. (Col. Chester's MS. List of Knights.) He was second son of James Basset, of Tehidy, co. Cornwall, by Jane, daughter of Sir Francis Godolphin, kt., but none of the pedigrees of the family give any further particulars about him.

SIR HUMPHREY BENETT. Of the Benetts of Pythouse, Wilts. Col. Thomas Benett was Prince Rupert's Secretary, and the family were staunch adherents to the royal cause.

SIR JOHN GRANVILLE. Son and heir of Sir Bevil Granville, who fell at the Battle of Lansdown, July, 1643. Created Baron of Kilkhampton and Bideford, Viscount Granville of Lansdown, and Earl of Bath, April 20th, 1661. He died August 22nd, 1701.

SIR JOSEPH WAGSTAFFE. Wounded at Lichfield, 1643. Engaged in the western rising, 1655, and was with difficulty persuaded by his companions from hanging the Parliamentary Judges and the High Sheriff of the County, who had fallen into their hands at Salisbury. After the ruin of the enterprize he escaped abroad.

SIR CHARLES LLOYD. Governor of Devizes. Knighted 8th of December, 1644.

SIR EDWARD WALKER. Author of the "Historical Discourses," &c., was successively, Rouge-Croix Pursuivant, Chester Herald, Norroy, and Garter-King-at-Arms, in which last office he was succeeded by Sir William Dugdale. See more of him in "Athenæ Oxonienses." He died 19 Feby. 1676, being then one of the Clerks of the Privy Council to Charles II.

COLONEL LEKE. Who fell at the Second Battle of Newbury, was the son of Sir Francis Leke, knt., of Sutton, co. Derby, elevated to the peerage, 26 Oct., 1624, as Baron D'Eyncourt, whose two sons both laid down their lives under the royal banners. Lord D'Eyncourt, who himself took an active part in the war, became so mortified (it is said) by the execution of Charles I. that he clothed himself in sackcloth, and, causing his grave to be dug some years before his death, laid himself therein every Friday, exercising himself frequently in divine meditation and prayer. The Barony of D'Eyncourt and Earldom of Scarsdale became extinct on the death of the 4th Earl, who died unmarried in 1736. Burke's "Dormant and Extinct Peerages," p. 319.

COLONEL ANTHONY THELWALL. "A branch of the Worshipful family of the Thelwalls of Plasyward, near Ruthin, in Denbighshire; known for his brave Actions at Cropredy (where his majesty trusted him with a thousand of the choicest men he had, to maintain, as he did bravely, the two advantageous villages, Burley and Nelthorp), and at the Second Newberry fight, where he did wonders with the reserve of Sir George Lisle's Tertia; and had done more, had he not been slain for not accepting of Quarter." Lloyd's "Memoires," p. 661.

COLONEL GILES STRANGEWAYS. "Of Melbury Sampford, in Dorsetshire. This worthy gentleman, who was descended from one of the most ancient and respectable families in Dorsetshire, was representative in Parliament for that County, and one of the Privy-Council to Charles II. In the time of the Civil War, he had the command of a regiment in that part of the royal army which acted under Prince Maurice in the West. In 1645 he was imprisoned in the Tower for his active loyalty, where he continued in patient confinement for more than two years and six months. There is a fine medallion of him, struck upon this occasion: on the reverse is represented that part of the Tower called Cæsar's, with the inscription—*Decusque adversa dederunt*. When Charles fled into the West, in disguise, after the battle of Worcester, Col. Strangeways sent him three hundred broad pieces; which was, perhaps, the most seasonable present the royal fugitive ever received. This, however, was but a small part of the sum which is to be placed to the account of his loyalty; for the house of Strangeways paid no less than £35,000 for its attachment to the Crown. He died 1675. The present Countess of Ilchester is descended from this family." Granger's "Biogr. Hist. Eng." vol. ii, pp. 272-3.

COLONEL HOUGHTON. Son of Sir Richard Houghton, Bart., of Haughton Tower, Lancashire. He fell in the Second Battle of Newbury.

CAPTAIN CATELYN. A member of a Norfolk family, one of whom, Sir Robert Catelyn, was Lord Chief Justice in the reign of Queen Elizabeth. Capt. Catelyn, commanding a troop of horse in Sir Edward Waldegrave's regiment, fell in the Second Action at Newbury, while engaged with the royalist force on the Speen side. He was buried at Speen, as the parish-register thus records:—"1644. Oct. 31, Thomas Catelyn a gentleman of Norfolke."

ROBERT STRADLING. This gentleman appears to have been a member of the ancient family of Stradling of St. Donat's. In a petition addressed to the Bishop of London, by Robert Stradling, shortly after the Restoration, desiring the Bishop's influence with Secretary Nicholas to obtain the petitioner the place of Messenger to the Queen, he encloses certificates in his favour from Sir John Boys, Sir John Robinson, Sir Edward Savage, and Sir Philip Musgrove, testifying to his services at Donnington Castle, in Ireland, Scotland, the Isle of Man, and Shetland. In a subsequent petition, the former not having received attention, the petitioner mentions that he went with the Countess of Derby to join his Majesty on his arrival in Scotland, but fell ill in 1651, and has suffered much by imprisonment, loss of estate, &c. He annexes the previous certificates, with another by Richard Egerton, to the effect that "Robert Stradling was Cornet of Horse in Sir George Booth's rising, and always ready for design in the King's service." The certificate of Sir John Boys is as follows:— "I doe Certify that this gent. Robert Stradlyn was under my command in the garrison of Dennington Castle, and did venture his life for his late Ma^{ts} service, and that he was faithfull in his Trust. Jo. Boys. July xviijth." State Papers, Domestic, Charles II, vol. 55, No. 3, i.

B.—PARLIAMENTARIAN OFFICERS.

EARL OF MANCHESTER. Edward Montagu, son and heir of Henry Montagu (first Earl of Manchester), M.P. for Huntingdon in the first Parliament of Charles I., was raised to the Upper House in 1626, with the title of Baron Montagu of Kimbolton was associated in the charge, and of high treason with Pym, Hampden, Strode, Holles, Hesilrige, whose arrest Charles attempted in his famous and fatal *coup d' état*. He defeated the Earl of Newcastle at Horncastle in June, 1643, and distinguished himself by his victory over Prince Rupert at Marston Moor, in which engagement Cromwell acted as his Lieut.-General, but in reality guided him. He refused to sanction the execution of the King, and retired from Parliament (where he held the office of Speaker) until 1660, when he assisted at the meeting of peers who voted for the restoration of Charles II. He was deputed by the Lords as their Speaker to congratulate the King on his return to the Capital, and shortly after the Restoration, was appointed Chamberlain of the Household, and held other posts of dignity strangely out of keeping with his antecedents. The Earl died at Whitehall, May 5th, 1671, at the age of 68 years. He had been five times married. The present ducal house of Manchester is descended from his second marriage.

SIR WILLIAM WALLER, son of Sir Thomas Waller, Constable of Dover Castle, and Margaret, daughter of Sampson Lennard, Lord Dacre, served in the Netherlands, in the same camp with Sir Ralph Hopton; and was in the army of the confoderate princes against the Emperor. He was one of the most able and active of the Parliament Generals; and, being for a considerable time victorious, was therefore called, William the Conqueror. He was defeated at the battle of Lansdown, near Bath; and afterwards wholly routed at Roundway Down, near Devizes. The "Conqueror's" fame sunk considerably from this time; but he afterwards had the credit of defeating his former fellow-soldier, Lord Hopton, at Alresford. A few months later, he was beaten by the royalists at Cropredy, in Oxfordshire; and repeated reverses led to his being deprived of his command in 1645. He was imprisoned by the Independent Parliament, and confined until the King's Restoration. He died at Osterley Park, near Hounslow in 1668. The Wallers of Newbury were descended from the youngest son of this eminent commander.

SIR ARTHUR HESILRIGE. Eldest son of Sir Thomas Hesilrige, of Nosely, co. Leicester. Sir Arthur Hesilrige brought forward in the House of Commons the suit for the attainder of the Earl of Strafford. The soldiers of Sir Arthur's troops were so completely armed that they were called by the other side "Hesilrige's Lobsters," because of their bright shells with which they were covered, being perfectly cuirassed. They were the first that made any impression on the King's cavalry. Hesilrige was one of the King's judges, but did not sign the death-warrant. He died in the Tower shortly after the Restoration.

Thomas, brother of Sir Arthur Hesilrige, married (at St. Luke's, Chelsea, Middlesex, 6th Sept. 1632) Rebecca, daughter of Thomas Sheafe, D.D., Prebendary of Windsor, and rector of Welford, near Newbury. Heath's "Chronicle" mentions Sir Arthur's brother, Thomas, as suborning witnesses to vilify the King; and he evidently served the Parliament so faithfully as to secure honourable burial within Westminster Abbey, and thus rendered his memory so obnoxious that his remains were included amongst those disinterred after the Restoration, and thrown into a common pit in the Churchyard. See notes to the burial in the "Westminster Abbey Registers," edited by Col. J. L. Chester, LL.D., p. 145. Dr. Sheafe, Rector of Welford, who died in 1639, at the age of 80, a short time before his death published a work entitled "A Plea for Old Age."

MAJOR-GENERAL CRAWFORD. Laurence Crawford, of the family of Crawfords, of Jordan Hill, Renfrewshire. The name of Crawford is rendered in some degree memorable from the circumstance of his being the original authority for imputing cowardice to Cromwell. The accusation is given at large in Holles's "Memoirs."

LIEUTENANT-GENERAL MIDDLETON. Fought in the First Battle of Newbury. Of Donnington Castle fame. "A person" says Clarendon, "who liv'd to wipe out the memory of his youth, for he was but eighteen years of age when he was first led into Rebellion." He quitted the service of the Parliament when they cashiered the Earl of Essex, and made their New Model Army. He was taken prisoner after the Worcester fight; and, when he was sufficiently recovered of his wounds, he was removed to the Tower, where his friend and comrade Massey, the defender of Gloucester, who had likewise joined the royalist party, and fought at Worcester, was daily expecting the vengeance of the Commonwealth. When the time of their trial approached, Middleton found means to make his escape and got safe to France; and within a few days after, Massey had the like good fortune, "to the grief and vexation of Cromwell," who, Clarendon states, "thirsted for the blood of those two persons."

LIEUTENANT-GENERAL LUDLOW. Edmund Ludlow was a native of Wiltshire, having been born at Hill-Deverill, or in its neighbourhood, where his father, Sir Henry Ludlow, resided. He was M.P. for the County of Wilts in the Parliament which began Nov. 3rd 1640, one of the Council of State,—Lieutenant-general of the horse,—and Commander-in-chief of the forces in Ireland. He entered with zeal into all the measures of the Republican party; and tells us himself, in his

"Memoires," that he "had the honour of being one of the late King's judges." About the time of the Restoration he retired into Switzerland, where he remained in obscurity until the Revolution in 1688, when he repaired with other deputies, to London, to offer to raise men for King William's service. His further progress, however, in this measure, was quickly arrested by Sir Edward Seymour, who moved a resolution in the House of Commons, that they should address his Majesty to bring Ludlow to trial as a regicide, which he no sooner heard of than he returned to Switzerland. He died at Vevay, in the year 1693; and his remains were interred in the church of that town, under a monument erected to his memory by his widow. His memoirs, which are curious and apparently accurate, were printed after his death.

COLONEL RICHARD NORTON. Of Southwick, near Portsmouth, Hants. He was Governor of Basingstoke, and Cromwell's favourite "Dick Norton." He witnessed the Second Fight at Newbury only as an amateur, but got so far in assisting Ludlow, who was in danger, that he was wounded. Richard Norton, the grandson of "Dick," was the last heir male of that family, and by his will bequeathed Southwick Park, Hants, and all his other estates, to the amount of £6000 a year, together with personal property of the value of £60,000, to the Parliament of Great Britain, in trust for the use of "the poor, hungry, thirsty, naked strangers, sick, wounded, and prisoners, to the end of the world." The will was, however, set aside; and the estates eventually devolved to the Thistlethwaytes, maternally descended from the Nortons. Charles I. was at Southwick when the Duke of Buckingham was assassinated by Felton at Portsmouth.

COLONEL SIR RICHARD INGOLDSBY. Second son of Sir Richard Ingoldsby, of Lethenborough or Lenborough, Bucks, by Elizabeth, daughter of Sir Oliver Cromwell, of Hinchinbrooke. Col. Ingoldsby was one of the Commissioners of the High Court of Justice for the trial of his Sovereign, and signed the warrant for his execution. He was one of the chief confidants of the Protector; Governor of Oxford Castle, and one of the Lords of the Upper House. When he found the cause of his relative Richard Cromwell desperate, he strenuously exerted himself in promoting the restoration of the exiled King Charles II.; and so effectually recommended himself to his favour, that he not only procured his pardon (being the only one of the regicides who received a free pardon), but was made a Knight of the Bath. He married Anne. daughter of Sir George Croke, one of the Judges of the Court of King's Bench, and widow of Thomas Lee, Esq., of Hartwell, near Aylesbury. He died in 1685, and was buried at Hartwell.

COLONEL JOHN BIRCH. "In the sphere in which he moved, he was among the remarkable personages of the time: by no means inferior to those whose names are better known, though not more deserving of being recorded. He attained to considerable distinction in the field and in the senate; and, after a long share of personal exertion and sufferings, survived the troubles and dangers of a stormy and eventful struggle, and ended his days in retirement and peace." Preface to the "Military Memoirs of Col. John Birch," edited by the Rev. T. W. Webb, M.A., F.R.A.S. See more of him in that work.

CAPT. MASON. In Webb's "Civil War in Herefordshire," (1879, vol. ii. p. 106), the following curious particulars are given of the dress of this officer:—"Capt. Mason, who afterwards acted as a sequestrator in Herefordshire, appeared at the Second Battle of Newbury habited in the following officer's uniform—'with a sword about his neck and a black scarfe about his middle, in a black velvett doublett, and a scarlett paire of breeches laced with two silver laces at the knees, being a Captain! He was supposed to have been there on the side of the King, which he afterwards denied, when it was necessary that he should vindicate his conduct against Parliamentary enquiry."

Note.—Many of the foregoing personal notices are based on biographical sketches given in various works—as Lloyd's "Memoires," Foss's "Judges of England," Granger's "Biographical History of England," the "Lives from the Clarendon Gallery," &c. Some modifications and several corrections and additions have necessarily been introduced.

XIII.—HISTORICAL NOTICES OF THE MANOR & CASTLE OF DONNINGTON.

So little is known of the early history of the Manor of Donnington, that it is hoped the following notices may prove an interesting addition to the later annals of its memorable Castle.

1086. *Domesday* shows that William Lovet held, in Berks, Aneborne and Mortune, also Deritone,* in the hundred of Taceham. The third place is that now called Donnington. These places were afterwards held of the Honour of Skipton-in-Craven, Yorkshire.

1166-7. The next earliest document in which the name of Donnington appears is the Pipe-Roll of the Exchequer, 13 Henry II. (about 1166-7), when, among the names of vills amerced, occurs that of Dunintona, held by Gervas de Sancrvilla, which is amerced at half-a-marc. In the account of the aid levied in the following year for marrying the daughter of Henry II., which is found in the Black-Book of the Exchequer,† it is stated that Wm. de Sandrevill holds four knights' fees of the said Honour of Skipton, and Gervard de Sandrevill has a fifth fee,‡ of which the lord of Skipton

---

* "Domesday Book:" Facsimile of the part relating to Berkshire, 1862, p. 11.
† Ebor., p. 22.
‡ For every grant of a certain quantity of land, called a knight's feud, fief, or fee, the grantee was bound to do personal service in the army of the granter or feudal lord, forty days in every year, if called upon. "But," says Blackstone, "this personal attendance growing troublesome in many respects, the tenants found means for compounding for it, by (first) sending others in their stead, and in process of time by making pecuniary satisfaction to the owner in lieu of it. This pecuniary satisfaction came to be levied by assessment, at so much for every knight's fee, under the name of 'scutages.'" It was first levied in 5 Hen. II., 1158, but was abolished by Statute, 12 Car. II. cap. 24. This was the origin of the modern land-tax.

could not have the service. From the previous extract, it is clear that this fee is Dunintona; and that even as early as this period the service for it had been alienated from the Honour of Skipton. It is to be remembered that the returns in the Black-Book of the Exchequer do not show the knights holding in different Counties, but those holding of different Honours. Many Honours had fees in several Counties, but the return for the whole is entered under the County in which was the *caput honoris*. There is a Manor still called Sandrevill in the parish of South Moreton, near Wallingford, which Lysons states to have belonged to a family of that name in the reign of Edward I.*

1213. In the fifteenth year of King John (1213) Donnington was in the hands of Gilbert Fitz-Reinfrid; and for some unexplained reason, on the 16th Nov^r· of that year † the Sheriff of Berks was directed to transfer it to the custody of Peter Fitz-Herbert, to whom also Philip de Columbar's neighbouring land of Sac (Shaw) was committed.

1216. In this year Gilbert Fitz-Reinfrid returned to his obedience; and his charter, submitting himself to the King, is entered on the Charter-Roll.‡ One amongst the things which he had to do, was that he should give the daughter of Richard de Copland as a hostage.

1232. In the sixteenth year of Henry III. there was a final concord between Philip de Sandrevill, Plaintiff, and Richard de Copland and Johanna, his wife, Defendants, for one knight's fee in Donnington, which was allowed by the Plaintiff to be the right of the Defendants and the heirs of Johanna, for which the Defendants gave the Plaintiff 60 marcs.

1237. Accordingly, in the "Testa de Nevill,"§ the collectors for the aid for marrying the King's sister account for 1 marc for one knight's fee, which Richard de Cocland held in Donington of the Honour of Wallingford; "Cocland" being either a mistake or misspelling for Copland.

The Honour of Skipton, or a great part of it, passed in the reign of Henry II. to the Earls of Albemarle;∥ and the "Testa de Nevill"¶ shows that Philip de Sandrevill held land of the Earl of Albemarle in South Moreton and Enborne.

These were two of the places held, at the taking of *Domesday*, by William Lovet (see above); but nothing is said of the third (Deritone), the Lordship of which had now passed from the Honour of Skipton. This, combined with the extracts from the Pipe-Roll and the Black-Book of the Exchequer, proves that by "Deritone" the modern *Donnington* is meant.

1243. In the third volume of the old "Monasticon,"** Robert, Bishop of Salisbury, is shewn to have confirmed to the Priory of Wallingford the tithes of the demesne of Richard de Coupland, in the vill of Davinton, and also of the mill there. By this, no doubt, Donnington is meant; and for this reason:—Shaw, which adjoins Donnington, is

---

* "Magna Britannia; Berkshire," vol. i. p. 316.
† "Close Roll," vol. i. p. 273. ‡ Ibid. 221, b.
§ "Testa de Nevill," p. 119. ∥ Dugdale's "Bar," vol. i, p. 626.
¶ Page 124. ** Dugdale's "Monasticon," vol. iii. p. 12.

not mentioned in the Charter, yet the "Taxation of Pope Nicholas"*
shows that the Priory had a pension of 13s. 4d. from Shaw. It is,
however, only a confirmation of the grant, which might have been,
and probably was, made a hundred years earlier.

It is far from improbable that the Berkshire Coplands were a
branch of the Cumberland family of the same name, and of whom
there is an Inquisition, 26 Edward I. (1298), † when one Alan was
found to be son and heir of a Richard Copland, and 21 years old.

1279. In an "Inquisitio post mortem" ‡ of this date mention is
made of another Richard de Copland; and, by reference to the
"Calendarium Genealogicum," ‖ it will be seen that Joanna de
Hertrugge, wife of Richard de Copland, was "soror" and "coüterina"
of Philip de Hertrugge, that is to say, she was sister by the same
mother. Joanna is said to be 40 years of age; she clearly therefore
could not be the Joanna mentioned in the fine of A.D. 1232; but that
age makes it probable that Richard, her husband, was the son of
Richard, Defendant in the fine. The next document which will be
quoted shows Richard to have held Donnington, and that he died
before 1284.

1284. On the Assize Roll, 12th Edward I.§ is a suit in which Alan
de Copland seeks from Nigel de Sandrevill, the manor of Donyngton
by Shaw, as that in which the Defendant had ingress by intrusion on
the death of Richard de Copland, to whom Plaintiff had demised it for
life. The Defendant did not defend the suit on its merits, but
demurred, pleading he did not hold the whole manor, two other
persons holding small portions of it. The Plaintiff could not deny
this, and was consequently nonsuited.

1288. It is evident that Alan had eventually got possession of the
Manor, for, by a fine, 18 Edward I., between Master Thomas de
Badburber, Plaintiff, and Alan de Copland, Defendant, for the Manor
of Duninton, Defendant allowed it to be the right of the Plaintiff.
This Plaintiff's name was derived from Adderbury in Oxfordshire,
and is spelt, as was that of the place, in many different ways.

1291. In the twentieth year of King Edward I., Thomas de
Abberbury had a grant of free-warren over Donnington and Bradley.
The following is a translation from the original charter:—

"For Master Thomas de Abberbury. The King to his Archbishops,
etc. greeting. Know that we have granted and by this our Charter
have confirmed to our beloved Master Thomas de Abberbury, that he
and his heirs for ever may have free-warren in all his demesne lands
of Doninton and Bradelee, Berks, provided however that those lands
are not within the bounds of our Forest. So that no one shall enter
those lands to hunt in them, or to take in them anything which
pertains to the warren, without the license and will of Thomas himself
or his heirs, under forfeiture to us of £10. Witnesses—the Venerable
Father Robert, Bishop of Bath and Wells; John de Vescy; Guy
Ferre; etc. Dated at Wigton, the eleventh of September, 1291." ¶

---

* Page 187 b.
† "Calend. Inq. post mortem," 25 Edw. I., No. 6.
‡ "Cal. Inq. post mort." 7 Edw. I., No. 28. ‖ Page 283.
§ Berks, m. 6. ¶ "Charter Roll," 20 Edw. I., No. 8.

1299. In an "Inquisitio post mortem"* concerning the lands of Edmund, Earl of Cornwall, of this date, mention is made of Donington among the rents and fees appertaining to the Honour of Wallingford, which confirms the opinion already expressed.

1306-7. The Inquisition upon Thomas de Abberbury furnishes us with a description of the Manor at this time. It is as follows:—†

Possessions of Master Thomas de Abbresbury, Dynynton, Berks. "Extent," dated 23 May, 35 Edward I.:—

Manor held in chief of the King of the Honour of Wallingford by service of half a knight's fee. A capital messuage with garden worth 6s. 8d. a year; 120 acres of arable land, 30s.; 50 acres of worse land, 4s. 2d.; 2¼ acres of meadow, 3s. 9d.; 3 acres of pasture, 3s. 6d.; sheep pasture, 12d. (?); wood, 2s.; two water-mills, 40s. At Miggham 3 acres meadow, held of the Prior of Sandelford, 3s. Water-mill there, held of the Prior, 30s. 2 acres of meadow in la Wydmede, held of the Abbot of Reading, 2s.

Two free tenants	..	..	11d.
Villani	Total of their rents	27s.	3½d,
"	their work	27s.	10¾d.
	Tallage	18s.	10½d.
Cotarii	Rents	12s.	10½d.
	Work	2s.	6d.

Profits of Court 12d.

Walter de Abbresbury, brother of Thomas, is next heir; 30 years of age and more.

22s. to be paid to the Prior of Sandleford by Miggham Mill.

Held also lands in Steple-Aston Manor } Oxon.
Sulthorne Manor }

" Migham } Berks.
Eneburne }

1323. Of Walter, brother of Sir Thomas Abberbury, we are enabled to obtain little information; but in this year (1323), in conjunction with his son Richard, he granted certain lands in the parish of Abberbury to the Cathedral Church of Winchester.‡

It is stated by Grose, in his "Antiquities of Berks" (p. 5), that Walter Abberbury gave the King (Edward II.) 100s. for the Castle.§ It was thought by the late Mr. Henry Godwin, F.S.A., that the license to build, given by the succeeding King (see further on), indicated that the new structure was a re-edification of a former building; and this doubtless was the case, since we see by the Inquisition of 1306-7, that "a capital messuage" was then attached to the Manor.

---

* "Cal. Inq. post mort.," 20 Edw. I., No. 44 (26 and 52).
† "Cal. Inq. post mort.," 35 Edw. I., No. 44: translated.
‡ Pat. 17 Edw. II., p. 1, m. 23.
§ Grose took his authority for this from Urry's "Life of Chaucer," published about 1726. In 1731 the fire took place at Ashburnham House where the Cotton MSS. were kept, and it is very probable that the original document from which Urry derived his information was destroyed at that time.

1385-86. At this time (9th Richard II.) the Manor was in the hands of Sir Richard dé Abberbury, who had been guardian to the King in his minority, and had obtained the license to build anew and crenellate his castle at Donnington. The license is expressed in these terms:—
"The King to all his bailiffs and faithful subjects, to whom, etc. greeting. Know that of our special grace we have granted and given license for ourselves and our heirs, as much as in us lies, to our beloved and faithful Richard Abberbury the elder, that he may build anew and fortify with stone and lime, and crenellate a certain Castle on his own land at Donyngton, Berks; and may hold that castle so built, fortified, and crenellated, to him and his heirs for ever, without disturbance or hindrance by us or our heirs, justices, escheators, sheriffs, or other bailiffs or officers of ours whatever. In testimony of which, etc." This instrument was acknowledged by the King himself at his Manor of Henley, 11th June, 1385.*

1397. It cannot be determined with certainty in what year Sir Richard de Abberbury the elder died, as the Inquisition taken after his death is not to be found at the Record Office. It may, however, be inferred that he was living in 1397, for he had a son of the same name, to whom, by the description of Mons. Ric. Abberbury le fils,† John of Gaunt, by his will, dated 3rd February, 1397, bequeathed a legacy of 50 marks.

There is some difficulty, owing to the similarity of christian names, in identifying the various members of this family; but we have evidence of the existence of a Richard de Abberbury, the younger, as late as the twelfth year of Henry VI., 1433, when the name occurs in the list of Berkshire Gentry returned by the King's Commissioners. He represented this County in the 17th and 20th Parliaments of Richard II. Alice, the wife of this Sir Richard de Abberbury, junior, was the only daughter and heiress of John Cleet, Knight of the Shire for Berks in the 36th Parliament of Edward III. Her first husband was Edmund Danvers.

1400. It has been asserted that the Castle and Estate of Donnington belonged to Geoffrey Chaucer, the poet, whose death is recorded to have taken place on Oct. 25th in this year; but there is no evidence to show that it was alienated by Sir Richard Abberbury, during the poet's life-time. A deed-poll of Thomas Danvers, son of Alice, Lady Abberbury, by her first husband, Edmund Danvers, is dated at Donyngton, 1414, 2 Hen V., which seems to imply that it still continued to be their residence.‡

We now arrive at a point where our researches are assisted by several important documents, some of which are printed *in extenso* in the late Mr. Godwin's paper on Donnington Castle in the "Archæologia," and in the second volume of Transactions of the Newbury District Field Club.

1414-15. From a Fine dated the second year of Henry V.,

---

* Rot. Pat. 9 Ric. II., pt. 2, m. 7.
† "Donnington Castle," by H. Godwin, Esq., F.S.A., "Archæologia," vol. xliv; and "Trans. Newbury D. Field Club," vol. ii.
‡ Clarke's "Hundred of Wanting," p. 88.

between Thomas Chaucer, Edward Hampden, John Golofre,* and William Beck (Plaintiffs), and Richard Abberbury, knight, and Alice his wife (Deforciants), of the Manor and Castle of Donnington, we ascertain that the said Richard Abberbury and Alice his wife conveyed to Thomas Chaucer and his Trustees the Manor and Castle of Donnington for 1000 marks of silver.†

By a Fine of a shortly subsequent date, Edward Hampden, John Golofre, and William Beck granted to John Phelipp and Alice his wife, for the like consideration (1000 marks of silver), the said Manor and Castle of Donnington, to them and their heirs for ever. In the event of Phelipp and Alice dying without heirs, remainder to Thomas Chaucer and his heirs.‡

At an *Inquisitio post mortem*, taken at Wallingford, 21st October, 1415, on the Monday after the feast of St. Luke, as to the estates of which Sir John Phelipp died seized, the Jury say that Edward Hampden, John Golofre, and William Beck (now deceased) were seized of the Manor and Castle of Donnington, and of one croft, one carucate, called Meredene, &c., and that they had given and granted the same to Sir John Phelipp and Alice his wife and their heirs.§

It appears from a Fine, dated Hilary term in the third year of Henry V., made between Thomas, Earl of Dorset, Hugh Mortemer, Will. Hankeford, knt., Thomas de Stonore, Henr. Somer, Rich. Wyot, Henr. Aston, John Warefeld, and Geoffry Prentys, clerk (Plaintiffs), and Thomas Chaucer (Deforciant), of the Manor and Castle of Donnington, that Alice Chaucer, the wife of John Phelip, knt., held the same for the term of her life, and that it ought to revert to Thomas Chaucer on the death of his daughter Alice. The effect of this document would evidently be a conveyance in trust. The remainder is conveyed to the Earl of Dorset and others for ever.‖

Alice, the only child and heiress of Thomas Chaucer and Matilda his wife, daughter of Sir John de Burghersh, was born in 1404; and, according to the frequent practice then prevalent, was married in her childhood to Sir John Phelip, Knight; the object of these early marriages being to secure the property of the heiress as soon as possible, and to provide against escheats.

Sir John Phelip and Sir William Phelip, Knight of the Garter, who in right of his wife was Lord Bardolph, were brothers. Their mother was Juliana, daughter of Sir Robert Erpingham, of Erpingham, in the County of Norfolk. It is shown by the Inquisition taken shortly after his death, that Sir John Phelip died on the 9th October,

---

* There were two John Golofres living at the same time. One, a Knight who married Philippa Mohun in 1389, and died before 2 Hen. V. (1414-15), when his relict married Edward, Duke of York. Another John Golofre died, seized of the manor of Fyfield, in 1443. In the late Mr. Godwin's article on Donnington Castle, these two persons appear to have been confounded. It is there said that John de la Pole, Earl of Lincoln, married the daughter of Sir John Golofre. No authority is given, but; as Lysons says the same, the statement was probably taken from him. The Inquisition on John Golofre shows this, however, to be erroneous.

† Pedes Finium, 2 Hen. V., No. 3, co. Berks.
‡ Pedes Finium, 3 Hen. V. No. 2, co. Berks.
§ "Cal. Inq. post Mort," 3 Hen. V., No. 42.
‖ Pedes Finium, 3 Hen. V., No. 1, co. Berks.

1415; and that he had attained the age of thirty-one years. His brother, Sir William Phelip, took a distinguished part in the French wars of Henry V., participated in the triumph of Agincourt, and was subsequently present at the storming of the Castle of Caen, and at the protracted siege of Rouen.

The exact degree of relationship between Thomas Chaucer and the Poet has yet to be discovered, and, as no fresh evidence has been advanced on the subject, it is not necessary to enter at length into this long-disputed controversy.

The following chronological notes, however, resulting from some recent researches, may be submitted to the consideration of those pursuing the enquiry.

Sir Payn Roet, knt., *alias* Guyn King-of-Arms, a knight of Hainault, had two daughters—
1.—Philippa, married to Geoffrey Chaucer.*
2.—Katherine, wife of Hugh Swinford, knt., and mistress (afterwards wife) of John, Duke of Lancaster. She died 10 May, 1403, and was buried at Lincoln (of which See her son Henry was Bishop).

The children of Katherine by the Duke were (besides others)—
1.—John de Beaufort, a knight in 15 Rich. II., (1391-2), and created Earl of Somerset 20 Rich. II., (1396-7): died 1409, leaving his son Henry 9 years old.
2.—Henry, made Bishop of Lincoln in 1397, and of Winchester in 1405: died 11 April, 1447, aged 80. It is needless to mention others.

If this be correct, Henry was born in 1367, and John, therefore at least in 1366.

Geoffrey Chaucer is said to have died in 1399 or 1400, that is, three or four years earlier than his wife's sister.

In the facsimile of National MSS., Part 1. ("Athenæum," 13 Jany. 1866), is a letter to Henry IV, from Henry, Prince of Wales, dated 1402 (and which cannot be before that year, as it speaks of the marriage of Henry IV. and Joanna of Navarre), wherein he says:— "As I trust to God your humble leige-man, my cousin Chaucer, hath plainly informed your Highness at this time."

If there be no good evidence to prove that Geoffrey Chaucer died before 1402, this letter shows that he must have left male issue by the sister of Katherine Roet, since no other Chaucer but such issue would have been of kin to the Prince.

Thomas Chaucer died 13 Henry VI., on the Thursday after St. Edmund (20 Nov.), 1434, leaving Alice, daughter and heiress, aged 30. We may suppose that Thomas Chaucer had married about 1400; and he could not have been married more than two or three years earlier than that. If this be so, and if he were son of Geoffrey, and about the age of his first-cousin John Beaufort, he was 34 years old when he married. Instead of this, may not Thomas have been the grandson of Geoffrey ? and, if so, who was his father ?

---

*The evidence on the *Issue Rolls* tends to prove that Chaucer married a namesake or cousin. The earliest payments of Philippa's pension (presumably *before* her marriage) were received by her as Philippa *Chaucer*, but the later payments were received by Geoffrey for her, who is *then* described as her husband.

Alice (daughter and heir of Sir Thomas and Lady Chaucer) soon after the death of Sir John Phelip married Thomas de Montacute, Earl of Salisbury, who was soon afterwards killed in the memorable siege of Orleans. The Earl was succeeded in the command of the English troops before that city by William de la Pole, Earl of Suffolk, who was forced by Joan of Arc to raise the siege, and was taken prisoner. He contrived, however, to escape to England, and married Alice (Chaucer), the widow of his comrade in arms, "The brave Earl of Salisbury." After enjoying great favour at Court, he was charged with treason, and beheaded at sea in 1450. The story of his death is a mournful episode in English history, and has been often told.

Alice (Chaucer) survived her last husband many years; and, dying in 1475, was buried near her parents in Ewelme Church. The altar-tomb bearing her effigy "is hardly surpassed in beauty," says Skelton, "and certainly not in the extreme excellence of its preservation, by any monument in England." It is one of the three known examples of female effigies decorated with the Order of the Garter. It is figured in Gough's "Sepulchral Monuments."

John de la Pole, son of Alice (Chaucer) and William, Duke of Suffolk, was confirmed in his father's estates and honours in 1463, and held the Manor and Castle of Donnington. He married Elizabeth Plantagenet, sister of Edward IV.; and died in 1491. John de la Pole and Elizabeth lie buried in Wingfield Church, in Suffolk, where, in the chancel, there is a large altar-tomb with effigies of herself and husband. Their arms are in a window of the south aisle of Iffley Church.*

John, Earl of Lincoln, eldest son of John de la Pole, by his wife Elizabeth Plantagenet, and consequently nephew to Edward IV., being engaged in the conspiracy to raise the impostor Lambert Simnel to the crown, fell at the battle of Stoke, in 1487, in the life-time of his father. In the first year of Richard III., 1485, he had obtained a grant of the manor of Woodhay, and of the Lordships of Basingstoke and Andover; but he being attainted, his next brother Edmund, succeeded to his father's titles and estates.

Edmund de la Pole, the last in lawful succession to the dukedom of Suffolk, was deprived of his title by attainder, and his honours were forfeited to the Crown. He was beheaded on the Eve of the Ascension in 1513, and left no male issue. His other brother Richard de la Pole, called the "White Rose," was afterwards slain, fighting in the French army, at the battle of Pavia in 1528.

1514. In February of this year, Charles Brandon, Viscount L'Isle, the friend of Henry VIII. from youth, was created Duke of Suffolk, in tail-male, and received from the King a grant of the Castle, Park, and Manor of Donnington, Berks, being part of the possessions of Edmund de la Pole, late Duke of Suffolk, attainted.†

Charles Brandon, Duke of Suffolk, was Henry's chief favourite, and had married secretly, Mary, the King's sister, and widow of Louis XII. In contracting this union without the permission of Henry VIII., both parties exposed themselves to the risk of his serious displeasure, which,

---

* E. Marshall's "Account of Iffley," pp. 102, 3. Oxf. 1870.
† Pat. 5 Hen. VIII., pt. ii, m. 28.

to Suffolk, as his own subject, might have proved fatal. But the French dowager-queen and her English husband crossed the Channel and took up their abode in their Manor in Suffolk, without venturing near the Court. A reconciliation was in a short time effected; the accomplishment of which was greatly owing to the good offices of Cardinal Wolsey, who appears to have been a staunch friend to the young couple.

In a letter from the Queen-dowager of France, to Henry VIII., dated Letheryngham, Suffolk, 9th September, 1515, she thanks him "for permitting 'my lord,' her husband, to repair to him on his coming to Donyngton, which had greatly comforted him. Had the time been convenient, she would gladly have accompanied her husband in this journey, but hopes they will both see his grace, as he wrote in his last letters, 'which is the thing that I desire more to obtain than all the honour of the world.' Desires to be remembered to her sister the Queen, and the Queen of Scots, and hopes to hear of the prosperous estate of her niece the Princess."*

Frances Brandon, Duchess of Suffolk, the eldest of the two surviving daughters of Charles Brandon by this marriage, on whose issue the Crown was settled by the will of Henry VIII., ended in prison a life, which for variety of wretchedness has had few parallels. She had seen her daughter, Lady Jane Grey, beheaded: her own and her daughter's husband had shared the same fate: her daughter Catherine, after having been repudiated by the Earl of Pembroke, was imprisoned in the Tower: and her youngest daughter Mary was most unequally matched to an inferior officer of the household.

The Duke of Suffolk, it appears from several letters addressed to Wolsey, from Donnington, and preserved among the State Papers, frequently resided at the Castle. Symonds, in his "Diary," mentions that the following quarterings were to be seen in many of the windows of the Castle in 1644:

Quarterly, 1 and 4, Barry of ten argent and gules, over all a lion rampant or, crowned per pale gules and argent [Brandon]; 2 and 3, Quarterly; 1 and 4, Azure, a cross moline or [Bruin]; 2 and 3, Lozengy, gules and ermine [Rokesley]. The whole within the garter, and surmounted by a coronet or [Brandon, Duke of Suffolk].

As also this impaling:

France; impaling, quarterly France and England; the whole surmounted by a crown [Louis XII. and Mary Tudor].

Divers lyons heads also, and this motto very often: LOIAVLTE OUBLIGE. [Crest and Motto of Brandon.]†

1535. By an Act, 27th Henry VIII. cap. 38, an exchange of lands was confirmed between the King and Charles, Duke of Suffolk; and by an Indenture bearing date 19 July of the same year, made between the Right Honourable Thomas Audeley, knight, Chancellor of England, Thomas Cromwell, Esquire, Chief Secretary to the King and Master of the Rolls, Sir Bryan Tuke, knight, Treasurer of the

---

* Cal. State Papers, Hen. VIII., vol. ii., pt. 1, No. 2347.

† Symonds' "Diary of the Marches of the Royal Army ;" ed. by C. E. Long, M.A., p. 143.

Chamber, Christopher Hales, Attorney-General, and Richard Ryche, Solicitor-General to the King, on the one part, and the Right Noble Charles, Duke of Suffolk, on the other part, the same Duke bargained and sold, &c., the Manors, Castles, and Lordships of Ewelme, Donyngton, Langley, West Bradley, West Compton, and Buckland, in the County of Berks, together with other Manors in the County of Oxford, the Manor-house and place of Southwerke, commonly called the Duke of Suffolk's Place, in the County of Surrey, with all Houses, &c., and the Park there, and also the offices of the High-Stewardship and Constableship of the Castle of Walyngford, Berks, in exchange for the reversion of the fee-simple of the Manors of Philberdes (otherwise called Phelbartes), Long Wittenham, Fiffed [Fifield], Eton, Frydysham (otherwise called Freleford), and Gartford, in the Counties of Berks and Oxon, the reversion belonging to and the Manors of Southwolde, Dysenage, and others in the County of Suffolk.

Donnington Castle was thus again acquired by the Crown; and Thomas Cromwell, writing to Sir Richard Rich, Solicitor-General to the King, from Tewkesbury Monastery, July 29th, 1535, states that he is ordered by the King to reply to Rich's letter respecting this transaction with the Duke of Suffolk, as follows:—As to the leases, which, it was supposed, were made by the Duke of Suffolk, the King says he does not know that the Duke or his officers have made any lease since the conclusion between them of this bargain. As he is informed that the Duke or his officers have offered to make leases since that time, he considers this to be unkindness and ingratitude in the Duke, if it can be proved. Touching the decay of Ewelme and Donnington, the King answered that, whatever the Duke had spent upon them, it will appear in what decay they stand; whoever views them will easily perceive that good sums of money will not easily repair them. The King himself hath viewed Ewelme when lately there, and for Donnington the house is not only in decay, but also the keeper of the same, Mr. Fettyplace, hath both consumed and destroyed the deer and game there, and also wasted the woods in such wise as it is thought he hath not only forfeited his patent, but also right ill-deserved to have either fee or thanks for any good service he hath done there. *

1547. Charles Brandon, Duke of Suffolk, died in 1545. Upon the death of Henry VIII., in 1547, the Castle passed to his son Edward VI., who in the fourth year of his reign (1550), in fulfilment of the will of his father, the late king, and with the advice of his Council, granted by Letters Patent to his sister, Lady Elizabeth, various lands in several Counties, including the lordship and manor of Donyngton, with all the deer and beasts in the park, and the liberty of park within the said park; the Castle of Donyngton, Berks, with all rights and appurtenances, the whole town of Newbury, with all appurtenances, formerly parcel of the lands and possessions of the jointure of Lady Johanna, Queen of England [Joanna of Navarre, Queen of Henry IV.], the Manor of Hamsted-Marshall, etc., the whole being of the yearly value of £3106 13s. 1½d. To be held by a yearly rent of £106 0 1½, to be paid to the Court of Augmentations,

---

* "Miscellaneous Letters," Series III, vol. ii., No. 96; Public Record Office.

or until the Councillors named in King Henry's Will shall arrange a marriage for her, in accordance with the said will.*

1551. The above-mentioned Letters Patent were surrendered on 23rd April of the following year (1551) by the Lady Elizabeth personally appearing before the King in his Court of Chancery; and the enrolment was accordingly cancelled. On this surrender, another grant was made to the Princess in substitution of the former grant, including, with other lands mentioned in the previous grant the Lordship and Manor of Donnington, the Castle of Donnington, and the Manor of Newbury—the annual value of the whole being estimated at £3064 17 8¼. To be held at a rent of £109 13 7, for life, or until marriage, as before.†

1600. On the 15th of May, in the forty-second year of Queen Elizabeth, a grant of the Castle and Manor of Donnington was nominally made to Nicholas Zouche, and Thomas Hure, Esquires, and their heirs, nominees of Charles, Earl of Nottingham, Baron Howard of Effingham, to protect it against escheat. In the following year, the said Nicholas Zouche, Esq., and Elizabeth his wife obtained license to alienate to the said Charles, Earl of Nottingham, and Catherine his wife, and the heirs of the said Earl, the Castle and Manor of Donnington, Winterborne-Davers (alias Winterborne-Danvers), Winterborne-Mayne, Leckhampstede, the Park of Donnington, and 40 messuages, 40 gardens, 20 tofts,‡ 4 water-mills, 3 dovecotes, 40 orchards, 1000 acres of arable land, 100 acres of meadow, 500 acres of pasture, 300 acres of wood, 300 acres of gorse, 100s. of rent, free warren, view of frankpledge in the town aforesaid, Bussock Courte, Speene mores, Uplamborne (alias Lamborne), Northcroft, Horspoole-Furlonge,§ Newbury, Shaw, Thatcham, Henwyke, Spynamlande, Shawborne, and other places, together with the presentation and free disposal of the Hospital of Donnington, and all tithes and oblations in Donnington, Newbery, Speene, Winterborne-Davers, and Winterborne-Mayne, and the Advowson of the Church of Newbury, co. Berks, the Borough of New Lymington, and the Manors of Old Lymington and New Lymington, with other lands in the Counties of Southampton and Surrey. All these were to be holden by the grantees as follows:—With the exception of the lands in Southampton, to the use of the said Earl and Catherine his wife for their lives; with remainder to William Howard, son and heir apparent of said Earl, and his heirs male, remainder to Charles Howard, Esq., son and heir of William Howard, knt., brother of said Earl deceased, and heirs male ; with remainder to Francis Howard, Esq., second son of the said Sir William Howard, knt., deceased, and heirs male; with remainder to the right heirs of said Earl for ever. Worth £40. Fine on alienation £13 6 8. *Note in the Margin:*—"The cause of this small rate was for y^t my Lo. purchased these lands in other men's names upon trust, and, all these dyinge but one, was forced to take ye same back from ye Survivor and his wiffe, as well for barringe of dower of ye wiffe

---

* Pat. 4 Edw, VI., pt. 3, m. 25. † Pat. 5, Edw. VI., pt. 4, m. 11.

‡ Toft: a messuage or house, or rather a place where a messuage once stood, that is fallen or pulled down.—*Bailey.*

§ A meadow belonging to Donnington Priory is still known by this name. The word "furlong" occurs often in the names of fields in Beds and Bucks.

of him that had y^t in trust, as also for my Lo. his further securyty." *

1603. Sir Thomas Edmonds, in a letter to the Earl of Shrewsbury, dated, Woodstock, Sept. 11, 1603,† says, "I suppose your Lordship is no less entertained with the pleasures of your hunting than we are here; so as you do not expect to hear any novelties from us during this time. Since the time that your Lordship left us, we have wholly spent our time in that exercise; but the Queen [Anne, of Denmark] remained at Basing till the King's coming hither, and she hath as well entertained herself with good dancing, which hath brought forth the effects of a marriage between my Lord Admiral [The Earl of Nottingham] and the Lady Mary Stuart. His Lordship, in his passage hither by the way of Newbury, hath recovered the possession of Donnington Castle from the Lady Russell,‡ she being absent in Wales with her daughter the Lady Herbert." §

This letter is also printed in Nichols' "Progresses of James I." In what way Lady Russell became interested in Donnington Castle is at present unknown; and, as Mr. Nichols remarks, we are not likely to gain further information as to the dispute than this letter gives us.

1615. In this year another dispute arose as to the ownership of the Castle and Manor, which at this time were in the hands of Lady Anne, widow of William, Lord Howard of Effingham. Being summoned to show by what title she entered upon and held the said Castle, &c., she stated that William, Lord Howard, was seized of the Castle and Manor of Donnington, &c., in demesne as of fee, &c.; and, being so seized, by Indenture, dated 10 October, 13 James I., between William, Lord Howard, of the one part, and Peter Vanlore, of the other part, he (William), bargained and sold to Peter Vanlore the said lands, &c., by which means Peter Vanlore became possessed of the same, but without having first obtained the King's license. (King James, however, by Letters Patent, dated 13 May, 14 James I., pardoned this alienation.)

She said further, that Peter Vanlore, senior, being thus seized, the King by Letters Patent, dated 1 April, 14 James I., gave license to Peter Vanlore, senior, to alienate the Castle and Manor of Donnington, &c., to Anne, Lady Howard, widow, late the wife of William, Lord Howard, of Effingham, for life; with remainder to Elizabeth, daughter and heir of William, and to the heirs of Elizabeth, and in default of such heirs to the right heirs of Anne.

Whereupon a fine was levied at Westminster in Trinity Term, 14 James I., between Anne, Lady Howard, Plaintiff, and Peter Vanlore, senior, Deforciant, of the Castle and Manor of Donnington, &c., which Peter Vanlore conveyed to Anne, as appears by an Indenture, dated 30 March, 14 James I., made between Peter Vanlore, senior, of London, Esq., of the one part, and Anne, Lady Howard of Effingham, late wife and sole-executrix of William, Lord Howard of Effingham, of the other part. By virtue whereof, Anne had entered

---

* Alienation Office: "Entries of Licenses and Pardons," v. 7, p. 313 d.

† "Memoirs of the Peers of England during the reign of James I.," by Sir Egerton Brydges; p. 171.

‡ Elizabeth, daughter of Sir Anthony Cooke, and widow of John, Lord Russell, second son of Francis, Earl of Bedford.

§ Wife of Henry, Lord Herbert, son of the Earl of Worcester.

upon and hitherto was seized in demesne as of free tenement for life. Judgment was therefore given in favour of Anne.

This Roll* contains a long list of places besides Donnington. It includes the Park of Donnington, also a meadow called Lorde's Meade, alias Horsemead, in Donnington, also two water-mills at Donnington, also a messuage near the bridge of Newbury between the tenement of Ralph Gunter, on the north part, and the Church Lane, leading to the Mill, on the south part, and extending in length from the High Street on the east part to the "Almes" on the west part, then or lately in the tenure or occupation of Catherine Lichpole and John Lichpole, otherwise Chaundeler, or their assigns, or the assigns of one of them. All the places mentioned passed under the conveyance here set out.

The two water-mills at Donnington are contiguous; and until recently they have been held by two different owners; one belonging to the Castle estate, the other to Mrs. Parry, whose family at one time were the proprietors of the adjacent Priory.

The messuage in Newbury comprised the premises well known in later years as the "Globe Inn," which before the dissolution of the Monasteries formed part of the possessions of the Priory of Wherwell, Hants.

William, Lord Howard of Effingham, who was summoned by writ to several Parliaments during his father's life, married Anne, daughter and sole heir of Lord St.-John, of Bletsoe. He died before his father, in 1615, and was buried at Chelsea, leaving Elizabeth, his only daughter and sole heir, who became the wife of John, Lord Mordaunt, afterwards Earl of Peterborough. Charles Howard, Earl of Effingham, the Lord High Admiral (which office, Fuller says, he resigned to the Duke of Buckingham, in the reign of James I), died at Haling House, Surrey, December 14, 1624; and was buried in the family vault in the chancel of Reigate Church.† He was succeeded in the title by Charles, his son by his first wife, Katherine Cary.

Lady Anne Howard died in June, 1638; and was buried in Westminster Abbey. In the letters of administration granted to her only child, Elizabeth, Countess of Peterborough, 20th of June, 1638, she is described as of Hawnes, Co. Beds; but she died in the parish of St. Bartholomew the Great in London. See Col. Chester's "Westminster Abbey Registers," p. 133.

Sir Peter Vanlore, above-mentioned, was a rich merchant, born at Utretch. He died in 1627; and in Tylehurst Church, near Reading, there is an elaborate and curious Jacobian monument to Sir Peter and his lady, with a long eulogistic inscription, commencing with the following lines:—

"When thou hast read the name, here lies Vanlore,
Thou need'st no story to inform thee more."

Further on, however, we learn, that Sir Peter was an industrious

---

* Memoranda Roll (Lord-Treasurer's Remembrancer), Hilary, 14 James I., Roll, 205.
† "Worthies," Surrey, pp. 83, 84.

merchant, beloved by three English Monarchs; and that he died very rich, having lived four-score years—

"The greatest part in one chaste wedlock spent;
Utrecht his cradle—Tylehurst loves his tomb."

Sir Peter is supposed to have had a temporary interest in the Manor of Tylehurst by alliance with the Kendricks.

1623-44. John Chamberlayne is described in the Rolls of the College of Arms for 1623, as of "Donnington Castle," Berks;* and Symonds, the writer of the "Diary of the Marches of the Royal Army," informs us that the Castle in 1644 was "the habitacion of Mr. Packer, who bought it of Mr. Chamberlayne." A diligent search at the Record Office has failed to find a license given to Anne Howard to alienate, or a transfer to Chamberlayne; but this is no reason for doubting Symonds's statement. There is a John Chamberlayne described as of Sherborne, Co. Oxon ("Close Roll," 22 James I., p. 16, m. 5); and another John Chamberlayne, as of Beaulieu, Co. Southampton ("Close Roll," 19 James I., p. 11, m. 7). The latter is most probably the person who was for a short time the owner of the Castle.†

At the commencement of the Civil War, the Castle was unquestionably the property of John Packer, Esq., and in his hands when it was garrisoned for the King. Mr. Packer was born at Twickenham, Middlesex, about 1572, and appears to have been in public employment (at one time in the Signet Office); and to have been of considerable social distinction. A letter, dated 17 January, 1610, addressed by him to Sir Thomas Edmonds, Ambassador at the Court of Brussels, will be found in the "Court and Times of James the First;" 1848, vol. i. p. 104: and Camden, in his "Annals," states that the Marquis of Buckingham, Baron Haye, and the Countess of Dorset were sponsors at the baptism of one of Mr. Packer's children, in Westminster Church, 24 June, 1618. It is probable that he acted as Secretary to George Villiers, first Duke of Buckingham. He was buried at St. Margaret's, Westminster, 15 February, 1649.

His will, dated 20th July, 1645, with a codicil, dated 2nd May, 1648, was proved, 27 Nov., 1649, by his relict Philippa. He was residing in a house within the College of Westminster, but described himself as of Shellingford, co. Berks, Esq.; and stated that his lands had been sequestered by the King's forces, excepting the Manor of Groombridge (in Speldhurst), Kent, where he had built a chapel, and which he bequeathed to one of his sons, who still held it in 1696. He had married Philippa Mills, of the city of Westminster, gentlewoman, daughter of Francis Mills, Esq., of Southampton.‡ In a letter, dated 12th Dec., 1604, written by John Packer to Sir Ralph Winwood, he speaks of his "good friend" Sir Thomas Lake (Principal Secretary of State to James I.), who first procured him the

---

* "Transactions of the Newbury District Field Club," vol. ii, p. 39.

† We may also mention that a John Chamberlayne had been Mayor of Newbury in 1601; and that this name frequently occurs in the town records about this period.

‡ See note to the baptism of Mr. Packer's daughter, in the "Westminster Abbey Registers," edited by Col. J. L. Chester, p. 65.

reversion to the Privy Seal; and he mentions that he is "now at the Court." Sir Dudley Carleton, writing to Sir Ralph Winwood in 1610, refers to Mr. Packer as having been sent as Envoy to Denmark, and alludes to "John Chamberlaine," with whom Mr. Packer was, it seems, familiar.

In 1647, 23 Charles I., John Packer, of Donnington Castle, was one of the Committee appointed by an ordinance of the Parliament for the "Visitation and Reformation of the University of Oxford." His sons, Robert and Philip, were members of University College, and subscribers to the new works at that College about 1675; and in one of the windows of the Hall are inserted the arms of the Packers—Gules, a cross lozengy, between four roses argent. Their brother, William, was one of the "Tryers for Approbation of Public Preachers" in 1653. The residence of the Packers at Shellingford, about two miles to the north-east of Faringdon, was an ancient stone building, called "Shellingford Castle." It remained unoccupied many years, and was at last taken down. A few outbuildings, a large walled garden and some plantations of yew, surrounding a fish-pond, are now all that remain to indicate the dwelling-place of this once important family. Mr. Robert Packer, M.P. for Wallingford in the Long Parliament, and who died in 1684, appears to have been among those members, some of whom were imprisoned or secluded, and others seized by the army on the 6th December, 1648, for having voted the day previously, "That the King's answers to the proposition of both Houses were a ground for peace."

After the Civil War was over, Mr. John Packer had some of the ruinous parts of the battered Castle taken down; and with the materials he erected the mansion now standing near it, and called "Donnington-Castle House."

FINIS.

INDEX.

Abberbury family, noticed, 199.
Abingdon, failure of Prince Rupert's attack on, 156.
Aldbourne Chase, fight at, 8; M. De Larrey's account of the fight at, 9; the forces at, 7; Royalists' account of the fight at, 10.
Aldbourne, parish registers of, 9 note; relics of the fight at, 13.
Aldermaston, Rupert's skirmish near, 50, 58.
Andover, fight at, 113; the King's march from, 116.
Anecdotes of the Battle on Wash Common, 44.
Armament of Donnington Castle, 118.
Army of the King in array on the Wash, 28; its condition in 1644, 111.
Army of the Parliament in array on the Wash, 29.
Ashburnham, Sir W., account of, 191.
Ashe, Rev. Simeon, account of, 131 note.
Astley, Sir Bernard, account of, 191.
Astley, Sir Jacob, account of, 76.
Aston, Sir Thomas, account of, 76.
Auxiliaries, Red Regiment of the, 57.

Bagehot, Col. Thomas, account of, 79.
Balfour, Sir William, account of, 86.
Balsdon (Balston, Balsome, Bolsome) House, near Kintbury, notice of, 180 note.
Balsome House, the Kentish Regiment at, 180.
Banbury, relief of, 117.
Basing House, relief of, 112; from Hungerford, 153.
Basset, Sir T., account of, 192
Battle at Speen and Shaw, 132, 136; first, at Newbury, 24, 30, 51.
Battle-march of the Puritans, 136.
Battle on Wash Common, near Newbury, 24, 30; political effects of, 51; relics of, 44, 46; second, at Newbury, 130.
Bear Inn at Hungerford, 153 note; Newbury, 83.
Bedford, Earl of, account of, 71.
Belasyse, Lord, account of, vii, 72.
Bennet, Sir H., noticed, 192.
Bennet, Sir Humphrey, his brigade of horse, 123
Berks, Agreement with King for support of army, 104; Commission for raising money and forces in, 95; Petition of Grand Jury against Ship-money, 100; political feeling in, 102; proportion of Ship-money, 100; protestatoirs, returns of, in, 90; sequestrators of estates in, 93.
Berkshire, Earl of, account of, 188.

Bertie, Hon. Henry, account of, 73.
Biggs' Cottage and Biggs' Hill, near Newbury, 21 note, 24 note.
Biographical Notices of Parliamentarian Officers, 85, 194; Royalist Officers, 67, 187.
Birch, Col. John, his account of the capture of Lady Brentford, 173; notice of, 196.
Blagrave, Daniel, account of, 98.
Boxford, parochial records of, 168; the Lambourne passed by Gen. Waller at, 128, 129.
Boys, Colonel, his defence of Donnington Castle, 109. 118, 145, 158, 183; raid upon Newbury, 154; replies to Col. Middleton, 109; reply to Col. Horton, 118; to summons of surrender, 145; surrender of Donnington Castle, 159; knighted on Red Heath, 117, 163, 165; Sir John, account of, 190.
Brandon, Charles, Duke of Suffolk, noticed, 204.
Brentford, capture of Lady, 173; Earl of, his escape from Donnington, 146; Lady, capture of, 146.
Bridge, old: at Newbury, 133.
Bristol, assault of, 1.
Brocas, Bernard, account of, vii, 75.
Brooke. Mr. Thomas, account of, 162 note.
Brouncker (Bronkerd), Sir W, account of, 191.
Browne, Mr., of Shefford, notice of, 155; Richard, account of, 98.
Buckingham, Duke of, death of, 71.
Bucklebury, parish registers of, 169.
Burden, Samuel, noticed, 186.
Burial of the dead after the Second Battle, 143; on the Wash, 45, 46.
Byron, Lord, his account of the Battle on the Wash, 35; attack at the Battle on the Wash, 31, 34, 35; letter to Lord Clarendon, 6; remarks on the fight at Aldbourne Chase, 8; position of troops at Newbury, 12, 27.
Byron, Sir John, account of, 67.

Caernarvon, Earl of, account of, 68; death of, on the Wash, 39.
Campaign of, 1644, 107.
Cannon, see Guns.
Capel, Lord, account of, 188.
Capture of Lady Brentford, 173.
Carleton, Rev. Guy, account of, 169.
Carnarvon, Lord, his description of the Royalists in array in Wash Common, 26.
Cary, Lucius (Viscount Falkland), account of, 71.
Castle and Manor of Donnington, history of, 197.

Casualties at the Battle on Wash Common, 42, 43, 49, 51; Second Battle of Newbury, 139, 141, 142.
Catelyn, Capt., notice of, 193.
Chamberlayne, John, noticed, 210.
Chandos, Lord, account of, 73.
Chaucer, family of, noticed, 201. 208, 204.
Chieveley, halt of Parliamentarians at, 128.
Chilton House and Chilton Lodge, account of, 20 *note*.
Cirencester, fight at, 5; flags taken at, 47.
Clare, Earl of, 71.
Clarendon, Lord, reference to his History, *passim*.
Clarke, gunner, account of, 78.
Clay Hill, Shaw, Parliamentarian Camp on, 125.
Cleveland, Earl of, account of, 70; taken prisoner, 134.
Clifton, Capt., account of, 79.
Codrington, Robert, account of, 89; on the retreat from Gloucester, 8.
Colepeper, Lord, account of, 189.
Colours, captured by Lord Essex, 47; of the London Regiments, 55.
Commissioners for raising money and forces in Co. Berks, List of, 95.
Committee, the Derby-House, 110, 114, 129.
Conditions of the surrender of Donnington Castle, 160.
Constable, Sir William, account of, 86.
Cope Hill, near Newbury, fight at, 34.
Corbet's relation of the Siege of Gloucester, 5.
Cox, Gabriel, of Newbury, noticed, 27, 103, 185.
Crawford, General, noticed, 195.
Criticism, military, on the tactics of the two armies at the Battle on Wash Common, 52.
Cromwell and Manchester, quarrel between, 157.
Cromwell, General, his cavalry charge in Speen Fields, 134, 135; flank march, 127, 129, 131; Information against Manchester, 115; joined Manchester's army as General of the Horse, 114.
Crosby, James, noticed, 186.

Dalbier, Col., his investment of Donnington Castle, 159, 183; notice of the career and death of, 161.
Dalton, Colonel, account of, 43 *note*.
Deane, General, account of, 87.
Defeat of the Royalists on Speen Hill, 132.
Defence of Donnington Castle, 109, 119, 145, 158, 183.
Delinquents, papists, spies, &c., 93.
Derby-House Committee, the, 110, 114, 129, 144.
Digby, Lord George, account of, 72: remarks on the defeat of the Royalists on the Wash, 44.
Dolman's house at Shaw, 122, 135, 164.
Donnington Castle, 19; armament of, 118; besieged by Col. Horton, 117, 119; in November, 1644, 145; Capt. Knight's account of the siege of, 177; defence of, 109, 119, 145, 158, 183; investment of, 109, 159; lead taken from, 184; regalia and treasure at, 149; strategical importance of, 19, 108; supplied with provisions, 154; supplies for the defence of, 108; surrendered, 160.
Donnington, history of the Manor and Castle of, 187; water-mills at, 209.
Dragoons, account of, 25 *note*.
Dunce (Daunce, Dance) family, noticed, 163.
Dunch, Edmund, account of, 97.

Elizabeth, Princess, her possessions at Donnington and Newbury, 206, 207.
Enbourne Heath, the fighting on, 38.
Essex, Lord, his arrangement of troops for the Battle on Wash Common, 24; conduct in battle, 32 *note*; his flag, 32 *note*; disaster in Cornwall, 110; march to Gloucester, 4; to Newbury, 20; movements in the campaign of 1644, 107, 110; relief of Gloucester, 3; success against the Royalists on Wash Common, 40; tomb in Westminster Abbey, 85; triumphal entry into London, 47; Prince Rupert's attack on his rear, 58; strength of his army, 6.
Essex, the Earl of, account of, 85.
Eure, Col. Thomas, account of, 78.
Ewhurst Church, burials in, 112 *note*.
Eyetons of Hendred, the, 103.

Falkland Farm on Wash Common, 36.
Falkland, Lord, account of, 81; his death, 35, 37, 49, 53, 82; his Will, 84; on Ship-money, 101; shot when charging across Dark Lane, 35 *note*.
Fawley, Little, Symonds's notice of, 155.
Fettiplace, Thomas, mentioned, 95.
First Battle at Newbury, the, on Sept. 20th, 4643, 1; the King present at the, 32 *note*, 186.
Flag, Lord Essex's, 32 *note*.
Flags taken at Cirencester, 47; the First Battle of Newbury, vii, 48.
Flank march, under Waller and Cromwell, 127, 129, 131.
Fleetwood, Capt. C., account of, 89.
Fleetwood, Dr. James, account of, 119 *note*.
Flight of the King from Newbury, 134.
Fogge, Rev. Robert, account of, 120 *note;* brings Mrs. Fleetwood's letter to the Castle, 119.
Forster, Mr., his account of the Battle on Wash Common, 39.
Forster, Sir Humphrey, his petition to Parliament, 124 *note;* military intrusion at his residence, 170.
Forth, Earl of, account of, 67
Frechville, Sir John, account of, 76.
Fuller on the Battle at Newbury, 48.

Gage, Col., his relief of Basing, 112; Sir H., his relief of Basing, 153.
Garrard family, notice of, 151 *note*.
Gerard, Col. Charles, account of, 78.
Gerard family, noticed, 79.

Gloucester, Capt. John Gwynne's account of the march from, 7; Corbet's relation of the siege of, 5; inscriptions on the south gate of, 4; siege of, 2.
Golofre, family of, noticed, 202 *note*.
Goodman, Rev. Dr., account of. 147.
Goodwin, Sir Arthur, account of, 86.
Goring, Lord, account of, 190.
Granville, Sir J., noticed, 192.
Greenham Manor-house, noticed, 181 *note*.
Grey of Groby, Lord, account of, 85.
Gryce, Gyles, noticed, 185.
"Gun" public-house on Wash Common, 25.
Guns, kinds of, used at Donnington Castle, 118; recapture of, at Speen, 132; old, at Shaw House, 137.
Gwynne, Capt., account of, 80; on the retreat from Gloucester, 7.

Hammond, Capt., account of, 88.
Henrietta Maria, not present at the Battle on Wash Commen, 61.
Hesilrige, Sir A. account of, 195.
Hoby, Peregrine, account of, 94.
Holland, Cornelius, account of, 92; Earl of, account of, 70.
Hooper, Sir T., notice of, 192.
Hopton, Lord, account of, 189.
Horton, Col., his blockade of Donnington Castle, 117; letter to Mr. Fogge, 120.
Horton, Col., summons Col. Boys to surrender, 118.
Houghton, Col., noticed, 193.
Howard, Lady, noticed, 208, 209; of Effingham, Lord, noticed, 207, 209.
Hungerford Park, account of, 20 *note*.
Hungerford, the King at, 153 *note*.
Hunt, Captain, account of, 88.
Hurry, Col. Sir John, account of, 77, 146.

Ingoldsby, Col. Sir. R., account of, 196.
Ives, Thomas, noticed, 186.

Jermyn, Lord, account of, 72.

Kingsclere, the Kentish Regiment at, 179; King at, 116.
Kingsmill, Henry, notice of, 162 *note*.
Kirke, Sir Lewis, account of, 75.
Knight, Capt., his account of the siege of Donnington Castle, 177.
Knight, Roger, noticed, 93.
Knight's feud, fief, or fee, 197 *note*.
Knollys, Sir Francis, account of, 93.

Land-tax, origin of, the, 197 *note*.
Largess from Parliament to General Massey and the garrison of Gloucester, 4.
Larrey, M. de, on the fight at Aldbourne Chase, 9.
Leaders of the Royalists at Shaw and Speen, 126; at the Wash, 28; Parliamentarian, at Shaw and Speen, 126; at the Wash, 29.
Leathern guns, 137.
Legge, Col. William, account of, 77.

Leke, Col., account of, 192.
Lenthall, William, account of, 95.
Letter by an Officer of Horse about the Battle on Wash Common, 33; John Saunders describing journey to Marlborough, 83; the Rev. R. Fogge, 120; from Anthony Vaux about the conduct of the soldiers, 172; Capt. John Gwynne, 7; Charles Murray to Sir John Berkeley, 167; Col. Dalbier to the Earl of Essex, 60; Col. Goodwin to Lady Wharton, 86; to Lord Wharton (?), 18; Col. Norton to Richard Major, 142; Col. William Ball to Mr. Speaker Lenthall, 170; John Ashburnham (for the King) to Prince Rupert, 13; King Charles I. to Prince Rupert, 111; Lord Byron to Clarendon, 6; Lord Digby to Prince Rupert, 115; Lord Essex to Colonels Godwin and Henry, 18; Lord George Digby (for the King) to Prince Rupert, 14; Lord Grandison to Prince Rupert, 17; Lord Sunderland to Lady Dorothea, 80; Mr. Roger Knight to the Astrologer Lilly, 181 *note;* Messrs. Johnston and Crewe from Thatcham, 125; Sir Thomas Edmonds to the Earl of Shrewsbury, 208; the Duke of Richmond (for the King) to Prince Rupert, 14; Earl of Essex to Col. Godwin, 60; Marquis of Newcastle to Prince Rupert, 62; Mayor of Newbury to Prince Charles, 133.
Letters from Henriette-Marie to the Marquis of Newcastle, 61; Prince Rupert to Gen. Waller and Lord Essex, 82.
License of War, 2, 154, 169, 172.
Lilly, Roger Knight's letter to, 181 *note*.
Lindsey, Earl of, account of, 69.
Lisle, Sir George, account of, 74.
Lloyd, Sir C , noticed, 192.
London, Trained Bands of, 31, 55.
Lucas, Sir Charles, account of, 74.
Ludlow, General, account of, 195; his account of the death of Gabriel Ludlow, 127; his "Memoires" quoted *passim*.
Luke, Sir Samuel, account of, 86.

Manchester and Cromwell, quarrel between, 157.
Manchester, Earl of, account of, 194; his friendly disposition towards the King, 115; march from Reading to Newbury, 124; march westward, 108, 110, 112.
Manor and Castle of Donnington, historical notices of the, 197.
Mansel, Sir Anthony, account of, 76.
Maple tree, old, near Donnington Castle, 182 *note*.
March, flank, under Waller and Cromwell, 127, 129, 131; of Lord Essex to Reading, 47, 49, 50, 59; the King from Andover to Whitchurch, 116; from Donnington Castle to Marlborough, Nov. 1644, 150; from Oxford to Donnington, 147; on Salisbury, 111; to Newbury from Andover, 162; the

INDEX. 215

Parliamentarians from Aldbourne to Newbury, 19; the Royalists from Gloucester to Newbury, 15.
Marlborough, the King's stay at, 152.
Marsh, fortifications in the, at Newbury, 148 *note*.
Marten, Henry, account of, 94.
Mason, Capt., noticed, 196.
Massey, governor of Gloucester, 2, 4.
Maurice, Prince, account of, 187.
Meldrum, Col. John, account of, 88.
Meyrick, Sir John, account of, 85.
Middleton, Col., before Donnington Castle, 109; General, account of, 195.
Milton, Christopher, account of, 103 *note*; John, on Charles's weakness of character, 113.
Molyneux, Lord, account of, 73.
Monkey Lane, name of, 50.
Moore, John, noticed, 106; Sir Francis, account of, 155 *note*.
Morgan, Col., account of, 78.
Movements of the opposed armies in the Spring of 1644, 107.

Needham, M., account of, 51 *note*.
Newberry, Earl of, the title of, 79; Manor of, in Co. Cork, 16 *note*.
Newbury, a "witch" murdered at, 63; Church used as a prison and hospital, 167; disposition of the people at, 17; flight of the King from, 134; fortified in Nov. 1644, 148; its history, 16; manor of, 16; old bridge of, 133; raid upon, from Donnington Castle, 154; the King's march to, from Andover, 162; stay at, 27, 163; value of its position to the Royalists, 19.
Newman, Capt., noticed, 16 *note*.
New Model Army, the, 157.
Newport, Earl of, account of, 188.
Northampton, Earl of, account of, 69; his relief of Banbury, 117.
North Heath, near Chieveley, 128, 129.
Norton, Col. R., account of, 88, 196.
Nottingham, Earl of, account of, 70.

Oak, the Queen's, in Donnington Park, 178.
Officers of the Trained Bands, lists of, 55; Parliamentarian notices of, 85, 144; Royalist, notices of, 67, 187.
O'Neill, Col. Daniel, account of, viii, 78.
Owen, Sir John, account of, 192.
Oxford, the King at, 43; the King's retreat to, 145.

Packer Family, noticed, 210; John, account of, 210; Phillip, his deposition concerning the removal and forcible detention of lead from the Castle, 184.
Page, Sir R., noticed, 192.
Parliamentarian Camp on Clay Hill, Shaw, 125; Officers and others, notices of, 85, 194.
Percy, Lord Henry, account of, 72.
Petition against Ship-money, Berks, 100; of — Daniel for redress, 47 *note*; John Bonwak for compensation for his sufferings, 167; people of Donnington for compensation for damages, 177

note; Robert Stradling for employment, 183 *note*; the Corporation of Newbury to purchase the Manor, 16.
Petitions of Sir Humphrey and Lady Anne Forster, 124 *note*.
Phelip family, noticed, 202.
Platt, Col. Richard, account of, 78.
Portage, Rector of Bradfield, trial of, 84.
Porter, Gen. George, account of, 77.
Potts, Michael, noticed, 186.
Powle, Henry, account of, 94.
Presence of the King at the First Battle of Newbury, 32 *note*, 185; Queen on Wash Common, disproved, 61.
Prisoners, Royalist, taken at the Second Battle, 141.
Protestation in County Berks, Returns of, 90.
Public feeling in Berks in 1643, 102.
Pye, Sir Robert, account of, 95.
Pyle, Sir Francis, account of, 93.
Pym, Capt. Charles, 89.

Queen Henrietta-Maria, not present at the Battle on the Wash, 61.

Red Field, near Clay Hill, Shaw, 125, 127, 128, 130 *note*.
Red Heath, its position near the Wash, 165; the King's camp on, 117.
Red Hill, its position near the Wash, 165.
Red Hill Field near Clay Hill, 166.
Reformadoes, 141.
Regalia and treasure at Donnington Castle, 148.
Regiments and Officers of the Trained Bands and Auxiliaries, lists of, 55.
Relics of a fight at Speenhamland, 83, 149; the Battle on Wash Common, 44 *note*, 46; skirmish at Aldbourne, 13.
Relief of Banbury, 117; Basing, 112; Gloucester, 4.
Removal of the communion-table at Boxford, 168.
Repulse of Parliamentarians at Shaw, 122, 125.
Results of the fighting at Shaw and Speen, 138, 144; First Battle of Newbury, 51.
Retreat of the Royalists from Newbury, 132.
Richmond, Duke of, account of, 187.
Rivers, Earl, account of, 188.
Robartes, Lord, account of, 85.
Royalist families in Berks, 102; Officers, biographical notices of, 67, 187.
Royalists, position of the, Oct. 26th, 1644, 121.
Rudyerd, Sir Benjamin, account of, 96.
Rupert, Prince, account of, 67; his attack on Essex's rear near Aldermaston, 50, 58.

St.-Barbe, Capt. F., account of, 88.
St.-John, Col., account of, 77.
St.-Leger, Sir W., account of, 191.
Second Battle at Newbury, Oct. 27th, 1644, 107.
Second Battle of Newbury, casualties at, 139, 141, 142; C. Murray's account of, 167; results of, 138, 143, 156.

Seeley, George, noticed, 186.
Self-denying Ordinance, the, 157.
Sequestrators, Co. Berks, list of, 93.
Seymour, Lord, account of, 152 *note*.
Shaw House and Park, occupied by the Royalists, and attacked by the Parliamentarians, 122, 135.
Shaw House, attack on, repulsed, 130; the King at, 164.
Shaw, skirmish near, 148; the fighting at, 135.
Sheffield, Colonel, 88.
Shefford, Great, the King at, 155.
Ship-money, account of, 99.
Siege of Donnington Castle, 117, 119, 159.
Skinner's Green, fight at, 32.
Skippon, General, account of, 87; advance of the Trained Bands on Wash Common under. 31, 38.
Skirmish at Aldbourne, 8; in Shaw Fields, 148; near Aldermaston, 58.
Slingsby, Sir Henry, account of, 75.
Smith, Lt.-Col., notice of, 181 and *note*.
Snelsmore Heath, near Donnington, 139 *note*, 147.
Speen and Speen Hill (proper) occupied by the Royalists, 123.
Speenhamland and Speen Fields in 1644, 122.
Speen Hill, the fight on, 131.
Stapleton, Sir Philip, account of, 85.
Stradling, Robert, account of, 183 *note*, 193.
Stradling, Sir Edward, account of, 76.
Strangeways, Col. G., account of, 193.
Strength of the Royalists on Oct. 26, 1644, 12.
Stuart, Lord Bernard, account of, 187.
Suffolk, Duchess of, noticed, 205; Duke of, noticed, 204, 206.
Sunderland, Earl of (Spencer), account of, 80.
Superstitious ornaments, ordered to be removed from Churches, 168 *note*.
Support of Parliamentary Garrisons, 95; Royalist Army, 104.
Surprise of Cirencester, 5.
Symonds, Capt., his account of the King's March from Salisbury to Andover, 114; his "Diary" quoted *passim*.

Tanfield, Sir Laurence, his monument, 81 *note*.

Thanksgiving Day for Gloucester, 4.
Thelwall, Col. A., account of, 193.
Tomb of Lord Essex in Westminster Abbey, 65.
Towers, Robert, account of. 162 *note*.
Trained Bands and Auxiliaries of London, list of the, 55.
Trial of Charles I., witnesses as to his presence at the First Battle of Newbury, 185.
Twisse, Dr., Rector of Newbury, account of, 51 *note*, 89.

Vachell, Tanfield, account of, 95.
Vanlore, Sir Peter, noticed, 209.
Vavasour, Sir William, account of, 76.
Villiers, Col. Edward, account of, 77.
Vinson, John, noticed, 185.
Vivile (Vieuville), Marquis of, taken prisoner, 9.
Vyne, account of the, vii, 48 *note*.

Wagstaffe, Sir J., noticed, 192.
Waldegrave, Sir Edward, account of, 75.
Walker, Sir Edward, account of, 192; his account of the fight at Speen, 133; Royalist position at Speen Hill, 123; his "Historical Discourse" quoted *passim*.
Waller and Cromwell, their flank march, 128.
Waller, General, Army under, 108, 112; his escape from Andover, 113; his success against the Royalists on Specu Hill, 132.
Waller, Sir W., account of, 194.
Warrant to draw provisions at Marlborough, 152.
Warwick, Sir Philip, his opinion on the march to Gloucester, 1.
Well of the Castle at Donnington, 146.
Will of Lord Falkland, 84.
Wilmot, Lord, account of, 68.
Windsor, John à, noticed, 182 *note*.
Witch-murder at Newbury, 63.
Witnesses at the Trial of Charles I., as to his presence at the First Battle of Newbury, 185.
Wodehouse, Sir Michael, account of, 76.
Woodd, Capt. Basil, account of, 79.

www.ingramcontent.com/pod-product-compliance
Lightning Source LLC
Chambersburg PA
CBHW031732230426
43669CB00007B/326